INDIA TODAY

INDIA TODAY

Economy, Politics and Society

Stuart Corbridge, John Harriss
and Craig Jeffrey

polity

First published in 2013 by Polity Press
Reprinted in 2013

Polity Press
65 Bridge Street
Cambridge CB2 1UR, UK

Polity Press
350 Main Street
Malden, MA 02148, USA

ISBN-13: 978-0-7456-6111-7
ISBN-13: 978-0-7456-6112-4(pb)

A catalogue record for this book is available from the British Library.

Typeset in 10 on 12 pt Adobe Sabon
by Servis Filmsetting Ltd, Stockport, Cheshire
Printed in the USA by Edwards Brothers Malloy

For further information on Polity, visit our website: www.politybooks.com

Contents

Part III: Society

Figures and Tables

Abbreviations

AIADMK	All India Anna Dravida Munnetra Kazagham
APL	Above Poverty Line
BJP	Bharatiya Janata Party
BJS	Bharatiya Jana Sangh
BKU	Bharatiya Kisan Union
BIMARU	Bihar, Madhya Pradesh, Rajasthan, Uttar Pradesh
BPL	Below Poverty Line
BSKSS	Bastar Sambhag Kisan Sangharsh Samiti
BSP	Bahujan Samaj Party
CEO	Chief Executive Officer
CM	Chief Minister
CMIE	Centre for Monitoring Indian Economy
CMP	Common Minimum Programme
CPI	Communist Party of India
CPI(M)/CPM	Communist Party of India (Marxist)
CPI(Maoist)	Communist Party of India (Maoist)
DFID	Department for International Development (UK)
DMK	Dravida Munnetra Kazagham
EPW	*Economic and Political Weekly*
EPZ	Export Processing Zone
EGS	Education Guarantee Scheme
FCI	Food Corporation of India
FDI	Foreign Direct Investment
GDP	Gross Domestic Product
HYV	High Yielding Variety
ICDS	Integrated Child Development Scheme
ICRISAT	International Crops Research Institute for the Semi-Arid Tropics

IIM	Indian Institute of Management
IIT	Indian Institute of Technology
INC	Indian National Congress
ISI	Import Substitution Industrialization
IT	Information Technology
ITeS	Information Technology-enhanced Services
JD	Janata Dal
KRRS	Karnataka State Farmers' Association
KSSP	Kerala Sastra Sahitya Parishad
LF	Left Front
LS	Lok Shakti
MBC	Most Backward Class
MDG	Millennium Development Goal
MKSS	Mazdur Kisan Shakti Sangathan
NAC	National Advisory Council
NAM	Non-Aligned Movement
NAPM	National Alliance of People's Movements
NBA	Narmada Bachao Andolan
NCAER	National Council for Applied Economic Research
NCEUS	National Commission for Enterprises in the Unorganised Sector
NDA	National Democratic Alliance
NEP	New Economic Policy
NFHS	National Family Health Survey
NGO	Non-Governmental Organization
NREGA	National Rural Employment Guarantee Act
NRI	Non-Resident Indian
NSS	National Sample Survey (Organisation)
OBC	Other Backward Class
OCI	Overseas Citizen of India
PAEG	People's Action for Employment Guarantee
PDS	Public Distribution System
RJD	Rashtriya Janata Dal
RSS	Rashtriya Swayamsevak Sangh
SAP	Samata Party
SC	Scheduled Caste
SEBI	Securities and Exchange Board of India
SEZ	Special Economic Zone
SHG	Self-Help Groups
SP	Samajwadi Party
SS	Shiv Sena
ShS	Shetkari Sanghatana
ST	Scheduled Tribe

TDP	Telegu Desam Party
UF	United Front
UNICEF	United Nations International Children's Fund
UNPA	United National Progressive Alliance
UPA	United Progressive Alliance
VHP	Vishwa Hindu Parishad

Preface and Acknowledgements

India Today builds upon and yet is significantly different from another account of contemporary India that was written by two of us, Stuart Corbridge and John Harriss, just over a decade ago. *Reinventing India* (Corbridge and Harriss, 2000–3) presented an analytical history of colonial and post-colonial India. It argued that economic liberalization and ascendant Hindu nationalism in post-1980 India could be understood as elite revolts against earlier assertions of popular (or subaltern) democracy.

India Today involves three authors in equal measure and is cross-sectional in its main design. Each of its substantive chapters seeks to answer a question. When and why did India take off? How did a weak state promote audacious reform? Is government in India becoming more responsive (and to whom)? Does India have a civil society? Has the rise of Hindu nationalism halted? Will India reap a demographic dividend? And so on. There are many more questions that we would like to have asked and answered. *India Today* is certainly not a comprehensive account of contemporary India. But the thirteen main questions that we have selected here seem to us to be important and in some respects interlocking ones. Together, they address significant new developments in India's economy, polity and society, while a brief Afterword considers India's emerging geopolitical ambitions.

The answers that we propose to these questions draw upon our training as students of South Asia, on the one hand, and of political economy, comparative politics or international development, on the other. We believe that analysis of contemporary India is at its best when it combines the insights of area studies with the more generic form of reasoning that is typical in economics or comparative politics. Accordingly, as we explain further in chapter 1, the structure of most chapters in *India*

Today is broadly T-shaped. We first consider what answers to our question(s) might be suggested by theoretical or comparative work in the social sciences. For example, if we want to know when and why the Indian economy took off, it helps to know something about the definition and frequency of growth accelerations in developing countries and something too about the main drivers of economic growth. The same logic holds when we ask 'How much have things changed for Indian women [whether since 1950 or 1990]?' Women in India are a heterogeneous group of people with different capabilities and identities. They also differ in key respects from women in Europe or North America. There are grounds for believing, even so, that processes of economic growth and development lead very often to higher literacy rates, create new opportunities for paid employment, and expand the public sphere – for women as well as for men. At any rate, this is one key intuition that is suggested by comparative political economy. Chapter 13 also takes on board some contrasting intuitions proposed by feminist scholars and South Asianists. The fact that there are over 1,060 men for every 1,000 women in India should caution us against simplistic – and overly generalized – views about empowerment through modernization.

India Today is an academic book and we trust it will earn the attention of our peers. At the same time, we hope the book will be of interest to lay readers and specialists in other world regions. We have done our best to adopt a prose style that is precise and not weighed down by long notes. We have also tried to minimize repetition across the chapters of *India Today*, although some points of overlap undoubtedly may still be found. We think this is inevitable in a book that allows readers to consult chapters out of order, if they wish, and that doesn't provide a minutely chronological account of economic, political or social life in contemporary India. Throughout, we draw on our own field studies in eastern India (Corbridge), south India (Harriss) and north India (Jeffrey).

India Today is, of course, also the title of a well-known Indian news magazine. There is no connection between the magazine and our book, although we happily acknowledge the value to all those of us who are interested in India of remarkable news magazines published in the country, most of which are now readily accessible online. We have drawn significantly on *Frontline*, published fortnightly by *The Hindu* group of newspapers, and also upon the weekly *Outlook* – as we have as well, extensively, upon India's extraordinary *Economic and Political Weekly*, which carries academic articles and commentary on contemporary affairs of very high quality. Our title, *India Today*, also repeats that of Rajni Palme Dutt's powerful indictment of British colonialism, published by the Left Book Club in Britain in 1940. India has changed enormously since the publication of Palme Dutt's book, and we hope that our book is as relevant to wider understanding of contemporary India as was Palme Dutt's work at the time of its publication.

Scholarship is always a collaborative enterprise and we are enormously indebted to all of the many authors whose work we draw upon here. Most of all, we are grateful to the work of the following academics, activists, friends and journalists who either took the trouble to read one or more of our draft chapters or provided more general commentary and inspiration: Bina Agarwal, Pranab Bardhan, Tim Besley, Neera Chandhoke, Sharad Chari, Jeff Checkel, Jane Dyson, Chris Fuller, Nandini Gooptu, Barbara Harriss-White, Himanshu, Robin Jeffrey, Sanjay Kumar, Stephen Legg, Sumi Madhok, Stig Toft Madsen, James Manor, Tamir Moustafa, Alf Gunvald Nilsen, Saraswati Raju, Sanjay Ruparelia, Alpa Shah, Manoj Srivastava, Ravi Srivastava, René Véron, Dhana Wadugodapitiya, Glyn Williams and Stephen Young. We have done our best to take on board their helpful comments and insights and we are confident that *India Today* is much stronger as a result. We are especially grateful to three anonymous referees and to the editorial staff at Polity Press, and most of all to Helen Gray, our copy-editor, and our indexer, Michael Solomons. Nikki Kalra and Thanh Lam provided excellent research assistance, which we are also delighted to acknowledge. John Harriss is grateful to the Institute of South Asian Studies at the National University of Singapore for the time and space in which he was able to start his work on this book, and then to complete it. Any errors of fact or interpretation are ours alone. Lastly, we are very pleased to salute our families for their patience, support and constructive commentaries, and of course for so much more: a big thank you, then, to Pilar and Joanne; Gundi, Kaveri and Ayaz, and Eli; and Jane, Florence and Finn.

London, Vancouver and Oxford: October 2011

1
Making Sense of India Today

1.1 Introduction

It can be difficult to avoid the use of clichés, not to mention hyper-bole, when discussing contemporary India. India as the world's largest democracy. India as a new regional superpower, an emergent economy, a BRIC – alongside Brazil, Russia and China. India as a poster child for managed ethnic pluralism: the fabled unity in diversity of a land that Churchill once declared to be 'no more a single country than the equator is a country'. As with most clichés, too, there is more than a grain of truth in all of these claims. India has maintained its geographical integrity since 1947, notwithstanding that many observers once predicted a future made up only of fissiparous tendencies, growing ethnic and linguistic chauvinisms (Harrison 1960), or even, as V. S. Naipaul (1990) would darkly put it, a million threatening mutinies. A country which, as late as 1990–2, advertised itself to the wider world mainly in terms of rising caste tensions, looming bankruptcy, and the extraordinary dismantling of a mosque in Ayodhya by militant Hindu nationalists, has been sub-stantially reinvented as one of the world's fastest growing economies and a beacon of hi-tech modernity.

India today is marked by increasing self-confidence, at least among its urban middle classes. There is a growing sense that the country has taken its place at the heart of an Asian growth machine, and that power is shift-ing away from Europe and North America towards what not so long ago was called, mainly pejoratively, the Orient, including South Asia and the 'Far East' (Quah 2011). Mohandas Gandhi (the Mahatma) would have been as shaken by this turn of events as his erstwhile tormentors in the colonial establishment, Churchill very much included. Jawaharlal Nehru, too, the first and longest-serving Prime Minister of India (1947–64), would have been surprised by India's recent embrace of an economic strategy that has begun to roll back the Licence and Planning Raj that he helped build up in the 1950s. He also would have been dismayed by the resurgence of militant Hinduism in India in the 1980s and 1990s, more than thirty years after the assassination of Gandhi, the acknowledged father of the nation, by Nathuram Godse, a Hindu fanatic and one-time member of the Rashtriya Swayamsevak Sangh (RSS), on 30 January 1948. (The RSS was founded in 1925 in Nagpur and remains the core organization of Hindu nationalism in India.)

One aim of this book is to convey how different India today can look from the India of twenty years ago, never mind the India of the 1940s or 1950s. A lot has changed since the crisis years of 1990–2, even if it is easy to exaggerate a sense of rupture between India now and India then. This is not a book, however, that is driven mainly by historical narrative, although we do provide some background material for readers who are new to India. Rather, *India Today* explores specific aspects of India's economy, politics and society as they have emerged in the period mainly since *c*.2000. We want to know how and why India has changed, and with what consequences. Distinctively, too, *India Today* has been written to take full account of new scholarship that has been emerging over the past decade or so from social scientists for whom India is just one area of interest among many.

Serious work on India must always have great respect for variations across the country in ecology, marriage patterns, regional political formations, cultural and linguistic traditions, land tenancy systems and so on. Social scientists who wish to explore current realities in India will also be at a disadvantage if they choose to dismiss the past as another country: if they brusquely separate India's post-reform growth story, for example, from the years of *dirigiste* economic management that preceded it. The same can be said of social scientists who hope to make sense of India in terms of normative counterfactuals that have little regard for political possibilities in the country they are studying. Not much is to be gained from saying that India in the 1960s should have been more like South Korea, regardless of how we might imagine South Korea to have been at that time.

We do strongly take the view, however, as we said in the Preface, that explorations of India's economy, politics and society that cling to ideas of Indian exceptionalism are deficient in important respects. There are very significant differences between the organization of the caste system in India and forms of social stratification that prevailed in the American South into the 1960s, or in apartheid South Africa, or indeed in contemporary Peru or Israel. But there are also some useful lessons to be learned from cross-country comparisons or more general theoretical models (see, for example, Cox 1948). The same can be said of the rise of Maoism in eastern India over the past decade or so. Maoism in India is different from Maoism in China and Nepal, not to say from rebel movements in parts of West Africa. Yet there can still be instructive points of comparison between these movements in terms of their funding and recruitment systems or in regard to some of their ideological pronouncements, and some common insights and hypotheses that are worthy of exploration: for example, on the relative importance of greed and grievance (Collier and Hoeffler 2004; Cramer 2006), on possible breakdowns in systems of state patronage (Di John 2009), or on the possibility of resource curse effects (Ross 1999) in states like Jharkhand, Orissa and Chhattisgarh.

Studies of Indian development in the first two decades after Independence commonly included contributions from economists, political scientists and sociologists who would never have thought to call themselves 'Indianists'. They believed nonetheless that serious study of India might help them make sense of more general debates about economic development or democratization. Joan Robinson (1962), Edward Shils (1961) and Albert Hirschman (1967) all come to mind, along with the demographer Kingsley Davis (1951), and Marxist historians like Victor Kiernan (1967) and Maurice Dobb (1963). In the 1970s and 1980s, and for much of the 1990s, India fell out of favour with comparativists, prompted in part by its growing isolationism. The resurgence of Hindu nationalism in the 1980s, or of a deepening subaltern politics, were more often examined by career Indianists, if we can put it this way, than by students of comparative religious nationalism or ethnicity. Even studies of democratic deepening in India, some of which were truly outstanding (Rudolph and Rudolph 1987), for the most part had little regard for more general debates on democratization and economic development. (There are, of course, some notable exceptions to this generalization. It is important to acknowledge that historians of India made tremendous contributions throughout this period to global debates on imperialism (Ambirajan 1978; Stokes 1980), nationalism (Bayly 1998; Chatterjee 1986), and the meanings and local practices of colonialism (Arnold 1993). Some of these studies have contributed to the new and emerging field of global or transnational history: see Bayly (2004, 2007) and Lake and Reynolds (2008). Exports of Indian academic expertise in key respects ran ahead of theoretical importations during these years.)

More recently, however, India's re-entry into the global public arena has brought mainstream social scientists flocking back to India, including large numbers of economists and political scientists trained in the United States. Some of their studies can betray a lack of familiarity with Indian realities, or with its diverse histories and geographies, and it is no part of our purpose to put comparative or theoretical studies on a pedestal. Inevitably, too, some of these studies rehearse arguments and present conclusions that are already well known to serious students of India. Novelty is sometimes in the eye of the beholder. At their best, however, these new studies provide welcome insights into many of the questions that we pose in *India Today*. So much so, indeed, that the reader will see that in each of the chapters that follow we begin with some intuitions that seem to us to flow from more general bodies of theory – that is, we aim to start each chapter with broad-based reasons for constructing answers to our questions in some ways and not in others.

We shall have more to say about the 'new Indianism' later in the chapter. At that point, too, we will comment further on the organization of our text and the goals we have set for ourselves. Before we pick up these threads, however, we want to provide a very brief account of how India in 2000 became India in 2000, if we can put it so crudely. Readers who require an in-depth account of India's changing political economy from *c.*1950 to *c.*2000 are encouraged to consult key sources flagged throughout the chapter. What follows is bound to be schematic, but we hope it provides readers with information they will find helpful in making sense of India post-2000, not least with reference to broader debates in social science.

1.2   Path-Dependencies and Present Histories

An important vein of work in contemporary social science – though one with a long ancestry – examines the influence of what has come to be called historical path-dependency. Acemoglu, Johnson and Robinson (2001), for example, are prominent amongst those scholars who hold that long-run patterns of economic growth and development are shaped very largely by the quality of a country's institutions (broadly, the rules of the game or incentive regimes, something they model in terms of property rights guarantees and respect for the rule of law: see also chapter 2). They argue that 'neo-Europes' like New England, Australia and New Zealand prospered because English and other European migrants to these shores brought with them high-quality institutions that were locally improved upon. Untroubled by dangerous tropical diseases, these migrants settled in their new countries, where they invested in their futures. In Jamaica, in contrast, or in some parts of Iberian America, and, later on, in much of West Africa, European migrants were less minded to put down roots. These lands were rife with dangerous infectious diseases, and wealth could be extracted at a distance with the aid of forced labour systems.

Sugar, coffee, gold and diamonds have all been mentioned in this regard, and later on oil. In a second and complementary paper, Acemoglu, Johnson and Robinson (2002) argue that many regions which reported relatively high average per capita incomes in *c*.1800 suffered a reversal of fortune in the nineteenth century. Locally autocratic regimes, created to meet the practical needs of plantation or mining economies, found themselves poorly equipped to take advantage of the new industrial technologies which began to emerge from capitalist North-west Europe. Instead, it was the settler colonies which imported these new technologies and which developed better industrial technologies of their own. They were able to do so, Acemoglu et al. conclude (following Marx (2008), Barrington Moore (1966) and Robert Brenner (1977) it should be said), very largely because of the quality of the institutions they had imported and developed two centuries previously. (For a more shaded account of this *longue durée*, see Austin 2008a.)

Clearly, history matters; indeed, it matters rather a lot. Mahmood Mamdani (1996) believes that many of the problems confronting post-colonial African states today – notably those of nation-building and 'tribalism' – can be traced back to systems of colonial indirect rule which accorded racial identities to citizens and ethnic identities to subjects. Ethnic fractionalization is a problem for Africa, but it is a manufactured one rather than an original condition (see also Laitin 2007). Partha Chatterjee (1993) and Nicholas Dirks (2001) have each made a parallel argument about British rule in India. The British may not have invented 'the caste system', but the colonial ethnographic state – and the Census of British India most of all – did much to harden identities around caste (or ethnic) categories which the British used alongside religious categories to govern and even produce their imperial subjects. An earlier generation of historians, not to mention nationalists, described this as 'divide and rule'. Politics in India continues to be informed by these caste identities, although, as we explain in chapter 12, hierarchical rankings of castes or *jatis* are far less commonly accepted now than fifty or a hundred years ago.

Geography also matters, as the AJR model begins to suggest. Institutions adapt in part to geographical conditions, even as they also modify those conditions over time. Recent work by Engerman and Sokoloff (1997) and Sokoloff and Engerman (2000), mainly on the Americas, as well as by Easterly and Levine (2003; see also Nunn 2009; and Austin 2008b), has resurrected the idea that at least some of the variation that we currently observe in global patterns of governance can be traced back to the land/labour ratios that take hold in different soil and climate zones (Goody 1971; Myint 1964). Crudely, in regions where land is scarce and labour is plentiful, highly centralized political regimes evolve to manage access to the limited resource. This is the story of East Asia (Wittfogel 1957; see also Pomeranz 2000). In regions where land is plentiful but labour is scarce, political systems emerge which seek control over labour in less territorialized ways. This is the story of Africa, slavery regimes very much included. As in East Asia, rule is coercive, but it is more decentralized and less conducive to the building of strong bureaucracies (Goody 1971; Herbst 2000; Hopkins 1973; see also Nunn 2008). Land markets are limited and incentives for agricultural innovation correspondingly are diminished.

Of course, this is not to say that history (or geography) is everything, or that the paths a country treads are always narrowly circumscribed or foreordained (Poteete 2009). The basic intuition of most path-dependency models is nonetheless supportive of a certain scepticism about the capacity of existing governments significantly to change the future history of a country: hence the importance of regime change in some models. We know, for example, that Africa's population growth rates have more than tripled over the past fifty years, and governments across the continent now have to adjust to new demographic and political realities. Employment growth is a critical issue and conflicts over land and resources are becoming more common, not least in parts of East and South Africa (Moore 2005). Whether these states have the capacity to act effectively is another matter. The demographic past still weighs heavily in the region. Discontinuous historical change, meanwhile, picks up on the importance of conflict and revolutions in changing previous historical paths. The French and American Revolutions are commonly cited in this regard: abrupt breaks with the past that paved the way for new institutional settlements. More recently, economic historians have signalled the importance of revolutionary and post-conflict settlements in Japan (in 1867 and again in 1945), as well as in China (1949 and possibly 1976–8), Taiwan (1949) and South Korea (1945). All are seen as turning points on the roadway to economic development (see Frieden 2006).

But what of India? India witnessed major institutional changes in the colonial era and immediately after 1947; albeit many of its post-Independence institutions grew out of British machineries of rule. Since the time of the Constituent Assembly (1946–9), however, India apparently hasn't suffered (or embraced) the sorts of upheaval that have been seen in many other post-colonial states. Continuity seems to be a more accurate watchword for post-Independence India. But, if this is true, how do we make sense of an apparent reversal of economic fortunes in India since about 1980? How do we explain India's take-off or its ability to sustain concerted economic growth for more than thirty years? One answer might be that India gives the lie to strong path-dependency arguments, or to arguments that focus in a very singular fashion on institutional quality (or change) as a precondition for a sustained growth acceleration. We shall have more to say on this in chapter 2. It is an argument that has some merit. Good policies and good leadership might matter more than mainstream social science currently allows. Another answer, however, and one to which we are more generally inclined, is that India *has* been going through a revolution of sorts over the past few decades – but it is a 'quiet', even a 'silent', revolution, and one with a much slower trajectory than most of the revolutions that we commonly identify (Ahluwalia 1994; Jaffrelot 2003). As ever, it is partly a matter of wording, of how we frame events and processes.

Regarding the present history of India, we believe this is best understood in terms of three key moments. First, there are the legacies of British rule, and indeed of earlier systems of rule. If we want to understand why Bihar has long been one of India's poorest states, it helps to know that its 'landlockedness' – a key factor in the model of geography and development advanced by Jeffrey Sachs and his colleagues (see, for example, Sachs, Mellinger and Gallup 2001) – became more of a burden as the economy of colonial India was reorganized to serve Britain's trading needs on a global stage. It also helps to know that rural areas of the Bengal Presidency, of which Bihar and Orissa were component parts until 1911, were subject to the Permanent Settlement of 1793 and systems of *zamindari* (not *raiyatwari*) rule: roughly speaking, landlordism and rack-renting rather than peasant farming. There was also a version of plantation farming in north Bihar, as in Champaran. Gandhi famously helped to organize indentured indigo workers there in 1918–19, adding his weight to a struggle that had begun locally a few years earlier. The strength of New Delhi in India's federal system of governance, meanwhile, owes a good deal to the Government of India Act, 1935, as well as to the mistrust of state and local politicians that was expressed in the Constituent Assembly debates (1946–9) by Nehru and Ambedkar. Both of the main drafters of the Constitution of India were sharply critical of the conservatism and even communalism of India's provincial elites. India's present system of affirmative action also has its roots in the decision of the colonial state, in 1943, to combine reservation of seats in legislative bodies with reserved jobs in government services for members of the Scheduled Castes, and in earlier reservations of seats for the 'Depressed Classes'. We refer to these and other colonial legacies at appropriate points in *India Today*, but readers wanting comprehensive treatments of this period should again look elsewhere (see, for instance, Washbrook (2004) on south India).

A second foundation stone of India's present history is the period of nation-building and economic development that was presided over, very largely, by Prime Minister Nehru and later by his daughter, Indira

Gandhi, and his grandson, Rajiv Gandhi. The Constitution that was adopted in 1950 committed independent India to a political model that embraced elements of the Westminster and Washington systems of government. The first Lok Sabha election of 1952 was based upon universal adult suffrage, as all elections have been since. Competing political parties and independent candidates aim to win parliamentary seats on a first-past-the-post basis. A similar electoral system was introduced into the second tier of India's democratic polity – the State Legislative Assemblies – and led in most of India's provinces to the formation of Congress governments, just as at the centre. The Bharatiya Jana Sangh, flying the flag for Hindu nationalism in the early post-Independence years, failed to win more than 10 per cent of the popular vote in Lok Sabha elections through the 1950s, 1960s and 1970s. Instead, the main opposition to Nehru's Congress governments came from various wings of the Indian National Congress itself, from the communist left in Kerala and West Bengal, and sporadically from pro-business and regionalist groupings, including the Swatantra Party nationally and the Jharkhand Party in Bihar (see also table 1.1).

It was common in the 1960s for commentators to describe India as a one-party democracy. Not least this is because a 40 per cent vote share translates into a much greater share of parliamentary seats in a winner-takes-all electoral system (table 1.2). But this depiction of the 'Congress system' fails to do justice to some further aspects of India's political landscape (Kothari 1964). While independent candidates and political parties are able to stand in all of India's electoral competitions, they can only contest 'reserved constituencies' by fielding individuals from the communities for whom the seat is reserved. What in India is called compensatory discrimination, and what elsewhere is called affirmative action, provides reserved seats in the Lok Sabha for India's Scheduled Castes (SCs or ex-untouchables) and Scheduled Tribes (STs or *adivasis*) in proportion to their share in the population of India more generally – roughly 15 per cent and 8 per cent respectively. In some of India's states, and most notably in the south where anti-Brahmin political movements had already gathered force in the pre-Independence period, attempts were also made to reserve seats for some other Backward Castes in Legislative Assemblies, just as jobs in government and the public sector (the latter from 1969) were reserved for candidates applying from India's hitherto subaltern communities.

The Constitution of India was constructed first and foremost to embrace democracy and federalism, and to provide individuals with Fundamental Rights against abusive government power. This liberal agenda was made to coexist alongside an agenda for social uplift that aims to compensate SCs and STs for injustices historically committed

Table 1.1: Distribution of votes of major parties, Lok Sabha elections, 1952–2009 (in percentages)

	BJP	BJS	BLD	BSP	CPI	CPM	INC	JD	JNP	PSP	SWA
1952		3.06			3.29		44.99				
1957		5.97			8.92		47.78			10.41	
1962		9.31			9.94		44.72			6.81	7.89
1967					5.11	4.28	40.78			3.06	8.67
1971		7.35			4.73	5.12	43.68			1.04	3.07
1977			41.32		2.82	4.29	34.52		28.36		
1980					2.49	6.24	47.97				
1984	7.74				2.71	5.87	49.10		6.89		
1989	11.36				2.57	6.55	39.53	17.79	1.01		
1991	20.11				2.49	6.16	36.26	11.84	3.37		
1996	20.29				1.97	6.12	28.20	8.08	0.19		
1998	25.59			4.67	1.75	5.16	25.82	3.24			
1999	23.75			4.16	1.48	5.40	28.30	3.10			
2004	22.16			5.33	1.41	5.66	26.53				
2009	18.80			6.17	1.43	5.33	28.55				

BJP   Bharatiya Janata Party
BJS   Bharatiya Jan Sangh
BLD   Bharatiya Lok Dal
BSP   Bahujan Samaj Party
CPI   Communist Party of India
CPM   Communist Party of India (Marxist)
INC   Indian National Congress
JD   Janata Dal
JNP   Janata Party
JS   Jan Sangh
PSP   Praja Socialist Party
SWA   Swatantra Party

Source: Election Commission of India.

Table 1.2: Distribution by party of seats won in Lok Sabha elections, 1952–2009

	BJP	BJS	BLD	BSP	CPI	CPM	INC	JD	JNP/JP	PSP	SWA
1952		3			16		364				
1957		4			27		371			19	
1962					29		361			12	18
1967		35			23	19	283			13	44
1971		22			23	25	352			2	8
1977			295		7	22	154				
1980					10	37	366		72		
1984	2				6	22	404		10		
1989	85				12	33	197	143	5		
1991	120				14	35	232	59			
1996	161				12	32	140	46			
1998	182			5	9	32	141	6			
1999	182			14	4	33	114	21			
2004	138			19	10	43	145				
2009	116			21	4	16	206				

Source: Election Commission of India.

against them. The Fundamental Rights of the Constitution are thus complemented by numerous non-justiciable Directive Principles of State Policy, many of which have the effect of reinforcing group identities based on caste or ethnicity (Galanter 1984). The Constitution of 1950 guaranteed reserved seats for India's SCs and STs only up to 1960. The dependence of the Congress Party on the votes of these two groups, however, as well as on those of many Muslims and members of India's Forward Castes (Brahmins, Kshatriyas and Vaishyas), helped persuade Nehru's government, and all governments in New Delhi since his time, to continue this policy for succeeding ten-year periods. Since the end of the 1980s, as we shall see in later chapters, demands for reserved seats in India's Lok Sabha and State Assemblies have widened markedly to include the country's Other Backward Classes (roughly, those castes or sub-castes between the Forward Castes and the Scheduled Castes: mainly the Shudra *varna*), and India's women.

Nehru clearly expected caste and religious identities to wither away in a progressively modernizing India. Most likely an atheist himself, Nehru famously described the Bhakra Nangal dam on the Sutlej river in Punjab (now in Himachal Pradesh), as well as dams along the Damodar river in eastern India, as India's modern temples (Klingensmith 2003). The Prime Minister shared, that is to say, a classic mid-century faith in the inevitability of traditional ways of life giving way to modern ways of being. Urbanization, compulsory state provision of secular education, and above all industrialization would call into being new Indian citizens who would have less need for pre-modern forms of identity.

It didn't quite work out this way, however. On the one hand, the political system constructed for independent India made it rational for people to mobilize as much on the basis of group identities as on the basis of a more individualized sense of self. Caste identities were not dissolved, but instead were valorized and reinvented: the traditional, so-called, was modernized (Rudolph and Rudolph 1967). We explore why and how in chapter 12. In addition, it was clear by the 1960s that the capacity of government to provide its citizens with public goods was less than had been expected when planned development began in India in the early 1950s. Myron Weiner (1962) argued that mobilization around ethnic or other sectional interests was increasingly induced by a 'politics of scarcity': the poor performance of the Indian economy at once deprived the Government of India of revenues while at the same time it ensured that the state would become more and more the focal point for organized groups bent on drinking such milk as it could offer (see also Chatterjee 2000). Here too was an opening for India's army of fixers, brokers and bosses: the *pyraveekars*, *dalaals* and *dadas* who for a commission connect ordinary people to the state, and who themselves very often play the role of patrons who provide services to their clients (Reddy and Haragopal 1985). Kanchan Chandra maintains that India's patronage democracy functions as a 'covert auction in which basic services, which should in principle be available to every citizen, are sold instead to the highest bidder' (Chandra 2004: 292). This may be a little exaggerated, but ideology does take a back seat in India's electoral politics – the communists and religious nationalists excepted in varying degrees. Politics is mainly about capturing scarce state resources. And in India, it turns out, this is still done most effectively by voting with one's fellow caste members.

More so than in some other countries in Asia and Africa, however, the skill with which successive governments in India have negotiated the politics of scarcity helped to maintain the unity of the country at times of low economic growth (Dasgupta 2001). Ballot rigging and booth capture probably did not disturb the overall fairness of India's elections even in the era before electronic voting machines. Governments have consistently been voted out of power, and this became more common in the 1970s and 1980s as the Congress Party began to lose shape and was 'deinstitutionalized' (Kohli 1990). Other parties started to challenge more confidently for the votes of different groups of Indians: caste-based parties, regional parties and religious parties. Once in power in India's multiform democracy, moreover, non-Congress politicians, or even new factions within the Indian National Congress (which itself split in 1969), used their patronage networks to bind disaffected groups into the broader project of building India (or *Bharat*, the Hindi word for India). A free press and an (in)convenient neighbour, Pakistan, also helped to manufacture an identity that Churchill had considered oxymoronic and which Nehru and Gandhi both saw as manifest destiny – albeit one which was torn asunder by Partition, a catastrophic sequence of events centred on 1947, which, as Sunil Khilnani (1997: 202) reminds us, still haunts the political imaginaries of both India and Pakistan. And where cooptation failed, there was always force, as Portuguese Goa discovered in 1961, and as generations of people have discovered since then along India's northern and eastern borders: in Punjab, in Assam, in Nagaland, and most of all in Kashmir (Brass 1994).

India's sense of self was also encouraged by the nuts and bolts of economic development, notwithstanding that the building of roads, schools, factories and dams happened more slowly than expected. Five-year plans were introduced in 1951. The first of these was broadly neutral in its treatments of rural and urban India, and agnostic between the public and private sectors. India's Second and Third Five-Year Plans, however, which spanned the years from 1956 to 1966, and which are often taken to embody the Nehru-Mahalanobis model of planned industrialization, committed India more definitively to a model of directed economic development which found favour at that time with most development economists (Hirschman 1981). (Prasanta Chandra Mahalanobis was a dominant figure in India's Planning Commission, a body that was set up in 1950 and chaired initially by Prime Minister Nehru. First and foremost, Mahalanobis was an outstanding statistician: see Rudra 1997).

Early development economics took shape in the 1940s and 1950s around three key ideas. First, there was a critique of comparative advantage theory. Hans Singer (1950) and Raoul Prebisch (1950) each took issue with the idea that latecomer countries could develop effectively as primary goods producers. In their view, there were both theoretical and empirical reasons to suppose that prices for non-primary goods would rise faster over time than the prices of primary commodities. Developing countries had to build up infant industries as a priority, even if this meant erecting tariff barriers around the domestic economy (see also Naoroji 1901). Second, this commitment to import-substitution industrialization (ISI) implied in the short term a run of balance of trade deficits. Developing countries first had to import the machine tools and other goods that would help them build up local manufacturing capacity. A foreign-exchange constraint would become especially compelling in a country like India where ISI was intended to privilege the production of capital goods: iron and steel, chemicals, heavy engineering, etc. Flows of foreign direct investment were thin on the ground in the 1950s and 1960s, and probably would not have been very welcome in India. Happily, Nehru's ability to position India at the head of the Non-Aligned Movement helped to unlock this constraint. India was able to build a steel mill at Bokaro (Bihar) with assistance from the USSR, and another at Rourkela (Orissa) with help from West Germany. Third, the very scarcity of foreign exchange in the 1950s and 1960s, coupled with poorly formed local stock markets and supposedly weak private trading systems (some of which were coded as 'oppressive' or exploitative), inclined the Government of India to think of economic development as a project that had to be planned for and delivered by a beneficent state. (This paragraph and the next five follow Corbridge 2010: 307–9.)

Thus conceived, India's model of development through most of the 1950s and 1960s made a virtue of deferred gratification. Nehru and Mahalanobis believed that high rates of economic growth would depend on high rates of personal and government savings and their efficient mobilization for purposes of large-scale industrialization. By definition, this first wave of capital-goods based production would not be labour intensive; it would not create large numbers of goods for the under-employed peasants who wanted to leave the countryside to find more productive jobs in the modern sector. This Lewisian transformation would have to await the second stage of India's industrial revolution

(Lewis 1955). Cheap steel, chemicals and power could then be plugged into a plethora of efficient Indian-run companies that would produce bicycles, radios, two-wheel tractors and such-like for the final consumer.

Put another way, the Nehru-Mahalanobis model presupposed that India would be governed by what later would be called a developmental state, of the sort that was even then taking shape in East or South East Asia (Wade 1990). This would be a state that was relatively autonomous of privileged local classes, as Marxist theoreticians liked to put it (see also Evans 1995). In India, it would be embodied in the Planning Commission and in the Five-Year Plans themselves. The state would specify a social welfare function for the future (five, ten, fifteen or twenty-five years away) and then deploy the best economic and planning instruments to match inputs to intended outputs. The model further supposed that the Government of India could funnel resources from the agricultural sector to the non-agricultural sector without provoking a backlash among India's rural population. Nehru believed that he could square this circle in two main ways: first, by making use of Public Law (PL) 480 food aid from the USA, and, second, by means of land-ceilings legislation that would break up unproductive estates and enfranchise efficient small farmers. Agriculture was a 'bargain basement' that would free up scarce resources for use elsewhere in the developing economy (Harriss 1992).

In practice, it did not work out this way. By the early 1960s, it was apparent that increases in grain production were barely keeping pace with population growth. Food-supply growth in the 1950s came mainly from increases in the area under cultivation, but that could not continue once the land frontier closed. By the mid-1960s, many farmers were bemoaning their lot. The great Jat farmers' leader, Charan Singh, had opposed Nehru's plans for cooperative farming in the 1950s. In 1967, he defected from the Congress, before setting up the Bharatiya Kranti Dal (Indian Revolutionary Party) in 1969. Singh anticipated Michael Lipton's (1977) claim that India was suffering from high levels of urban bias. Government spending decisions were denounced as inequitable, inefficient and unsustainable. In a country where more than 75 per cent of the people still lived in the countryside – agriculture's share of GDP was as high as 61 per cent in 1950, and not much less than 50 per cent in the mid-1960s – it apparently made little sense to waste capital on inefficient urban and industrial projects. The need instead was to fund new irrigation systems and off-farm employment growth in the countryside.

This view gained currency at the end of the 1960s, following the failures of the 1965 and 1966 monsoons, and in the wake of new data showing that the incidence of absolute poverty in the Indian countryside had remained stubbornly high through that decade (Dandekar and Rath 1971). Nehru died before the crisis in Indian agriculture was fully exposed and before the suspension of planning in 1966–9. But his death also came after a disastrous war with China in 1962, and these events taken in the round continued to inform the difficult political and economic atmospheres in which first Lal Bahadur Shastri (1964–6) and then Indira Gandhi had to make their way as Prime Ministers.

Indira Gandhi has many times been compared unfavourably with her father (Nehru), and very often for good reason. She deserves to be condemned above all for the disastrous way that she fought religious fire with fire in Punjab in the early 1980s, when she covertly supported separatist forces led by Sant Bhindranwale, and for her government's suspension of democratic rule in India during the Emergency (1975–7). But what is sometimes forgotten in these comparisons is that Mrs Gandhi came to power at a time when India's democracy was deepening, when the dominance of the Congress Party/System was for the first time being challenged in New Delhi and the states, and when state–society relations more generally, in the words of Lloyd and Susanne Rudolph (1987), had moved from a pattern of 'command politics' to one of 'demand politics'. The new political landscape of the 1970s and 1980s saw not only the deinstitutionalization of the Congress Party and the rise of credible opposition parties; it also marked a period in India's political economy when a prospectively developmental state was undermined in key respects from within. That state had always been an uneasy construct in India, as Partha Chatterjee (1997, 2004) and Sudipta Kaviraj (1984, 1991) have several times reminded us. Nehru mobilized large sections of the English-speaking 'progressive' elite in support of his modernizing agenda. This elite, however, was fated to see its ambitions translated at local level by power brokers who rarely shared its stated commitments to the 'greater good' or the 'long run'. Local worlds were more often vernacular worlds, or worlds where commitments were most often forged at the level of a household, kin group or caste community. As Kaviraj (1984: 227) so memorably puts it, India's high modernist state 'had feet of vernacular clay'. At the national level, too, the highest reaches of government were captured in large degree by sectional interests, including well-to-do farmers, powerful civil servants, and business leaders who had grown used to state patronage and high tariff regimes.

Partly as a result of these compromises, GDP growth in India in the 1970s averaged only 3.1 per cent per annum, notwithstanding some good individual years (as we shall see in chapter 2). India's poverty-reduction agenda suffered in the wake of this so-called 'Hindu rate of growth', although here too the story is not a simple one: the headcount incidence of poverty declined in the 1970s as rural labour markets tightened amidst the Green Revolution (see chapter 3). By some accounts, too, the greater costs of participating in India's competitive politics led a growing number of politicians to finance their campaigns illegally and/ or through abuses of office. Civil servants, for example, were forced to stump up greater rents to acquire a desirable posting, or to head off an undesirable one. Criminals, for their part, moved into politics, both to milk the system and to deflect unwelcome attention from the justice system. This was most evident in north India, although it was hardly unknown in the south.

In the 1980s, there was a pro-business tilt in government economic policy in India. This was spearheaded first by Indira Gandhi, on her return to power in New Delhi in 1980, after less than three years in opposition (to two Janata governments), and then by her elder son, Rajiv Gandhi. GDP growth rates in the 1980s were consistently positive and ran on average close to 5.9 per cent per annum. Social scientists are still struggling to explain this upturn in the economy's performance and its possible relationships to the diversification and decentralization of manufacturing, and the burgeoning of India's higher education sector, in the 1950s and 1960s. Telling a coherent story about India's growth trajectory from 1950 to 2000 and beyond is no easy matter, as we shall see in chapter 2. It is too easy to dismiss the Nehru-Mahalanobis years as a missed opportunity, pure and simple, or to ignore some very real improvements in worker productivity in the late 1970s and 1980s. At the same time, it is clear that a growing proportion of India's economic growth through the 1980s was funded by foreign and domestic borrowing. Fiscal probity was not a first-order priority for the governments of Indira and Rajiv Gandhi, or for the Janata Dal governments which ruled India either side of 1990 and which came to power promising their mainly rural supporters farm-loan waivers and cheap power, among other things.

By early 1991, India was facing bankruptcy. The country barely had sufficient foreign-exchange reserves to cover more than a month or two of imports. There was a widespread feeling that India's political institutions were no longer robust enough to manage, let alone reform, the economy. Strong farmers' movements had emerged in the 1980s to lobby for still greater public support for India's rural economy, an objective that no political party felt able publicly to talk down (Varshney 1995). Many of these farmers, too, came from India's Other Backward Classes (OBCs), including those from communities like the Jats and the Yadavs in northern India. Northern India's OBCs had grown in strength through the 1970s and 1980s, finally catching up with their counterparts in the south of the country (Jaffrelot 2003). Many of their members were mobilized in the Lok Sabha election of 1989 by V. P. Singh, the first leader of the Janata Dal coalition government that swept Congress from power.

In 1990, Prime Minister Singh chose to act upon some of the key recommendations of the report of the Second Backward Classes Commission. The Mandal Commission Report had been commissioned by the Janata government in 1979 and then promptly shelved by Mrs Gandhi when she returned to power in New Delhi. Crucially, Singh extended the reservation of central government jobs to include most of India's OBCs. This ensured that about half, rather than just under a quarter, of such posts were now reserved for India's Scheduled Communities and the OBCs (collectively known as India's Backward Classes).

Voting along caste lines now made more sense than ever for the non-Forward Castes. This in turn inclined India's traditional elites to pursue their interests in one or both of two ways: either by pressing for the greater privatization of India's economy, and/or by swelling the ranks of India's growing Hindu nationalist movement. That movement had come alive in the 1980s in part because of the vigorous reinvention of the Bharatiya Jana Sangh as the Bharatiya Janata Party (the BJP, fronted by Lal Krishna Advani and Atal Bihari Vajpayee), and also because of some imaginative political campaigning by the *Vishwa Hindu Parishad* (VHP). The VHP, or the Worldwide Hindu Council, was formed in 1965 and is another member of the family of militant Hindu nationalist organizations (alongside the BJP and RSS) known as the *Sangh parivar*.

The attractions of Hindu nationalism have always had a strong cultural dimension, as we report in chapter 9 (see also Rajagopal 2001). This does not mean, however, that militant Hinduism wasn't also attractive to India's upper castes for more obviously material reasons. Corbridge and Harriss (2000) suggest that Hindu nationalism and economic liberalization in India must each be seen in part as an 'elite revolt' against the claims of assertive subaltern movements in India through the 1970s and 1980s. The demolition of the Babri Masjid in Ayodhya in December 1992, by *kar sevaks* (volunteers) of the VHP, dramatized these tensions further, Muslims having become a convenient enemy for political forces determined to discount inter-caste conflicts. The bombings which followed in Mumbai in March 1993, another stronghold of militant Hindu forces – here in the shape of the nativist *Shiv Sena* (the reference is to the seventeenth-century Maratha king, Shivaji Bhosle, not to the Hindu deity Lord Shiva) – also suggested to the wider world that India was in turmoil, if not in danger of falling apart.

At this juncture, most foreign observers were ill informed about the ongoing reform of the Indian economy, which in any case is commonly – if not quite accurately – dated to actions taken by the new Congress government of Narasimha Rao and Manmohan Singh in summer 1991. Even in India, it is fair to add, few observers of the country in the early 1990s would have been prepared to forecast any or all of the following: (a) that India would become one of the world's most rapidly growing

economies early in the new millennium; (b) that the forward march of
Hindu nationalism would seemingly reach a high-water mark around
2000, or that Hindu nationalist forces, once in power in New Delhi, as
they were from 1998 to 2004, would largely embrace and carry forward
India's reform agendas; (c) that violence against Muslims in India would
decline after 1993 and into the new millennium, with the horrific exception to date of the anti-Muslim pogrom that shook Gujarat in 2002; or
(d) that India's growing economic self-belief would take hold and harden
under a succession of coalition governments (from 1989 onwards), and
notwithstanding the continuing rise in many states of governments that
can be described in key respects as casteist, regionalist or even strongly
criminalized.

And yet all of these things came to pass. Taken together, they
constitute a third moment in the construction of India up to *c*.2000.

1.3   Towards a Comparative Understanding of Contemporary India

How should we understand the consequences of these reinventions
for particular constituencies in India: the poor, women, rural people,
businesses, the young, city-dwellers, *adivasis*? How did successive
governments – each of which had supposedly been captured by sectional
interests – drive a slow but apparently permanent revolution in India's
economic and political fortunes post-1980 (or 1991)? Why has the transformation of rural India been so difficult to secure? To what extent, too,
has government in India been able to re-engineer not only its relationships with business and capital, but also with ordinary men and women
through a revitalized third tier of India's democracy: the *panchayati raj*
(local government) institutions that were shocked into life in most states
by the 73rd and 74th Constitutional Amendment Acts of 1993? These
institutions have created new spaces for popular participation in local
government assemblies (including village-level public meetings, or *gram
sabhas*), as well as new oversight mechanisms through which citizens can
better track how government funds are being spent in their *panchayats*,
Blocks and districts. They have also brought women more firmly into
India's local government. One third of all seats in *panchayati raj* institutions are reserved for women. Is affirmative action working, and how
would we know? Is government becoming more responsive to citizens?
Does India even have a civil society in the Western sense: rights-bearing
individuals who can make claims on state officials in an impersonal and
transparent manner? Or is India today still a patronage democracy, as

Kanchan Chandra suggests? And what happens when a citizen can't access the state, or indeed a reasonably well-organized political party: whether the Communist Party of India (Marxist) in Kerala and West Bengal, Shiv Sena in Mumbai, the Dravida Munnetra Kazhagam in Tamil Nadu, or caste-based parties like the Rashtriya Janata Dal or the Bahujan Samaj Party in north India? Do they find new protectors from among local criminal gangs or even rebel groups? Does this help to explain the rise of Maoism in eastern India – by common consent the biggest threat to India's internal security for many decades?

These are some of the thirteen major questions which organize our account of *India Today*. Most of our chapters are T-shaped. We construct detailed answers to our questions on the basis of various broad intuitions that are suggested to us by comparative social science. In the case of chapter 2, these intuitions are provided by standard growth theories and work on the deeper determinants of economic growth. In chapter 3, they are provided by cross-country comparisons of the relationships between economic growth and poverty reduction, both cross-sectionally and over a period of years or even decades (the Kuznets hypothesis). We don't set out formally to test these models against Indian realities. Rather, we aim in each chapter to tack back and forth between our starting intuitions – what might also be called our theoretical priors – and our understanding of a large and growing empirical literature on India's changing economy, polity and society.

Chapters 2–14 are always comparative but only rarely are they written around in-depth comparisons of India with one or more countries: be it Pakistan, South Korea, China, Brazil or Russia. When we refer to comparative politics or comparative social science we have in mind an intellectual apparatus in which rigorous analysis of one country is strongly informed by an accumulating body of cross-country work of a more theoretical nature. Why do rebel movements form? What are the main preconditions for effective democratic governance? Why do people bother to vote? How do governments push through audacious reforms? Why might we expect women to benefit from an expansion of the public sphere? There is an enormous and contested body of work on all of these questions. We have necessarily drawn upon it selectively, but, we believe, in such a way as to have shown both how comparative social science illuminates the India case, and how analysis of this case contributes to more general theorizing.

PART I
ECONOMY

2
When and Why Did India Take Off?

2.1 Introduction

India's gross domestic product (GDP – the market value of all goods and services made within a country in a given year) grew at an average annual rate of 3.7 per cent from 1950–1 to 1979–80, and at about 6 per cent a year in the period from 1980–1 to 2000–1. On the face of it, something must have happened around 1980–1, or just before then, to cause the economy in India to take off. Economic theory tells us that income growth is determined by some combination of capital deepening, human capital accumulation and productivity growth, with high population growth rates pulling down per capita figures. Standard theory also tells us that the deeper determinants of growth – the reasons, in other words, for higher levels of capital accumulation or productivity growth – will most likely be found in some combination of geography, trade integration and institutional quality (Rodrik 2003). If we assume that India's basic geography hasn't changed much since 1980, we are left with trade integration and institutional quality as the two most plausible drivers of growth. Presumably one or both of these variables, both of which are partly endogenous to the growth process (that is, they are not wholly independent of high prior levels of income growth), must have changed, which is to say improved, around 1980.

In fact, matters are not quite this simple. We begin this chapter with a brief account of the empirics of India's recent growth acceleration(s), bearing in mind that it is possible that another one began in 2003–4. It is clear that rates of per capita income growth in India are now higher than they were in the 1970s and that India is performing much better in international league tables of GDP growth rates (Krueger and Chinoy

2002). It is also clear that worker productivity in India has increased since 1980 and that savings and investment rates have continued to rise (Mohan 2008). We can accept, in short, that something significant happened around 1980, and that sustained economic growth in India since that time has been pushed forward by an accumulating and more consistent set of pro-business and pro-market policies. India has entered the global marketplace more fully since the 1990s and this also helps to explain a step-up in growth rates since 2003–4. Exports of software and other high-technology products are often proposed as symbols of the New India.

Where our analysis departs from mainstream accounts of India's growth take-off is not in regard to these broad and very substantial accomplishments, but in respect of three points of omission, emphasis and interpretation. In terms of omission, first, we challenge the view that economic growth in India from 1950 to 1980 can reasonably be described either as straightforwardly failing and/or as non-contributory to India's post-1980 growth acceleration(s). This is a commonly held view, but there is no need to hold a strong version of it alongside an upbeat assessment of post-1980 (or post-1991) developments. There are good reasons, in fact, to believe that economic growth rates in India in the first three decades after Independence were close to international norms; they were also in line with what standard growth theory predicted, not least given India's starting position at the end of British rule. It is important as well to emphasize the cumulative dimensions of the growth process in India, including, for example, in the fields of technological change and infrastructural provision. This argument holds true notwithstanding that some poor policy choices undoubtedly were made by successive governments – not least by Mrs Gandhi – and that the economy in India did a poor job of pulling people out of poverty before c.1970 (very poor, if we believe that India inherited good institutions at Independence: see section 2.4 for discussion). We also dispute the view that India was blighted by a so-called Hindu rate of growth throughout the entirety of the 1950s, 1960s and 1970s, or even through all of the late 1960s and 1970s. The year 1980–1 is undeniably one turning point in India's recent economic history, but we should be cautious about characterizing growth in India from 1950 to 1980 on the basis either of standard decades or without proper regard for the difficulties – economic and political – of the 1970s. (Oddly, too, as we note later in this chapter, the economy performed quite well during the Fifth Plan period from 1974 to 1979.) Where we don't compare like with like, we sometimes draw inappropriate public policy conclusions.

Second, we note, with others, that the causes of India's economic turnaround are not yet the subject of consensus among economists. To the contrary, there is much that we still don't understand. Some economists are emphatic that growth in India in the 1980s was chimerical and debt-fuelled. Sustained economic reform and growth only begins with Narasimha Rao and Manmohan Singh in 1991. This is roughly the line of T. N. Srinivasan and Jagdish Bhagwati, not to mention domestic and foreign boosters like Gurcharan Das (2002) and Thomas Friedman (2005). Others disagree and place less emphasis on supposedly binding external constraints or the balance of payments crisis of 1990–1. They highlight productivity growth in the 1980s, particularly in the industrial sector. What remains unclear from this perspective, however, which we associate with Atul Kohli, Dani Rodrik and Arvind Subramanian, among others, is what sparked the 1980s upturn. Why should a shallow pro-business tilt in government policy produce such dramatic economic effects? Did these same attitudinal effects continue into the 1990s? Or must we explain post-1991 economic growth in other terms?

Third, in terms of the deeper determinants of economic growth, it is widely argued that institutional quality is key (Acemoglu 2009; North 1990; Rodrik and Subramanian 2004b). Markets work best where property rights are enforced, where monopolies are broken up, where transactions are properly regulated, where bureaucracies function impartially, and where there is the rule of law. But herein lie two further dilemmas. To begin with, there is the matter of timing. Do we have good reasons to suppose that the quality of India's institutions improved some time around 1980, or perhaps again in the early 2000s? (In the latter case India's growing integration into global markets might be a better *primum mobile*, as we discuss.) And if not, second, should we be heaping praise instead on heroic policymakers and economic policymaking? If so, why did small (in the 1980s) and larger (in the 1990s) policy reforms – trade policy reforms, industrial policy reforms, financial policy reforms, etc. – have such significant and sustained effects on India's underlying rate of economic growth? One possibility that we shall consider, which might be of significance for other developing countries, is that policy changes in India had sizeable GDP effects precisely because of the underlying (good) quality of India's institutions. India was a wilting sunflower waiting to be watered. This is an argument made by De Long (2003) and Subramanian (2007), and it is an interpretation of events that we find suggestive, albeit not without problems of its own. Another argument pays more attention to class and politics – very often the main drivers of institutional change, as Adam Przeworski (2004) reminds us. It characterizes recent economic changes in India as an elite revolt against *dirigisme* that has come increasingly to be led by big business interests. What has been unbound in India since the 1980s is a more vital process of capitalist accumulation and dispossession. This is most apparent in the country's small formal sector, but it is presumably evident as well in the informal sector where nine out of ten Indians make a living (though the mechanisms here are less well understood). Writing in the *Wall Street Journal* on 8 November 2007, James Robinson declared 'that solving the problem of underdevelopment is all about "getting politics right" in poor countries'. Broadly speaking, that is the line we adopt here, and that we explore further in chapter 6. Since around 1980, albeit with gathering force, India's business elites have set Prometheus free. Corporate capitalism has been unbound.

2.2   Years of Failure?

A common counterpart to today's *India Shining* story is the suggestion that the economy in India performed very badly in the decades that followed the founding of the Republic in 1950 (save perhaps for the 1950s themselves). 'Thirty years of failure' is the charge made by those who believe that economic growth in India in the 1980s was largely debt financed, and thus in some senses illusory.

The failure thesis has been proposed most stridently by pro-market reformers such as Deepak Lal (1999) and Jagdish Bhagwati (1993), both of whom suggest that 'development economics' itself, which they associate with a mistrust of the market mechanism and a romanticization of government capabilities, was significantly to blame for India's apparent under-performance under Nehru and (more so) Indira Gandhi. It is a thesis, however, that finds broad support within the academy and among policymakers. The conventional view of economic growth in India from the 1950s to the cusp of the 1990s is that India's planners neglected agriculture, which then as now was the main provider of jobs for Indians, paid scant heed to the importance of micro-economic efficiency, not least because of the over-protection of workers in the organized sector (Besley and Burgess, 2004; but see also Miyamura 2010), misused scarce public monies to build up capital-intensive industries, and managed the whole sorry edifice behind increasingly autarkic trade barriers. Instead of moving swiftly on from import-substitution industrialization to export-led growth in the mid-1960s, when a balance of payments crisis and pressure from the United States opened a door in that direction (Mukherji 2000), India's economy under Indira Gandhi took on the characteristics of the Licence-Permit-Quota Raj. Indian entrepreneurs found themselves drowning in red tape or mired in rent-seeking activities. Government failed to direct the market or substitute efficiently for it. Instead, it came to be known most of all for its partiality and venality.

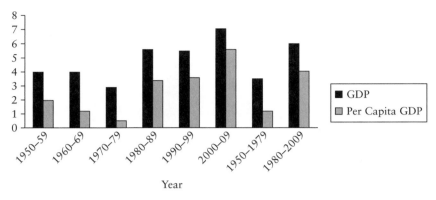

Figure 2.1: India's long-term growth, 1950–2009.

Source: World Bank data.

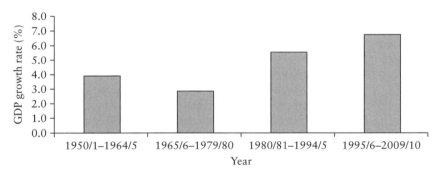

Figure 2.2: Phases of growth: command and demand politics.

Source: World Bank data.

Evidence for this story of expectations unmet – of optimism in the early Nehru years giving way to the darkness of India's Emergency years (1975–7) and beyond – has never been hard to find. Indeed, standard treatments of India's growth story are set up precisely to highlight such changes of gear. One common procedure is to group data by decades: the 1950s, 1960s and so on. The decadal averages are then plotted as in figure 2.1. Another procedure exploits the crisis years of the mid-1960s: the death of Nehru in 1964, the crop failures of 1965 and 1966, the suspension of planning and the balance of payments crisis of 1966. This gives us a narrative of rise and fall (1950/51–1964/65 versus 1965/66–1979/80), or a rise-fall-and-rise-again narrative that updates to 1990 and beyond (see figure 2.2). This chronology is consistent with the idea that the state was largely in command of society up to the mid-1960s,

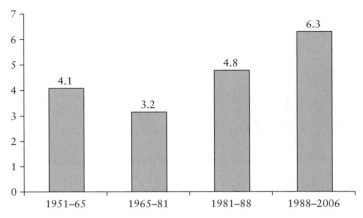

Figure 2.3: Panagariya's four phases of growth.

Source: Panagariya (2008).

but thereafter was forced to respond, often unwisely and with a large measure of profligacy, to various politically powerful demand groups (see Rudolph and Rudolph 1987; and discussion in chapters 1 and 7). Lastly, and more idiosyncratically one might think, there is the fourfold division of India's post-1950 economic history that is reproduced here as figure 2.3. This figure is taken from Arvind Panagariya's important book from 2008, *India: The Emerging Giant.* Panagariya's aim is to downplay the scale of the growth upturn that Kohli and others describe for India in the 1980s.

A powerful narrative emerges from all of these figures that seems to confirm that India suffered from at least fifteen and possibly twenty-five years of economic failure – depending on whether we think that the 'Hindu rate of growth', so-called, lasted until *c.*1980 or (with inflationary disguise) until *c.*1990. Scholars generally prefer not to go all the way back to 1950 or 1951, on the basis that the First Five-Year Plan was (a) under-financed, and/or (b) reasonably liberal in its treatments of trade and foreign investment (this is Panagariya's view: 2008, chapter 2).

We need to be careful, however, when proposing a narrative that claims to make sense of these summary tables or figures. Decades beginning with year 0 and ending with year 9 have an immediacy that can be hard to resist: the 1950s, the 1960s. But there is generally nothing more profound going on. Unless we have good reason for supposing that activity A begins in Year 0, or lasts for just ten, twenty or thirty years, we should be sceptical of the value of constructing time-series data that are grouped into conventional decades. Even econometricians are at odds with one another on when (or if) there is a sharp break in India's growth figures: Wallack (2003) spotlights the beginning of the 1980s, while Ghate and Wright (2009, cited in Ghate, Wright and Fic 2010) plump for the mid-1980s.

The basis for periodization in figures 2.2 and figure 2.3 *is* given in part by an underlying logic or hypothesis (command versus demand politics; styles of economic management). But suppose we end Phase 1 with 1966–7? We might do this on the basis that the crop failures which largely caused a decline in GDP from 1965–7 were a necessary corollary of the urban bias that was hard-wired into the Second and Third Five Year Plans (1956–66). The overall growth rate figures for Phases 1 and 2 of the Panagariya graph become 3.54 per cent and 3.85 per cent: much harder then to tell a simple story of rise and fall (the good Jawaharlal, the bad Indira). Or suppose we have Phase 2 end in 1975–6 and not in 1979–80? The steep contraction of India's economy in 1979–80 then goes in Phase 3. And what of Panagariya's choice of 1988–9 as the start of a brave new world of real reform and growth – what he calls the 'Triumph of Liberalization'? It is unclear what intellectual basis there is for starting his fourth phase with the one year to date when the Indian economy saw double-digit growth (10.2 per cent). The presentational effect, however, is clear as daylight. (Note: the average annual growth rate from 1976–7 to 1987–8 is 4.05 per cent. From 1979–80 to 1987–8 it is 3.82 per cent.)

William Easterly maintains that 'Humans are suckers for finding patterns where none really exist, like seeing the shapes of lions and giraffes in the clouds' (Easterly 2009, referring to *The Drunkard's Walk* by Leonard Mlodinow (2008)), and this is partly what we are driving at. Of course, there is no denying that the economy in India has picked up since the 1980s in terms of sustainability and improvements in per capita income growth, and even more so in terms of how it has been faring relative to other developing countries. Statistical legerdemain should not blind us to the fact that Indira Gandhi enacted policies from 1969–73 that were *dirigiste* and anti-business to an extraordinarily unhelpful degree. Irritated and humiliated by the Americans in 1966–7, when President Johnson exploited India's extreme dependence on PL 480 food aid, and determined to outflank her rivals in the Congress Party by tacking left, Mrs Gandhi instructed senior civil servants like I. G. Patel to nationalize many of India's leading banks (in 1969), sought the regulation of big business houses through the Monopolies and Restrictive Trade Practices (MRTP) Act, also in 1969, and struck hard at inflows of foreign investment and technology with the Foreign Exchange Regulation Act (FERA) in 1973 (for an excellent summary, see Panagariya 2008: chapter 3). We find it helpful, even so, to acknowledge that the 1970s was a difficult decade for many developing countries, not least in the wake of the oil price rises of 1973–4 and a global economic downturn. Mrs Gandhi's governments did little to improve the lives of ordinary Indians before the Emergency (1975–7), save for her important sponsorship of the Green Revolution, but India was very far from being the only country to suffer from lower than expected growth in the 1970s. It is almost too easy to condemn India for its 'Hindu rate of growth', and too easy to assume that the economy failed more generally throughout the pre-reform period. At the very least, we need to push harder at the counterfactual logic that informs the failure story, and why this logic might be flawed. Four issues stand out.

First, there are reasons to think that the Indian economy took off most visibly not in 1980–1, or indeed in 1991, but in 1950 after 'a near stagnation in per capita income . . . during the first half of the twentieth century' (Nayyar 2006: 1452; see also Clark and Wolcott 2003). Deena Khatkhate brusquely dismisses this suggestion of Deepak Nayyar as 'fatuous and facetious . . . any policy, statist or otherwise, with India's interests at the centre, would have achieved better results than under a colonial regime' (2006: 2204). In terms of simple figures, however, Nayyar is clearly right, and we need to keep his argument in mind when we return later on to broader arguments about colonial legacies and institutional quality. India's platform for higher rates of growth from 1980 onwards was more secure than the platform bequeathed to India by the British in 1947. Low rates of family-planning knowledge and uptake into the 1960s and 1970s further ensured that more downwards pressure was placed on per capita income figures before 1980 than afterwards. Population growth rates of close to 2.0 per cent in the 1950s and 1960s slowed to less than 1.6 per cent in the 2000s. Even if we agree with Mamdani (1973) that some poor families had large numbers of children because they were poor – both as a form of insurance against growing old and to take advantage of inter-generational flows of wealth from children to their parents – it can hardly be denied that low levels of information flow and human-capital formation in India in the 1950s and 1960s, especially, and most of all in rural areas, were contributory factors to low household-income growth and were still another legacy of British rule. As Pranab Bardhan further points out (personal communication), 'the most damning commentary on the colonial legacy is that, at the end of British rule, life expectancy at birth was about 29 years'.

Second, as Jessica Wallack (2003) reminds us, economic growth is bound up with broad processes of structural transformation. Savings rates are generally low in very poor countries – India is an exception here – and value-added opportunities can be limited in the dominant primary-producing sectors of the economy. Poor countries are often locked in poverty traps (Collier 2007). The 'Big Push' theories of economic development that took hold in the 1950s, and that were expressed in some degree in India's Second and Third Five Year Plans, recognized this point. In retrospect, we might agree they were a little crude, or that they paid less attention than they should have done to the quality and capacity of the pusher (the state, mainly). But the idea that development is likely to shift people out of low value-added occupations into higher-value activities (notably manufacturing industry, latterly some service jobs) is as relevant today as it was when W. Arthur Lewis was writing in the 1950s, or Ricardo, Marx and Marshall before him. It follows then, as Wallack suggests, that there are good a priori reasons for expecting lower rates of GDP growth in India in the 1950s and 1960s, when agriculture still dominated the economy, than in the 1980s or 1990s, even allowing for a much slower than expected reduction in agricultural employment in India post-1980 (see chapter 4). There is a danger that we may not make valid comparisons. In Wallack's view, India's growth acceleration in the 1980s was caused less by improvements in sectoral growth rates (within agriculture, industry or services) than because of shifts from 'slow-growing toward faster-growing areas of the economy' (Wallack 2003: 4312).

Third, there is the matter of anachronism and the plausibility of the assumed counterfactual. We have partly dealt with this by raising the issue of Big Push theories of economic development. Many of the policies that were informed by these models took at face value the conventional economic thinking of the 1950s: for example, about market failure or absence, about the importance of economic diversification and industrialization, about the need for strong and enlightened state actions. And in large degree they did so for good reason. Few voices were raised against the orthodoxies of 'development economics' in the mid-1950s or early 1960s. In India, arguably the first sustained intellectual critique of planned industrialization was published in 1970 by Bhagwati and Desai (though see also Singh 1964). More recently, some proponents of a strong failure thesis have argued that India should have changed course economically in 1966. Perhaps so: but then the question arises as to why India didn't change course.

Strong versions of the failure thesis assume two points that should not go unchallenged. On the one hand, they assume that Indira Gandhi could simply have selected a new economic model in 1966. They put to one side the very real political difficulties that Mrs Gandhi was facing at this time, and that drove her increasingly towards left populism in the late 1960s. After all, it is widely recognized that Mrs Gandhi was more of a pragmatist than an ideologue (Patel 2002). On the other hand, they make the strong assumption that nothing good came of planned industrialization. This assumption neglects the fact that India's development model in the 1950s and 1960s was not simply about economic growth, but was also about nation-building – about building a stronger, more independent, and more geographically inclusive country. It also had to deal with difficult colonial legacies: of weak industrialization, for example, and of different land tenure regimes. An activist regional policy fed into this model and secured benefits over the longer run that are not considered in narrow failure models.

These models generally also neglect the fact that Nehruvian investments in heavy engineering and infrastructure, or indeed in Indian institutes of management or technology, can be shown over a period of fifty or so years to have delivered significant benefits to long-run economic growth. It is not just a matter of costs, or of bad policy choices. (T. N. Srinivasan does acknowledge this legacy. We return to his preferred counterfactual later in the chapter.) A recent IMF Working Paper prepared by Kochhar and colleagues concludes that, 'in 1981 India had approximately the normal share of output and employment in manufacturing [relative to all developing countries]' (2006: 22). They accept that policy distortions helped shape a manufacturing sector that used too little labour and too much capital (ibid.17: a common description of Indian industrialization). But they also contend that 'In this cloud of distortion may well have resided a silver lining – in creating capabilities that did not exist in the typical poor country, India may have created potential sources of growth that would allow it to follow a different growth path from other countries as policy distortions were removed' (ibid.: 18). Specifically, Kochhar et al. cite investments in the Nehruvian era in 'skilled human capital, built through the technology, management and research institutes, as well as through the public sector' (ibid.: 27) as one building block of India's post-1990 IT boom. Another positive legacy that they point up is improved state capacity across India as a result of deliberate diversification policies. Again, the (unintended?) benefits of this diversification would be reaped, they argue, 'when the constraints placed on the states were lifted in the post-1980s period' (ibid.).

Fourth, there is an argument deployed most forcefully by Bradford De Long. The novelty of De Long's essay is that it develops an approach from basic growth theory to investigate how 'odd' India's economy looked c.1992. The failure thesis argues that India's economy became something of an outlier in the 1960s and 1970s, mainly because of pervasive economic distortions and bad policy choices. De Long constructs a cross-country regression of the average growth rate of output per worker against three proximate determinants of growth in a standard Solow model: the share of investment in GDP, the population growth rate, and the log of output per worker in 1960 (a proxy for the prospect for rapid catch-up, or of a technology gap). The regression was run for eighty-five economies, using data from 1960 to 1992, and De Long finds that 'there is very little that appears unusual about India's economic growth between independence and the late-1980s. . . . from 1960 to 1992, India lies smack in the middle of the scatter of world growth rates' (2003: 189). Just to make the point crystal clear, De Long concludes by noting:

> the extraordinary thing about India's post-World War II growth is how ordinary and average it seemed to be – up until the end of the 1980s. It is not nearly as bad as growth performance in Africa. It is not nearly as good as growth performance in East Asia. It is average – suggesting either that India's poor growth management policies were not that damaging, or rather that they were par for the course in the post-World War II world. (Ibid.: 193)

2.3   Economic Reform and Liberalization

Let us now return to our first question: when and why did India take off? The long-run perspective that Nayyar, Wallack, De Long and others set out is a useful antidote to what might be called heroic presentism, and is of a piece with our efforts to reconsider the pivotal importance of 1980 (or 1991). To repeat: if India's growth transition since c.1980 is mysterious to some economists (Rodrik and Subramanian 2005), it is so in part because too much effort has been expended in developing overdrawn and sometimes misguided comparisons with the years of 'Hindu Growth' which came before it. We should not ignore the difficulties facing India after colonial rule; nor should we discount the role played in India's post-1980 growth story by investments made cumulatively in the 1950s, 1960s and 1970s in human and physical capital accumulation. Basu and Maertens (2007) also note that one of India's very best single years of GDP growth (9 per cent) came in 1975–6. The fact that this happened – distastefully – during the Emergency may have directed attention away from the fact that annual average growth was only a touch short of 5 per cent throughout the Fifth Plan period (1974–9).

Of course, none of this means there isn't an important and rather dramatic story to tell about India's growth surge since c.1980 – a surge that has few peers within the global economy, whether in terms of rates or longevity. Annual GDP growth rates in India in the period 1950–80 never climbed above 4 per cent across a full run of ten years, and often were below 2 per cent in the early 1970s. Compare this with the period from 1980 to 2010. The Indian economy has not contracted since

Table 2.1: The world's fastest-growing countries, 1980–2003 (per cent per year)

Country	1980–90	Rank	1990–2003	Rank	1980–2003	Rank
China	10.3	2	9.6	1	10.0	1
Botswana	11.0	1	5.2	6	7.6	2
Korea, Rep. of	9.0	3	5.5	5	7.3	3
Singapore	6.7	6	6.3	2	6.5	4
Oman	8.4	4	4.3	8	6.3	5
India	5.7	8	5.9	3	5.8	6
Thailand	7.6	5	3.7	9	5.6	7
Mauritius	6.0	7	5.2	6	5.6	7
Malaysia	5.3	9	5.9	3	5.6	7

Source: Ahmed and Vashney (2008).

1979–80 (when it shrank by fully –5.2 per cent, following earlier contractions in 1972–3, 1965–6 and 1957–8), although per capita incomes did fall back slightly in 1991–2 when the economy was subjected to a more concerted round of pro-market adjustments. Hausmann, Pritchett and Rodrik (2005: 305) describe eighty-three growth accelerations in the global economy from 1950–92 (including India from 1982). They define a growth acceleration as an increase in per capita growth of 2 percentage points or more, where the increase in growth has to be sustained for at least eight years and the post-acceleration growth rate has to be at least 3.5 per cent per year. They further note that the global incidence of growth accelerations declines sharply across this period. India, then, which may be on the brink of recording two growth accelerations within a period of thirty years, as well as maintaining continuous economic growth, has outperformed most countries in the global South. Other countries have exceeded India's rate of GDP growth on an annualized basis, or perhaps over five years, but only China among large developing countries has been India's peer since 1980. India has a vibrant economy that now ranks in the top 10 per cent of global performers (table 2.1).

Some clues as to what has been driving this growth surge are apparent as soon as we link empirics to theory. Capital accumulation will increase where domestic and foreign savers spot profitable investment opportunities. Interestingly, India has long enjoyed high savings rates. As figure 2.4 indicates, savings rates of between 10 per cent and 20 per cent were common even in the 1960s and 1970s. Investment rates ran ahead of domestic savings rates then because of external capital inflows. In the 2000s, however, savings rates in India jumped closer to 30 per cent, taking them up to levels seen previously only in East

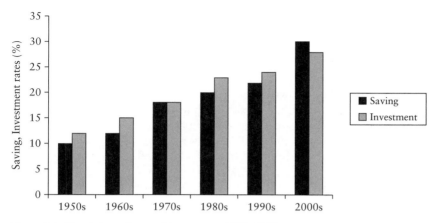

Figure 2.4: Trends in savings and investment, 1950–2008.

Asia. India has become both a significant exporter of capital and a destination that is better able to attract high-quality technologies from abroad. Partly for this reason, a number of recent studies have found that total factor productivity (TFP) in India has increased significantly since 1980 (as compared to the years from 1950–80). Roughly defined, TFP is a measure of efficiency gains in the use of capital and labour, including from technical progress. Barry Bosworth, Susan Collins and Arvind Virmani, (2007, table 3) in a study prepared for the US National Bureau of Economic Research, estimate that output per worker in India increased by 1.3 per cent per annum on average from 1960–80, with TFP growth during that period barely positive (0.2 per cent). In the period from 1980 to 2004, in contrast, they estimate growth in average output per worker at 3.8 per cent per annum and TFP growth at 2 per cent, or just over half of total output per worker growth. They identify the other proximate drivers of growth as physical capital formation (1.4 per cent per annum) and education (0.4 per cent) (see also Bosworth and Collins 2007; and Virmani 2006).

The larger question, however, is: 'what has been driving higher rates of capital accumulation and TFP, the proximate causes of India's growth acceleration'? Happily, there is now a fair amount of agreement on the basic causal chain. According to Rodrik and Subramanian, 'When Indira Gandhi returned to power [in 1980] . . . she aligned herself politically with the organized private sector and dropped her previous [socialist] rhetoric' (2005: 195). Much like Atul Kohli (2006a, 2006b), they go on to suggest that Indira and Rajiv Gandhi adopted macro-economic policies through the 1980s that increasingly were pro-business, but not pro-market: that is, they eased restrictions on capacity expansion for incumbents, removed price controls and reduced corporate taxes, but did little to boost trade liberalization (ibid.). Significantly, they also maintain, with Bosworth and Collins, that TFP increased sharply in the 1980s – to an average growth rate of 2.49 per cent per annum. This rate of growth is not only much higher than in the 1970s, for which they report negative TFP growth overall, but is also higher than in the 1990s (1.57 per cent per annum) – all of which leads Rodrik and Subramanian to conclude that there was a productivity surge in India in the 1980s. India's growth through the 1980s was not simply an effect of structural transformation, or 'catching up' (*pace* Wallack). Rather, it was powered by research and productivity improvements that eclipsed those in all other world regions save for East Asia; these improvements were mainly centred, moreover, in India's manufacturing economy (Madsen et al. 2010).

Rodrik and Subramanian recognize that further and more pro-market rounds of economic reform became necessary in India after the crises of internal and external indebtedness that hit the country in 1990–1. They also acknowledge that India remained one of the more closed economies in the developing world in 1990. Indeed, they describe India's reforms in the early 1980s as 'more import substitution, [which was] attractive from a political economy perspective because they created virtually no losers' (ibid.: 225). They insist, even so, that economic growth in India in the 1980s was driven as much by productivity gains as by deficit financing, and that the growth surge that revived India after the crisis of 1991–2 was powered very substantially by the 'strong base of manufacturing and productivity growth' (ibid.) that was put in place in the 1980s. Finally, Rodrik and Subramanian tackle head on the conundrum that seems to be at the heart of their explanation: why such big gains from such limited policy changes? Their answer, which has been taken up at greater length by Arvind Subramanian (2007), is that India's strong underlying institutions and high rates of savings, together with its position as an outlier in the 1970s in global terms – a country 'far inside its possibility frontier' (ibid.: 217) – allowed small 'attitudinal' changes on the part of government to 'unleash . . . the organized and incumbent private sector sometime in the early-1980s' (ibid.).

We shall come back to this 'trigger' argument shortly. Needless to say, it is not an argument that sits well with scholars who write off the 1980s as a period of 'hesitant and limited' rather than 'systemic' reforms (Srinivasan, 2005; see also Bhagwati 1993), or who argue that growth in the 1980s was powered mainly by public-sector employment growth and real-wage expansion, none of which could be sustained beyond the debt trap that closed in India c.1990–1. Williamson and Zagha echo a more general line when they declare that the Indian economy in 1991 was in urgent need of further and more radical reform. 'The central government fiscal deficit increased rapidly, to 8.5 per cent of GDP at its peak in 1986–87' (2002: 8), and, while it fell back at the end of the decade, the combined deficits of the centre and India's states reached 9.9 per cent in 1990–1. External debt, meanwhile, had shot up from just under $20 billion in 1980 to just under $70 billion in 1990, with much of the increased indebtedness taking the form of relatively short-term loans from private creditors at high interest rates. By the early summer of 1991, India had sufficient reserves to pay for barely a few weeks' worth of imports and its international credit rating was down-graded by Moody's and by Standard and Poor (Corbridge and Harriss 2000: 152).

In these circumstances, India probably was required to make more deep-seated economic reforms, and certainly was wise to do so (see chapter 6). This was the case notwithstanding that some of the country's reserve problems had been caused by events that were more contingent than structural in nature (the Gulf War, for example, and an associated loss of remittance incomes from Non Resident Indians (NRIs)). Initially, the 'systemic' reforms that Srinivasan likes to celebrate were enacted mainly to stabilize an economy in crisis. The rupee was devalued by about 18–20 against major currencies in the summer of 1991, and spending cuts were proposed in Manmohan Singh's first budget. Thereafter, successive governments have moved more or less purposefully to reform India's investment regime, its trade policy regime, its tax system and its financial sector. Arguably, less progress was made at the end of the 1990s than either before or after that time.

Details on particular reform policies can be found elsewhere (Ahluwalia 2002; McCartney 2009a; Panagariya 2008), but the scale of what has been achieved can be indicated easily enough. The most remarkable changes were engineered in the trade and industrial policy arenas. India's share of trade in GDP was 14.6 per cent in 1990–1, at which time too the importation of consumer goods was strongly regulated. Average weighted tariff rates were as high as 72.5 per cent in 1991–2. By the mid-1990s, import licensing had been abolished and average weighted tariff rates had fallen to almost 25 per cent. India's share of trade in GDP jumped to 21.4 per cent in 2001–2 and by the end of the 2000s was over 45 per cent. Neither in terms of trade openness nor foreign investment received is India anything like as globalized as China, but, on the plus side, the country now has a reduced debt burden (as a share of GDP) and ample foreign reserves, something which served it well during the Great Recession of 2008–9.

As is well known, too, India's service exports have grown sharply since the 1990s, including those of software. High-tech India benefitted not only from trade liberalization after 1992, but also from a foreign investment regime that was liberalized almost year on year in the 1990s, notwithstanding early resistance from a few domestic firms that were opposed to foreign competition. Industrial licences, meanwhile, were abolished in July 1991 for all bar eighteen industries, a number that has been much reduced since. Progress has been slower to effect in agriculture, in the power sector and in regard to the reservation of certain goods for production by small-scale industries. As several observers have pointed out, this is mainly because economic reform in India has had to be negotiated in a multi-party democracy. What Varshney (2000) calls 'elite reforms' – those affecting trade, industrial licensing and foreign direct investment – could be pushed through quickly by Rao and Singh because they did not directly threaten the livelihoods of ordinary Indians (see chapter 6 for discussion).

By the time of India's fourteenth and fifteenth Lok Sabha elections, in 2004 and 2009 respectively, it was clear to most observers that economic reform no longer had to struggle hard to secure its own legitimacy or to demonstrate its apparent benefits. Debates focused more on the distributional consequences of reform – could growth be more inclusive, or pro-poor (see the Eleventh Five-Year Plan (Government of India 2006a))? – as well as on the likelihood that the reform process could finally be extended to labour-market rigidities, privatization and agriculture, to name just three widely identified candidates for liberalization. Significantly, too, observers of the Indian economy had to come to terms with an apparent second upturn in the country's GDP growth rate. After a period of steady (5–7 per cent) growth from the mid-1990s to 2002–3, the economy grew at close to 9 per cent annually in the five-year period from 2003–4 to 2007–8 (Harriss and Corbridge 2010). Clearly, such a growth acceleration, if this is what it is, has not been powered by agriculture. As Chandrasekhar and Ghosh report (2007), 'Agriculture has languished at a time when the trend rate of growth has been rising' (see also table 2.2). Export revenues have surged, including from some manufactured goods (chemicals, metals, transport equipment, etc.), but the main driver of integration has continued to be service-sector growth, with IT exports doing well again alongside a domestic boom in real estate, business services and insurance – all in part underpinned, according to Chandrasekhar and Ghosh (2007), by reduced interest rates and debt-financed consumption.

Table 2.2: India's sectoral composition of growth, 1950–2009 (per cent per year)

	Agriculture	Industry	Services	Total
1950–60	3.0	6.2	4.3	3.9
1960–70	2.3	5.5	4.8	3.7
1970–80	1.5	4.0	4.4	3.1
1980–90	3.4	7.1	6.7	5.6
1990–2000	2.5	5.6	7.6	5.6
2000–09	3.0	7.9	9.5	7.6

Sources: Ahmed and Varshney (2008); Economic Survey of India, 2010–11.

2.4   Plausible Arguments for Take-off

It is still too early to tell whether India's growth rate will settle down at close to 8–9 per cent per annum, or even higher. Public-sector deficits have been reducing, but capacity constraints might yet prefigure higher rates of inflation. Still, Rodrik and Subramanian believe that the prospects are good at least for 7 per cent per year on a sustained basis (say, to 2020), and this is a reasonable best guess. In their view, India remains significantly inside its production possibility frontier. It suffers from low rates of human-capital formation, can do more to close a technological gap with the developed world, and is about to reap a demographic dividend: the ratio of dependants to workers is set to decline from just over 0.6 in 2000 to just under 0.5 in 2025 (though see chapter 14). Couple these observations with two others – that India has strong democratic institutions, and (yet) is increasingly being fronted by a new class of self-confident business people and entrepreneurs (see Nilekani 2008) – and it is easy to be confident about India's macro-economic future, and possibly also about its prospects for catching up with China (Humang and Khanna 2003; see Bardhan 2010 for a more considered assessment).

But what about the take-off: how, finally, should we explain it? Srinivasan and Bhagwati present what in essence is an 'enlightenment' model of India's post-1947 economic growth. The gist of their argument is that India took a wrong turn in economic policy in the 1950s that should have been corrected in the 1960s. Srinivasan is very clear about this – about the 'one counterfactual [that] has always intrigued me' (2004: 13).

> Had the brief liberalization and opening that followed the 1966 macro crisis been in place thereafter, and greater attention been paid to agriculture and social sectors, would India have replicated and exceeded the

performance of the East Asian miracle economies that switched to an export-oriented strategy at that time? I believe that it would have, and there would have been no one living under India's modest poverty line by now. (Ibid.)

Unhappily, things didn't turn out this way, and it took a further twenty-five years before enlightened policymakers were forced to begin a systematic dismantling of the License-Permit-Quota Raj that had held India back prior to 1980 (and that was given a new lease of life in the 1980s only by unsustainable borrowing). Happily, once perverse government regulations and incentives were taken off the backs of India's business people – a slow and continuing process that should have been much quicker – the economy was 'unbound', to use Gurcharan Das's (2002) phrase, and high and sustained levels of economic growth could be driven forward by a revivified private sector.

No doubt there is something to be said for this line of argument. Srinivasan's contention that 'by the time Nehru died in 1964, many of the problems with infrastructure at the time of independence had been addressed, schools of higher education in engineering and management (the Indian Institutes of Technology and Management) had been established, and appropriate and inexpensive import substitution in consumer goods had been completed' (ibid.: 13), is a serious one – and signposts points of agreement between theoretical and political positions that sometimes are too sharply distinguished from one another. The idea that India had essentially thrown off the worst legacies of colonialism by 1964 is intriguing (if not wholly convincing: cf. Nayyar), and Srinivasan's broader experiments with counterfactual histories underline what we think is most interesting about current debates on economic reform – or the take-off – in India: namely, and precisely, that they force us to evaluate the recent past in longer perspective.

This might sound horribly academic when most debates about Indian economic policy are forward-looking or closely concerned with the distributional effects of growth. But this is to misunderstand the importance of thinking counterfactually, or, better, making explicit the counterfactuals that necessarily inform our interpretations of the present and future (Hawthorn 1991). What we have called the 'enlightenment argument' works by and large to deny the significance of long-run path-dependencies (colonial legacies, for example), and to enfranchise the wise and committed policymaker who is reasonably free to choose another course of action. The years between the ending of 'unchosen' path-dependencies – roughly 1964 – and the choosing of the right path (systemic reforms, since 1991) are then coded as years of failure and regret.

In contrast, the Kohli and Rodrik and Subramanian arguments work on the basis of different counterfactuals and to different ends. Kohli (2006a, 2006b) argues more strongly than Rodrik and Subramanian that India's economic growth rate simply did not pick up after 1991, as compared to after 1980. Neoliberal or pro-market reforms were no more effective than the pro-business reforms effected in India in the 1980s, the latter of which began as well to hint at the formation of a developmental state in India (along East Asian lines). This argument becomes more difficult to sustain, in our view, to the extent that we look at the full run of GDP growth rates in India from 1992–3 to *c*.2010. Kohli's argument also downplays the cumulative signalling effects of reform consistency.

Rodrik and Subramanian (2005), and more recently Subramanian (2007), develop an argument that is less open to refutation in this way. They agree with Kohli that economic growth took off in the 1980s and was underpinned by real productivity gains, notably in manufacturing. They also challenge the view that growth in the 1980s was straightforwardly unsustainable or fuelled wholly by fiscal expansionism (ibid.: 205–7).

Arguably, Rodrik and Subramanian are less insightful than Kohli on the ways in which political power in India has been seized since 1991 by particular class interests. But where they add significant value is in the development of what we would call a 'trigger' model of India's take-off. India, in the view of Rodrik and Subramanian, was an outlier in 1980 (contra De Long and looking at the deeper determinants of growth). Given the underlying strength of its core institutions – fairly well-defined property rights, reasonable rule of law, functioning elections, effective conflict-resolution mechanisms – India's growth performance before 1980 was significantly below where cross-country regressions (of growth against institutional quality) would have predicted it to be. Why? Because of bad or perverse government policies. *Ergo*, a small change in policy direction – the attitudinal shift that they and Kohli rightly detect under Indira and Rajiv Gandhi in the 1980s – has a growth effect that is seemingly out of proportion with real policy shifts.

Rodrik and Subramanian add to this insight a willingness to be open-minded about the legacies both of the British and of Nehru. After all, the institutions that they are keen to salute were mainly founded or consolidated in these two periods. India's inheritance from the British included functioning stock markets, a strong tendency to political centralism, and a powerful administrative service, while the Nehruvian legacy includes the Constitution of India, high savings rates, and strenuous efforts to devise a workable solution to demands in the 1950s for new states. Subramanian notes that these and other public institutions perform four important economic functions: they help to create markets and an 'environment in which business and private investment can flourish'; they regulate and/or substitute for markets (as when the state provides water to the needy); they help to stabilize markets (through monetary and fiscal policies); and, crucially, they legitimize markets by providing 'mechanisms of social protection and insurance' (2007: 197–8).

The problem for this trigger argument, however, is not so much its 'distance to frontier' component. It is not difficult to argue that India's strong institutional basis for flourishing private markets was undermined until recently by *dirigiste* economic policies. Indira Gandhi's notorious MRTP is just the most egregious example of what might be called institutional undermining – and it is worth recalling that Mrs Gandhi embarked on further bank nationalizations when she returned to power in 1980. Rapid recent increases in TFP are also consistent with a trigger argument. The more pressing problem is to explain how a pro-business or pro-market policy regime had this gap-closing effect when there is evidence to suggest that the quality of many of India's inherited institutions weakened over the same period (*c*.1980–2010).

Subramanian addresses this issue in his 2007 paper. He accepts that measures of institutional quality rely largely on proxy variables – for example, murder conviction rates as a guide to judicial performance – and are remarkably difficult to track consistently over time. He concludes, nonetheless, that whether we use proxy variables of institutional quality, or 'subjective, perception-based measures of economic governance' (ibid.: 205), the best evidence that we have suggests that 'the picture . . . is one of decline – substantial decline – since the 1960s' (ibid.). Ethnographic evidence on corruption and the criminalization of politics largely confirms this picture (Jeffrey 2001; see also Kapur 2005; and chapter 8 in this volume). Subramanian, however, maintains two further points: first, that India was so much an outlier in 1980 that the underlying quality of its institutions still trumps evidence of institutional decline and hesitant policy reforms when explaining why India has done so well since that time. 'India is well below the regression line . . . given its level of institutions, its income should have been much greater in 1980, by a factor or four or so' (ibid.: 211); and, second, that the supply of improved institutions in India is now lagging significantly behind demands for institutional reform – demands that are bound to increase as per capita incomes rise.

The first of these two points is a difficult one to test, except perhaps in cross-country terms. To our way of thinking, it is a suggestive – and most likely plausible – element in a trigger story that is alert to the cumulative and variegated nature of the reform process in India. Indeed, we would add to it by being more explicit about the pro-business reforms that were enacted in India in the Fifth Plan period, as well as about the inconsistencies in Mrs Gandhi's policymaking from 1980 to 1984. It is possible, as well, that Subramanian makes rather too much of the institutional decline thesis. India's higher courts and its electoral system are functioning better now than twenty years ago (the Election Commission has been strengthened), and some NGOs are performing a more active watchdog role than was the case previously. The second of Subramanian's points is important because it highlights the need for further government actions in India to support a process of institutional strengthening. It also points up critical areas of political market failure, or what non-economists might call the damaging effects both of uneven economic development and of a political project – deepening economic reform – that has been driven very largely by India's business elites and urban middle classes.

Subramanian acknowledges this point when he notes a growing tendency among these elites to exit the public system. Where 'growth is concentrated at the upper ends of the income spectrum . . . the rich [might turn] to the private sector to get essential services (for example, gated communities with private policing, private generators for power, private schools for their children's education, and so on). The normal pressures for improving the provision of public goods become attenuated' (ibid.: 217). This is undoubtedly the case and we comment on these exit strategies and their effects in subsequent chapters. Where we part company from Subramanian is in regard to his – and many economists' – willingness to confine debate to the relative growth effects of institutions and policies. We do so, first, because it is not always clear where an institution ends and a policy begins. The standard Northian definition of institutions refers to 'the rules of the game', or the incentive regimes that both formally and informally guide the actions of agents. Property rights and the rule of law are often cited in this regard. It is not clear, though, that actions to ensure low inflation and macroeconomic stability, or indeed 'central banks or fiscal institutions' (2007: 198), are institutions in this sense. Couldn't they just as well be described as policies or policymaking bodies?

We also believe that institutions are themselves the products of underlying political settlements and are changed by politics or political struggle. As Przeworksi (2004) points out, institutions are not distributed randomly across space, but instead are induced by what he calls the underlying 'conditions' or structures of rule. If we are properly to account for the whys and whens of India's economic reform we have to recognize, as Kohli clearly recognizes, that the real driving force behind 'take-off' – one that has emerged slowly on occasions, in the states sometimes as much as in New Delhi, and in various incarnations (pro-business, pro-market) – has been the consolidation of a state machinery that increasingly is in the service of the corporate sector (see also chapter

6). This is where India is most coming to resemble China – just as much, we would maintain, as in terms of its high savings and investment rates. India is booming because the state has been actively facilitating processes of creative destruction that have the very real effects of increasing both economic growth and social inequalities.

Subramanian rightly notes some of the limits of this strategy, or at least of its counterparts of institutional decline and the criminalization of politics. For our part, we want to suggest that a decline in some measures of institutional quality during a growth spurt is not a puzzle that needs explanation. Rather, it is something that is predictable in fast-developing countries. It happened in the UK and the USA, and it is happening now in China and India. Indian capitalists have been taking advantage over the past thirty years of an 'elite revolt' (Corbridge and Harriss 2000) in the country's politics that has liberated them from a *dirigiste* state and many laws they didn't wish to see applied (Harriss-White 2003; Roy 2009). This is how vibrant forms of capitalism actually work, notwithstanding homilies to the contrary (Chang 2010). Institutions matter, but politics matters more – and by politics we mean struggles over the production and distribution of wealth. 'India Inc.' has been doing well of late, mainly because these struggles have been won by key members of India's business elites and their backers among the urban middle classes. What Subramanian calls the pro-market function of institutions has triumphed in large degree over the legitimizing functions of institutions and politics. When that calculus changes we will see fresh changes in India's growth trajectory and its regimes of accumulation.

2.5   Conclusion

We will pick up various challenges to the hegemony of India's ruling elites in later chapters. We will also explore some of the problems that will face those elites when it comes to maintaining high rates of economic growth. Reclaiming eastern India from the Maoists is one pressing problem, but more general ones have to do with investments in infrastructure and human capital. To sustain high rates of growth in the medium-term, India will have to upgrade its labour force, and this has implications for the country's tax-raising powers and public debt (Topolova and Nyberg 2010).

For the moment, let us summarize our answer to the question 'when and why did India take off?'. Our first contention is that we need to soften the idea of a singular take-off. We have argued strongly that the years from 1950 to 1980 (or 1960–90) cannot simply be characterized as years of economic failure in India. This characterization is misleading empirically and also in terms of its counterfactual reasoning. India may not have matched East Asia in this period (few countries did), but it very significantly upped its rate of economic growth compared to the late colonial period. Under Nehru, too, and even under Mrs Gandhi, some solid foundations were laid for the later acceleration of the Indian economy. The IITs and IIMs are often mentioned in this regard, but we would make a larger argument: the possibility of take-off in post-reform India was also made possible by the fact that India was made to hang together in the 1950s and 1960s. This was no mean achievement of Prime Minister Nehru and it was not unconnected to his economic policies in these years.

Second, we largely agree with the contention by Rodrik and Subramanian that India's accumulated institutional advantages were sufficiently great by the 1970s, in comparative terms, for the country to turn even small pro-capitalist policy shifts into large economic gains in the 1980s, and then into the 1990s. This remains true notwithstanding that some of India's institutions have been in decline since Nehru's time, and notwithstanding some obvious economic policy failures under Mrs Gandhi. India has boomed over the past thirty years because India's business classes have progressively been set free to behave as capitalists are wont to behave. In this enterprise they have been hugely aided by the consolidation of a state in New Delhi, and in many leading states – Andhra Pradesh under Chandrababu Naidu comes to mind, along with Narendra Modi's Gujarat – willing to take the part of corporate capital both within and against the rule of law. It should not be thought, however, that the liberation of capital is anything like complete in India or that there are not countervailing forces. We consider some of these forces later in the book. Nor should it be assumed that the successes of private capital in contemporary India are unrelated to the achievements – intended or otherwise – of previous political regimes (the British, the Nehrus and Gandhis), or have put those achievements completely in the shade.

Finally, we note that an economy that grows at 10 per cent per annum, which was very nearly the case for India in the mid-2000s, ahead of the global recession, will double in size in just over seven years. Unsurprisingly, then, as Arvind Subramanian points out, 'Whereas "midnight's children" [Indians born close to August 1947] saw their standard of living double over 40 years, midnight's grandchildren – the "India shining" generation – can expect five or six-fold improvements in their lifetime' (Subramanian 2007: 196). Here is where we want to signal – and celebrate – the importance of discontinuities in India's economic management, as well as the continuities we have sought to highlight. India as a whole may have benefitted from some of the legacies of Pandit Nehru and Indira Gandhi, but the country has also benefitted greatly from a willingness to recognize the inappropriateness of some of their policy assumptions as the world economy changed and became more open. This has been the great achievement of Manmohan Singh and his colleagues and supporters. In chapter 6, we consider how successive governments were able *politically* to promote audacious economic reform in India in the 1990s and 2000s. Before that, in the next three chapters, we examine the unevenness and the social consequences of the reform programme that Dr Singh, especially, has done so much to initiate and promote.

3

How Have the Poor Fared (and Others Too)?

3.1 Introduction

Growth accelerations in low-income countries are generally thought to reduce extreme income poverty and to increase social and spatial inequalities, at least in the short run. The intuition connecting growth to poverty reduction is straightforward. We have few reasons to suppose that all of the benefits of higher growth will be captured by individuals or households above a poverty line. Even if the non-poor population captures a large initial share of increased income or wealth – because of a greater capacity to access the more productive jobs that power higher growth – they are likely to spend their new riches in ways that trickle down to the poor. Construction would be a good example. This creates work for unskilled labour, whose real wages can be expected to rise. (Exceptions to this argument are when rich households spend their money on houses abroad, or park their funds in offshore bank accounts.) Some economists believe that poor households don't have to wait for crumbs from the rich man's table. In a much cited paper, David Dollar and Aart Kraay argue that 'Average incomes of the poorest quintile rise proportionately with average incomes in a sample of 92 countries spanning the last four decades. This is because the share of the income of the poorest quintile does not vary systematically with average incomes' (2002: 195). In this case, it is not trickle-down spending that drives up the incomes of the poor, but rather the wave of growth itself: its benefits wash evenly across the population, or evenly enough that the incomes of the bottom quintile rise and fall with average incomes.

The intuition that links growth and inequality is the Kuznets hypothesis or the inverted U-shaped curve (Anand and Kanbur 1993; see also

Banerjee and Duflo 2003; Fosu 2009). This is the idea that social and spatial inequalities will increase in the early stages of growth because of the capture and access effects to which we have referred. New factories will be located in some cities and regions and not in others, and employers may demand skill sets only supplied by well-educated people. In time, though, either in response to public protests against rising inequalities, and/or because of greater factor mobility – capital moving to poor areas, labour to rich areas – and/or because of increased investment in human-capital formation, a process of income convergence begins. In some versions of this model, inequalities automatically correct themselves. In others, greater attention is given to public policy interventions.

India's recent experiences with poverty and inequality are very broadly in line with these predictions. The incidence of extreme income poverty declined significantly between 1980 and 2010, following three decades of sustained economic growth. Income and wealth inequalities increased socially and geographically over the same period. States in the west and south of India have benefited more from economic reform than have initially much poorer – and often less well-governed – states in the north, centre and east.

Still, the similarities between what is happening in India and what our intuitions might suggest are not so precise that we can ignore locally important facts. What is arguably most interesting about the growth-poverty-inequality story in contemporary India is the following: (a) the pace of poverty-incidence decline stalled in the mid/late 1980s after fifteen years of 'pro-poor' growth; (b) the pace of poverty reduction picked up again from the mid-1990s and was arguably greater in the second half of the 1990s than in the 1970s; (c) a shift to a more unequal growth trajectory in the late 1980s or early 1990s reduced the effectiveness of the growth–poverty reduction transmission belt: distribution-neutral growth from c.1990–2010 would have pulled tens of millions more Indians above the government's official poverty line; (d) poverty reduction per unit of growth from 1980 to 2010 was barely more than half that achieved by China over the same period; (e) economic growth has not yet pulled more than a quarter of Indians above a two dollars a day poverty line, and in some parts of the country the conditions of the very poorest – the bottom decile not the bottom quintile – have improved hardly at all since 1980; (f) some of India's poorest states in 1990 saw little or no improvements in average real incomes between 1993–4 and 2004–5, while average real incomes in some western states improved by over 60 per cent in the same period; and (g) in regard to some human-development indicators, the gap has begun to close between richer and poorer states, but overall achievements in reducing non-income measures of poverty have been mixed at best and often poor.

In the next two parts of the chapter, we review the Great Indian Poverty Debate. Basic definitions and data sets are provided and we consider problems that emerged in the late 1990s in the interpretation of income poverty trends. We also note that the Government of India looks set to change its definition of extreme income poverty as this book goes to press (with exchanges over this definition between the Supreme Court and the Planning Commission; see *The Hindu*, 22 September 2011). The Planning Commission's Expert Group to Review the Methodology for the Estimation of Poverty (the Tendulkar Committee Report) recommended in 2009 that consumption estimates of a minimum standard of living in rural India should be brought more squarely into line with those for urban India; they should also have greater regard for education and health-care costs. The official all-India urban poverty estimate of 25.7 per cent of the population for 2004–5 would remain unchanged, but the estimate for rural India would rise from 28.3 per cent to 41.8 per cent (Himanshu 2010: 38).

We next consider why income poverty has been reducing more slowly in India than in many East Asian countries, and perhaps least of all in India's historically poorest states. The blunt answer is that social and spatial inequalities are much higher in South Asia than in East Asia. Initial conditions matter (assets, incomes, literacy rates, quality of governance, etc.). To make matters worse, in India the share of growth accruing to the poorest households has diminished sharply since the early 1990s. In part, this reflects higher returns to talent and entrepreneurialism and to better government policies. We might refer to this as 'good inequality'. Rather more so, though, it reflects the inability of many poor people to access new circuits of growth. 'Bad inequalities' are the result of low levels of education, high dependence on farm incomes, weak non-farm income growth, social discrimination, deteriorating public services, and, in some cases, conflict and weak or even absent government. All of these points are well known, including to India's politicians. Many of them highlight the importance of non-income dimensions of poverty, an issue we briefly outline. (We return to this issue in chapters 4, 5, 10, 13 and 14, where we consider some of the different ways in which people experience and speak about poverty, distress, destitution and vulnerability).

Lastly, we consider the prospects for more inclusive growth in India. Dollar and Kraay express scepticism about the possibility of pro-poor growth and indeed of 'policies intended to benefit the poorest in society' (2002: 195). Many other scholars, however, picking up on the pro-rich bias of India's recent growth path, are less impressed by cross-country averages and talk of equiproportional growth. They note the very different effects of growth on poverty reduction in countries like China and India, or indeed between Indian states like Kerala and Bihar – what economists call 'the growth elasticity of poverty' – and they push hard at the reasons for these 'residuals' from the regression line (Donaldson 2008). Instead of endorsing the true but trite notion that 'growth is good for the poor', they prefer to ask 'when and by how much', and 'can poverty be bad for growth'? We address these questions here.

3.2   The Great Indian Poverty Debate: Part One

Social scientists, planners and politicians have long been interested in mapping changes in the incidence of poverty and well-being. Debates around destitution and the Poor Laws in the United Kingdom were central to some of the formative exchanges in nineteenth-century political economy. More recently, the World Bank and many large bilateral donor agencies have insisted that international development must be in the service of poverty reduction, especially income-poverty reduction. Governments in developing countries also feel a need to be seen as active combatants in the war on poverty. Social scientists who have contributed to what Deaton and Kozel (2005) call the 'Great Indian Poverty Debate' have confined their attention overwhelmingly to trends in aggregate income or consumption poverty measures, as we do here. Their focus has been on the total numbers of people living below a given poverty line and changes in those numbers over time. Debate has also focused on the likely drivers of poverty reduction. We should recognize, however, that the poverty debate has other more directly political dimensions to it, some of which we pick up in later chapters. Politicians want to know not simply that 45 per cent or 33 per cent of their citizens live in extreme income poverty. For reasons both of patronage and of public policy, they also want to know exactly who these people are and where they live. Policymakers in India are required to designate people as below (or above) the poverty line: BPL. This is not something that the Great Indian Poverty Debate is set up to discuss. It is one thing to say that X per cent of a population is poor. It is quite another thing to say just who the poor are. Social scientists can advise governments on the latter – we know in India, for example, that many more Scheduled Caste men and women are poor than are members of the Forward Castes – but the labelling of individuals and households is always, finally, a political act.

We return to this issue in Part II of *India Today*. Here, we begin our account of the Great Indian Poverty Debate with some definitions. Attempts to track changes in poverty in developing countries are for the most part focused on extreme income or consumption poverty – often called absolute poverty – rather than measures of relative poverty or deprivation, or broader measures of empowerment or capabilities (though Sabina Alkire and her colleagues have recently developed a multi-dimensional poverty index which aims to provide such a broader measure: see Alkire and Santos 2010, which includes measures for Indian states). Poverty lines are set at different levels, but domestic and international poverty lines concerned with extreme poverty generally have regard to income, and/or consumption levels, required to provide people with a minimally adequate diet *and* command over at least some non-food commodities and a small number of government services.

The World Bank did much in the 1990s to fix in the public imagination the idea that people were poor if they lived on less than one dollar a day. In work conducted for the 1990 *World Development Report*, Ravallion, Datt and van de Walle 'compiled data on national poverty lines across 33 countries and proposed a poverty line of $1 per day at 1985 PPP as being typical of low-income countries . . . they estimated that one third of the population of the developing world in 1985 lived below the $1 a day standard' (Chen and Ravallion 2008: 3, citing Ravallion, Datt and de Walle 1991). PPPs, or Purchasing Power Parity rates, are used in international comparisons instead of market exchange rates to capture the fact that many non-traded goods and services, including some food staples, are relatively cheap in developing countries (though see Reddy and Pogge 2002 for critical commentary). No one in the USA could have hoped to live long on less than one dollar a day in 1985. Indeed, extreme income poverty there was effectively zero. But, in the thirty-three countries that Ravallion et al. surveyed, a dollar a day seemed enough to keep body and soul together.

Over time, the World Bank has revised its poverty lines as more data have become available and as more countries have begun to participate in the national price surveys carried out as part of the International Comparison Program (ICP). India and China participated in the ICP for the first time in 2005. Estimates proposed for the World Bank's 2000–1 *World Development Report: Attacking Poverty* used an international poverty line of $1.08 a day at 1993 PPPs (ibid.). Using this poverty line, the Bank announced in 2004 that slightly under 1 billion people in the developing world were 'poor'. In 2008, however, the World Bank had to qualify this story of global poverty reduction. Using new and improved data from the 2005 ICP, bank researchers now proposed that people needed $1.25 a day to escape from poverty. They would have needed $1.45 a day if living costs in poor countries had increased as rapidly as in the US, but this was thought not to be the case. Still, the daily figure was adjusted upwards because the Bank accepted new research on how poverty was understood by people in fifteen of the poorest countries in the developing world. Earlier estimates of the total value that poor people gained from government services – including education and housing – were judged to have been too high and had led to discounting of real poverty levels. The World Bank maintained in 2008 that 1.4 billion people lived below an international poverty line of $1.25 a day in 2005. This figure included 456 million people in India – still the country with the highest number of people living in extreme income poverty, thus defined (Chen and Ravallion 2008: table 6).

World Bank figures also show that the Headcount Index of poverty in India for 2005 – that is, the percentage of people below a given poverty line: here an international poverty line of $1.25 dollars a day – was 41.6 per cent, a much higher figure than the Government of India (GoI) was reporting in 2008 for the same year. GoI data suggested that 27.9 per cent of Indians, or around 300 million people, were living in poverty in 2004–5. The Asian Development Bank (ADB), for its part, released figures in 2008 that showed even higher poverty levels in India. 'According to the ADB, the number of poor in India was anywhere between 622 million and 740 million people in 2005 [the former figure being defined against a daily poverty line figure of $1.35], well over double the Planning Commission Estimates' (Himanshu 2008: 39).

How could this be? The answer, of course, is that the Government of India has historically defined poverty in much harsher terms even than the World Bank, let alone the ADB. (As we have suggested, this is soon set to change: see also below.) The official poverty estimates prepared by India's Planning Commission rely on regular consumer expenditure surveys carried out by the National Sample Survey Organisation (NSSO). NSS data, as they are commonly called, are collected annually from a smallish sample of households (n = 30,000–40,000), and about every five years from larger surveys – or 'thick rounds' – of around 120,000 households (75,000 rural households and 45,000 urban households). Only data from the major surveys are used in official accounts of poverty trends in India. India's poverty lines historically had close regard for the number of calories that were deemed necessary for rural and urban bodies to function effectively. An Expert Group in 1979 suggested minimum levels of 2,400 calories a day in rural areas and 2,100 in urban areas. In money terms, this was thought to equate to Rs 49 a month in rural areas and Rs 57 a month in urban areas at 1973–4 prices. As Himanshu notes, however, the calorific basis of India's poverty estimates has assumed less significance over time. What is really being measured is 'consumption poverty, not calorie deficiency'. Indeed, 'NSS estimates of [the] proportion of people with less calorie intake than these [1979] norms (79.8 per cent rural and 63.9 per cent urban) . . . [was by 2004–5 hugely at odds with] . . . the official poverty headcount (28.3 per cent rural and 25.7 per cent urban)' (Himanshu 2010: 40; see also Usha Patnaik 2010, for a blistering commentary on rising levels of calorific distress in India). Poverty lines vary across states and sectors (urban and rural), and are updated periodically using data from state price surveys and from the consumer price indices for industrial workers and agricultural labourers respectively. 'All-India urban and rural poverty lines are then set so that when they are applied to urban or rural households without differentiation by States, the total number of urban and rural people matches the sum of the State counts' (Deaton and Kozel 2005: 178).

Deaton and Kozel believe that 'NSSO statisticians are highly skilled, and field staff are disciplined and well trained' (2005: 194). This is very probably the case, although ethnographic work on the production of NSS household data is sorely missing and would be very welcome. Who is reporting what to whom, according to which protocols, and in line with which incentive systems? It is a feature of NSS data, however, that problems can be caused for the estimation of poverty levels and trends if a thick round coincides with an unusual year (a bad harvest or a recession), or if the results can be disputed on technical grounds. This will have significant implications for government anti-poverty policies. It can affect who gets defined as Below Poverty Line and who is eligible for targeted government benefits. Unfortunately, this is exactly what happened with the 55th Round of the NSS, which was carried out in 1999–2000. Previous thick rounds of the NSS had collected information on consumer expenditure on the basis of a uniform reporting period of thirty days. The Planning Commission instructed the NSS in 1999–2000, however, to use a mixed reporting system in its 55th Round. This was so notwithstanding that it might cause comparability problems for anyone working back from the 55th Round to the 50th, 43rd and earlier major Rounds. Food, *pan* and tobacco consumption were to be reported over both a seven-day and a thirty-day period, while the 'traditional 30-day reporting period for durables, clothing, education and institutional medical services [not all of which were used to estimate consumption poverty] was replaced by a 365-day period only' (ibid.) When the survey results were compiled and processed, the Planning Commission adopted the thirty-day responses 'as the basis of the new official poverty totals, although Planning Commission press releases also provided (lower) estimates of poverty using the 7-day reporting period results (ibid.: 186). Scholars, however, were not slow to dispute the government's claim that poverty in India had fallen by 10 percentage points from the time of the 50th NSS Round in 1993–4 to the 55th Round in 1999–2000 – an extraordinary rate of decline by India's historic standards, as we shall see. Led at first by Abhijit Sen (2000), a compelling argument took hold in the first part of the 2000s, which charged that reported household consumption over thirty days had been upwardly biased by the fact that households were simultaneously reporting data for a seven-day period. This contagion effect led to falsely optimistic assessments both of poverty levels in 1999–2000 and the scale of poverty reduction in India following the Rao-Singh economic reforms of the early 1990s.

To complicate matters further, another argument took hold, which pointed in the opposite direction: to lower poverty levels and faster rates of poverty reduction. Surjit Bhalla (2002, 2003a, 2003b), in particular, has noted that the estimates of mean consumption reported in India's National Accounts are significantly above those provided by NSS survey data. He has also pointed out that the gap between the two figures has grown significantly since the 1960s. Bhalla maintains that 'poverty in India was below 15 per cent' by 2000, according to National Accounts data. He further believes that 'pro-poor growth' in India in the 1990s was sufficiently rapid that India had met its Millenium Development Goal target for absolute poverty reduction by 2000.

Bhalla is right to highlight the growing gap between survey and national accounts data. This is not an exclusively Indian problem, but the fact that survey estimates of mean consumption are now only about two thirds those of national accounts estimates *is* something that needs explanation. On balance, though, we find ourselves in agreement with Sundaram and Tendulkar (2003) when they maintain that 'survey data are to be preferred because they measure living standards directly, as opposed to national accounts statistics, which derive consumption as a residual at a long chain of calculations' (as reported by Deaton and Kozel 2005: 182; see also Minhas 1988). We also note that Bhalla's assessment of poverty levels in India is conjured from an optimistic reworking of National Accounts data – what Martin Ravallion (2003) calls 'fanciful numbers' – and uncritical use of an official poverty line in India that has long been significantly more harsh than the World Bank's international poverty line: in 2008, very close to $1 a day, not $1.25 a day. If and when the Government of India finally accepts a new definition of minimum rural living standards, something like 100 million people will be added to the country's official poverty totals for 2004–5. This ballpark figure (408 million) is still below the World Bank's baseline figure for India in the same year – 456 million people – but it is a long way removed from Bhalla's estimate of 150 million poor Indians in 2000.

3.3   The Great Indian Poverty Debate: Part Two

Given these instabilities in the production of poverty estimates – World Bank 1 versus World Bank 2, India 1 versus India 2, World Bank versus

India, ADB versus World Bank, Bhalla versus the rest – it might seem reasonable to conclude that there is little of value to be said about poverty in India, or about who has been benefiting from thirty years of sustained economic growth. But this is not the case. It is important that we gain familiarity with some of the intricacies of the Great Indian/International Poverty Debates, and it is certainly important to recognize that levels of reported poverty are the product in large degree of which poverty lines we choose. Bhalla's claim that less than 15 per cent of Indians were poor in 2000 will not impress many observers of India, but it tells us something important about how Bhalla thinks of poverty. So long as estimates of poverty are produced consistently and effectively over time we can say something useful about trends. Hopefully, we can then explain these trends with reference to various causal factors: that is, we can aim to tell a plausible story about why the incidence of poverty is declining (or, on the other hand, getting worse).

Several things have happened since 2000 to make our understanding of India's poverty story more robust. First, a number of important corrections were proposed to the 'contaminated' data outputs of the 55th Round of the NSS. Abhijit Sen and Himanshu (2004a) took the most pessimistic view of what had happened to consumption poverty in India in the 1990s, in what was then often called the post-reform period (after 1991–2), or between 1993–4 and 1999–2000 (the 50th and 55th Rounds). In their view, the rural headcount figure fell by only 2.7 percentage points between the 50th and 55th Rounds, while the corresponding urban figure dropped by 3.1 points. This rate of poverty reduction was both much slower than was observed in the 1980s (see below) and barely enough to reduce the total number of Indians living in poverty. More optimistic corrections were proposed by Deaton (2003) and Sundaram and Tendulkar (2003). In place of official claims of a 10 percentage point poverty reduction from 1993–4 to 1999–2000 – from 37.3 per cent to only 27.0 per cent, or a drop of about 60 million people – Deaton suggested a reduction of 7.1 percentage points in rural areas and 7.5 in urban areas. Sundaram and Tendulkar suggested a decline of 5 percentage points in rural areas and 3 in urban areas.

The different findings of these corrective studies clearly have significant implications for how we should understand India's poverty performance in the 1990s, not least when it comes to the total numbers of people pulled out of extreme consumption poverty. They also inform debates on the designation of BPL households. Rather than spend further time on these differences, however, we note, second, that the collection and publication of new poverty data from the 61st Round of the NSS, in 2004–5, has allowed a more stable picture to emerge of absolute poverty trends in India. (We write, too, as the processing of the 66th Round of

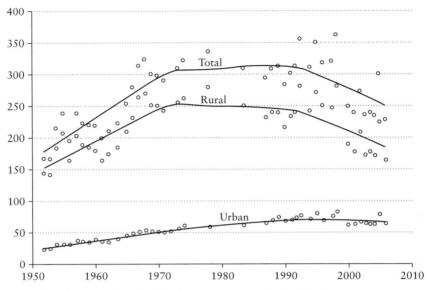

Figure 3.1: Number of people living below the poverty line (millions).

Source: After Datt and Ravallion (2010).

the NSS, 2009–10, is being completed.) Finally, we note that while different poverty lines give rise to different estimates of the total number of Indians living in extreme poverty, the trends that can be observed in post-Independence India's poverty story hold in large degree, irrespective of the choice of particular poverty lines. The gradient of a poverty line that reduces from N to 250 million people will be different from one that reduces to 350 million people. However, what might be called the direction of travel will look broadly similar, and this similarity allows us to piece together more or less convincing accounts of why poverty in India increased or reduced in different time periods.

For convenience we work mainly with India's official poverty estimates as they were produced before new protocols were scheduled for introduction in 2011. Datt and Ravallion (2009, 2010) provide a credible data set on poverty measures for rural and urban India from 1951 to 2006 that is adjusted where necessary for mixed-recall period bias. Figure 3.1 displays the numbers of people in India 'living in households with consumption per person below India's national poverty line (fixed in real terms over time)' (Datt and Ravallion 2010: 56). Trend lines smooth out annual and minor NSS Round data point variation. The graph shows that the total number of people in rural areas living in

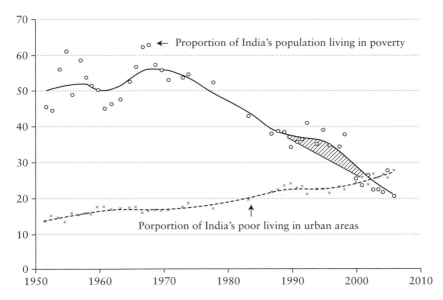

Figure 3.2: Headcount index of poverty using the national poverty line (percentage).

Source: Adapted from Datt and Ravallion (2010).

poverty peaked around 1970, then declined slowly to the early 1990s, before declining more rapidly to the mid-2000s (to less than 200 million people against this tough metric). The number of people living in poverty in urban areas rose slowly from the early 1950s to *c*.1990 before stabilizing.

Figure 3.2 tracks the headcount index of poverty over the same period. The dotted line shows the steady increase of urban dwellers among India's poor. About a third of India's below poverty-line population in 2010 lived in towns and cities, and this percentage will rise rapidly in the coming decades. India will come more consistently into line with a global trend towards the urbanization of poverty (Jones and Corbridge 2010). The continuous line shows how the incidence of poverty ebbed and flowed in India in the 1950s, before it peaked at nearly 60 per cent in the crisis years of the late 1960s. From around 1970 to the mid/late 1980s, the incidence of poverty in India came down sharply: from about 56 per cent to about 40 per cent in 1986–7. The scale of poverty incidence reduction then fell back sharply from the later 1980s to the mid-1990s, before it resumed a trend line closer to that from 1970 to 1987 in the years from 1997 to 2006. We have added to Datt and Ravallion's original graph a shaded area from *c*.1987–2000. Crudely speaking, this shaded area allows us to estimate a 'loss of poverty reduction' in this period that is equivalent to 5 percentage points at the widest point (1993–4).

3.4   Plausible Stories of Poverty and Inequality

What are we to make of these numbers and trends, and how should we explain them? The World Bank concluded in 2008 that 'The developing world is poorer than we thought, but no less successful in the fight against poverty' (Chen and Ravallion 2008). It acknowledged, that is to say, that 1.4 billion people were extremely poor in 2005 (at less than $1.25 a day), as opposed to previous estimates of 1 billion people. At the same time, the Bank insisted that the global incidence of extreme income poverty halved from 1980 to 2005 in $1.25 a day terms (52.0 per cent to 25.7 per cent) and more than halved in $1 a day terms (41.7 per cent to 16.1 per cent).

The Government of India has sometimes been keen to make similar claims, but it generally lacks the data to back them up. World Bank data and poverty lines suggest that 296.1 million people in India lived on less than $1 a day in 1981. This figure reduced to 266.5 million in 2005. Corresponding numbers at $1.25 a day are 420.5 million and 455.8 million, or a rise in total numbers over twenty-four years. The headcount index figures at $1 a day moved from 42.1 per cent in 1981 to 24.3 per cent in 2005, or not far short of the halving that the Bank reported globally. At the $1.25 a day international poverty line, however, India reduced only from 59.8 per cent to 41.6 per cent, a reduction of less than a third. According to the Government of India's own data, the incidence of poverty in India reduced from about 43 per cent in 1983 to about 28 per cent in 2005. These numbers are close to the World Bank's $1 a day figures, as we would expect.

Why has India underperformed against recent global poverty reduction trends? Proximately, the main reason is that growth has been less effective in India than in many other countries in pulling people out of poverty. Much less effective we can say, given that growth rates in India over the past thirty years have been bettered by only a handful of countries, China most notably. We will discuss the reasons for India's low growth-poverty elasticities shortly. First, though, we consider some more facts and figures.

Burgess and Besley (2003) provide estimates of the elasticity of poverty with respect to income per capita for the developing world as a whole from 1990 to 2015, and for six constituent regions (see table 3.1; see also

Table 3.1: Growth and Poverty Across the Globe, 1990–2015

	Whole sample (1)	East Asia and Pacific (2)	Eastern Europe and Central Asia (3)	Latin America and Carribean (4)	Middle East and North Africa (5)	South Asia (6)	Sub-Saharan Africa (7)
Elasticity of poverty with respect to income per capita	−0.73 (0.25)	−1.00 (0.14)	−1.14 (1.04)	−0.73 (0.29)	−0.72 (0.64)	−0.59 (0.36)	−0.49 (0.23)
Annual growth rate needed to halve world poverty by 2015	3.8%	2.7%	2.4%	3.8%	3.8%	4.7%	5.6%
Historical growth 1960–1990	1.7%	3.3%	2.0%	1.3%	4.3%	1.9%	0.2%
Total growth needed to halve world poverty by 2015	95%	70%	61%	94%	95%	117%	141%

Note: Robust standard errors in parenthesis.

Source: Burgess and Besley (2003).

Bourguignon 2003). India dominates the score for South Asia, which is minus 0.59. Separately, Besley, Burgess and Esteve-Volart (2007: 62) estimate the average elasticity score for India as –0.65 (though see the standard error terms). These scores are bettered by all regions save for sub-Saharan Africa. According to these calculations, and assuming constancy in other factors, growth in East Asia and the Pacific – dominated by China, of course – is likely to be almost twice as effective in reducing poverty as in South Asia over the same period. For South Asia to meet its first Millenium Development Goal (MDG) target of halving extreme income poverty [$1 a day] from 1990–2015, its annual average GDP growth rate would have to be 4.7 per cent – significantly up from the rate achieved from 1960 to 1990, but something India will achieve very comfortably. At the same time, economies in East Asia and the Pacific are required only to grow collectively by 70 per cent from 1990–2015 to meet MDG1. In South Asia, required growth is 117 per cent.

These figures are inevitably rather crude and prospective. Petia Topolova (2008) has deepened this line of enquiry in a recent paper for the International Monetary Fund (IMF). Her analysis picks up the important point that growth in India, in the 1970s and most of the 1980s, pulled more people out of poverty per unit of growth than it has done since the late 1980s. We know this intuitively from looking at figure 3.1. The pace of poverty reduction in India slowed from the mid/late 1980s to around the mid-1990s. We know, however, that average annual rates of GDP growth in India were very similar in the 1980s and 1990s (see chapter 2), and that both rates were higher over the course of each decade than they were in the 1970s. We also know that India's growth performance picked up for a second time around 2003–4, in which case we might expect to see a steepening trend-line reduction from around 2005 (we await conclusive data on this).

How do we explain an observable slowing down of the growth-poverty reduction engine in the late 1980s and into the 1990s? Growing inequality is a large part of the story. Tables 3.2 and 3.3 are taken from a paper published by Himanshu in 2007. They also provide a foundation for thinking about Topolova's work. Both tables provide data we have considered before on the incidence (Headcount Index) of poverty in India as reported in four comparable thick rounds of the NSS. They report the Government of India's official line that rural poverty reduced from 46.5 per cent in 1983 to 28.7 per cent in 2004–5, while urban poverty reduced from 43.6 per cent to 25.9 per cent in the same period. They also confirm that by far the highest rates of rural and (less so) urban poverty were to be found by 2004–5 in central and eastern states like Bihar, Madhya Pradesh, Jharkhand, Orissa and Chhattisgarh.

Table 3.2: Comparable estimates of rural poverty and inequality, 1983–2004/5 (Official Poverty Lines)

Rural	Headcount Ratio				Poverty Gap			
	1983	1987–88	1993–94	2004–05	1983	1987–88	1993–94	2004–05
Andhra Pradesh	26.8	21.0	15.9	10.8	5.86	4.35	2.9	2.0
Assam	44.6	39.4	45.2	21.7	8.75	7.45	8.3	3.5
Jharkhand	65.5	52.8	62.3	42.9	22.00	13.56	16.2	8.9
Bihar	64.7	54.2	56.6	42.2	19.54	12.74	14.2	8.3
Gujarat	28.9	28.3	22.2	19.4	5.64	5.44	4.1	3.4
Haryana	21.9	15.3	28.3	13.6	4.28	3.62	5.6	2.2
Himachal Pradesh	17.0	16.7	30.4	10.9	3.58	2.63	5.6	1.5
Karnataka	36.3	32.6	30.1	20.0	9.73	7.88	6.3	2.7
Kerala	39.6	29.3	25.4	13.2	9.98	6.30	5.6	2.8
Chhattisgarh	50.6	46.7	44.4	42.0	12.49	10.38	8.6	9.4
Madhya Pradesh	49.0	40.1	39.2	35.8	13.95	10.64	9.8	7.8
Maharashtra	45.9	40.9	37.9	30.0	11.95	9.56	9.3	6.4
Orissa	68.5	58.7	49.8	46.9	22.72	16.30	12.0	12.1
Punjab	14.3	12.8	11.7	10.0	3.03	1.97	1.9	1.3
Rajasthan	35.0	33.3	26.4	19.0	9.65	8.64	5.2	2.9
Tamil Nadu	54.8	46.3	32.9	22.7	17.39	12.65	7.3	3.7
Uttaranchal	25.2	13.2	24.8	14.9	4.00	1.99	4.4	1.9
Uttar Pradesh	47.8	43.3	43.1	33.9	12.70	10.25	10.6	6.7
West Bengal	63.6	48.8	41.2	28.5	21.06	11.58	8.3	5.4
All India	46.5	39.0	37.2	28.7	12.36	9.29	8.5	5.8

Rural	Squared Poverty Gap				Gini			
	1983	1987–88	1993–94	2004–05	1983	1987–88	1993–94	2004–05
Andhra Pradesh	2.00	1.41	0.87	0.65	29.7	30.9	29.0	29.4
Assam	2.63	2.04	2.21	0.90	20.0	23.0	17.9	19.9
Jharkhand	9.8	5.03	5.59	2.55	27.2	26.6	23.4	22.7
Bihar	7.86	4.32	4.9	2.30	25.9	25.2	22.2	20.7
Gujarat	1.69	1.59	1.16	0.91	26.8	26.1	24.0	27.3
Haryana	1.37	1.30	1.75	0.61	28.5	29.2	31.4	34.0
Himachal Pradesh	1.16	0.71	1.62	0.35		27.1	28.4	31.1
Karnataka	3.69	2.80	2.01	0.63	30.8	29.7	27.0	26.5
Kerala	3.62	2.05	1.85	0.98	32.0	32.1	30.1	38.3
Chhattisgarh	4.47	3.36	2.47	3.43	24.4	24.5	21.7	29.8
Madhya Pradesh	5.54	3.97	3.58	2.31	31.5	30.6	30.0	26.8
Maharashtra	4.3	3.21	3.35	1.99	29.1	31.2	30.7	31.2
Orissa	10.17	6.24	4.07	4.24	27.0	26.9	24.6	28.5

Table 3.2: (continued)

Rural	Squared Poverty Gap				Gini			
	1983	1987–88	1993–94	2004–05	1983	1987–88	1993–94	2004–05
Punjab	1.06	0.51	0.48	0.26	29.2	29.7	28.1	29.5
Rajasthan	3.81	3.40	1.56	0.72	34.7	31.5	26.5	25.1
Tamil Nadu	7.52	4.80	2.50	0.96	36.7	33.0	31.2	32.2
Uttaranchal	1.04	0.46	1.08	0.42	29.2	28.3	24.4	28.5
Uttar Pradesh	4.7	3.4	3.64	1.93	28.9	28.5	28.3	29.0
West Bengal	9.46	3.99	2.45	1.42	30.0	25.8	25.4	27.4
All India	4.87	3.23	2.84	1.76	30.0	29.9	28.6	30.5

Source: 2004–5 estimates are calculated from grouped data from NSSO Report 508; estimates for 1983, 1987–8 and 1993–4 are calculated from the unit level data respectively; Himanshu (2007).

(We come back to this.) In addition, tables 3.2 and 3.3 furnish time-series data on India's Poverty Gap figures and inequality. Poverty Gap and Squared Poverty gap figures measures the severity and depth of poverty respectively. The poverty gap is the average, over all people, of the gaps between poor people's living standards and the poverty line. The squared-poverty gap index takes inequality among the poor into account (see Foster, Greer and Thorbecke 1984 for details). Transfers from poorer people to even poorer people reduce the index score. As Himanshu notes, what is troubling about the poverty gap figures is that things got worse in Chhattisgarh and Orissa in the period from 1993–4 to 2004–5, notwithstanding slow improvements in rural Headcount Index scores. Some of the very poorest Indians have not been making progress (a point strikingly confirmed by Krishna and Bajpai's finding that 'in villages located more than five kilometres from the nearest town – home to more than half of the entire population of India – inflation-adjusted per capita incomes fell between 1993 and 2005' [2011: 44]). Finally, Himanshu provides Gini coefficient scores by state and sector. Higher coefficients denote higher levels of inequality. Table 3.2 suggests that rural India as a whole became somewhat more equal from 1983 to 1993–4. Growth favoured the poor. Since 1993–4 these gains have been reversed. In urban India, inequalities have increased more markedly since 1993–4.

Topolova confirms this analysis, albeit some of her index figures for consumption are slightly different from those in Himanshu's paper (see table 3.4). The main innovation of her paper, however, derives

Table 3.3: Comparable estimates of urban poverty and inequality, 1983–2004/5 (Official Poverty Lines)

Urban	Headcount Ratio				Poverty Gap			
	1983	1987–88	1993–94	2004–05	1983	1987–88	1993–94	2004–05
Andhra Pradesh	41.2	41.1	38.8	27.1	10.9	10.6	9.3	6.1
Assam	25.9	11.3	7.9	3.7	5.6	1.5	0.9	0.5
Jharkhand	40.5	34.6	26.5	20.7	10.9	7.8	5.2	4.7
Bihar	61.6	63.8	40.7	38.1	18.5	16.6	9.7	9.3
Gujarat	41.9	38.5	28.3	14.2	9.7	8.2	6.2	2.5
Haryana	26.4	18.4	16.5	15.6	5.8	3.6	3.0	3.2
Himachal Pradesh	11.0	7.2	9.3	5.0	2.8	0.7	1.2	1.0
Karnataka	43.6	49.2	39.9	33.3	13.3	14.1	11.4	8.9
Kerala	48.0	38.7	24.3	20.6	14.7	10.0	5.5	4.7
Chhattisgarh	50.7	36.0	44.2	40.7	14.5	9.8	11.5	12.9
Madhya Pradesh	56.1	50.0	49.0	42.3	16.1	14.5	13.9	12.4
Maharashtra	41.1	40.5	35.0	32.8	12.1	12.4	10.2	9.2
Orissa	54.0	42.6	40.6	43.7	16.7	11.1	11.4	14.1
Punjab	22.9	13.7	10.9	5.0	5.9	2.3	1.7	0.6
Rajasthan	41.2	37.9	31.0	28.5	11.5	9.6	7.0	6.2
Tamil Nadu	51.9	40.2	39.9	24.1	15.4	11.5	10.2	5.3
Uttaranchal	22.4	20.4	12.7	17.0	5.9	4.2	3.2	3.0
Uttar Pradesh	52.7	46.4	36.1	30.7	15.1	12.7	9.3	7.2
West Bengal	33.5	33.7	22.9	15.4	8.5	7.4	4.5	2.6
All India	43.6	38.7	32.6	25.9	11.4	10.2	8.0	6.2

Urban	Squared Poverty Gap				Gini			
	1983	1987–88	1993–94	2004–05	1983	1987–88	1993–94	2004–05
Andhra Pradesh	4.1	3.9	3.2	1.9	33.2	36.1	32.3	37.6
Assam	1.7	0.3	0.2	0.1	26.1	31.0	29.0	32.1
Jharkhand	4.2	2.6	1.6	1.5	30.9	32.1	32.5	35.5
Bihar	7.1	5.9	3.4	3.0	28.5	26.6	28.2	33.3
Gujarat	3.6	2.6	2.0	0.7	28.5	27.8	29.1	31.0
Haryana	1.9	1.1	0.9	1.0	34.8	28.7	28.4	36.5
Himachal Pradesh	1.1	0.1	0.3	0.3	35.8	29.2	46.2	32.6
Karnataka	5.5	5.7	4.4	3.1	34.2	34.0	31.9	36.8
Kerala	6.2	3.9	1.9	1.6	38.9	36.9	34.3	41.0
Chhattisgarh	5.6	3.6	4.1	5.4	32.2	32.1	30.6	44.0
Madhya Pradesh	6.2	5.6	5.3	4.8	29.8	33.3	33.6	39.7
Maharashtra	4.9	5.2	4.2	3.5	34.6	34.8	35.7	37.8
Orissa	7.1	4.2	4.3	5.8	29.0	31.0	30.7	35.4

Table 3.3: (continued)

Urban	Squared Poverty Gap				Gini			
	1983	1987–88	1993–94	2004–05	1983	1987–88	1993–94	2004–05
Punjab	2.3	0.6	0.4	0.1	33.9	28.8	28.1	40.3
Rajasthan	4.7	3.4	2.2	1.9	33.9	34.6	29.3	37.2
Tamil Nadu	6.3	4.6	3.9	1.6	35.1	35.8	34.8	36.1
Uttaranchal	2.0	1.2	0.9	0.7	30.5	35.1	27.5	32.9
Uttar Pradesh	5.9	4.7	3.4	2.3	31.5	33.5	32.6	36.9
West Bengal	3.2	2.4	1.4	0.6	33.5	34.6	33.9	38.3
All India	4.4	3.8	2.9	2.0	33.9	35.0	34.4	37.6

Source: World Bank database, United Nations Development Program; Himanshu (2007).

from an attempt to decompose the sources of poverty reduction in India since 1983–4. The basic question that Topolova asks is this: 'How much more or less poverty reduction might have been achieved had growth occurred without changes in the income distribution?' (Topolova 2008: 7). Interestingly, what she calls her 'counterfactual simulation' – what would have happened if X not Y – 'suggests that in the 1980s changes in the distribution of income enhanced the effects of growth on poverty reduction. In rural India, poverty reduction from "growth alone" would have been 27 percent lower had the distribution of income not changed in favour of the poor. In urban India "growth alone" accounts for the entire poverty decline' (ibid.: 8). As can be seen from table 3.5, the direction of the sign for Urban India, 1983–1993/4, is very slightly positive in the column for Contribution of Change in Distribution. When it comes to the second growth period, however, we see that all the signs in this column are positive – which is to say they all indicate a shift in the distribution of income against the poor (or officially Poor). Topolova concludes that 'Distribution neutral growth would have generated a poverty decline in rural India that was 22 percent higher; in urban areas, the decline in poverty would have been 76 percent higher' (ibid.).

These are startling numbers and they indicate a similarly stark shift in the trajectory of India's economic growth since the early 1990s. Topolova also provides graphical representations of the same phenomena. Figure 3.3 plots what economists call 'growth incidence curves' – of real monthly consumption per capita – for India as a whole, and for rural and urban India separately. There are two panels: one for 1983–93/4 and another for 1993/4–2004/5. The horizontal thick and

Table 3.4: India: evolution of inequality

	Gini			Theil Index			Log (PCE 95/PCE 5) 1/			Variance of Log Consumption		
	All India	Rural	Urban	All India	Rural	Urban	All India	Rural	Urban	All India	Rural	Urban
1982/83	0.319	0.312	0.340	0.198	0.191	0.215	1.774	1.740	1.866	0.303	0.290	0.342
1987/88	0.313	0.301	0.349	0.200	0.186	0.241	1.688	1.621	1.887	0.279	0.258	0.348
1993/94	0.303	0.285	0.343	0.191	0.171	0.235	1.638	1.537	1.878	0.263	0.234	0.345
2004/05	0.325	0.298	0.378	0.228	0.196	0.288	1.692	1.541	2.029	0.285	0.240	0.402

Source: Topolova (2008).

Table 3.5: India: decomposing changes in poverty

	Initial Level of Poverty	Change in Poverty	Contribution of Growth	Contribution of Change in Distribution
1983–1993/94				
Rural	0.4617	−0.0933	−0.0683	−0.0249
Urban	0.4208	−0.0925	−0.0973	0.0047
All India	0.4524	−0.0940	−0.0808	−0.0132
1993/94–2004/05				
Rural	0.3684	−0.0880	−0.1071	0.0191
Urban	0.3283	−0.0702	−0.1237	0.0536
All India	0.3585	−0.0837	−0.1151	0.0314

Source: Topolova (2008).

dashed lines provide benchmark data on annualized growth in mean and median incomes, respectively, for each period. As can readily be seen, the curves for rural India and India as a whole, in the earlier time period, show that 'growth in consumption at the bottom of the income distribution [especially the bottom decile] outpaced growth at the top' (ibid.: 10). In the second time period, we see that these relative gains are reversed for all but the very poorest households in rural India. The big beneficiaries of real consumption growth are the top 15 or 20 per cent of India's urban households and less than 10 per cent of India's best-off rural households.

Figure 3.3 also points towards an explanation of what has been driving these changes in the effectiveness of India's growth-poverty reduction transmission belt. A commonly heard complaint about economic growth in the 1970s holds that it was too anaemic, while a commonly heard complaint about growth in the 1980s suggests it was unsustainable (because debt financed: see chapter 2). There is more than a grain of truth in both these charges, but what each of them misses is that Indian agriculture was significantly transformed through these decades by the Green Revolution and the broader consolidation of agrarian capitalism (Harriss 1982). Increased private and public investments in the rural economy (irrigation, electrification, farm price-support policies, grain subsidies) helped tighten labour markets and reduced the real cost of food. There was also significant expansion in the rural non-farm sector through this period (Lanjouw and Stern 1998), and considerable political pressures were brought to bear on governments by 'new farmers' movements' (Varshney 1995). All of these developments helped to secure sharp declines in the incidence of

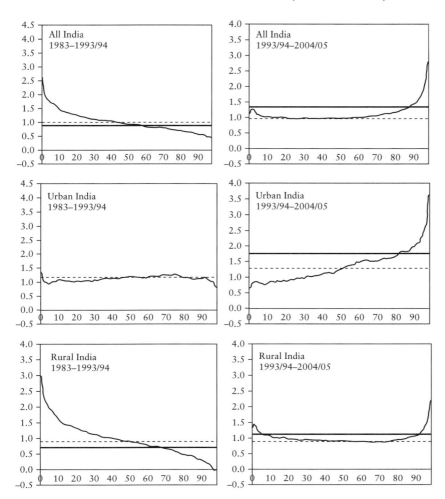

Figure 3.3: India: patterns of real consumption growth.

Source: NSSO various rounds and Fund staff estimates (Topolova 2008).

poverty in the countryside. Study after study has told us that most poor people in rural India are landless labourers or marginal farmers. The overwhelming majority of these people are net purchasers of food. Their living standards are thus extremely sensitive to the real price of grain and other staples. They generally hope to escape poverty by working more days in a year (whether in local labour markets or further afield: Breman 2010c), and/or by seeing their wages rise faster than the price of food and other basic items.

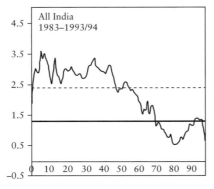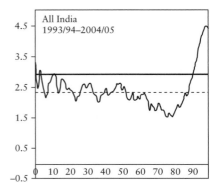

Figure 3.4: India: patterns of real wage growth.

Source: Topolova (2008).

Topolova confirms this intuition in the first panel of a graph that is reproduced here as figure 3.4, which pools data on urban and rural workers aged fifteen to sixty-five engaged in regular salaried or casual wage labour (the thick and dashed horizontal lines are as in figure 3.3). As she reports, 'Between 1983 and 1993/94, real wage growth at the bottom generally outpaced the growth of wages at the top' (ibid.: 13). In the second period, however, we see far greater returns to the top 15 per cent of households, and particularly to graduates working in the manu-facturing and service sectors. Topolova also finds that Scheduled Caste (SC) and Scheduled Tribe (ST) households failed to keep pace with the growth rates in average per capita consumption recorded by members of non-SC/ST households after 1993–4. Indeed, after matching non-SC/ST households through the first time period, SC and ST households saw their consumption levels rise after 1993–4 by about half as much as non-SC/ST households (ibid.:14).

Exactly when the poverty efficiency of India's growth trajectory changed is impossible to say if we rely on consumption data from four thick rounds of the NSS – somewhere between 1987–8 and 1993–4, we can assume. We should be careful, however, in how we seek to interpret the poverty reduction effects of India's economic reforms. It is not clear that a long period of 'systemic' economic reforms which has been dated back to 1991 (Srinivasan) or 1988–9 (Panagariya) has yet delivered a pace of poverty reduction that is significantly better than that achieved in the 1970s or the first half of the 1980s. The most optimistic gloss that can be put on 'post-reform' poverty reduction is that: (a) trade liberali-zation came slowly to India before the new millennium and might only now be improving elasticities of poverty reduction; (b) there are growing signs that urban and non-farm growth is becoming a more efficient vehicle than previously for raising agricultural wages (Lanjouw and Murgai 2009); and (c) India's rate of poverty incidence reduction since the mid-1990s is as impressive as in the 1970s, notwithstanding greater inequalities in the distribution of incomes. More broadly, of course, it is perfectly reasonable to argue that poverty in India is focused increasingly in eastern and northern states, not because of liberalization but because of its absence: a failure to connect and take part. Others will argue that poor starting conditions in these states made the adoption of pro-reform policies unlikely. The hard work of poverty reduction needed to begin elsewhere: with asset redistribution, greater investment in infrastructure and human capabilities, and with governance reforms. Simply put, India – and not just eastern India – could and should have done better.

3.5   Inclusive Growth?

Wherever we come down in these debates, it is clear that economic growth in India since 1990 has worked extremely well for its best-off households. This is consistent with the Kuznets hypothesis and with the suggestion that India's incentive regimes before the late 1980s were stacked against private capital accumulation. By these lights, it is neither surprising nor very alarming. Economic reform in India necessarily took the form of an elite revolt against *dirigisme*.

Still, the degree to which India's reforms have delivered tremendous benefits to the country's richest individuals is worth noting. Banerjee and Piketty have calculated that 'the average incomes of the top 0.01 percent of [India's] income distribution was about 150–200 times larger than the average income of the entire population during the 1950s. The difference fell to less than 50 times larger than the average income in the early 1980s, but then rose again to 150–200 times larger during the late-1990s' (2005: 7). Jayadev et al. (2011) suggest that inequalities in wealth have increased at least in line with inequalities in income. In this case, the main driver is not returns to talent or entrepreneurship in new product markets; rather, it reflects blossoming returns on assets like gold, land and shares. All this happened, meanwhile, as some states, or some parts of states (the interior areas of Orissa more so than its coastal belt, for example), were effectively left behind amid India's long post-reform growth acceleration. Arguably, some left themselves behind. Per capita net state domestic product at constant 1993–4 prices actually fell in Bihar from Rs 4,474 in 1990–1 to Rs 3,396 in 2003–4 (probably because of the loss of Jharkhand), while the residents of Uttar Pradesh, including the richer western parts of that state (but not Uttaranchal), saw their real incomes rise from Rs 5,342 in 1990–1 to a meagre Rs 5,975 in 2003–4 (Government of India 2006b). Matters were slightly better in Orissa and Madhya Pradesh, where per capita net state domestic product increased from Rs 4,300 to Rs 7,176 in the former state, over the same time period, and from Rs 6,350 to Rs 8,038 in the latter. In Maharashtra, meanwhile, the corresponding figures show more than a 60 per cent increase in real terms over thirteen years, from Rs 10,159 to Rs 16,765. In Gujarat, the rate of economic expansion was even greater, with a per capita net state domestic product of Rs 8,788 nearly doubling by 2004–5 to Rs 16,878 (after Corbridge 2011).

Since 2005, there have been signs of economic improvement in Bihar, which is very much to be welcomed, but it is too soon to start speaking about convergence of incomes in India, either socially or spatially. Divergence remains the order of the day and will do for some time to come. In another important paper, Topolova makes use of a quasi-natural experiment to assess the effects of trade liberalization on poverty and inequality in districts across India. Her basic intuition is that trade liberalization in India began after the balance of payments crisis of 1991 and has proceeded more and less rapidly in different industries. This being so, it is possible to measure changing levels of exposure to foreign trade on a district by district basis. So long as we know the share of a district's population employed by various industries on the eve of economic reform, and also the level of reduction of trade barriers in these industries, we can link district 'poverty and inequality . . . [to] district-specific trade policy shocks' (Topolova 2005: 4). Topolova finds that

> trade liberalization led to an increase in poverty and poverty gap in the rural districts where industries more exposed to liberalization were concentrated. . . . According to the most conservative [of her] estimates, compared to a rural district experiencing no change in tariffs, a district experiencing the mean level of tariff changes saw a 2 percent increase in poverty incidence and a 0.6 increase in poverty depth. This setback represents about 15 percent of India's progress in poverty reduction over the 1990s. (Ibid.: 3)

This is a significant finding and it helps us to understand why India's growth engine in the 1990s was less effective in reducing poverty than might have been anticipated. Many workers fared badly in industries that were strongly and suddenly exposed to foreign competition. As Topolova recognizes, however, negative trade liberalization effects are most evident in the poverty reduction stories of richer – or at least more industrialized – states. And in many of these states – Maharashtra and Gujarat, for example – losses to labour are being compensated by new firm openings (Hasan, Mitra and Ural 2007). This is true notwithstanding evidence of jobless growth (or continuing high rates of investment in physical capital accumulation; we return to this issue in the next chapter, and in chapter 14). Topolova's paper has less to say about the gap that widened through the 1990s and 2000s between India's more entrepreneurial states and those states in the centre and east of the country that remained dependent on primary commodity production, whether from fields or mines. Her key observation in this regard, which is controversial (she may have underestimated especially the seasonal labour flows that we discuss in the next chapter), is that 'migration [in India] is remarkably low, with no signs of an upward trend after the 1991 reforms' (ibid.: 4, and see also Topolova 2004). Neither capital nor labour are flowing in India as fluidly as standard theories would predict.

Topolova ends her paper by suggesting that government policies may be needed to redistribute the gains of liberalization from winners to those who do not benefit as much. Like many economists, she has in mind reforms that will enhance labour mobility. It is not obvious, however, that this is the best place to begin to address labour supply (or demand) issues. There probably is a 'pervasive bias . . . against the employment of unskilled labour' in some of India's leading firms, and this is bound to hurt the poor (Joshi and Little 1994: 221). It is less clear, however, that pro-labour legislation in India – notoriously, for some economists, the Industrial Disputes Act of 1947 and its later Amendments (1976, 1982) – has significantly distorted the country's emerging industrial structure. It is at least as likely that the cartelized and capital-intensive (formal) industrial economy that emerged in India under British rule induced forms of labour legislation that suited both capital and labour. In any case, only around 10 per cent of Indians work in the formal economy and their employers find all sorts of ways to escape 'rigid' labour laws (Harriss-White 2005).

What really holds back factor mobility in India is a lack of transferable skills in poor labouring households and an under-supply of infrastructure and security in poor regions. It is because of the collapse of the state and the rise of an organized Maoist movement that capital is not flowing to Jharkhand or Chhattisgarh (see chapter 10). With a few obvious exceptions – mining companies, for example – the attractiveness of doing business in this part of India has reduced markedly since c.2000. Too many arguments about mobility and poverty traps fail to register the important point that geography is not joined up in eastern India. Not only are there poor air and rail connections to India's leading cities, but there is also a dearth of safe or metalled roads in India's Red Belt and more or less an absence of functioning public and

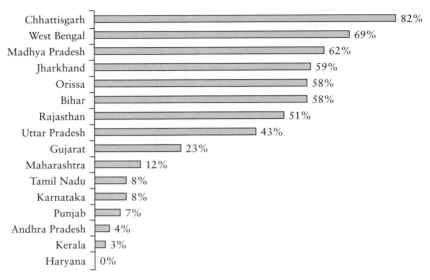

Figure 3.5: Percentage of habitations not connected by roads, by Indian state.
Source: World Bank (2006).

private services: everything from working Block Development Offices to working petrol stations (Corbridge, Williams, Srivastava and Véron 2005; and see figures 3.5 and 3.6). Under these circumstances, labour laws that might privilege a labour aristocracy elsewhere in India would seem to be the last thing on the minds of poor householders in eastern India.

Failures of governance – of rule, in effect – are amplified in many of India's poorest districts by an appalling under-supply of public goods like power, water, sanitation, health care and education, something we take up at length in chapter 8 (World Bank 2006; Pritchett 2008). Once we begin to think about poverty in terms of capabilities – of what people are able to do with their lives (Sen 2000) – instead of just in terms of consumption, we see very quickly that it is the continuing over-production of 'bad inequalities' that is holding back both poverty reduction and poverty convergence across India. Consider education, for a start: almost half of all adult women in India are illiterate, compared to around 10 per cent of women in China (Bardhan 2010: 112). Even among young people aged twenty-five to twenty-nine 'about 30 percent are still illiterate' (ibid.). We discuss problems regarding education in India later (in chapters 8 and 14), but note here that although total spending on education in India has been rising since 2000, most of this increase has been in the private sector. The exit of well-off urban (and some rural) families from a

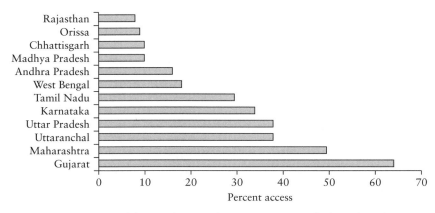

Figure 3.6: Percentage of the population with access to sewerage facilities, by Indian state
Source: World Bank (2006).

public education system that lacks both funding and strong accountability mechanisms does little to put pressure on policymakers to improve matters for the poor.

We will have more to say on youth employment/unemployment later in the book (chapter 14). Unemployment isn't just a problem for men and women without formal educational qualifications or skills. There is also a growing problem of unemployment among educated Indians, or among formally educated Indians (which is not always the same thing: certificates are very often awarded to people with limited problem-solving capabilities: Jeffrey 2008, 2010). In health-care provision, too, we see large and widening gaps between the quality of care available to people with medical insurance, on the one hand, and those who need (or hope) to use public hospitals and clinics, on the other (Jeffery and Jeffery 2008). Efforts are being made to universalize rural primary health-care through the National Rural Health Mission. Nonetheless, the World Bank (2006: table 1.3) reports that the percentage of children receiving immunization for polio and measles fell between 1998–9 and 2002–3, in both cases to less than 60 per cent coverage. Even in metropolitan Delhi, as Das and Hammer (2004) have shown through experimental work, the ability of well-qualified doctors to diagnose simple conditions like diarrhoea can be alarmingly low. Women in India continue to die in childbirth at rates that are similar to or above corresponding rates in sub-Saharan Africa, and India's progress against most of the United Nation's non-income Millenium Development Goal targets is lamentable. Evidence of this is provided in table 3.6 and little by way of interpretation is required.

Table 3.6: India's progress against non-income Millennium Development Goals

Achieve universal primary education	Improve maternal health
Target: Ensure that, by 2015, children everywhere, boys and girls alike, will be able to complete a full course of primary schooling	*Target: Reduce by three-quarters, between 1990 and 2015, the maternal mortality ratio*
Total enrolment, primary (% net)	**Maternal mortality ratio (per 100 000 live births)**
2008: 96 2015 target: 100	1990: 570 2008: 230 2015 target: 142
Current status: *Possible to achieve only if changes are made*	Target: Achieve, by 2015, universal access to reproductive health
	1990: 34 2008: 47 2015 target: 100
	Current status: *Possible to achieve only if changes are made*
Promote gender equality and empower women	Ensure environmental sustainability
Target: Eliminate gender disparity in primary and secondary education, preferably by 2005, and in all levels of education no later than 2015 **Ratio of female to male primary enrolment (%)**	*Target: Halve, by 2015, the proportion of people without sustainable access to safe drinking water and basic sanitation* **Improved sanitation facilities (% population with access)**
1990: 74 2008: 97 2005 target: 100	1990: 18 2008:31 2015 target: 59
Ratio of female to male secondary enrolment (%)	**Improved water source (% of population with access)**
1990: 58 2008: 86 2005 target: 100	1990: 72 2008: 88 2015: 86
Ratio of female to male tertiary enrolment (%)	Current status: *Insufficient information*
1990: 52 2008: 70 2015 target: 100	

Table 3.6: (continued)

Promote gender equality and empower women	Ensure environmental sustainability
Current status: *Possible to achieve only if changes are made*	
Reduce child mortality	Combat HIV/AIDS, malaria and other diseases
Target: Reduce by two-thirds, between 1990 and 2015, the under-five mortality rate	*Target: Have halted by 2015 and begun to reverse the spread of HIV/AIDS*
Mortality rate, under-fives (per 1000)	*HIV prevalence among population aged 15–49 years (%)*
1990: 118 2008: 39 2015 target: 68	1990: 0.1 2008: 0.3
Current status: *Off track*	Current status: *Insufficient information*

Source: World Bank database, United Nations Development Program.

When it comes to the regional distribution of these impaired capabilities, moreover, it is overwhelmingly the case that India's poorest states in income/consumption terms are precisely the ones that are most damaged by a continuing under-supply of infrastructure and collective goods. With their multi-dimensional poverty index, which takes account of these vital elements of well-being, Alkire and Santos (2010: 31) show that in eight states of India with high levels of income poverty – West Bengal, Orissa, Rajasthan, Uttar Pradesh, Chhattisgarh, Madhya Pradesh, Jharkhand and Bihar – multi-dimensional poverty is as acute as in the poorest twenty-six African countries. The state of Bihar, for instance, which on some measures was the poorest state in India in the mid-2000s (in terms of Gross State Domestic Product), was also then among the worst three of fourteen major states in terms of rates for literacy and underweight children. (Still, even Bihar performed better than some rich states in the north-west of India (Punjab, Haryana and Gujarat) when it came to imbalanced sex ratios – see table 3.7, and see also chapter 13). Boys and girls born into India's poorest households face enormous problems in equipping themselves for work in India's formal sector

If India is 'shining for the poor too' (Datt and Ravallion 2010), it is not mainly because of sustained capability improvements in

Table 3.7: Ranking of India's poorest states by GSDP per capita and human development indicators

	Rank by GSDP per capita	HDI rank[a]	Literacy rate[b]		Infant mortality[c]		Under-weight children[d]		Sex ratio[e] (0–6 years)	
			Diff.	Rank	Diff.	Rank	Diff.	Rank	Diff.	Rank
Bihar	13	13	-17.9	13	-5.3	9	-7.4	11	15	5
Orissa	12	10	-1.8	9	-13.4	11	-7.4	12	26	3
Uttar Pradesh	11	12	-8.0	12	-19.1	13	-4.7	10	-11	8
Madhya Pradesh	10	11	-1.3	8	-18.5	12	-8.1	13	5	7
Rajasthan	9	8	-4.4	11	-12.8	10	-3.6	9	-18	10
West Bengal	8	7	3.8	5	18.9	3	-1.7	7	33	2
Andhra Pradesh	7	9	-4.3	10	1.8	8	9.3	4	34	1
Karnataka	6	6	1.6	7	16.1	4	3.1	5	19	4
Tamil Nadu	5	2	8.1	2	19.4	2	10.3	3	15	6
Haryana	4	4	3.2	6	10.8	5	12.4	2	-108	12
Gujarat	3	5	4.6	3	5.0	7	1.9	6	-44	11
Punjab	2	1	4.6	4	10.5	6	18.3	1	-129	13
Maharashtra	1	3	11.9	1	23.9	1	-2.6	8	-14	9
All-India (avg.)			**65.4**		**67.6**		**47**		**927**	
Kerala	7	1	25.5	1	51.3	1	20.1	1	33	3

Note: GSDP refers to Gross State Domestic Product. Diff. refers to the difference between state-level indicator and All-India average. a: HDI ranking refers to the Human Development Index methodology in the UNDP Human Development Report 2011. Ranking across sixteen major states, including Assam, b: 2001, per cent of population seven years and older, c: 1998/9, per 1,000 live births, d: 1998/9, per cent of children under three years of age, e: 2001, girls per 1,000 boys in zero to six years group.

Source: 2001 National Human Development Report; 2001 Census, 1998/9 National Family and Health Survey, 1999 Sample Registration System; World Bank (2006: 21).

the post-reform era. Rather, it is because Backward Class political movements in north and central India began in the 1980s to deliver some of the gains around honour and dignity (*izzat*) that had been struggled for much earlier in India's southern states (Jaffrelot 2003). Many Scheduled Caste and Other Backward Caste people, and some Scheduled Tribals too, are less prone now than a generation ago 'to feel shame in public' – a change in status that matters hugely (Narayan, Pritchett and Kapoor 2009). At the same time, many of the parents of these boys and girls – and especially now among India's *adivasi* (ST) communities – have seen their livelihoods come under attack from food price inflation (a big problem in 2007–8 and again in 2011) and from the continued privatization of many common or open-access property resources. As Pranab Bardhan points out, we should 'recognize that private consumer data of the NSS that are used in poverty estimates . . . do not capture the declining access to environmental resources (such as forests, fisheries, grazing lands, and water both for drinking and irrigation) on which the daily lives and livelihoods of the poor depend' (2010: 94).

3.6 Conclusion

The good news that we have reported in this chapter is that the incidence of extreme income poverty has fallen significantly in India since 1970 and can be expected to fall much further, and possibly rather faster, in the rest of this decade and the next one. It is clear, too, that economic growth is a very powerful driver of poverty reduction. Had per capita incomes risen at only 1 per cent per annum over the past three decades, or had there been no per capita income growth, the percentage of Indian households below any given poverty line would almost certainly have been much higher now than it already is. Growth of the economy also allows governments to raise public spending and we are now seeing evidence of this in India. Government revenues are rising at about 1 or 2 percentage points ahead of GDP growth. Money is increasingly available, therefore, for some of the huge infrastructural projects that India must get to grips with over the next ten, twenty or thirty years, if high rates of economic growth are to be sustained. Money should also be available for investments in human capital projects, or for the building up of those 'capabilities' which Amartya Sen (2000) rightly insists must be at the heart of any meaningful account of 'development as freedom' (and see our discussion in chapter 5).

Pranab Bardhan further reminds us, however, that, 'of India's children under the age of three, as many as 46 percent are underweight, compared to China's 8 percent' (ibid.: 105), and the three larger stories emerging from chapter 3 cut against the grain of a growing boosterism about poverty reduction in India. We need to recognize, first, that while the incidence of extreme income poverty is being reduced in India, it was still the case in 2005 that nearly 830 million Indians lived on less than two dollars a day (Chen and Ravallion 2008: table 6b). A journey from Delhi to Kolkata still takes a traveller through the global epicentre of extreme income/consumption poverty, notwithstanding common conceptions that conditions for the poor are much worse in sub-Saharan Africa than in South Asia. Life is desperately hard and uncertain below this poverty line, the more so when people lack access to efficiently provided public services and well-targeted social protection spending. In the next two chapters, we report some recent improvements in employment relief provision (under the National Rural Employment Guarantee Act), but we also document the phenomenon of 'jobless growth' and changes in the workings of the Public Distribution System which threaten the food security of poor households. Employment growth is key to poverty reduction and we have reasons to be concerned about the slow structural transformation of the Indian economy.

Second, there is a 'missing middle' in India today. This claim will come as a surprise to academics and others who like to comment on India's 300 million-strong middle class, and who write at length, and often insightfully, about their new lifestyles and consumption patterns (Fernandes 2006; Brosius 2010; see also chapter. 14, where we offer similar commentary of our own). Nancy Birdsall (2010), however, writing for the World Bank, has recently proposed a definition of 'the middle class in the developing world to include people with an income above $10 a day, but excluding the top 5% of that country. By this definition, India, even urban India alone has no middle class; everyone at over $10 a day is in the top 5% of the country' (Srinivasan 2010). In a very real sense, we are seeing the emergence today of 'two Indias'. Perhaps this was to be expected – cf. Kuznets – but it might also bring in its wake increased political mobilizations against some remarkably visible and growing forms of social and spatial inequality.

Third, it bears saying that Dollar and Kraay's picture of distribution neutral growth holds little traction in India. For one thing, the bottom quintile of India's households has not been holding its own since c.1990, as Topolova very clearly demonstrates. For another, the gap between the bottom quintile and average incomes is not terribly meaningful in a country where almost half the population in 2005 was living on less than $1.25 a day. We also dispute Dollar and Kraay's suggestion that 'policies intended to benefit the poorest in society' are unlikely to improve the incomes of the poorest by raising growth rates. On the one hand, this downplays the importance of direct improvements in human development index scores, of the sort that are well documented for Kerala. Besley, Burgess and Esteve-Volart (2007: 62) suggest that Kerala's poverty elasticity with respect to growth was four times greater than that of Bihar in the period 1960–98 (–1.23 against –0.30). (Only two other states had scores better than -1.00: Punjab at -1.03 and West Bengal, –1.17; see also Kohli 1987; Ravallion and Datt 1999; and Harriss 2003b.) On the other hand, it discounts the historical importance of strategies that have promoted redistribution for growth (Chenery et al. 1974). It is frankly hard to see how India will sustain high rates of per capita income growth in the long run unless and until actions are taken to bring effective governance to India's poorest districts and states (a receding horizon as we write), and to supply India's poorest households with the capabilities that would allow them to access reasonable employment opportunities.

4

Why Hasn't Economic Growth Delivered More for Indian Workers?

4.1 Introduction

Social and regional inequalities have been increasing in India during the recent period of rapid economic growth, as we argued in the last chapter. There remains controversy over the extent to which income poverty has been reduced, but there is no doubt about the fact that significant non-income indicators of well-being remain depressingly low. Economic growth is certainly necessary for poverty reduction, but we believe that there are strong reasons for thinking that, thus far, India's rapid economic growth has not delivered commensurate benefits in terms of improved levels of well-being. This has been so not least by comparison with China where the poverty-reducing effects of economic growth have been greater. In this chapter, we will explore further the question of why high rates of economic growth haven't delivered more for Indian workers. We ask who the people are in India who have been missing out on the benefits of growth, and why.

Those who have been losing out are, first, most of those very many people in the country who depend directly or indirectly upon the agricultural economy, which has lagged increasingly behind the rest of the economy; and, second, most of the very large numbers of people who depend upon 'informal' or 'unorganized' employment outside agriculture, and whose share of the labour force as a whole has been increasing. The material disabilities of all these people may be compounded by factors of social marginality and exclusion that have to do with caste and religion. All indicators of well-being show that members of the

Scheduled Castes, or Dalits, and people from the Scheduled Tribes of the central and eastern Indian states – who together make up very nearly a quarter of the population – are much worse off than are others who share with them the same or similar positions in the economy. Agricultural work has become more distinctly 'Dalit' in the major agricultural regions of the country because they are often excluded from better-paying non-agricultural jobs; most members of the Scheduled Tribes have little chance of participating in the modern economy, given the very low levels of education that prevail amongst them, except as vulnerable casual workers. Very many Muslims suffer from similar disabilities.

We begin by explaining the context of all these problems in the limited structural transformation of India's economy, or what some refer to as failed transition. We go on to explain the particular problems of the agricultural economy, and of employment trends. As we shall explain, high rates of economic growth in India have not generated very many 'good jobs'.

4.2   The Context: India's 'Lopsided', 'Failed' or 'Tortuous' Transition

One of the most fundamental assumptions about economic development is that it must entail a major transformation in the structure of an economy. In early stages of development, it is usually the case that the primary, agricultural sector is overwhelmingly dominant, and the great majority of the population is engaged directly in agricultural production. The process of development involves an historic shift away from agriculture to industry and a wide range of service activities, and of labour out of agriculture and into employment in these sectors. In many agricultural economies, small-scale, household-based 'peasant' farming is widespread, and it has often been assumed that the process of structural transformation is likely to involve the more or less gradual consolidation of many of these small farms into larger, more highly capitalized units. 'Development' therefore involves the dispossession of many peasant producers – they lose control of their own land and other assets – and those affected by dispossession move into dependence upon wage labour for others, both on the larger, capitalist farms and increasingly outside agriculture altogether. Of course, this is a highly stylized account, based on an understanding of what went on in Western industrial economies starting in the eighteenth century or even before. But the ideas of the structural transformation of economies and of the societal transition

Table 4.1: Employment structure in India – daily status (per cent)

Year	Agr	Mfg	CTT	G&P	Total
2004–05	53.9	12.8	21.8	09.00	97.5
1999–2000	58.0	12.1	18.9	08.90	97.9
1993–94	61.1	11.4	14.8	10.80	98.1
1983	63.4	11.8	13.3	09.90	98.4

Agr=Agriculture; Mfg=Manufacturing; CTT=Construction, Trade and Hotels, Transport, Storage and Communications; G&P=Government Services, Education, Health, Community Services, Personal Services. Total less than 100 per cent because employment shares of mining and of real estate and finance are not included.

Source: After Eswaran *et al.* (2009: table 6).

associated with it have been fundamental in thinking about development within different theoretical frameworks, from that of the modernization school to those of Marxist thinkers.

The three adjectives of the heading above are the different ways in which different authors (Government of India (2009b), Partha Chatterjee (2008) and Pranab Bardhan (2009), respectively) refer to a cardinal fact about India's economy. This is that the structural transformation of the economy has not been completed, in spite of years of high rates of economic growth – and India's 'transition to an enlarged and dominating sphere of capital in the economy' (Bardhan 2009: 31) is correspondingly problematic. In India, the declining relative share of income from the agricultural sector has not been accompanied by an equivalent decline in employment in that sector. In 1950–1, agriculture accounted for 61 per cent of GDP and for 76 per cent of employment (Chandrasekhar 2007), while it now contributes less than 20 per cent of GDP (16 per cent in 2007–8) but still employs around 60 per cent of the labour force, according to census data from 2001, or 54 per cent in 2004–5, according to data from the National Sample Survey (NSS), showing the daily employment status of individuals by activity (see table 4.1, but note that NSS data for 2007–8 show the share of farm employment as 55.4 per cent (Himanshu 2011: 47)). The lowest share of agriculture in GDP across states is 9.5 per cent, in Maharashtra, where the level of agricultural employment, however, remains at more than 53 per cent (Dev 2008, table 7.11).

The shift of labour from agriculture in India has been less than in some comparator countries (table 4.2), though there is less sharp a contrast with China than Bardhan suggests (2009: 33). An important point of difference between India and China is that in China 55 per cent of the cumulative increase in GDP between 1990 and 2005 was accounted for by manufacturing, which has generated relatively more employment than

Table 4.2: Distribution of GDP and of employment across sectors in India and comparator countries

Country	GDP (2007)			Employment(2005/2006)		
	agriculture	industry	services	agriculture	industry	services
India	**17.7**	**29.4**	**52.8**	**53.9**	**12.8**	**30.8**
China	11.3	48.6	40.1	42.6	23.8	32.2
Brazil	5.5	28.7	65.8	19.3	21.4	57.9
Indonesia	13.8	46.7	39.4	42.0	18.7	37.2
Pakistan	20.6	26.6	52.8	43.4	20.3	36.6
Bangladesh	19.0	28.7	52.3	48.1	14.5	37.4

Note: 'Employment' refers to distribution of the labour force by occupation/sector.

Source: World Bank Data (accessed at: <http//www.worldbank.org/data> September 2011).

the services sector that accounts for 60 per cent of the increase in GDP over the same period in India – though in China, too, labour is now being absorbed increasingly into services.

Dispossession of small-scale agricultural producers has gone on, and continues to go on, for industrial, mining and infrastructural projects across the country, and has increasingly encountered resistance from them in actions that may involve the Maoists who are now organized across about a third of the districts of the country (see chapter 10). The Indian agricultural economy, however, is still characterized by extensive small-scale, household-based production. The distribution both of ownership and of operational holdings is distinctly pear-shaped, and what are described as 'marginal' operated holdings (of one hectare, or less, in extent) now account for 70 per cent of the total. Most such holdings are unlikely to be capable of 'providing enough work or income to be the main livelihood of the household' (Hazell et al. 2007: 1). Estimations made by Vikas Rawal (2008), using data from the 59th Round of the National Sample Survey (NSS) for 2003–4 show that 31 per cent of rural households across the country as a whole own no land at all, and another 30 per cent own less than 0.4 hectare (or about one acre of land), while only a little over 5 per cent of households own more than three hectares (and just 0.52 per cent own more than 10). The absolute numbers and the relative share in the rural population of households without land – which have for long been considerable – have been increasing. The data from 2003–4 are not strictly comparable with those from an earlier round of the NSS, for 1992, but Rawal suggests that they show an increase of as much as 6 percentage points in landlessness, while inequality in land ownership also increased. Still, over most of

Table 4.3: Employment by type and sector (millions)

	1999–2000			2004–05		
Sector	Informal workers	Formal Workers	Total workers	Informal Workers	Formal workers	Total workers
Informal	341.3	1.4	342.6	393.5	1.4	394.9
Formal	20.5	33.7	54.1	29.1	33.4	62.6
Total	361.7	35	396.8	422.6	34.9	457.5

Source: Sanyal and Bhattacharyya (2009), citing NCEUS

the country, landlordism, where small producers depend for access to land and other assets upon the owners of large estates, has declined. The share of leased-in land in the total operated area, according to the NSS, declined from 10.7 per cent in 1960–1 to just 6.5 per cent in the *kharif* (summer) season of 2002–3. Traces of classic 'landlordism' remain, however, and inequality in land ownership still gives considerable power locally – economic, social and political – to the relatively small numbers of larger landowners and the increasing numbers of capitalist farmers.

At the same time, those depending upon wage employment have not, generally, been able to find what we might label as good jobs in the organized or formal sector, and the most dynamic and productive sectors of the economy, and they take up activities in the unorganized or informal economy, outside the purview of most employment legislation, which are often not very productive. Workers who are informally employed have no protection – against the loss of their jobs, or in event of illness – and receive no benefits from employers. They are usually low paid, and their work and their incomes are commonly irregular, though they may also work very long hours and in hazardous workplaces. It is reliably estimated that about two thirds of India's GDP comes from such unregistered, informal activity, and that it accounts for more than 90 per cent of livelihoods – more than half of them being generated from self-employment (see Lerche 2010 for discussion of the informal economy and classes of labour). Meanwhile, according to data presented by the National Commission for Enterprises in the Unorganised Sector (2009b) the absolute numbers of protected 'formal sector' jobs actually *declined* marginally from 33.7 million to 33.4 million between 1999–2000 and 2005–5 (table 4.3) – though they have increased again since then (Himanshu 2011: 56).

While a classic theory, associated with Marx, holds that those employed (often self-employed) in informal activities constitute a reserve army of labour, necessary for the development of industrial capitalism over the longer run, it has been suggested (in an argument that will be considered further below) that in India now a large share of the labour force as a whole is better described as 'excluded', being unnecessary for the growth of the economy as a whole, and surviving in a wide range of activities that are of only marginal significance for the dynamic, corporate sector (Sanyal and Bhattacharyya 2009). Whatever one makes of this argument it is clear that the narrative of structural transformation and societal transition breaks down in regard to modern India. This chapter analyses the implications of the 'failed' transition.

4.3   What is Wrong with Indian Agriculture?

The fact that there has been such little movement out of agricultural employment, even as the share of agriculture in GDP has declined, means that the majority of the people of India still depend on agriculture for their livelihoods. So if the agricultural economy is not doing well – if productivity is not increasing – then it follows that most of the people won't be doing very well either. As the London *Economist* puts it (13 March 2010: 15): 'the [Indian] government cannot achieve the "inclusive" growth it aspires to without robust progress in agriculture'.

Yet, as Pranab Bardhan argues forcefully, 'the agriculture sector is in bad shape' (2009: 31) after a decade – 1994–5 to 2004–5 – of the lowest growth rates in the sector (0.6 per cent per annum, according to his calculations) since Independence. This is the result of the very high incidence, now, of marginal holdings, of the costs of inputs, the degradation of the natural resource base, declining public investment, and decreased access to public-sector credit. One tragic but powerful marker of the fact that many cultivators have not been doing at all well in recent times is the high rate of suicides amongst them, which began to be reported in the later 1990s. A systematic study of this phenomenon, by K. Nagaraj (2008), based on an analysis of the data on 'Accidental Deaths and Suicides in India', published by the National Crime Records Bureau, for suicides amongst those described as 'self-employed in farming/agriculture' over the period 1997–2006, confirms that the rate of suicides amongst farmers is high by comparison with that for the general population. More significantly, Nagaraj believes that the suicide rate amongst farmers has been increasing, at least from the year 2001 onwards, while the general rate has been more or less stable. The five states of Maharashtra, Karnataka, Andhra Pradesh, Chhattisgarh and Madhya Pradesh are the ones that have been most affected (accounting for two thirds of the national total of farmer suicides), and Nagaraj argues that 'there is a contiguous, dry, semi-arid, poor, backward region within these states . . . where the problem must be very severe'. This is a region, he suggests, in which agro-ecological conditions make for high levels of vulnerability, where under the impact of policies of economic liberalization agriculture has been particularly badly affected by the withdrawal of state services, and where there is a lack of alternative livelihood opportunities. Arvind Panagariya, on the other hand, though he refers to comparable findings about the trends, argues that 'existing studies do not systematically connect the dramatic rise in farmer suicides in certain regions to the reforms' (2008: 154). This follows from his reliance on sources that analyse reasons given for individual suicides by close relatives and friends – an approach that is sensibly critiqued by Nagaraj, drawing not least on the authority of Durkheim's arguments in his classic *Suicide*. Structural, social conditions – in this case having to do at least in part with changes relating to liberalization – underlie the enormously diverse reasons that are attributed to individual acts of suicide (Kumar 2010).

'Farmers' suicides' is an emotive indicator of the existence of an agrarian crisis. But what of other evidence to justify this idea with reference to the current state of Indian agriculture? While it is extremely difficult, given the considerable variance in the performance of the agricultural economy from year to year – due to the highly uncertain climatic conditions characteristic of most of India – to draw clear-cut conclusions about growth trends, and much depends of course on which years or groups of years are taken for comparison over time, there is no doubt about the fact that the growth of agriculture has lagged behind that of the rest of the economy. That this has been particularly marked in the period of high overall growth after 2003 was recognized both by the Prime Minister, Manmohan Singh, and by Montek Singh Ahluwalia, the Deputy Chairman of the Planning Commission, in speeches made in 2010 (see reports in *The Hindu* 18 June and 20 June 2010). Both regretted that agriculture had been growing at a rate of only about 2 per cent per annum (though see also Bardhan 2009, cited above), as against the target of 4 per cent per annum set in the Eleventh Plan, and both spoke of the need to raise the growth rate. Table 4.4 sets out two different estimates of growth rates by acknowledged authorities.

Other estimates suggest, like those calculated by Bhalla and Singh, that the period of India's economic reforms has been marked by lower rates of growth of the agricultural economy (see Eswaran et al. 2009; Mathur et al. 2006; Vaidyanathan 2010: chapter 1). The noted agricultural economist A. Vaidyanathan argues, however, that 'Rigorous statistical tests on official time series do not provide strong corroboration of a progressive deceleration of agricultural growth' (2006: 4011). But he points out as well that these data also show that the average of

Table 4.4: Agricultural growth rates

Bhalla and Singh (2009)
Annual compound growth rate (%) of value of output

1980–83/ 1962–65	1990–93/ 1980–83	2003–06/ 1990–93	2003–06/ 1962–65
2.24	3.37	1.74	2.36

Panagariya (2008)
Annual growth rates (%) of agricultural output (at factor cost)

1951–5	1965–81	1981–8	1988–2006
2.9	2.1	2.1	3.4*

*But 2.3% in 2000–2006.

Source: Calculated from data in the RBI *Handbook of Statistics on the Indian Economy.*

Source: Calculated from Ministry of Agriculture data.

Table 4.5: Classification of rural households according to major earnings source, 2005

Income source	Non-poor households	Poor households
Self-employed in non-agriculture	16.5	12.9
Agricultural labour	22.1	41.8
Other labour	10.3	12.1
Self-employed in agriculture	38.4	26.7
Others	12.7	6.5

Source: Calculated from NSS data by Eswaran et al (2009).

annual changes in total output, area and yields are lower, and much more volatile, over the fifteen years since 1989 than they were in the preceding period of twenty years.

Agrarian distress is reflected in Prabhat Patnaik's calculation (cited by Jha 2007) that over the period from 1994–5 to 2003–4 the real per capita incomes of India's agriculturally dependent population remained stagnant, when per capita incomes for the country as a whole increased by more than 4 per cent (see also the similar findings of Krishna and Bajpai (2011), reported in chapter 3). The point is brought home in findings of the Foundation for Agrarian Studies, from village surveys in Andhra Pradesh, Uttar Pradesh and Maharashtra, that it was virtually impossible in 2005–6 for households with operational holdings of two hectares of land or less (who account for all but a small share of all the cultivators in the country, remember), to earn an income sufficient for family survival. The net annual incomes from crop production of very many households were actually negative (Ramachandran and Rawal 2010).

The rural poor include large numbers of cultivating households, but an even greater share of agricultural labour households, as we show in table 4.5. They might be expected to have been even more badly affected by the agricultural crisis than have been cultivating households. The NSS data suggest that agricultural wage employment increased at about 1 per cent per annum between 1993–4 and 1999–2000 (a lower rate than in the 1980s), even while total agricultural employment stagnated, but that it has subsequently declined. In line with these trends, the NSS data show that the annualized rate of growth of weekly earnings in agriculture declined from 3.27 per cent during 1983 to 1993–4, to 1.82 per cent during 1993–4 to 1999–2000, and to 1.11 per cent in the period from 2000 to 2004–5. The series *Agricultural Wages in India* shows a similar path of declining wage increases, and also that real wage rates in most operations actually fell in many districts across the country in the

1990s. In line with these trends, there is evidence of increasing indebtedness amongst agricultural labourers, especially to informal lenders, and of weakening of school attendance amongst children from agricultural labour households (Eswaran et al. 2009; Jha 2007; but see also Pangariya 2008: 148, for a contrary view, depending on data from the annual Costs of Cultivation surveys – there is uncertainty about wage trends).

Where real agricultural wages have increased, as in some parts of rural Tamil Nadu, it is in circumstances in which there has been an increase in non-agricultural employment opportunities (Harriss et al. 2010). Agricultural labour itself has become increasingly feminized, and – most likely – increasingly 'Dalitized', as those from the Scheduled Castes confront particular barriers in entering even many casual laboring jobs outside agriculture (Harriss-White 2003; Heyer 2010). The rate of growth of rural non-agricultural employment in India, however, over the period from 1993–4 to 1999–2000, at 2.26 per cent per annum, was more than twice the rate of growth of agricultural employment (1.06 per cent), and was higher still in the period to 2004–5, at 5.27 per cent per annum, according to NSS data (Himanshu 2007: table 8). Such increases in agricultural wages as have taken place have probably followed from tightening in rural labour markets where non-farm employment is available. Rural distress, following from the crisis in agriculture that is attested most tragically in farmer suicides, but shown up in the evidence on declining trends in the growth of agricultural output and productivity, has been offset, no doubt, by the growth in non-farm employment opportunities. This is often associated, however, with increased migration, both rural–rural and rural–urban, much of it circular (when people move to and fro between village homes and distant work sites). One recent estimate is that the numbers of such circulating migrants have reached 100 million, though the National Commission for Enterprises in the Unorganised Sector estimates that the number of seasonal migrants is of the order of 30 million (Bird and Deshingkar 2009; Deshingkar and Farrington 2009). What we know of the conditions of life and work of this mobile labour force is limited (though see Rogaly et al. 2002), but shows that though workers may earn more than in agriculture, their livelihoods are characterized by high levels of vulnerability – exactly as are those of the larger numbers of people in the mobile labour force of China. Thus far, however, as we explain in chapter 10, there has been less political mobilization in protest against rural distress in the major agricultural regions of India than there has been in China, where the widespread occurrence of violent incidents has led the government to elevate rural development as a national priority (Dong et al. 2010).

4.4   Why Such a Crisis?

The proximate causes of the problems of the Indian agricultural economy are quite well understood. The sector has depended historically on substantial state intervention, including investment in research and infrastructure, and the provision of extensive subsidies, both for key inputs (fertilizers, electricity and water supplied through public irrigation schemes) and underpinning the prices that farmers receive for their products. It also benefited from legislation requiring major banks to open rural branches and to meet certain targets for the supply of credit to agriculture. In the context of India's economic reforms all these have been reduced or eliminated, and at the same time domestic agriculture has been progressively opened up to the world market, exposing some cultivators to much greater price volatility (see Vakulabharanam 2005 for an account of liberalization measures in agriculture).

As Ramachandran and Rawal (2010) have pointed out, government expenditure in the countryside has declined in relative terms; investment in agriculture as a proportion of GDP fell from 1.92 per cent in 1990 to 1.31 per cent in 2003, and gross capital formation in agriculture, again as a percentage of GDP, declined from 3.8 per cent in 1980–1 to 1.7 per cent during 2004–5. The same authors explain how financial liberalization meant that the expansion of public-sector rural banking was brought to an end, and many rural branches of commercial banks were shut down; the credit–deposit ratios of rural commercial banks fell sharply; advances to small farmers, to Dalits and to *adivasis* declined – while the share of informal credit in the principal borrowed by rural households increased. There has been some reversal of these trends in the most recent past, under the United Progressive Alliance Government after 2004. At the same time, however, the costs of inputs have increased sharply, because of the decline in administrative price support, while the Minimum Support Prices offered by government to ensure remunerative prices for farmers' output 'have not compensated the actual costs of production per unit of output for most crops in a majority of states' (Ramachandran and Rawal 2010: 74) – so farmers have been subjected to a severe costs–prices squeeze. Until 2007–8, the prices of most agricultural commodities in world markets witnessed a secular downward trend, though not without fluctuations. Vaidyanathan has argued that 'Available evidence does not corroborate apprehensions that liberalization has adversely affected domestic prices of farm products' (Vaidyanathan 2006: 4010). Other economists, however, believe that price volatility, in particular, has increased the vulnerability of many cultivators. Altogether, policy changes inspired by a liberal approach in economic policy – particularly the slowing down of public investment – have had an adverse impact upon agriculture, certainly in the short term.

Neither liberalization policies, however, nor the earlier mode of state intervention in agriculture, effectively addresses fundamental problems having to do with the inefficient and often wasteful use of agricultural resources – including the failure to use irrigation water efficiently, partly because of neglect of the maintenance of irrigation structures and limitations of their design; excessive use of chemical fertilizers; and degradation of soils. There is a long history of poor use of key agricultural resources in India, by comparison with China and elsewhere in East Asia. This was a theme developed years ago by Myrdal in his monumental *Asian Drama* (1968). In the early 1950s, Myrdal showed, the overall productivity of agriculture (in relation to land) was roughly twice as high in China as in India – and it remains so still. In 1999–2000, yields of rice per hectare in China stood at 4.1 tonnes, while in India they were just under 2 tonnes (and still only 2.1 tonnes in 2009–10). The problems of agricultural productivity are connected with institutional weaknesses, as in irrigation management – which is also generally much more efficient in East Asia – and in credit and marketing organization, that are in turn compounded, argues Vaidyanathan, 'by government policies for pricing of water, electricity, fertilizers and credit which induce demand growth far in excess of available supplies . . . and encourage inefficient use of scarce agricultural resources' (Vaidyanathan 2006: 4013; and, for detailed corroboration, Harriss-White and Janakarajan, eds, 2004). Tackling such problems calls for more than just increasing public investment (see also Vaidyanathan 2010: chapters 4 and 5).

4.5   And What Is To Be Done about It?

The critical policy questions, therefore, are not well addressed either by a dogmatic adherence to economic liberalism or by the restoration of older policies of state intervention in agriculture. Arvind Panagariya (2008: especially chapter 14) is a champion of the broader liberal policy framework, but his advocacy of reducing subsidies and increasing investment in agriculture is shared by other economists, who are not. His point that the policy of setting Minimum Support Prices for agricultural products mainly subsidizes farmers in the relatively rich states of Andhra Pradesh, Punjab and Haryana, is also well taken, and there are strong arguments in favour of using direct cash transfers for poverty reduction – which Panagariya supports, but which, until very recently, Indian policymakers generally rejected – to replace the Public Distribution System that supplies rations of essential commodities at controlled prices to those who are defined as being Below Poverty Line (BPL). We shall have more to say on this in chapter 5.

What is most controversial in Panagariya's policy argument is his advocacy of contract farming and, with it, much more corporate involvement in agriculture – bound up with the supermarket revolution that continues to encounter political resistance in India – and supported by reversal of the policy of redistributive land reform to which the Indian state has been formally committed historically. He believes that the development of contract farming is severely constrained if it has to involve transacting with large numbers of marginal and small farmers, and that the fragmentation of agricultural holdings has negative effects on productivity. The policy of redistributive land reform has largely failed – by 1992 the total area of land redistributed amounted to only 1.25 per cent of operational holdings across eighteen major states – and the protection of user rights of cultivators is now much more important, in Panagariya's view, than is redistribution.

There are strong arguments, no doubt, in favour of contract farming. A group of leading Bengali economists, for example, in proposing a 'Strategy for Economic Reform in West Bengal' in 2003, noted the achievements of agrarian reform in the state, but – given the long-run demand constraints on rice agriculture and the need for agricultural diversification – argued forcefully in favour of exploring the potential of contract farming in the production of vegetables, fruit and flowers (Banerjee et al. 2003). They, and others, argue that contract farming can be 'win-win' under appropriate institutional conditions that ensure transparency and provide some protection for farmers (see Haque 2003); but a recent report from the Government of India on supermarket retail chains reaches rather negative conclusions, arguing that 'the noise about smallholder benefit in high value crops due to retail chain linkage is exaggerated and the linkage is either weak or absent' (Singh 2010: 17). Exactly as Panagariya suggests, supermarkets and other corporates are not interested in transacting with large numbers of small farmers. So what is the future for the vast majority of Indian farmers? The sequencing here is all important – and there are very good reasons for fearing that in the absence of employment opportunities outside of agriculture, their exclusion from contract farming, and, even more, the displacement of small farmers by the corporate takeover of agricultural land, will lead to further impoverishment.

On the other hand, the fact that land redistribution has not taken place to any very great extent does not mean there is no longer a case for it. We noted earlier the extent of inequality in the distribution of agricultural land, and that inequality has been increasing; Vikas Rawal provides 'ballpark estimates', on the basis of the admittedly crude assumption of a uniform ceiling on ownership holdings of 20 acres, to show that 'there is about 15 million acres of ceiling surplus land in India'. As he goes on to say, 'this is more than three times the total amount of land that has ever been redistributed under land reform programmes in all states' (2008: 47). This is not to say that there is a large potential for redistribution, given the fact that only a very small proportion of agricultural land in India has been redistributed hitherto, but it does lend weight to Michael Lipton's conclusion in his recent comprehensive restatement of the case for land reform, that '*In South Asia*, still containing half the world's poor, 10ha is in most countries a large owned farm [and] there is scope for some further land reform, but land shortage and growing [though still, surely, seriously inadequate] non-farm work opportunities may largely limit it to creating tiny 'home-gardens' for increasingly part-time rural farmers' (Lipton 2009: 9, emphasis added). Legislation is being considered, however, and some has been passed that actually raises ceilings on the size of agricultural landholdings, and facilitates absentee farming by large owners and corporations. As Ramachandran and Rawal say, 'Such policies reduce the extent of land for redistribution, accelerate the loss of land by poor peasants and worsen inequalities in the distribution of land' (2010: 57).

At least as controversial as the matter of contract farming, is the question of whether or not genetic modification ('GM') has an important part to play in the future of Indian agriculture (see Herring 2007). Opponents of GM (more accurately, transgenic varieties) have very successfully framed the matter in negative terms, in the face of evidence suggesting quite strongly that cultivation of genetically modified varieties may drastically cut both farmers' expenditure on agro-chemicals, and the environmental and health hazards entailed in their use. Thus, in 2010, the Environment Minister Jairam Ramesh was persuaded to impose a moratorium on the release of a transgenic brinjal hybrid (*The Hindu* 10 February 2010).

Panagariya argues that the sustainable solution to poverty lies outside agriculture and depends upon moving a much larger share of the total labour force of the country out of agriculture altogether. Reducing the ratio of labour to land, he claims, offers a greater potential for increasing agricultural wages than any conceivable productivity-enhancing reforms in agriculture. These arguments are strong ones, but while there is no such movement of labour out of agriculture it surely is imperative to improve agricultural productivity and incomes. We return, then, to the problem of the failure of structural transformation in India.

4.6   Employment Trends, 'Jobless Growth' and Workers' Responses

One significant indicator of employment trends in India in the period of economic liberalization is that the highly successful information technology industry, which now contributes such an important share of GDP and of export earnings, generates so little employment. According to NSS data, the IT sector accounted for just 0.7 per cent of the non-agricultural labour force in 2004–5. The sector's revenues by that time accounted for 4.5 per cent of GDP, while contributing only 0.21 per cent of aggregate employment (Chandrasekhar 2007). In the following discussion (some parts of which are taken from Harriss 2011: 129–31), it should be noted that the numbers of those in the Indian workforce grow at the moment by about 10 million persons per year (or more, see Himanshu 2011: 52), a figure that greatly exceeds the one for *all* current employment in 'private-sector establishments' (8.8 million in 2006 – of which the IT sector makes up only a small part, according to figures from the Directorate General of Employment and Training: see Government of India 2008).

It has been widely argued that India is experiencing 'jobless growth' – a view supported by National Sample Survey (NSS) data showing that the rate of growth of the workforce as a whole, in the later 1990s, fell below the rate of growth of population, and well below its rate of growth in the 1980s and early 1990s (table 4.6; see also Dev 2008: chapter 7; Himanshu 2007; and Unni and Raveendran 2007, all of whom estimate the total growth of the workforce between 1993–4 and 1999–2000 at less than 1 per cent per annum).

This notion is contested, however, in interpretations of more recent NSS data that show acceleration of employment growth in 2000–5, within both urban and rural areas and amongst both men and women (the authors referred to immediately above all estimate employment

Table 4.6: Annual rates of employment growth for usual status workers (per cent)

Period	rural	urban
1983 to 1987–8	1.36	2.77
1987–8 to 1993–4	2.03	3.39
1993–4 to 1999–2000	0.66	2.27
1999–2000 to 2004–5	1.97	3.22

Source: Calculations from National Sample Survey (Chandrasekhar 2007).

growth over this period at a little less than 3 per cent per year). The jobless growth thesis was apparently refuted, and official claims were made that the employment problem had finally been resolved (Himanshu 2011: 44). It was also argued by Sundaram (2007) that there had been a marked increase of 'good quality employment'. The essential points in this case were that self-employment had grown markedly in urban non-agriculture, especially amongst women; casual employment generally had declined; and regular salaried non-agricultural employment had increased, especially for women – at over 5 per cent per annum in the recent decade. This argument depended heavily upon the assumption that self-employment represents good-quality employment because, over the period in question, there had actually been a decline in all wage employment and a very significant increase in self-employment among all categories of workers. All told, about half of those in the workforce were by that time self-employed. The idea that this is good-quality employment reflects the emphasis in current development thinking, internationally, about the virtues of self-employment, which is understood as 'enterprise' (a way of thinking that is reflected in the title of India's *National Commission for Enterprises in the Unorganised Sector* (Government of India 2009b)). But there are many reluctant entrepreneurs among the poor, and the NSS data show that just under half of all self-employed workers do not find their work remunerative, in spite of their usually low expectations of reasonable returns. Chandrasekhar concludes that a large part of the increase in self-employment has been distress-driven, and that 'the apparent increase in aggregate employment growth may be more an outcome of the search for survival strategies than a demand-led expansion of productive employment opportunities' (Chandrasekhar 2007).

For Unni and Raveendran, too, the apparently rosy picture painted by Sundaram has to be qualified by recognition that some of the increase of regular salaried jobs was in a subsidiary capacity, indicating part-time working; while the increase in female participation was of women mainly at lower levels of education, implying that their access to employment was either in self-employment or at the bottom of the wage/salaried employment hierarchy. There was evidence, too, from the NSS that the extent of home-working had increased quite significantly, especially amongst women. The increased employment of women in particular in subsidiary, part-time occupations, some of them involving home-working, and large numbers of them being poorly remunerated, are developments that have been characteristic of economies that have participated in economic globalization (Castells 1997). Most significant of all, however, for Unni and Raveendran, was the fact that the average daily real wages of regular workers declined in 2004–5, by comparison with 1999–2000 (particularly for females), indicating the growth of poorly remunerated jobs in urban areas in regular salaried employment. It is altogether likely that the growth of employment in the first five years of the new millennium was driven by distress, at a time when the agricultural economy was in crisis – as Himanshu has shown (2011: 53–5).

The estimates contained in the report on the 64th Round of the NSS for 2007–8, and then in those of the 66th Round of 2009–10, confirm the misgivings of other scholars as against Sundaram's optimism about the creation of 'good quality employment' ('Editorial' 2010a: 7). Total employment increased at a rate of only 0.17 per cent per year between 2004–5 and 2007–8 (the lowest rate of employment generation of the last three decades, and occurring in the context of very high rates of growth of GDP); and rural employment actually declined. The 66th Round of the NSS shows that between 2005 and 2010 usual status employment increased by just 0.1 per cent per annum. In this period, the deceleration in urban employment (from 4.22 per cent per annum in 1999–2005, to 1.36 per cent in 2005–10) and the decline in rural areas (the rate was -0.34 per cent per annum in 2005 to 2010) was accounted for largely by the sharp fall in female labour-force participation.

> What seems to have happened is that a large majority of women workers moved into the labour force during 1999–2005 and looked for work outside the home due to the agrarian crisis and distress in rural areas. And it is these women workers who have moved back into their homes as soon as the situation improved because of higher agricultural productivity. ('Editorial' 2010a: 7)

There is evidence, as Himanshu points out (2011: 56), that there is an inverse relationship between output growth and employment growth.

'Informalization' of employment is, of course, greatly to be desired according to the advocates of economic liberalization, for labour-market regulation beyond an absolute minimum is held to give rise to inflexibility, and this in turn to reduce employment, because it increases labour costs. Besley and Burgess have concluded from comparison across Indian states that those 'which amended the Industrial Disputes Act in a pro-worker direction experienced lowered output, employment, investment, and productivity in registered or formal manufacturing' (2004: 91). Their arguments have been subjected to significant criticism (Bhattacharjea 2009), however, and neither theoretical nor empirical work, in relation to India and to other countries, leads to unequivocal conclusions regarding the impact of employment protection legislation. As Bardhan says, 'there is hardly any study on the labour absorption question that conclusively shows that any adverse effect of labour laws is particularly large compared to the effects of other constraints on labour-intensive industrialization' (2009: 33; see also Kannan and Raveendran 2009). There is also substantial evidence that 'employers have been able to find ways to reduce the workforce even with "restrictive" provisions in place' (Sharma 2006: 2081) – such as that on the retrenchment of workers – by using the mechanism of the voluntary retirement scheme in the later 1990s. The increase in the numbers of contract workers in the total number of workers in manufacturing, from about 12 per cent in 1990 to over 20 per cent by 2004–5, shows that employers have been able to achieve greater flexibility by effectively informalizing a part of the labour force (Sharma 2006: 2081; and see also Nagaraj 2004).

Informalization/'flexibilization' has certainly been taking place, and its negative consequences for workers are attested in a number of case studies. It is not necessarily the case that total household incomes decline, partly because of increased workforce participation on the part of women, and in some cases of children, but livelihoods have become much more vulnerable. Jan Breman's analysis of the impact of informalization in Ahmedabad makes this point very forcefully (Breman 2001); and it is shown up as well in Nandini Gooptu's studies of once permanently employed workers in Kolkata (Gooptu 2007). In both cities, the decline of 'permanent' formal employment in cotton (in Ahmedabad) and jute mills (in Kolkata) has led to what Mike Davis (2006) has referred to – with reference to cities throughout the erstwhile 'third world' – as 'urban involution', meaning the crowding of workers into such activities as local petty trade, transport and construction, and (generally in relatively smaller numbers) into small manufacturing workshops. Coping with their changed circumstances has meant, in many households, that women, and children, have entered the labour force in larger numbers (contributing to the phenomenon of increasing self-employment, especially amongst women, that we noted earlier). It is for this reason that household incomes have not necessarily declined, but livelihoods have become more vulnerable and – according to Breman's observations in Ahmedabad – living standards have declined. Karin Kapadia, from fieldwork in low-income households in Chennai, too, thinks it is likely that in many of them women have become the main breadwinners – though this coincides with evidence of decline in the status of women in Tamil society (Kapadia 2010). Amongst men affected by labour-force changes in all these cities, there has developed a strong sense of their powerlessness and of loss of dignity. Some have responded to their material and identity crises through resort to criminality, and some to violence. Domestic violence may have increased. But these are not the only or necessarily the dominant responses. Some men have turned rather to clubs, and some of these to social-service activities. There are signs, too, of increasing religiosity, and both Gooptu and Breman think that religious ideologies are gaining ground (see chapter 9).

4.7   Conclusion: 'Excluded Labour'?

The evidence and argument that we have reviewed show that India's 'lop-sided transition', with the limited movement of labour out of marginal smallholding agriculture as the economy grew over the first five decades from Independence, has continued through the more recent years of very high rates of growth and in the context of India's partial pursuit of economic liberalism. These years are fairly described as a period of 'jobless growth', in spite of claims based on the apparently contrary evidence for the period 1999–2005. Himanshu sums up:

> The acceleration of GDP growth from an average of six per cent to eight per cent after 2005 has not been accompanied by any corresponding gen-eration of decent employment . . . [and] . . . with over 80 per cent of all new jobs created being in casual work, overwhelmingly in construction, there are serious questions about the ability of the growth process to offer sustained employment as the cornerstone of inclusive growth. (2011: 58–9)

Perhaps the most critical question, therefore, about labour in India, is that of whether the argument proposed by Sanyal and Bhattacharyya, that a very large share of Indian labour is 'excluded', carries weight or not. What are the prospects for incomes and welfare for those in informal employment?

Both Sanyal and Bhattacharyya, and Tania Li (2010), warn against the easy assumption of the inevitability of the linear pathway of structural transformation – such as appears, for example, in the arguments of the *World Development Report* for 2008 on *Agriculture for Development* (World Bank 2008) – and critique the residual functional-ism (as Li puts it) in the idea of the reserve army of labour. They refer to (and Li describes in some detail, from across Asia) the 'new round of enclosures that have dispossessed large numbers of rural people from the land, and the low absorption of their labour, which is "surplus" to the requirements of capital accumulation' (Li 2010: 66). Of course, there are informal activities that are integrated within the circuit of capital, as they may be through subcontracting and outsourcing, but a great deal of informal activity, which – as we have seen – involves extensive self-employment, constitutes a non-capitalist production space (in Sanyal and Bhattacharyya's view). This is the economy of surplus or 'excluded' labour, which does not contribute to capital accumulation.

As Bardhan has pointed out, the problem with this argument is that the authors suggest that the non-capitalist space accounts for the great majority of informal workers, when the evidence on the point is scanty. This is a fair criticism, though Bardhan's own further arguments certainly provide no convincing rebuttal of the idea that there is an extensive force of excluded labour. He refers to data showing that 'the all-India average market value of fixed assets owned per enterprise was Rs 58 000 in 2005–6 [$1200+] in the informal manufacturing sector' – but the conclusion that he draws when he says 'so the average informal enterprise is not run by destitute people' (2009: 34) is misleading. The great majority of informal enterprises, after all, are *not* in the manufacturing sector. Those that *are* may well include units that have become more capital-intensive over time, as Dibyendu Maiti and Kunal Sen report. But these authors also say that 'Whether the informal sector can be a source of robust and productivity driven employment growth in the future, in the face of weak employment growth in the formal manufacturing sector, is a question that remains to be answered' (2010: 8). The further question, of course – posed by Li, Sanyal and Bhattacharyya – is that of just how much informal activity really can be considered to be the site of capital accumulation. Isn't much of it reasonably seen as lying altogether outside the sphere of capital accumulation?

We have no means for mapping the distribution of informal economic activity and employment between that which is firmly within circuits of capital accumulation and that which can be held to be outside them, and the notion of exclusion is, to say the least, tendentious when we do know that garbage pickers, say, often are linked in ultimately to circuits of capital (as when they supply scrap metal for industry). Rather than referring to a large share of the labour force as being outside the sphere of capital accumulation, therefore, it is probably more sensible to think in terms of its being 'excluded' from the dynamic sectors of the economy, and engaged in activities of such low productivity as barely to allow for survival. There is no question that India's transition is indeed 'tortuous'; and there remains a 'marginal mass' of labour that barely survives without welfare provisioning on the part of the state, now through the National Rural Employment Guarantee and (it is to be hoped) through enhanced support for food security and more adequate public health. Such welfare provisioning is the subject of chapter 5.

5

Is the Indian State Delivering on Promises of 'Inclusive Growth' and Social Justice?

5.1 Introduction

'Inclusive Growth' is the theme of India's Eleventh Five-Year Plan, for the period 2007–12, and it is the title of the first main volume of the Plan document. The Prime Minister, Manmohan Singh, speaks of the Plan in his Foreword as 'a comprehensive strategy for inclusive development', and it is said that:

> The central vision of the Eleventh Plan is to build on our strengths to trigger a development process which ensures broad-based improvement in the quality of life of the people, especially the poor, SCs/STs, other backward castes (OBCs), minorities and women. (Planning Commission 2008: 2)

We have shown in the last two chapters that there are many ways in which this vision is not being realized. The Prime Minister, in his Foreword to the Plan, talks of the need to ensure that 'income and employment are adequately shared by the poor and weaker sections of our society', and we have shown that there is a lot of evidence that suggests this is not happening. The most recent findings of the National Sample Survey – referred to in the last chapter – show that productive jobs are not being created at anything like the rate required for 'inclusive growth'; and even if income poverty, as this is conventionally defined, has been declining – and there is, of course, much debate over this, as we showed in chapter 3 – other indicators of the quality of life of the people have hardly improved and some have shown deterioration. India's failure, so far, to reduce under-nutrition amongst small children (from birth to age five) – the proportion of such children who are under-weight declined by less than 1 percentage point between 1999–2000 and 2005–6, from 46.7 to 45.9 per cent – is one particularly poignant marker of the still very poor quality of life of a great majority of the people.

Successive governments have promised that, in the words of Finance Minister Yashwant Sinha in his Budget Speech of 2000, India's economic reforms will be 'guided by compassion and justice'. But this rhetoric is hardly reflected in budget allocations to social programmes. Certainly, the absolute amounts of money dedicated to these programmes have increased, as the volume of government revenues has grown with the growth of the economy. Budget allocations to social expenditure, as a share of GDP, however, have changed very little (Harriss 2011; Mooij 2011). Most significantly, commitments that were made in the Common Minimum Programme (CMP) that the new Congress-led government agreed with its supporters in 2004, to increase expenditure on educa-tion, as a share of GDP, to 6 per cent and that on health to between 1 and 2 per cent, are still far from having been honoured. The emphasis, in practice, has been to encourage the privatization of these services, and now, in the proposals for the Twelfth Five-Year Plan (for 2012–17), public-private partnerships (see *The Hindu* 13 April 2011). India's public spending on both education and health remains low by comparison with other, similar, countries, and as we show in other chapters of this book, the delivery of these vital social services by the state also suffers from very serious weaknesses (see chapters 8 and 14). Further, the practical out-comes of India's long-standing, constitutionally mandated commitment to social inclusion, through affirmative action for social groups deemed to have been discriminated against historically – the Scheduled Castes and Scheduled Tribes, and the Other Backward Classes – have been quite limited (as we show in chapter 12; and see de Haan 2008). The failures of the state in regard to the Scheduled Tribes, in particular, are reflected in the current strength of the Maoist insurgency in the country (as we explain in chapter 10). In these, and in other ways, India's record regarding inclusive growth and social justice seems poor indeed.

But this is far from being the whole story. India has also seen, latterly, some remarkable policy innovations, intended to deliver economic and social rights, which have come about largely as a result of pressures from within civil society. The most striking and the best known of these is the National Rural Employment Guarantee Scheme (NREGS) – now known as the Mahatma Gandhi National Rural Employment Guarantee Scheme – that was legislated for in 2005. This provides for up to 100 days of guaranteed wage employment per year to all rural households. NREGS, making employment a right, is almost certainly the world's largest rights-based safety-net programme. The right to education, too, is now recognized in a Bill that came into effect in April 2010. A Food Security Act – designed to guarantee that people will not henceforward go hungry – to which the present UPA government committed itself in 2009, is now in draft (in early 2011). The government has also sought to address the problems and the needs of the huge numbers of unorganized workers in the country, first through the appointment in 2004 of the National Commission for Enterprises in the Unorganised Sector (NCEUS), and then in the passage of the Unorganised Workers Social Security Act of 2008, which marks a step towards the formalization of such work, and the protection of workers, even if the legislation falls far short of what the NCEUS had advocated.

These really are all remarkable developments. In the context of the evidence and argument that we reviewed in the last chapter concerning the effective *exclusion* – rather than inclusion – of a large share of the labour force in India, under present circumstances, the legislation that has been passed and the programmes that have been introduced bear out Partha Chatterjee's contention that 'under conditions of electoral democracy [it is now] unacceptable for the government to leave these marginalized populations without the means of labour to fend for themselves'. He goes on to say 'That [leaving them to fend for themselves] carries the risk of turning them into the "dangerous classes"' (Chatterjee 2008: 62). The validity of this last point is perhaps shown in the Maoist insurgency that has gained such strength in those parts of India with the most marginalized populations.

Chatterjee's argument is supported even more clearly in the case of China. Shaoguang Wang has traced China's moves towards a market economy from the 1980s, showing how they shattered social safety nets that had been provided under the earlier regime headed by Mao Zedong. 'Against such a backdrop', Wang says, 'came a protective counter-movement. An increasing number of people, including government decision-makers, have realized . . . [that] . . . The market is necessary but it must be embedded in society. And the state must play an active role in the market economy to prevent a disembedded and self-regulating market from dominating society' (Wang 2008: 58). Wang refers here to Karl Polanyi's idea of the 'double movement' of modern history. Moves to establish the self-regulating liberal market economy (like those in nineteenth-century Britain in Polanyi's own analysis, or in China after 1978, and in India after 1991) are met, Polanyi argued, by a counter-movement from within society as people seek to protect themselves from the effects of the commodification of their labour, and of the environment (Polanyi 1944). Wang focuses on the responses of the state in China, through recent regional and health-care policies, to the very high levels of inequality that now exist in the country and the increasing intensity of unrest – which have led the leadership to talk in terms of the need for establishing a 'harmonious society'. Wang describes, in effect, a Polanyian counter-movement, though one largely directed from above (see Harriss 2010a).

Similarly, in this chapter, we trace movements and counter-movements in policy and politics, associated with economic liberalization in India. We begin by explaining the background, in India's constitutional commitments, to the recent attempts to realize economic and social rights, as through NREGS and now the proposed Food Security Act. We analyse the political forces that drive them. We briefly consider their practical outcomes – though we recognize that it is still too early to judge these with any certainty. We show in the end that there is no simple answer to the question of whether the Indian state is delivering on promises of social justice. Some progress has been made, no doubt, but in the face of serious obstacles. Social justice remains a field of contestation that shows up fault lines in contemporary Indian society.

5.2   Background: Economic and Social Rights and the Indian Constitution

The idea of 'rights-based development' is by now well established, having been given considerable impetus by the very influential work of the great Indian economist and philosopher, Amartya Sen, who won the Nobel Prize for Economics in 1998. A summary synthesis of his thinking is found in the book *Development As Freedom* (1999). Development, for Sen, is understood in terms of people's abilities to plan for and to lead full human lives. People possess sets of capabilities – as Sen calls them – which they are able to realize, or not, according to the circumstances of their lives. In this, freedoms, both negative ('freedom from . . .') and positive ('freedom to . . .'), are clearly indispensable – and freedom is, for Sen, both a condition for and an outcome of development. Those who are subject to arbitrary arrest or who are denied political freedom – who do not enjoy, in other words, civil and political rights, and who are prevented thereby from planning their own lives – are unable to realize their capabilities as human beings. But those who, say, through malnutrition in childhood (the lot of so many children in India), suffer neurological damage are also prevented from 'life-planning' and leading full human lives. There is a strong case, therefore, for the argument that economic and social rights – such as rights to adequate nutrition and to health and to livelihood – are also essential for, even constitutive of, development, though many scholars do not agree with this position. This is at least partly because many states lack the capacity to satisfy these rights (e.g., Little 2003: chapter 5), and there are those in India now who argue that governments simply cannot supply food security, or wages in NREGS, at the level that is demanded by activists.

Rights-based thinking in public policy internationally was both reflected in and furthered by the Universal Declaration of Human Rights of 1948, to which India was, of course, a signatory. Even at that time, however, a good deal of largely independent thinking was going on in the country, in the deliberations of the Constituent Assembly that was responsible for drawing up the Constitution of India, promulgated at last in 1950. In the end, in the Constitution, an important distinction was drawn between Fundamental Rights (in Part III) and what are called Directive Principles (the subject of Part IV of the Constitution), which substantially reflects that between civil and political rights, on the one hand, and economic and social rights, on the other. It seems, however, that the drafting history of the Constitution shows that 'the non-enforceable nature of the Directive Principles was intended to be temporary and modifiable when the country became ready to enforce them' (Birchfield and Corsi 2010: 711) – and, indeed, as we go on to explain below, the distinction between the Fundamental Rights and the Directive Principles has been whittled away by orders of the Supreme Court. The Fundamental Rights, which are justiciable, include the Right to Equality (here there is, amongst others, an article (No.17) on Abolition of Untouchability); and the Right to Freedom, including – of particular significance in the present context – Article 21 on the right to protection of life and liberty; as well as rights against exploitation, right to property, to freedom of religion and cultural and educational rights. The Directive Principles, however, are said (in Article 37) not to be 'enforceable in any court (though) the principles therein laid down are nonetheless funda-mental in the governance of the country and it shall be the duty of the state to apply these principles in making laws'. They include, amongst others, the 'right to work, to education and to public assistance in certain cases' (Article 41); 'living wage etc. for workers' (Article 43); and (Article 47) 'duty of the State to raise the level of nutrition and the standard of living and to improve public health'.

What has happened has been that judgments of the Supreme Court, extending back over many years, but especially some that have been passed in the course of the last decade, have in effect rendered non-enforceable Directive Principles justiciable in a court, and upgraded the status of social welfare to that of fundamental right (Birchfield and Corsi 2010: 713; and Chandhoke 2008). A judgment of 1970, for instance, argued that 'The mandate of the Constitution is to build a welfare society in which justice, social, economic and political, shall inform all institutions of our national life. The hopes and aspirations aroused by the Constitution will be belied if the minimum needs of the lowest of our citizens are not met' (referred to by Birchfield and Corsi 2010: 711; but see also Chopra 2009, citing a judgment of Justice Bhagwati in 1981). Since then it has been interpretations of Article 21 of the Constitution, on 'right to protection of life and liberty', that have been especially significant. Those who drafted this Article may have had in mind protection against arbitrary arrest and detention, but the judges have interpreted it to mean the right to life with dignity and to embrace both the right to education and the right to food.

5.3   The Right to Education

In the Constitution that came into effect in 1950, the right to education was relegated – as we may put it – to the Directive Principles. These committed the state to provision 'within a period of ten years from the commencement of this Constitution, for free and compulsory education for all children until they complete the age of fourteen'. The Indian state's failure to satisfy this Directive is perhaps the most damning of all its failures in the post-Independence period (possible reasons for it, relating significantly to the values of India's political elites, are discussed by Weiner 1991). Now, thanks in part, at least, to the engagement of the National Alliance for Fundamental Right to Education (an alliance initially of nine NGOs and now of more than 2,000 voluntary organizations), in 2001 the 93rd Constitution Amendment Bill was passed by the Lok Sabha, intended to enter a new sub-clause into the Constitution (that is, Article 21A, amongst the Fundamental Rights) guaranteeing that the state shall provide free and compulsory education to all children aged six to fourteen. Though the implementation of the Act was long held up, due to further mobilizations by civil society groups over the neglect of early childhood development and failure to provide for those aged over fourteen, and over a clause that introduces compulsion of parents or guardians of young children, in August 2009 the Lok Sabha finally passed the Act implementing the new Constitutional provision, and it came into effect in April 2010. The legislation was stimulated in the first place by a ruling of the Supreme Court in 1993, to the effect that 'though right to education is not stated expressly as a fundamental right, it is implicit in and flows from the right to life guaranteed under Article 21'.

5.4   The Right to Food

Even though India has not experienced a widespread famine (as opposed
to famine conditions in particular areas of the country) for many years,
hunger remains endemic. The Global Hunger Index for 2010 (prepared
by the International Food Policy Research Institute) places India at 106
of 122 countries for which data are available (in other words, there are
only sixteen countries in which hunger is estimated to be worse than
it is in India). This is the context of debates about food security in the
country.

A Supreme Court judgment of November 2001, in a case brought by
the People's Union for Civil Liberties (PUCL) against the Government of
India, through the instrument of public interest litigation – in a context
of famine in parts of Rajasthan at a time when it was well known that the
Food Corporation of India held massive stocks of food grains – explicitly
established a constitutional right to food.

> [The Court] not only held that specific government food schemes con-
> stituted legal entitlements . . . setting out in detail minimum allocation
> levels of foodgrains and supplemental nutrients for India's poor, but also
> outlined how those government schemes [including the Targeted Public
> Distribution System, the Midday Meals Scheme for schools, and the
> Integrated Child Development Services programme, amongst others that
> are less well known] were to be implemented. (Birchfield and Corsi 2010:
> 695)

Essentially the Court's judgment rested on the view that the right to
life under Article 21 includes the right to food; and the judgment has, in
the view of the lawyers Birchfield and Corsi, 'set India apart and made
it a leader amongst nations seeking to legally enforce the human right to
food' (2010: 718). Subsequently, the relationships between the judicial
system, the Right to Food Campaign – a loose coalition of civil society
groups, the establishment of which was stimulated by the action of the
PUCL in bringing its case – and the Commissioners whom the Court
required to be appointed to oversee the implementation of its orders,
have worked quite effectively, and in such a way as to act at least as
a check upon the actions of the government to deregulate and liberalize the economy, where these moves conflict with food security (see
Birchfield and Corsi 2010: 732–51). The struggle since 2009 over the
Food Security Bill (and that continues at the time of writing in September
2011) illustrates the strength of opposition from many in government to
the objectives of the Right to Food campaigners.

In order to understand the tussle over the Food Security Bill, it is helpful to backtrack a little and consider the history of India's Public Distribution System (PDS), set up to ensure people's access to essential commodities, especially rice and wheat, at controlled prices, through so-called Fair Price Shops. In effect, it is a public rationing scheme. The operation of the PDS requires that the government, through the Food Corporation of India (FCI) purchases food grains from farmers, at a price that is remunerative for them, and that it then releases these food grains into the PDS at a controlled rate. Clearly, determining and juggling the prices received by producers, and consumer prices, is a complex task, and it involves the government in paying out substantial subsidies. On the other hand, the PDS has been the most important element in such basic welfare security as the Indian state has provided, and there is good evidence that those states that have operated the PDS most effectively – generally, the southern states – have, on the whole, done better in reducing poverty than others (Harriss 2003b).

The introduction of the economic reforms from 1991 onwards led to pressures, however, to contain India's fiscal deficit and, therefore, to reduce the cost of food subsidies. It was argued that subsidies could be cut back and the PDS maintained if it were better targeted, rather than being, as it had been, a universal programme. This reasoning was supported by studies showing that the universal PDS was inefficient, not reaching the poor for whom it was intended, and involving high levels of corruption through leakage (as happens, for example, when owners of Fair Price Shops find ways of making profits by selling on PDS grain in the open market). The Targeted PDS was introduced in 1997. Households had to be classified as either 'Below Poverty Line' (BPL) or 'Above Poverty Line' (APL) – as if the idea of the 'poverty line' represented some well-defined truth rather than being, as it is, an arbitrary construct – and then prices were to be kept low for the BPL while APL prices were raised substantially. The supply of food grains to the PDS was also reduced, and the consequence of the different measures was that off-take from the Food Corporation of India declined in the context of increasing stocks. It was also recognized by researchers that there were entirely understandable and predictable but still very serious problems associated with the definition, and then with the administrative identification, of BPL households, and that large numbers of people who should have been entitled to cheap food grains were denied their entitlements. A most egregious example of the failures of targeting came from Dharavi, supposedly Asia's largest slum, with a population of half a million, where only 151 families had been issued BPL cards (Swaminathan 2000a: 97).

All these problems were then compounded by the BJP-led government in 2001 when it sharply increased prices in the Fair Price shops, effectively removing the APL households altogether from the PDS. It was true that the monthly allocation to BPL families was increased from 10 kg to 20 kg, but the requirement for the purchase to be made at one time put it beyond the reach of many poor families. The changes that were introduced at this time also linked increases in procurement prices (paid to farmers) with increase in issue prices in the Fair Price Shops to ration-card holders. Madhura Swaminathan correctly anticipated, in an article written at the time, that the new scheme would leave the FCI with even larger stocks of grain. 'Are the stocks going to rot in warehouses?', she asked (Swaminathan 2000b). This was exactly what did happen in the succeeding years – and the sense of moral outrage at food going to waste in government stores, while people went hungry, led the PUCL to bring its action against the Government of India in 2001. There was really no more eloquent testimony to the subordination of the needs of poverty reduction and of social equity to the dictates of neoliberal fiscal rectitude. The undercutting of this most important component of social security provision in India continued, outside the state of Tamil Nadu, which maintained a universal system when other states did not (athough recently Chhattisgarh has reverted to at least near-universal distribution). Data from the 61st Round of the National Sample Survey show very high rates of exclusion of the most needy from the system (at least 50 per cent of BPL households do not have ration cards) – even though, contrary to the arguments of politicians, the costs of the food subsidy as a share of GDP have actually been falling (Swaminathan 2008).

It has now become quite commonplace for the PDS to be dismissed as corrupted and ineffective. An example comes from work by senior scholars such as Devesh Kapur, Partha Mukhopadhyay and Arvind Subramanian, who argue that 'Given the long and egregious mis-management of the PDS, (a) call to "reform the PDS" is puzzling' (Kapur et al. 2008: 86). But how is the right to food to be implemented if not through a set-up like that of the PDS? The Right to Food Campaign argued as follows, after a series of consultations in 2009:

> The campaign's 'essential demands' sets the [proposed] National Food Security Act in the context of the nutritional emergency in India and the need to address the structural roots of hunger. In concrete terms, the campaign demands a comprehensive 'Food Entitlements Act', going well beyond the limited promise in the [ruling] UPA manifesto of 25 kgs of grain at Rs.3/kg for BPL households. . . . essential provisions of the proposed Act include a universal Public Distribution System (providing at least 50kgs of grain per family with 5.25kgs of pulses and 2.8kgs of edible oils); special food entitlements to destitute households . . . consolidation of all entitlements created by recent Supreme Court orders (e.g. cooked mid-day meals in primary schools and universalization of ICDS); support for effective breastfeeding . . . Further, says the Campaign, the Act must

include strong accountability and grievance redressal provisions, including mandatory penalties for any violation of the Act and compensation for those whose entitlements have been denied. (From <http://www.rightto-foodindia.org>; last accessed 1 May 2011)

The government, however, drafted a Bill early in 2010 that was described by the *Economic and Political Weekly* in an Editorial as perhaps best being seen 'as a design of how *not* to end malnutrition and hunger' (Editorial 2010b: 7). Its overriding concern appeared to be with cutting the fiscal deficit – though it was calculated that a universal scheme, supplying all households in the country with 35 kgs of food grains per month, would cost the equivalent of only 0.5 per cent of GDP per year.

Subsequently, the National Advisory Council (NAC), the body set up under the UPA government in 2004, initially to monitor the implementation of the Common Minimum Programme, chaired by the Congress President, Mrs Sonia Gandhi, and including leading representatives of civil society organizations, came up with a distinctly moderate but also administratively quite fiendishly complicated set of proposals in October 2010. These suggest providing subsidized food grains to 75 per cent of the total population (including 90 per cent of the rural population and 50 per cent of the urban), but with different levels of provision for a Priority group of households as against a General group – effectively reproducing the distinction between 'BPL' and 'APL' households of the Targeted PDS. Thus, the NAC would leave a quarter of the households of the country outside the provisions of a National Food Security Act, despite evidence that nearly 20 per cent of women and children even in the *richest* fifth of all households in the country are undernourished (Himanshu and Sen 2011: 39). The economist and NAC member Jean Drèze, who as a member of the first NAC had played a major role in the formulation both of NREGS and of India's Right to Information Act – and who has been active in the Right to Food Campaign – was led to issue a dissent note. Drèze described the NAC proposals as 'minimalist', involving a framework that 'fails to abolish the artificial distinction between APL and BPL households' and as representing, in the end, 'a great victory for the government – they allow it to appear to be doing something radical for food security, but it is actually more of the same' (as reported by *The Hindu* 24 October 2010).

The government, nonetheless, appointed an expert committee, constituted by officials and chaired by the economist C. Rangarajan, to reconsider the NAC proposals – and the committee's recommendations amounted to a further dilution of them, restricting eligibility for food security to only the NAC's 'Priority' households. This effectively excludes 60 per cent of the population – even though the committee itself argued that 'to ensure the genuinely needy are not left out, universalisation is the only way' (cited by Himanshu and Sen 2011: 38). But universalization, it was argued, is not feasible – the government simply cannot procure and pay for sufficient quantities of food grains. The Right to Food Campaign described the Rangarajan Report as 'the first step to finish off the subsidized foodgrains scheme' (*The Hindu* 11 January 2011).

At the time of writing (September 2011), the draft National Food Security Bill is reported to incorporate most of the recommendations of the NAC, and provide for a legal entitlement to cheaper food grains for about 70 per cent of the population (*The Hindu* 17 August 2011). It is the subject of swingeing criticism from the Right to Food campaign, which describes it as making 'a complete mockery of the idea of food security for all' (Right to Food Campaign 2011: 21). As Himanshu and Abhijit Sen have argued, is anything other than a universal PDS consistent with a rights-based approach? As they say 'Since a legal right must apply to all citizens with any exclusion defined precisely, targeting the "poor" or "priority" will involve definition of these terms and possible litigation' (2011: 39). They go on to present evidence showing that the targeting of the PDS has actually *increased* inefficiency and leakage (leakage of rice and wheat together from the PDS is estimated to have been 28 per cent in 1993–4, before targeting was introduced, but as high as 54 per cent in 2004–5). Meanwhile, Tamil Nadu, which alone amongst the states has maintained the principle of universalism, has 'by far the largest percentage of the population accessing the PDS and almost no leakage' (Himanshu and Sen 2011: 40). The Tamil Nadu case also shows that self-targeting (many people opt out of the PDS) limits the fiscal burden imposed by the system on the state. Himanshu and Sen go on to marshal evidence and argument to demonstrate the feasibility of at least a near-universal PDS as the means to realize food security in India. But the draft Food Security Bill shows that the government has resisted such ideas. As Jean Drèze has said, there appears to be 'a fundamental resistance to the idea that the ambit of the Public Distribution System should be expanded' (Drèze 2011).

In its place there is mounting official support for the expansion of Direct Cash Transfers (as Panagariya has advocated: see chapter 4; and Kapur et al. 2008), partly following from what is seen as having been the success of such programmes in Latin America, notably in Brazil where the *Bolsa Familia,* a cash transfer scheme that is conditional upon children's minimum school attendance, is believed to have lifted many out of poverty. The attractions of such schemes are fairly obvious. They seem to be administratively much simpler (than running something like the PDS), and they are less paternalistic, giving people choice, allowing them to access whatever goods and services they want in private markets – which is ideologically much to be desired on the parts of economic liberals (and absolves government of the responsibility for ensuring public provision). One major flaw in this reasoning is that it assumes there are no supply-side difficulties, particularly in regard to basic services of education, health – and food. As Jayati Ghosh puts it, 'Providing small amounts of cash to allow people [for example] to visit private local quacks will hardly compensate for the absence of a reasonably well-funded public health system' (2011a). But beyond this practical point there is also a normative aspect to it. As Pratap Mehta has argued, the danger with direct cash transfer is that 'it is seen as a substitute for governance, rather than instrument of governance. It gives up on the state' (2011: 15). This matters greatly, of course, to social democrats, but it is precisely why direct cash transfer is so attractive to others, for example, those policy-makers in India who are inclined to economic liberalism. Now the draft Food Security Bill has a clause committing the government to 'strive for . . . introducing (the) scheme of cash transfers in lieu of entitlements' (quoted by the Right to Food Campaign, 2011: 21) – which seems to the Right to Food campaign to presage the dissolution of the PDS.

We have spent so much time elaborating the arguments over the right to food in India because the controversy reflects so well the politics of these times. The case for establishing the right to food was made initially by a civil society organization, the PUCL, and by the means of appealing to judicial activism through the instrument of public interest litigation (a specifically Indian legal innovation of the 1980s, described by Birchfield and Corsi as 'a judge-made human rights mechanism' (2010: 715)). The case has subsequently been carried forward by a coalition of civil society organizations, the Right to Food Campaign, and an important forum of debate about it has been the non-constitutional National Advisory Council, an ad hoc grouping of, mainly, intellectuals and activists which interfaces, however, with regular politics through its links with the Congress Party. For its part, the government has sought to reduce the problem to a technical one, to be settled by technocrats. What is so striking is that all of this is taking place largely outside the institutions and the processes of formal democratic politics.

5.5   The Right to Work

The same sorts of informal politics were involved in the setting up of the National Rural Employment Guarantee Scheme. The Act setting up the scheme was passed by Parliament in September 2005, and extended to all districts in the country in April 2008, providing for up to 100 days of guaranteed wage employment to rural households. This was actually an outcome that was significantly influenced by the activities of the Right to Food campaign, following the events of 2001 that we discussed earlier. Later the campaign began to press the UPA government to deliver on its commitment to the Common Minimum Programme (CMP) that it had agreed with other parties, notably the left parties, in order to maintain a ruling majority. The CMP included a commitment to a national employment guarantee, and key activists with the Right to Food campaign – Aruna Roy, a former officer in the elite Indian Administrative Service, and a driving force in the Mazdur Kisan Shakti Sangathan (MKSS) that led the campaign for the Right to Information (also invoking a ruling of the Supreme Court), and Jean Drèze – who were also members of the National Advisory Council, presented a draft Bill at its first meeting. There was subsequently considerable conflict between different government departments over the Bill, with both the Ministry of Finance and the Planning Commission questioning the financial feasibility of a national employment guarantee. The subsequent considerably diluted draft brought eventually before Parliament by the Ministry of Rural Development was subjected to fierce criticism by civil society actors, articulated primarily through the NAC. Some of the civil society organizations, together with individuals, many of them with links with parliamentarians and bureaucrats, formed a campaigning organization, People's Action for Employment Guarantee, which – amongst other actions – organized a 'bus yatra' through ten states to mobilize popular support. The Act that was finally passed reflected the success of the PAEG in securing the restoration of most of the provisions of the original proposals – but also the vital support of the left parties in Parliament. The story shows, as Deepta Chopra argues in her analysis of the making of NREGA, the significance of (1) the creation of a new forum and network, outside regular political institutions – the NAC; (2) powerful and sympathetic state actors and networks – notably Mrs Sonia Gandhi, and some high-ranking officials; (3) civil society actors and their networks; and (4) political compulsions – the importance of left support, from the outside, for the UPA (Chopra 2011: 102). Only in regard to the last of these did conventional party politics enter in. The significance of the support of the left parties must not be ignored, however, and the current weakness of the left in Parliament is perhaps one factor that helps to account for blocks to the passage of a meaningful National Food Security Act.

Early studies of the NREGS in action show up the considerable difficulties of implementation, and that its effectiveness varies considerably between states. At best – in states such as Rajasthan and Madhya Pradesh – evaluations show that there has been fair success in meeting the objectives of the legislation, particularly in opening up employment opportunities for women, in spite of the mounting evidence of the diversion of vast sums intended for the scheme as a result of the corruption of local elected and other officials (Subrahmaniam 2009a, 2009b). An evaluation study conducted in 2008 in the states of Bihar, Chhattisgarh, Jharkhand, Madhya Pradesh, Rajasthan and Uttar Pradesh showed that the number of days of employment generated per rural household in NREGS ranged from seventy-seven in Rajasthan to twenty-two in Bihar (Drèze and Khera 2009). The participation of women in NREGS employment ranged from 71 per cent in Rajasthan to 5 per cent in UP; and the authors of the study argued that employment in NREGS was making a modest contribution to changing gender relations, and to greater gender equity (Khera and Nayak 2009). In general, NREGS has had a positive impact in tightening rural labour markets and raising wages:

> Data from the National Sample Survey Organisation for 2007–08 indicate that even by then the NREGS had made a difference to wage rates for rural casual work. Between 2004–05 and 2007–08, average real wages apparently increased by around 13 per cent, and more rapidly for female workers. In NREGS there is hardly any gender gap in the wages, while such gaps are very large in all other work, and in urban wages. Further, on average wages received in NREGS were significantly higher than those received by casual labour in other kinds of work. (Ghosh 2011b)

Increased wages led to protests in some parts that NREGS has made cultivation uncompetitive. This is most significantly an indication of potential that the scheme has in transforming agrarian social relations; and NREGS has led to increased popular awareness of rights (Drèze and Khera 2009).

But NREGS has also been the cause of another dispute that seems to show, on the other hand, the reluctance of government fully to support economic rights. From the beginning of 2009, the government froze daily wages paid under the scheme at Rs 100 and delinked them from the Minimum Wages Act, 1948; and then, on 31 December 2010, rejected a plea from the NAC for payment of statutory minimum wages to workers employed under the scheme. This was in spite of rulings by the Supreme Court that 'any remuneration which was less than the minimum wage was "forced labour" . . . It sets the lowest limit below which wages cannot be allowed to sink in all humanity'. Vidhya Subrahmaniam said of this decision, 'The poor had always been underpaid in the Indian labour market. But now . . . they were officially condemned to subhuman status, fit not even to earn subsistence-level wages' (this, and the preceding quotes, from Subrahmaniam 2011). This failure to comply with the Directive Principles of the Constitution regarding wages is of a piece, however, with other government actions in regard to workers.

5.6   The Rights of Workers

The 'inflexibility' of labour markets in India, resulting from the country's labour laws, is commonly supposed to be a major constraint on economic growth (though see our remarks questioning this view in chapters 2 and 4). It was in the light of these ideas that the Second National Labour Commission, reporting in 2002, sought to enhance the rights of employers to close establishments and to legitimize the use of contract labour, while expressing criticism of 'the increasing tendency on the part of trade unions to get together in *ad hoc* struggle committees' (Rajalakshmi 2002: 101). The weakness and the disunity of organized labour in India, divided by the political party affiliations of the major federations, is notorious (though may be exaggerated – see Teitelbaum 2006). Still, the unions have effectively resisted and have staved off the policies advocated by the Commission. In 2003, however, a series of Supreme Court verdicts on democratic rights and labour issues went against labour, and seemed to call into question the fundamental right to strike that had been upheld in earlier judgments (Venkatesan 2003a).

More recently, decisions of the Court have gone the other way. In January 2010, the Supreme Court 'expressed anguish at courts' apathy to the plight of workers being retrenched in the guise of globalization and economic liberalization'. In the judgment referred to here, Justice Singhvi pointed out that: 'It needs no emphasis that if a man is deprived of his livelihood, he is deprived of all his fundamental and constitutional rights and for him the goal of social and economic justice, equality of status or opportunity, the freedoms enshrined in the Constitution remain illusory.' In a separate judgment, Justice Ganguly said:

> this court should make an effort to protect the rights of the weaker sections in view of the clear Constitutional mandate. Social Justice, the very signature tune of our Constitution and being deeply embedded in our constitutional ethos, in a way is the arch of the Constitution which ensures rights of the common man to be interpreted in a meaningful way so that life can be lived with human dignity. (Venkatesan 2010)

The significance of Article 21 of the Constitution, and of the deeper interpretation of the right to life, is again reflected in these judicial statements.

The reluctance, however, of the government to act in line with the position taken by the justices was shown in its less than positive responses to the arguments of the National Commission for Enterprises in the Unorganised Sector (NCEUS), which was established by the new UPA government in 2004. The focus on 'enterprises' in the title of the Commission was a reflection of the government's view, in line with recent international development policy arguments, that the key to poverty elimination lies in the entrepreneurial enterprise of the poor. In practice, the members of the Commission engaged much more substantially, and critically, with the problems of unorganized workers than the title might lead one to suppose – evidently to the annoyance of the Prime Minister (according to personal communications to us from members of the Commission). They prepared two draft Bills which included proposals for legal protection of the labour rights of unorganized workers, as well as for protection of their livelihoods. These were, however, set aside by the UPA government in May 2007, and replaced by a single Bill (passed into law in December 2008), much watered down in comparison with the NCEUS proposals. The members of the NCEUS, themselves critical of the Act passed in 2008, point to the systematic underfunding of all the programmes introduced by the UPA government, during the process of its fulfilment of obligations agreed with other parties in the Common Minimum Programme of 2004 (and see Breman 2010a).

5.7 Conclusion

The recent history of struggles over economic and social rights in India that we have recounted in this chapter is aptly summed up by the London *Economist* (20 March 2010):

> Over the past two decades, in a radical response [to the widespread, massive problems of destitution in their society], India's Supreme Court judges have increasingly demanded action. They have typically done so by redefining economic and social rights as fundamental and legally enforceable. That should make the government enforce them. In a few cases, however, the judges have gone so far as to dictate how they should do so.

This eventually led Prime Minister Manmohan Singh, in September 2010, to take on the Court, specifically in regard to food security. He was reported as saying:

> I respectfully submit that the Supreme Court should not go into the realm of policy formulation. I respect the sentiments behind the [court] decision that when foodgrains are rotting and people are suffering from deprivation, then some way should be found to ensure that the food needs of the deprived sections are met. But quite honestly it is not possible in this country to give free food to all the poor people. (Varadarajan 2010)

The points at issue reflect the tensions between the executive and the judiciary that are an important feature of current Indian politics.

The moves and counter-moves of the different actors that are involved in these struggles over rights – which do seem to represent a Polanyian double movement – reflect a distinctive kind of politics. Polanyi, indeed, would probably not be surprised to learn how little the working classes, rural and urban, have been concerned in the politics of modern societies, given his reservations about the extent to which class adequately explains such involvement – 'class interests offer only a limited explanation of long-run movements in society,' he said (2001: 159). Even if Teitelbaum (2006) is right about the relative strengths of the Indian labour movement – contra conventional arguments – it is still the case that lock-outs (of workers by management, that is) have claimed more person days in India than have strikes, over a period extending back into the 1980s (Nagaraj 2004: 3389). And while it is true, as Rina Agarwala has shown (2006), that informally employed workers are now becoming more organized, their demands are targeted on the state, for welfare benefits as citizens, rather than being directed against employers and for workers' rights. Workers are struggling, she says, not against informality (the historical objective of trades union organization) but for rights within this status. Supriya RoyChowdhury is less sanguine about the character and performance of informal workers' organizations. The political edge of the movement is limited, she argues, noting that unorganized labour as a category 'is not an important constituency for any of India's major political parties' (RoyChowdhury 2003: 5283). The recent story of the National Commission for Enterprises in the Unorganised Sector, as we have explained, rather confirms this analysis. Rural workers, meanwhile, outside the tribal belt of central India and some parts of Bihar, where the Maoists have organized (chapter 10), have been notably passive over the last two decades in spite of – or perhaps because of – the crisis of agriculture that we discussed in the last chapter. The farmers' movements that became politically powerful in the 1980s have been weakened, as the richer, commercial farmers who led them have become more interested in gatekeeping activities – roles in which they mediate between other people and the state, and which enable them to secure resources for themselves (for example, from the allocation of ration cards). They are, one observer argues, 'looking after themselves' (Pattenden 2005: 1982); and poorer cultivators, and agricultural labourers, are generally involved more in caste politics. The horizontal solidarity of India's tribal societies is generally more conducive to enduring political mobilization.

The struggles over economic and social rights that we have discussed involve, rather, different fractions of the middle classes – amongst which we may include members of judiciary. The sphere of the civil society organizations that have been such important drivers of the struggles for rights to education, to food and to work, is essentially one of middle-class activism (see chapter 11) and, as Jean Drèze noted on one occasion, with regard to the Right to Food campaign of which he was a leading member:

> The 'leaders' almost invariably come from a privileged social background. However sensitive they may be to the viewpoint of the underprivileged, they cannot but carry a certain baggage associated with their own position. The bottom line is that, with few exceptions, social movements in India (or for that matter elsewhere) are far from democratic. This lack of internal democracy jars with the values we claim to stand for, and creates a deep inconsistency between means and ends. (Drèze 2004: 128)

This may seem an overly negative, pessimistic point of view, but it is a fair reflection of the historic ambiguities of the politics of the middle classes – which have been supportive of democratization in many societies, but only up to the point at which rising lower-working classes threaten to take away their power. There certainly are fractions of the Indian middle classes now that are withdrawing from formal democratic politics and looking for technocratic solutions to social problems (Fernandes and Heller 2006). And, as Jean Drèze has also written, 'It is hard to imagine how midday meals could have been extended to 100 million children without the firm intervention of the Supreme Court [but] the fact that it took public interest litigation to get political leaders to focus on children's nutritional rights is a telling reminder of the lopsidedness of Indian democracy' (Zaidi 2005: 52).

The current battle of ideas in India today, primarily amongst the middle-class elites, between contending projects for Indian society – one distinctly liberal, the other broadly social democratic – indicates there is no straightforward answer to the question of social justice that we have addressed in this chapter. Social justice remains a field of contestation.

PART II
POLITICS

6

How Did a 'Weak' State Promote Audacious Reform?

6.1 Introduction

In the first part of *India Today*, we discussed how and why India took off. We also paid close attention to the distributional consequences of sustained economic growth. We noted that India's recent economic trajectory presents a challenge to strong path dependency arguments. It creates problems as well for arguments that assume sustained growth accelerations are dependent upon local improvements in institutional quality. Incentive systems in India today are more efficient than they were twenty years ago, mainly as a consequence of reform. It would be difficult, even so, to argue that the quality of India's key underlying institutions has improved significantly over the past thirty years. In any case, an even larger question remains, one that goes far beyond standard growth theories. Suppose we accept that the state in India was something less than developmental in the years up to 1980 or 1991, whatever it might have been in the 1950s (see Corbridge and Harriss 2000, chapter 3). Perhaps it was a 'weak–strong state' (Rudolph and Rudolph 1987). Suppose we further agree that government in India delivered substantial largesse to the country's dominant proprietary elites through the 1960s and 1970s, and indeed the 1980s. How then do we explain the willingness and capacity of that same state to promote a long period of 'audacious' economic reform (after Grindle 2000)? Was it, indeed, mainly the state that drove the reforms, and if so why did it face so little organized resistance? And when we say the 'same state', what do we mean by that phrase? How has the state been changed by the process of reform? In what sense was it ever a weak state?

In the absence of revolution or significant institutional change, a number of drivers of audacious reform have been identified in the wider literature (Haggard and Webb 1994; Nelson 1990; Przeworski 1991; Stallings 1992). One of these involves economic and/or political crises, or 'events'. The debt crises that hit Latin American and African countries in the 1980s can be counted in this category. Following an unprecedented decline in their foreign reserve holdings, many of these countries were forced to adjust the deeper structures of their economies and were pushed to do so by the World Bank and the International Monetary Fund (IMF). One key function of the IMF that was strengthened at this time – and indeed at the time of Britain's economic crisis in 1976 – was to serve as a lightning rod for local opposition to austerity programmes. The IMF played a similar role in Greece in 2010. According to this argument, governments make audacious economic reforms most effectively: (a) when they are faced by an external crisis (or a crisis that can be made to appear to have at least some external origins); and (b) when the Bretton Woods institutions help push through a reform agenda, both by providing much-needed loans and by serving as a convenient scapegoat for aggrieved local parties. India, arguably, was in just this position in 1991.

A second argument pays attention to the role of reform champions and convenient enemies. Arnold Harberger maintains that real changes in the way we live can be brought about by a critical mass of brave and talented individuals – 'a handful of heroes' (Harberger 1993) – and there is clearly something to be said for the importance of public leadership and simple force of personality. Margaret Thatcher comes quickly to mind, and so too does Lee Kuan Yew. Both leaders also benefited from the real or imagined threat of a well-organized enemy: workerist fifth columnists or communists at the gate. In India, too, as we shall see, the Rao-Singh government of 1991–6 was able to raise the spectre of the BJP coming to power to shore up support for economic reform. More diffusely, perhaps, Keynes (1973 [1936]: 384) liked to insist that ideas matter as much 'for good or evil' as vested interests, and, in the case of Margaret Thatcher, it is worth recalling that her sometimes empirical approach to government was underpinned by an understanding of economics taken very largely from a 'free market' think tank in London, the Institute of Economic Affairs.

A third argument is focused on the costs and benefits of reform. The basic intuition is that turkeys don't vote for Christmas. How were people who benefited significantly from one system of economic management persuaded to 'vote' for a system that apparently threatened their economic standing? A number of answers suggest themselves.

Different elites are picked off or dealt with at different times. (This begs a question about who is doing the picking off and what is driving the reforms. We come back to this.) Various members of these elites don't fully recognize (or anticipate) what is happening to their income sources, and/or they discount these changes on the basis that they are happening slowly, giving agents time to adjust. This picks up the idea that there can be benefits to reforming cautiously, or at least not by means of shock-therapy. Well-placed losers from economic reform may also capture new income streams, whether legal or illegal. Even as economic reform takes away some rents, it provides access to others. For example, instead of exploiting a system of construction licences, an agile and reasonably well-informed agent might capture new benefits from booming real-estate transactions. In the long run, too, there is the possibility that economic reform is a positive sum game. High-income growth rates might confer gains on most well-off households, even if some households gain more than others. When it comes to ordinary people, or families Below the Poverty Line, two key issues to remember concerning India are as follows: (a) the difficulties they often face in organizing collectively; and (b) their low rates of involvement in the mainly formal or export-led sectors of the economy that were the first targets for economic reform.

Fourth, there is the matter of visibility, or of stealth. It is often supposed that democracies are less able to effect audacious reforms than are non-democracies. Organized labour, a free press and effective parliamentary scrutiny impose real costs on politicians who have to go back to the voters every few years. The seeming failure of the Obama government in the US to make substantial headway in cutting US debt, following the crisis of 2008–9, is sometimes explained in these terms. Members of the Senate and the House of Representatives benefit from delivering 'pork' to their constituents. They don't have much to gain from voting for higher taxes or local school closures. And yet changes clearly do take place in the US, as in India, including some quite audacious changes. President Obama managed to pass a health-care Bill in 2010 in the teeth of determined and well-financed opposition. There is an art to government, and politicians in functioning democracies are generally highly skilled in this art. Deals are made and votes are bought, one way or another. Much of this is done behind the scenes and out of the limelight. Raghuram Rajan (2010) argues that American politicians have strong incentives to pump money into the US economy to keep voters in work. In the absence of strong social security systems, politicians are acutely aware of the full-employment imperative. When the economy overheats, however, as it must do when credit remains cheap for too long, the US government often finds that inflation is the best way to write down debt. This way, the pain is less visible than when it is inflicted in the form of higher taxes or lower public spending. The distribution of losers is also changed: crudely, it is shifted to those on fixed incomes and, with luck, also to foreign holders of US government debt. In short, reform is effected by stealth. As we shall see later, this has also been the case in India – less in this case by inflation than by means of various off-stage investment deals, or bargains that are struck behind the backs of those charged with keeping government transactions open and accountable.

Lastly, there is the not insignificant matter of demonstration effects and jurisdictional competition. India is a federal democracy and it is misleading to think of the reform process there as being either a singular event or something that was effected entirely by central government. Regional political leaders have also played a key role, along with some members of provincial, as well as national, business groups. As in other federal systems, there can be significant prime mover advantages. Some states and cities capture the benefits of higher rates of economic growth and innovation more than others. This in turn can generate pressures among voters elsewhere to join the new game. Regional political groupings that strongly set their stall against reform can be punished at the polls. Rob Jenkins (1998) refers to this process in India as 'Provincial Darwinism'.

In the rest of this chapter, we draw on these five linked insights to address our central puzzle: how did a 'weak' state effect audacious economic reform, and why did opposition to reform fail to exploit a widely generalized mistrust of economic liberalism in India in the early 1990s? In proposing a solution to the puzzle, we also hope to build a more effective understanding of the 'state in India' and 'state effectiveness' – something we consider further in chapters 7 and 8, and which we foreground here in the next section.

6.2   The Crisis of 1990–1991 and India's Distributional Coalition

It is widely agreed that India's efforts to create a robustly modernizing state were compromised even in the 1950s, and were substantially defeated by the time of Nehru's death in 1964. By that time, India's development plans had been derailed in large degree by three dominant proprietary groups: the country's richer farmers, higher-level bureaucrats and big business houses. Land to the tiller land reform was blocked by the first group, while many bureaucrats earned rents on the licences and permits that were set up, in part, to protect the country's limited industrial bourgeoisie against domestic and foreign competition (Bardhan 1984; see also

Bhagwati 1993; and Chibber 2003). In the 1980s, this distributional coalition was widened to include various mercantile interests (Harriss 1981, 1985) and India's middle peasantry. Formal-sector labourers were also beneficiaries of government policies which gave significant advantages to incumbents – high wages and dearness (or cost of living) allowances, for example – and which blocked entry by new aspirants into elite private- and public-sector labour markets. By the time that Rajiv Gandhi came to power in 1985, the power of the dominant proprietary interests was sufficiently great that a government with a huge working majority in the Lok Sabha was unable to promote the market-led liberalization of the Indian economy beyond a few minor initiatives announced in 1985–7 (Corbridge 1991; Harriss 1987; Manor 1987). In the words of Lloyd and Susanne Rudolph (1987), a formally strong state in India was unable to enforce its will except territorially: it had become a 'weak–strong state'. In James Manor's view, just as pithily, India had become 'increasingly democratic and increasingly difficult to govern' (Manor 1988: 72).

Unsurprisingly, the strength of India's distributional coalition was reflected in the country's public-spending patterns. We reported in chapter 2 that there were some productivity gains across the Indian economy in the 1980s. But the economy grew as well because of increased deficit financing. Rising defence spending contributed strongly to a fiscal deficit that was equivalent in the mid-1980s to 8 per cent of GDP, but this was more than matched by growth in subsidies to India's food economy (including fertilizers and the Public Distribution System: see also Mooij 1999) and to various Public Sector Enterprises (PSEs).

The failure of any one member of the distributional coalition to gain hegemony over the Indian state also fanned the flames of government spending. K. N. Raj, writing in 1973, drew on the work of Michal Kalecki (1972) to suggest that corporate India formed part of a governing 'intermediate regime' with the country's lower middle classes and rich peasantry. This expensive and finally unsustainable regime provided few incentives for any one party to embrace less cloistered economic relationships (see also Denoon 1998). It also imposed significant costs on the social majorities who were locked out of the ruling distributional coalition. They bore a heavy burden in terms of public expenditures foregone, high prices for non-food consumption goods, increased corruption, and simple shortages. Overwhelmingly, such people were concentrated in India's non-formal economies (see chapter 4 on India's informal sector; and Harriss-White 2003). Many households in this group benefited from cheap grain in Fair Price Shops, and indeed from some targeted anti-poverty interventions (including food-for-work (Jawahar Rozgar Yojana) and housing schemes (Indira Awas Yoyana)). Taken in the round, however, these subventions failed to compensate poorer households for a more general lack of investment in health and education, or for the relative absence of the tighter labour markets that might have been brought about by higher and more sustainable rates of GDP growth.

In the end, it was not growing fiscal imbalances that led directly to the crisis that prompted significant changes in the macro-economic management of India, but rather an external payments crisis. India's trade deficit in the first half of the 1980s was quite low at around 3–4 per cent of GDP, and was largely balanced out by remittances from migrants in the Persian Gulf and by foreign aid inflows. In the second half of the 1980s, however, India's current account position worsened markedly, notwithstanding that merchandise exports grew sharply from 1985–6 to 1990–1, and it became more difficult to fund a balance of trade deficit from invisible earnings and capital inflows, including from Non-Resident Indians. From 1985 onwards, India was forced to deplete its reserves of foreign exchange, and also to take out increasing levels of short-term commercial debt. Matters worsened significantly at the end of the decade when foreign investors became nervous about the stability of India's government. The Gulf War of 1990–1 pushed up the price of oil and led to reduced remittances from the Middle East. By early 1991, India's short-term borrowings in the international capital market were worth as much as 140 per cent of foreign exchange reserves – compared to just 5.3 per cent in 1988 (Tendulkar and Bhavani 2007: 81) – and this prompted leading rating agencies to downgrade India's bonds. By the spring of 1991, India was unable to rollover its short-term commercial debts and could finance little more than a few weeks' worth of imports: 'an unprecedented default on international debt loomed large' (ibid.).

The key question, of course, is whether this external crisis was bound to lead to significant reform of the Indian economy (Ghosh 1998). India was required to take a loan of $1.8 billion from the Contingent Compensatory Finance Facility of the IMF in January 1991, and this caused political problems for the Chandra Shekhar government. As Tendulkar and Bhavani point out, however, the government fell before it could pass a budget that would satisfy the qualification criteria of the IMF loan. It was left to the incoming Congress-led minority government of Narasimha Rao to propose a budget – presented to Parliament by the new Finance Minister, Dr Manmohan Singh – that would begin the task of bringing India's external finances back into order. Interestingly, Dr Singh proposed to do this not just by devaluing the Indian rupee, but also by attending to the country's underlying fiscal imbalances, much as the IMF had been calling for. Taxes were raised in the budget, and cuts were proposed for defence, India's PSEs and the fertilizer subsidy. All told, there was a 'very sharp fiscal contraction equivalent to a reduction of 2.3 percentage points of GDP in [the] gross fiscal deficit between the crisis year of 1990–91 and 1991–2' (ibid.: 87). This in turn led to a contraction of the real economy in 1991–2, and to India's first – and so far only – reduction in per capita incomes since 1979–80.

How was this budget passed? Rajiv Gandhi, after all, had found it next to impossible to tackle India's food-grain, kerosene and fertilizer subsidies in the mid-1980s, notwithstanding that Congress MPs occupied three-quarters (415 of 542) of Lok Sabha seats during his premiership. The crisis of 1991 has to be a key component of our explanation, and with it the loan conditions imposed by the IMF. Changes were now required: they were not optional, for all the talk at the time about resisting the IMF. Even industrial houses that had grown fat under a regime of import-substitution industrialization (ISI) had to withhold their opposition for a while to more open economic policies. They needed IMF money to finance their own imports. More positively, Rajiv Gandhi's efforts in the late 1980s to woo 'segments of . . . modern . . . manufacturing India' (Mukherji 2010: 490) now started to pay off. Many large-scale business groups were keen to respond positively to the opportunities that were opened up by the crisis of 1991. Here was a chance to fight back against the power of rural (and subaltern) India, which had been flexing its muscles throughout the 1980s (see chapters 4 and 5), and possibly also to muscle in on the territory of small-scale industry. Rahul Mukherji reminds us, too, that 'The Federation of Indian Chambers of Commerce and Industry (FICCI), representing domestic capital, the Associated Chambers of Commerce and Industry (ASSOCHAM), with ties to foreign capital, and the Confederation of Indian Industry (CII [from 1986 to 1992 the Confederation of Engineering Industry]), all supported the trade and investment liberalization from 1991 to 1993' (ibid.). ISI might have been comfortable terrain for some of their members, but greener pastures now seemed to beckon – just so long as India's business elites could help steer the process of economic reform itself.

The crisis of 1990–1 was also catalytic of reform in other more subtle ways. It gathered force just as the Soviet Union was collapsing. There was mounting evidence, too, that China's embrace of pro-market reforms was paying substantial dividends, a fact not lost on New Delhi (Baru 2007). New economic instruments had also been pioneered in the West in the 1980s, not least in the UK: deregulation and privatization pre-eminent among them. Intellectually, the ideas of Milton Friedman and Friedrich Hayek were in the ascendance in some countries where Keynesianism had until recently been quite dominant. In addition, Indians who visited the West were increasingly impressed by the wealth and work habits of their erstwhile countrymen and women. It was less obvious to some well-travelled middle-class Indians by 1990 – as compared, say, to 1970 or even 1980 – that bureaucrats should be running dreary hotels in Delhi or other big cities, or that India's consumers were best served by state-run car plants. As Rajan has acidly observed, the Ambassador car – a local version of the 1954 Oxford Morris – came in 'only five different models [over nearly four decades] . . . and the sole differences between them seemed to be the headlights and the shape of the grill' (2010: 60).

It is never easy to quantify the role that changing ideas play in the production of new realities, but our strong sense is that the Kafkaesque qualities of a bloated public sector in India loomed more sharply into view in the 1980s, along with a sense that things could be different. If this was indeed the case – and we still await a first tranche of autobiographies from some of the prime movers of economic reform – it helps to explain why Manmohan Singh was able to push at an opening door in his first two budget speeches. There have been very few 'true believers' – committed neoliberals – in India's post-1991 governments (Manor 2011b). At the same time, it seems clear that Prime Minister Rao backed the judgements of Manmohan Singh, his close lieutenant Montek Ahluwalia, and some other professional economists who came to the reform process without the traditional Indian baggage of economic nationalism. These reform champions took the view that India's national interest was not best served by an economic mindset that trumpeted the virtues of self-reliance while promoting autarkic policies that mainly served the interests of powerful minorities. As the reform process deepened in the 1990s and 2000s, the faith of these men (and some women) in the virtues of micro-economic efficiency and internationalization was replenished by their contacts with professional economists such as Jagdish Bhagwati, T. N. Srinivasan, Amartya Sen, Nicholas Stern, Anne Krueger and (later) Lant Pritchett, as well as with successful members of the Indian diaspora (Kapur 2007). Over time, too, their reforming instincts were bolstered by many of India's new private media outlets, including by some sources – such as *India Today* on occasions, or the *Business Standard* – which urged India to reform itself less hesitantly. The possibility of further reform was also made easier in the 2000s by a growing recognition that poor Indians would not have been better off under a distorted version of state socialism. Even the global downturn in 2008–9 did little to dampen the by now conventional view among India's elites that the country's future lay with less encumbered forms of capitalism.

6.3   Elite Politics, Political Stealth and Reform Payoffs

The economic crisis of 1990–1 undoubtedly was a key factor in India's embrace of a more concerted agenda of economic reform in the 1990s.

On its own, however, it is a weak explanandum, even if we factor in the role of committed reform champions and a significant shift in public and intellectual affairs, including the end of the Cold War and a diminution of foreign aid to India from the socialist bloc. We need a more robust explanation of why pro-market economic reforms were enacted in the early–mid-1990s, when they were widely expected to be unpopular and were not the inevitable outgrowth of a stabilization package that was designed to deal with an external payments crisis. Import-substitution industrialization, after all, had been a viable option for post-1950 India in a way that it wasn't for smaller countries. Why did leading business leaders move so rapidly after 1991 to ditch ISI and embrace a broad agenda for economic reform? Was it simply circumstance, or did they spot new opportunities for economic and political advancement? Did they ever really press the pedal on liberalization? More generally, why wasn't India's handful of heroes overcome by a much larger gang of villains?

An interesting answer to this last question, which has been proposed by Ashutosh Varshney, is that economic reform in India during the 1990s largely played out in the arena of elite politics. It did not spill over much into the life-worlds of ordinary people, or into the landscapes of mass politics. Varshney points out that:

> In the largest ever survey of mass political attitudes in India conducted between April–July 1996, only 19 per cent of the electorate reported any knowledge of economic reforms, even though reforms had been in existence since July 1991. Of the rural electorate, only about 14 per cent had heard of reforms, whereas the comparable proportion in the cities was 32 per cent. Further, nearly 66 per cent of the graduates were aware of the dramatic changes in economic policy, compared to only 7 per cent of the poor, who are mostly illiterate. (Varshney 1998: 303, citing Yadav and Singh 1996)

In contrast, 'close to three fourths of the electorate – both literates and illiterates, poor and rich, urban and rural – were aware of the 1992 mosque demolition in Ayodhya' (ibid.), while just as many people expressed strong opinions on caste-based affirmative action and the merits of secularism.

Varshney concludes that economic reform meant little to ordinary Indians. It was not a big issue in the sphere of mass politics. This in turn reflected the fact that India's leading economic reformers were wise enough in the mid-1990s to confine their reforms to trade and industrial policy, and largely steered clear of direct and visible threats to existing labour laws, agriculture or public ownership. Even fiscal policy remained lax in the 1990s and well into the 2000s. Indeed, the gross fiscal deficit of India's central and states governments was slightly higher in 2001–2 than in 1990–1: 10.3 per cent of GDP against 9.4 per cent. Tax collection improved somewhat in the 1990s, which allowed the government to make some improvements in public spending while remaining revenue neutral. But the persistence of high government deficits up to the middle part of the 2000s mainly demonstrates the reluctance of government to cut spending programmes that were important to the countryside or other organized interests.

Varshney's argument is consistent with what we know about the sequencing of economic reforms in post-1991 India. Progress was made first in the industrial policy arena, where investment licences in organized manufacturing were quickly removed from all but a handful of industries, and where sectors like power and insurance, both of which had been reserved hitherto for public-sector enterprises, were opened up to private-sector competition. Small-scale industries, meanwhile, which remain by far the biggest employers of industrial labour in India, were allowed to maintain local monopolies over more than 800 products as late as 1997. This was not significantly changed until the mid-2000s, despite pressures from big business houses. Meanwhile, foreign direct and portfolio investment, which up to that point had been largely discouraged from finding a home in India – recall the de facto expulsion of IBM and Coca Cola from India in 1978 by the Janata government, and discounting here some important joint ventures in the 1980s: as, for example, between Hero and Honda – were courted once again by a country that was slowly opening itself up to world market forces. But even in this sphere, where foreign companies were now allowed to have majority equity shares in (some) Indian industries, the scale of direct foreign investment that flowed into the country in the 1990s was small beer, and far below the levels of direct foreign investment that were attracted into China in the same period. Varshney reports that it 'went up to $600 million in 1993–94, rising further to $.1.3 billion in 1994–95, $2 billion in 1995–96 . . . and $3 billion in 1997–98' (ibid.: 310). China received about twenty times as much in the late 1990s (Winters and Yusuf 2007; see also Sharma 2009).

The reform of India's economy has been a limited and stop-go process, albeit now a long and continuous one, and it is precisely these qualities that helped to ensure that the benefits of reform exceeded its costs for many key players. Even organized labour has continued to receive some legislative and political protection, although these provisions should be seen in perspective. Only between 2 and 5 per cent of workers in India are members of trade unions (see Bhowmick 1998), and even in the formal sector employers have not found it difficult to deal with the lack of an official exit policy. Meanwhile, big business houses were slowly able to colonize sectors of the Indian economy which had been reserved for public-sector enterprises, and which in many cases – telecommunications and automobiles are both good examples – were characterized by the existence of artificially induced shortages. Once the lid was lifted on these industries there was more than enough effective demand, it turned out, for private and foreign capitals to enter the market alongside PSEs that could be cosseted still in other ways. The privatization of India's economy was thus procured mainly by stealth, much like its labour markets. A Disinvestment Commission was established in 1996 and, in 1999, it proposed some management and other changes for fifty-eight PSEs (Nayak 2010: 370), including plans for reduced government stakes. For the most part, though, state-owned companies have not been put up for public sale – airlines like Air India, for example, or even some banks – and India's preferred means of privatization has been to create spaces for new or old private enterprises to flourish alongside PSEs. The restructuring or eventual sale of PSEs has often been postponed until another day, and with it, perhaps, unnecessary political conflict (Bhattacharyya 2007; see also Alfaro and Chari 2009 on incumbency bias in non-service sectors).

Of course, this doesn't mean that everyone gained from reform, or that a long process of reform was designed and sequenced from Year Zero (1991), or indeed that reform was always designed with a view to minimizing political opposition to it. It is not an oxymoron to say that radical policies sometimes evolve slowly and even by accident – as has certainly been the case in India. Nevertheless, while a first round of economic reform in India did produce some losers – inefficient private capitals, for instance, some fractions of organized labour, many lower-middle-class youths, importing houses that had taken for granted an overvalued rupee, even industrial groups that wanted to run faster – the unwillingness of the state to deal strenuously with India's fiscal deficits both at the centre and in the states cushioned the blow of economic restructuring, as indeed did economic growth itself. Possibly the main losers from industrial and trade policy reform were India's legions of licence-wallahs in the bureaucracy: no permits, no rents. But even here the damage was limited. Licences for small-scale industries remained, and new opportunities opened up for some bureaucrats to extract payments from private-sector firms that were anxious to gain privileged access to better-serviced public infrastructure. Meanwhile, rent-seeking in domains such as higher education has probably expanded, both in the public and private sectors (Kapur and Mehta 2007; and see chapter 14).

It is also significant that many of the key policy changes that were introduced into India in the 1990s were effected by changes to existing laws (for example, the Foreign Exchange Regulation Act, 1974, or the Monopolies and Restrictive Trade Practices Act, 1968), and/or by an agency outside what is usually thought to be central government. For example, devaluations and financial sector reforms were pushed through by the Reserve Bank of India, the country's central bank. The need for a coalition government to pass legislative amendments was correspondingly minimized, as Tendulkar and Bhavani point out (2007: 105). And when parliamentary approval was required – as it was in the case of Manmohan Singh's first two budgets, both of which galvanized opposition forces – the threat of the government falling was one that could be used to discipline coalition members and those parties – like the Communist Party of India-Marxist (CPM) and the Janata Dal – who preferred to support the government from without. Varshney (1998, Section III) astutely observes that the left was persuaded not to defeat the Congress's reform strategy because it feared the effects of a no-confidence vote in the Lok Sabha. Bluntly, the BJP could be brought to power. This is where mass and elite politics intersected to the advantage of India's reform champions in a way that it had not done in the mid-1980s. India's federal democracy, meanwhile, allowed the CPM to speak loudly against neoliberalism from the Writers' Building in Calcutta, where ideological purity appeared to be maintained, even as it backed off confrontation with the Congress-led government in New Delhi.

6.4   Provincial Darwinism

In the longer run, even the CPM in West Bengal has come to embrace economic reform, not least in respect of a more liberal industrial investment regime. Indeed, one of the more shocking political stories in India in the second half of the 2000s centred on the small settlements of Singur and Nandigram, in the Hooghly and Medinipur districts of West Bengal respectively. In Singur, the government of West Bengal used provisions from the 1894 Land Acquisition Act to purchase land from mainly small farmers for a Tata Nano car factory. Opposition to the project led to the Tatas pulling out in 2008 and moving to Guajarat. Nandigram, meanwhile, became infamous in 2007 as a village where at least fourteen people were shot dead by state forces determined to crush opposition to government plans for the acquisition of land for a Special Economic Zone (SEZ). The SEZ was meant to host a chemical plant that would be owned and developed by the Salim Group from Indonesia.

How did the CPM allow this state of affairs to happen? Part of the answer is to be found within the CPM itself and with various power struggles that have taken place in the broader left front parties in West

Bengal under the general stewardship both of Jyoti Basu (Chief Minister 1977–2000) and Buddhadeb Bhattarcharya (Chief Minister 2000–11). The story of how an avowedly left of centre political party/regime came to embrace economic reform while maintaining its socialist rhetoric is one that has yet to be written (though see Das 2012), notwithstanding some obvious parallels with China and Vietnam (Hayton 2010). More broadly, the answer lies in the fact that reform in India has acquired a good deal of its momentum since the mid-1990s, and has had many of its most visible effects in the states and not simply in New Delhi.

Prior to the 1990s, the commanding heights of the Indian economy were mainly in the public sector, and thus largely under the control of the centre, which 'dominated anything related to industrialization' (Sinha 2004: 28). The centre also commanded by far the largest share of India's most robust and elastic sources of revenue. It is hardly surprising therefore that most states were forced to take out grants-in-aid from New Delhi under Article 275 of the Constitution, and were inclined to define their political battles in terms of the fairness of centre–state relationships, including battles with other states for a greater share of the pie that New Delhi was able to distribute. Non-Congress state governments maintained they were especially vulnerable during periods of Congress rule in New Delhi. However, an emerging body of work on the political geography of grants-in-aid is agnostic in its conclusions. There is some evidence to suggest that Congress governments in New Delhi funnelled money most generously to those states where they felt the local Congress Party was facing strong local opposition (see Rodden and Wilkinson 2004; see also Rao and Singh 2005). But whatever was the case before c.1990, matters have changed a great deal since that time. For one thing, the geography of centre–state transfers has been complicated since 1989 by the failure of any one party to achieve power in New Delhi, as well as by the very considerable growth of caste-based and regional parties in both national and provincial elections. More importantly, however, the green light that was given to India's states in the mid-1990s to court foreign capitals directly, and to compete with other states in India to make their provinces more business-friendly, has gone a long way to reshape the nature of India's federal polity. Saez (2002) contends that economic reforms have led in India to 'federalism without a centre'.

Others might not go quite this far, but there can be little doubt that some of India's richest states now see themselves as 'competition states', fronted very often by a Chief Minister (CM) who sees himself or herself as a Chief Executive Officer (CEO). Chandrababu Naidu, the Chief Minister of Andhra Pradesh from 1995 to 2004, was the very model of a CM as CEO. Naidu committed considerable funds and energy to the task of building up Hyderabad as a technopole which could rival Bangalore (in Karnataka), and was taken to task by his critics both for neglecting rural Andhra Pradesh and for allegedly cutting deals that were favourable to major industrial houses, including Reliance Industries. Naidu was by no means the only CM who played this role, however. Narendra Modi has been the Chief Minister of Gujarat since 2001 and he has played an especially active role in bringing investment to Gujarat from its extensive diaspora, just as he courted the Tatas when they ran into difficulties in Singur. Further south, the states of Tamil Nadu and Maharashtra were in competition with one another in the mid-1990s to host a factory for the Ford Motor Company, a battle that was won on that occasion by Tamil Nadu in 1996. In all of these cases, the need for land clearances or some helping hand from the government – the expedited approval/building of upgraded sites and services, for example – created new sources of rent for government bureaucrats and politicians, whether or not they availed themselves of these opportunities.

In rather broader terms, the formation of competition states in India was necessarily bound up with increased regional inequalities, as we reported in chapter 3. Aseema Sinha (2004, 2005a) suggests that a brief window of opportunity existed from c.1950 to 1990 for India's eastern states to catch up with their richer neighbours to the south and west. The Nehru-Mahalanobis model of economic development placed great faith in heavy industries, as we have seen, and India's regional policy in this period was intended to add to an ostensible comparative advantage in manufacturing among India's resource-rich states: the coal, copper and iron-ore producing states of Bihar (or at least south Bihar: now Jharkhand), Orissa, West Bengal and Madhya Pradesh (particularly the districts that today are in Chhattisgarh). Unfortunately, these fine intentions were undone almost entirely by Freight Equalization Acts which delivered a single price across India for key raw materials. Value-added activities were very often located outside India's resource triangle, which suffered a version of a resource curse in consequence. It might also have been the case that India's eastern states lacked the trading and manufacturing expertise that earlier had provided the basis for private-sector economic growth in the Bombay presidency. There are certainly good reasons to think that Aseema Sinha is right when she contends that 'Leading states in the reform process (Gujarat and Maharashtra, for example) have utilized their previous linkages and institutional skills developed under the old [pre-Independence] regime to leverage crucial advantages in the new policy regime' (Sinha 2004: 27). In her view, India has returned to a form of strong federalism that was last apparent in the country before 1935: that is, a form of federalism where the powers of the centre are sharply circumscribed by those of the Provinces/states.

Rob Jenkins adds significantly to this argument by considering the pressures that build up in less reformed states because of the increasingly visible success of states that have made themselves attractive to private capital. Jenkins is a firm proponent of the view that economic reform in India has proceeded largely by stealth and in the provinces. New Delhi played its part by creating a better policy environment for business development. But the harder work of building a more vibrant economy has been performed mainly by a new generation of business leaders – Reliance Industries for sure, but also Infosys, the Bajaj and Bharti Groups, the Oberoi hotel chain, and many others, including the Tatas – with support from their backers in the CII and FICCI, as well as from an allied group of entrepreneurial politicians and political brokers. Pressures then build in less reforming states to keep pace with the early reformers. States are now subjected to new technologies of comparative governance, including an 'Economic Freedom Index' which takes as its starting point some of the work on business environments pioneered by *Transparency International* and the *Heritage Foundation-Wall Street Journal* (Debroy, Gangopadhyay and Bhandari 2004). Interestingly, Modi's Gujarat was ranked Number 1 in 2004, just two years after the anti-Muslim pogrom in that state.

A process of provincial Darwinism is thus set in train which seemingly forces weaker (or poorer) states to adopt the same or even more robust pro-business policies to catch up with their stronger (or richer) rivals. This jurisdictional competition, moreover, is played out not only at the inter-state level, but also at smaller spatial scales through the promotion of Special Economic Zones (SEZs). By early 2010, close to 600 SEZs had been approved under the terms of India's Special Economic Zone Act, 2005. As Jenkins points out, 'the ostensible purpose [of them is] to attract large volumes of investment by providing world-class infrastructural facilities, a favourable taxation regime, and incentives for sectoral clustering. The benefits for the wider economy are, in theory, more exports, particularly in high-value-added sectors, increased employment, and ultimately faster economic growth' (Jenkins 2011: 50).

More broadly still, India's SEZs represent for Jenkins 'a third generation of economic reforms' (ibid.), following efforts to liberalize the macro-policy environment and to create institutions to regulate a market economy. They also signal that economic reform in India is a work in progress. The crisis of 1990–1 might have triggered pro-market economic reforms in India, but their continuation has to be explained with reference to a broad raft of factors. Committed leadership, stealth, modest pacing, high net benefits for many among India's elites, and provincial Darwinism, are simply the most significant among them, alongside the growing self-confidence of India's leading business houses.

6.5   Conclusion: Making Sense of the State

Jenkins's work on provincial Darwinism needs to be tempered in one respect. His model of jurisdictional competition suggests that the political costs for state elites of not embracing reform are so high that pro-reform agendas must spread ineluctably across India. The evidence for this thesis is fairly compelling, not least when we consider recent shifts in this direction in West Bengal (already mentioned) and in Bihar under Nitish Kumar. It is worth recalling, even so, that Lalu Prasad Yadav was able to get himself (or his wife) re-elected as Chief Minister of Bihar on more than one occasion without making the slightest effort to improve the investment climate in his state. Lalu's vote-banks came from the Yadavs, the Kurmis and the Koeris, all of whom he rewarded handsomely with state funds, and the Muslims, whom he rewarded with effective government protection against organized Hindu violence (Nambisan 2000). More worryingly, perhaps, the failure of Lalu Yadav's governments to invest in basic infrastructure and local state competency helped to create a power vacuum that was filled by Maoist forces, as has been the case elsewhere in eastern India (Corbridge 2011). Their presence in turn has made inward investment into states like Jharkhand and Chhattisgarh extremely difficult, notwithstanding the Darwinian pressures that Jenkins describes. The slow leaching away from these states of an indigenous middle class has made eastern India less attractive to business interests. It has also weakened the very constituency that can be expected to speak most loudly for economic reform.

It is possible that Bihar has turned a corner under Nitish Kumar. The economy of Bihar reportedly grew at over 10 per cent per annum in the last two or three years of the 2000s, and there is growing evidence that middle class and professional Biharis – including doctors and business people – are now returning to a state where the law and order situation has improved in several key districts. Unhappily, this is not yet the case in Jharkhand or elsewhere in India's 'red corridor', including in some parts of Uttar Pradesh. Whatever economic and political pressures there might be for capital to flow to these regions, they are more than offset by the pressures of a low-level civil war and a rapidly degrading infrastructure. Ironically, too, when capital does reach this part of India it often takes hold under the sign of a different form of secessionism: that of the SEZ. Jenkins insists that India's SEZs 'represent a desire by both political elites and those who aspire to middle-class status to, in a sense, secede from the rest of India – that is, to escape the consequences of India's recent "democratic upsurge"'(Jenkins 2011: 64). Because their construction very often involves accumulation by dispossession, however, India's mining compounds and SEZs threaten to bring economic reforms into the terrain of mass politics, as was clearly seen at Nandigram. As Jenkins puts it, 'in implementing the SEZ policy, India's policy-making establishment seems to have run up against the limits of what can be achieved by practicing "reform by stealth"' (ibid.).

If this is the case, the progress of economic reform in India going forward is likely to be more contentious than it has been so far. (The Maoist insurgency alone will ensure that this is so: see chapter 10.) At the same time, the fact that 600 SEZs are already on the books points up both a remarkable deepening of the reform process and the continuing effectiveness of government in edging it forward. Indeed, if we attempt to read the post-1991 (or 1980) reform process as a guide to politics in India, three significant conclusions emerge.

First, it is not obvious that three dominant proprietary classes, or a broader distributional coalition, were ever fully able to bend the political process in India to their will (see also Pedersen 2000; Shastri 1997). In a sense, this takes us back to the path-dependency arguments we discussed in chapter 1. We said there that strong path-dependency arguments rarely gain much traction in South Asia, and similar difficulties are evident as soon as we think about state–society relations in India. It would be a nonsense to imagine that Nehru's developmental ambitions post-1950 were not blown off course by big business houses, the salariat and well-to-do farmers. But it is probably also true that the capacity of the state in India to command society was stronger in the Nehru-Mahalanobis years than at any time since, the Emergency years excepted. What the post-1991 reforms have just as clearly shown us, however, is that the seemingly immovable interests of India's winning distributional coalition(s) are more plastic than was previously thought. A long and continuing process of pro-business and pro-market economic reforms has been edged forward by the state in India in part because some things had to change (cf. the crisis of 1990–1), but mainly because a new political leadership was able to make deals with its supposed bosses in big business, the bureaucracy and the countryside. India's ruling political elites have shown great skill in proposing reforms that allowed India's emerging economic elites to take advantage of new opportunities to accumulate wealth. More obstructive business groupings were quickly sidelined in the 1990s. At the same time, India's rulers have taken care not to provoke confrontations where confrontations can easily be avoided – something that might now be changing, as Jenkins indicates. What Pranab Bardhan (2009) calls 'India's tortuous transition' can, of course, be read as a sign of state weakness; in our judgement, however, the slow speed of the reform process in India is a very significant reason for it being so cumulatively audacious.

Second, while stealth, backhanded deals and carefully calibrated reform payoffs all speak to the very skilled nature of India's ruling political classes, this isn't to say that we should think about politics in India entirely in terms of plural interest groups and multiple bargains. Economic reform in India initially exposed some conflicts of interest among India's big business houses (Kochanek 1996; Sinha 2005b). The Birlas, for example, and some other well-established family firms, seemed to drag their feet in the early years, at least when compared with the Tata Group or Reliance. But things changed fairly rapidly in the mid-1990s and since then leading business groups have been the major winners from the ongoing process of reform. In this particular sense, then, economic reform in India has displayed the qualities of an elite revolt (Corbridge and Harriss 2000: chapters 6 and 7), albeit this was a revolt against a form of economic management that had provided substantial benefits to corporate India before – as well as after – the process of liberal reform. Put another way, the ongoing process of pro-market reform in India has been designed so as not to prompt significant opposition at any one time from more than a small fraction of India's ruling elites. Great care has been taken to ensure that few of their members lose out because of the reform process or are uncompensated for their losses by new sources of income (or rent). One major consequence of this 'audacious conservatism' is that the state in India has become increasingly dominated over the past two decades by corporate capital, or what Bardhan calls 'the corrupt grip of the corporate oligarchy in Indian political life' (2009: 32). Kochanek provides a very early indication of this tightening grip – corrupt or otherwise – when he notes that the 1993–4 budget was referred to by the Revenue Secretary of the Government of India as the 'Tarun Das Budget' – Tarun Das being the dynamic Secretary-General of the CII (Kochanek 1995–6: 547). Bluntly put, the intermediate regime has become less intermediate.

Third, when it comes to questions of government responsiveness and accountability in India today, we need to tread carefully when reading the lessons of the reform years. Government in India is ever more responsive to the needs of big business, both at the centre and in the states. The processes of provincial Darwinism described by Jenkins are one reason why this should be so; another, increasingly, is the presence within government of business leaders who want to get to grips with the 'over-politicization' of public life in India by remaking government in the image of capital. (Some of these same business leaders also want government to be anything but transparent and accountable when it is required to turn a blind eye to unenforced labour laws or illegal real-estate deals.) When it comes to those people who inhabit the worlds of mass politics, however, it is not at all clear that government has become more responsive to their needs. We have considered this argument at some length in Part I of *India Today*: for example, we discussed the ways in which the years of economic reform in India have not reduced income or non-income measures of poverty by anything like as much as standard theory has been predicting. We observe now that these outcomes are consistent with an account of audacious reform in India that highlights its distinctly binary qualities and effects: those evident in the world of elite politics and those evident in the world of mass politics.

It remains to be seen whether the next phase of economic reform in India will blur the boundary between elite and mass politics, and will as a consequence stir up significant battles over land rights, labour laws and the future of agriculture. This seems likely to us, and it is more likely to the extent that government fails to compensate potential losers with new income streams or assets. Governments in India have proven themselves to be far more capable and responsive than was indicated in many of the studies of democracy and discontent that were published at the end of the 1980s or in the early 1990s – but this has mainly entailed a responsiveness to elite interests. How responsive government has become to the interests of ordinary Indians is the subject of chapter 8. Before that, in chapter 7, we discuss a prior question: whether and how effectively democracy works in India as a substantive (and not just formal) means of holding public officials to account in accordance with the wishes of the people.

7

Has India's Democracy Been a Success?

7.1 Introduction

The last quarter of the twentieth century witnessed a remarkable shift from authoritarian to democratic rule across the world, and recent events in Libya, Tunisia and Egypt appear to point to a new wave of democratization. Many post-colonial political regimes now exhibit the hallmarks of formal democracy: regular fair elections, universal suffrage and freedom of expression. But not all democracies have survived, and many formal democracies have not seen shifts towards substantive democracy, defined in terms of broad-based participation, inclusive social policy and a positive feeling of involvement in politics among the masses.

India – the world's largest democracy – provides a fascinating example of the marked, albeit partial, success of democratization in the global South. In comparison with its neighbours, Pakistan and Sri Lanka, democracy in India has been a notable success. The Indian Constitution was enacted in January 1950. It established India as a sovereign democratic republic. Building on Western traditions of liberal democracy, the Constitution specified the structures, procedures and duties of government. It defined the 'fundamental rights' of all citizens, including equality before the law, freedom of speech and association, personal liberty, and protection against exploitation. The 'directive principles of state policy' in the Constitution – as we explained in chapter 5 – pressed the new state to promote people's welfare and uphold a range of entitlements, such as the right to work, the right to an adequate means of livelihood, legal aid, and free and compulsory education. The Constitution also contained measures to ensure that quotas within government educational institutions and public-sector employment would be reserved for

India's 'Scheduled Castes' (SCs – those formerly termed 'untouchable') and 'Scheduled Tribes' (STs): castes and communities thought to have suffered historically from discrimination and that had been listed on government schedules in the 1930s.

This chapter examines the capacity of the post-colonial Indian state to make good on the promise of democracy contained with the Constitution. We consider first formal democracy and then the more complicated question of India's success in terms of promoting substantive democratization.

7.2   Is India's Formal Democracy a Success?

It is commonly held that for a country to effect a transition to democracy, specific conditions must exist (Lipset 1994: 6; see also Linz and Stepan 1996; Przeworski et al. 1996). Scholars frequently argue that democracy requires a culture of equality, high levels of public education, strong well-organized political parties and a vibrant civil society. Linz and Stepan (1996) add to this list of prerequisites a need for a strong bureaucracy, a political society that is autonomous of dominant groups and an 'institutionalized economic society': norms, institutions and regulations that mediate between the state and market.

Political scientists also argue that democracy tends only to thrive in countries that are capitalist, wealthy and growing economically (Lipset 1994; Przeworski et al. 1996). For example, Przeworski et al. (1996: 50) draw on comparative survey data to suggest that a country must maintain an annual economic growth rate of at least 5 per cent in order to consolidate itself as a democracy. A robust capitalist economy discourages distributional conflict. It also reduces the importance of the state as an economic resource and therefore discourages power holders from trying to monopolize government positions. In addition, a sound economy decreases the possibility that those in power will illegally retain office when voted out by an electorate. Capitalist growth may lead to the emergence of a working class, which can demand an expansion of rights and democratic freedoms (Lipset 1994: 3).

India lacked most of the presumed prerequisites for democratic transition and consolidation. In 1947 it was a poor, mainly agricultural country. The economic growth rate was well below 5 per cent through the 1950s and 1960s. In the social and political realm, India did not possess the culture of equality and inclusive civil society held to be necessary for democracy. The colonial power made no effort to educate the mass of the population in India, and colonialists systematically reinforced caste and class inequalities (Dirks 2001). But India possessed some features that would facilitate democratic deepening. The nationalist movement in India had fostered some sense of 'unity in diversity' and a commitment to adult franchise (Sarkar 2001). The role of the Indian National Congress in the anti-colonial struggle in India bestowed upon the Congress Party popularity and legitimacy. The Muslim League, on the other hand, the dominant political party in Pakistan in 1947, was not nearly as well integrated into wider society as was the Congress. Moreover, the Congress Party was fairly socially heterogeneous in terms of region, language and caste, as compared to Pakistan where there was tension between a Punjabi-dominated army and administration, on the one hand, and a majority population of Bengalis, on the other. The differences, then, between their leading political parties substantially explain the contrasting political trajectories of India and Pakistan (Adeney and Wyatt 2004; Oldenburg 2010).

The British also helped in some ways to prepare the ground for democratic consolidation. While neglecting to prepare the mass of the population for democracy, the British bequeathed a system of representative government on India that emphasized legal equality, civil rights and a judiciary independent of the executive (see Washbrook 1988; Sarkar 1996). David Washbrook (1988: 37–9) argues that the British also established a regime of colonial rule that served as a foundation for the strengthening of formal democracy. The British placed power in the hands of a small coterie of rich leaders at the centre, while buying off local bigwigs. In this system, elected 'native' boards, comprised mainly of powerful sections of society, were responsible for multiple aspects of governance. Local elites, for example, rich peasants in the countryside, became key intermediaries in patronage networks extending down to the local level.

This patronage system assumed a new form under the Congress Party, which ruled India between 1950 and 1967. During the 1950s and 1960s, dominant castes at the local level, mainly upper or middle castes, acted as brokers or bosses for the Congress Party. They transferred money up through the organization to politicians and cultivated clients at the village level through the offer of posts, contracts and access to public resources (Bailey 1957, 1963; Brass 1965; see Corbridge and Harriss 2000: 49ff.). This patronage system effectively suppressed popular dissent. Relatively untroubled by threats to its power, the Congress was able to concentrate on consolidating formal democracy.

Linz and Stepan (1996) emphasize the deleterious effects on democratic consolidation associated with elite dominance of political institutions. In India's case, however, a fairly benign and committed leadership used an elite-led patronage system to strengthen democratic institutions. Among

Nehru's key achievements in the arena of democracy were his ability to see through the enactment of the Constitution, establish a civil service on the foundations of the British model (Potter 1986), and ensure that elections were held regularly and to a large extent fairly during his term in office. In Pakistan, meanwhile, it was not until 1956 that a Constitution was enacted.

The success of India's formal democracy since Independence is reflected in four key spheres. First, the country's principal democratic institutions have been strengthened. India's new Indian Administrative Services (IAS), which was constructed along British lines, contributed to effective government and political stability during much of the post-colonial period (Potter 1986). India's Supreme Court also played a constructive role. It guaranteed people's right to basic needs, encouraged public interest litigation and assisted victims of state lawlessness (Rudolph and Rudolph 2001; Mooij 2011). The Supreme Court has sometimes assumed responsibility for matters outside its remit, such as the setting of school fees, and there is rightly concern over such abrogation of power (Mehta 2007; see chapter 5 of this volume). But this should not detract from the part that the Supreme Court has played in democratic consolidation. The Election Commission in India has been another guarantor of India's democratic strength, especially in the 1990s, when election commissioner T. N. Seshan significantly tightened oversight of elections.

Clouding this picture of democratic institutional strength is the problem of intra-party democracy. Political dynasties have become prevalent within major parties, and the procedures through which individuals are promoted within parties, appointed to vacant seats and chosen as candidates for elections are mired in corruption, secrecy and cronyism (see Sridaran 1999). The dominance of entrenched interests prevents newly mobilized groups and dissenting voices from acquiring power within parties. This is a pressing issue, but it should not detract too much from the general argument that India's main democratic institutions are robust.

A second sphere in which the strength of Indian democracy has been apparent is with respect to human rights, though it is true that the Indian state's ability to uphold human rights has come under considerable strain (e.g., Drèze and Sen 2002). A major problem has been that of Hindu majoritaranism. At the national level, and in several states, Hindu right-wing political parties and organizations have been able to usurp people's citizenship rights by seizing the reins of power and justifying unconstitutional action on the ground that they act on behalf of 'the people'. The anti-Sikh pogrom in Delhi in 1984 and the anti-Muslim pogrom in Gujarat in 2002 are two of the most obvious instances of aggression, and these and other incidents have created widespread minority anxiety and resistance.

The Indian state's capacity to sanction the abuse of human rights takes other forms, too. In its efforts to suppress secessionist movements, especially in Kashmir and the North East, the Indian government has resorted to draconian legislation, justified often in the name of national security. Such an approach has then come to influence state operations in other parts of India, as evident in the enactment of the Prevention of Terrorism Activities Act (POTA) in March 2002. This law permitted detention of a suspect for up to 180 days without the filing of charges in court. It also allowed law enforcement agencies to withhold the identities of witnesses and to treat confessions made to the police, which are commonly made under duress, as an admission of guilt. Other worrying dimensions of the Indian state's abuse of citizenship rights are the government's tendency to deploy paramilitary units to control the public (see chapter 10), extra-judicial police assassinations of suspected criminals (see Jalal 1995) and the militarization of India's borders (Jones 2009).

But against such observations of the state's abuse of human rights must be placed other evidence. Indian citizens often mobilize to guarantee their rights. In 1975, Indira Gandhi imposed a Political Emergency, elections were suspended, political and civil organizations were disbanded, and the media was gagged. These moves generated widespread popular resentment, which, in turn, contributed to Mrs Gandhi's losing national elections in 1977. Also indicative of Indian public intolerance of state coercion was popular opposition to POTA, which the government was forced to repeal in 2004.

Rights-based public activism has become marked over the past decade, as especially evident in the launch, in 2001, of the Right to Food Campaign that we discuss in chapter 5. Campaigners focused on employment as well as food, and they were important, as we explained, in the emergence of the National Rural Employment Guarantee Scheme. Other rights-based campaigns have concentrated on children and education (see chapters 5 and 14), urban land use, and corruption (see chapter 11).

Third, popular involvement in democratic politics is evident in the sphere of elections. Table 7.1 points to rising participation in central government (Lok Sabha) elections between 1957 and 1998. State-level data typically point in similar directions (see Yadav 1999; Yadav and Palshikar 2009).

There is also evidence that elections have become fairer (Robinson 1988; Singh; 1992; Wilkinson 2007). Marguerite Robinson (1988), in a study carried out between 1952 and 1977 in a village in rural Andhra Pradesh, found that a former system of elite-controlled 'vote-bank'

Table 7.1: Turnout in Lok Sabha Elections, 1957–1998

Year	Women (per cent turnout)	Men (per cent turnout)	Rural (per cent turnout)	Urban (per cent turnout)
1957	38.8	55.7	n/a	n/a
1967	49.0	61.0	n/a	n/a
1977	54.9	65.4	60.3	62.1
1989	57.5	66.4	62.6	60.0
1998	61.0	65.9	63.0	56.7

Source: Centre for Developing Societies survey, adapted from Yadav (1999: 2398).

politics collapsed in the 1970s. Jagpal Singh (1992) and Jan Breman (1993) note similar declines in vote-bank politics in western Uttar Pradesh and Gujarat, respectively. In a rather different vein, Steven Wilkinson (2007: 35) argues that the central government in India became increasingly unwilling to rig elections in politically sensitive regions during the 1990s and early 2000s.

It is not only that people participate in elections, but they also invest powerful meanings in the act of voting. This point comes across in the comparative nationwide study headed by Mukulika Banerjee on the 2004 elections in India. Banerjee and her team collected stories about how people vote, what they feel about the act of casting their ballot and what elections mean to them more broadly. They uncovered people's deep attachment to the practice of voting in widely varying parts of India. From poor women in central India to male landless labourers in the south, to frustrated youth in the sensitive north-eastern areas of India, there was a consensus that voting was a citizenship 'right', and constitutive of one's individuality and humanity. The contrast here with Pakistan is notable: Pakistanis have never had the opportunity to vote a government out of office (Adeney and Wyatt 2004).

There have also been moves in the past twenty years to extend the reach of representative government in local areas. In 1992, the passing of the 73rd Amendment Acts increased both the power and representativeness of local government in India. The Act implemented a three-tier system of local government in all states of India with populations of over 2 million people. Under this new system, *panchayat* councils would play a central role in the provision of public services, the creation and maintenance of public goods, and the planning and implementation of development activities. The Act stipulated that *panchayat* elections should be held every five years and provided a periodic 33 per cent reservation of *panchayat* seats for women, STs and SCs. Summarizing studies over the 1990s, Drèze and Sen (2002) argue that *panchayat* elections have tended to elicit keen public interest, and voter turnout has been high.

The increasing fairness of elections, people's investment in the act of voting, and the decentralization of representative government are dynamics intimately linked to a fourth key strength of India's democracy: the emergence since the 1960s of a genuinely competitive multi-party system. It is convenient to divide the history of Independent Indian politics into three periods: 1950–67, 1967–90, and 1991–present. The first period is one of Congress hegemony. Between 1950 and 1967, the Congress Party dominated Indian politics, winning the national elections of 1952, 1957 and 1962. A second phase of Indian politics (1967–90) was associated with the rise of political parties expressing regional demands, socialist parties such as the Communist Party of India (Marxist), and organizations, parties and movements representing specific sectional interests, for example, those led by prosperous farmers in Uttar Pradesh (UP). The Congress Party continued to be successful in central government elections. But it faced important challenges from other parties: Congress was out of power between 1977 and 1980, when the Janata Party exploited public discontent with Indira Gandhi, and in 1989, when a Janata Dal-led National Front coalition in alliance with the Left Front coalition won the elections.

Indira Gandhi responded to the more competitive democratic environment by moving away from the former Congress strategy of ruling through district and local party organizations. She also delinked State Assembly and Lok Sabha (central government) elections, which increased the frequency of elections that took place in India. Alongside these changes came a populist approach to politics. Indira emphasized direct links between her and the populace, for example, by promising to 'banish poverty' (*garibi hatao*), a populist strategy memorably satirized by Rohinton Mistry (1995) in his novel *A Fine Balance*.

A final period of Indian politics, beginning in 1990, has been associated with the rise of low-caste political parties and Hindu nationalist political organizations. The parties most successful in challenging the Congress in the 1970s and 1980s tended to be ones that represented middling sections of Indian society rather than those at the base of caste and class hierarchies. But in the early 1990s in India, a more profound democratization of electoral politics occurred, what Yadav (1996) terms a 'second democratic upsurge' (to distinguish it from the first upsurge, beginning around 1967). In the late 1970s, the ruling Janata Party had investigated strategies for extending positive discrimination to 'Other Backward Classes' (OBCs): castes above the SCs and STs in the Hindu caste hierarchy but nevertheless suffering from social and economic deprivation. The resulting Mandal Commission Report, published in

1980, outlined a programme for reserving seats in educational institutions and government bureaucracies for OBCs. In August 1990, Prime Minister V. P. Singh found it expedient to act on the Mandal Commission's recommendations. V. P. Singh's move had the effect of reorganizing political coalitions: strong and assertive regional blocs of OBC voters emerged (see chapter 12).

The rise of OBC politics was intertwined with two other notable forms of democratic expression that emerged in the early 1990s. First, there was an upsurge of politics among Dalits. The rise of Dalits was especially obvious in India's most politically influential state of Uttar Pradesh, where the pro-Dalit Bahujan Samaj Party (BSP) formed coalition governments in 1993, 1995, 1997 and 2002, and won a landslide victory in the state elections in 2007. Mayawati, a Dalit woman and former schoolteacher, has led the BSP since 1995. A second and more reactionary form of democratic expression, relating in complicated ways to both the rise of OBC and Dalit politics, was the emergence of the BJP and associated social and political mobilization among organizations representing the Hindu right. The forces of Hindutva sponsored a series of high-profile political campaigns in the 1990s, and the BJP held power at the centre between 1999 and 2004 (see chapter 9).

In sum, India's consolidation as a democracy has occurred in several spheres: via formal institutions such as the Election Commission, by means of increased public action in the sphere of rights, through the electoral process and by way of increased participation of low-caste groups in competitive politics. In each sphere, there are reasons to enter qualifications and caveats. It is important to highlight human rights abuses in Kashmir and against minorities, the problem of intra-party democracy and the unconstitutional role now being played by the Supreme Court in some aspects of governance. But India's achievements remain impressive.

Formal democracy has had further positive implications for the Indian population. Five key points stand out. First, democracy has played a role in guaranteeing the territorial integrity of the Indian nation. India's competitive democratic system has enabled regional forces to press demands while allowing the centre to remain in its position of overall authority. That several regions have been able to campaign successfully for status as separate states within the Indian federation is indicative of this point.

Second, formal democracy has had a positive effect on people's freedom from organized violence. Steven Wilkinson (2007) has argued that political competition, especially the intensification of competition in India since the early 1990s, acts on the whole to discourage political parties from alienating minorities. He gives the example of the state governments in Maharashtra and Uttar Pradesh, which were quick to prevent attacks on the city of Mumbai from sparking off wider communal conflict in 2006, 'because they recognized the electoral damage that communal violence could cause in terms of alienating Muslim votes and fragmented support from Hindus' (2007: 36). More broadly, the state's commitment to secularism and human rights has militated against widespread overt state oppression of the type that has occurred in Sri Lanka.

Third, democracy has precipitated a vibrant, noisy and diverse media. The state has little influence over the media in India, and the opening up of formal democracy has intersected with the growth of new forms of democratic expression. In a notable study, Manuel (1993) discusses how the increasing availability of the portable cassette player enhanced opportunities for political dissent in India in the 1970s. More recently, Assa Doron (2010) has traced how the success of the BSP in Uttar Pradesh was closely related to activists' use of mobile phones. Dia Da Costa (2010) has examined increasing democratization through the lens of political theatre in eastern India. Ranjani Mazumdar (2007) offers a parallel account of cinema, discussing the representation and production of democratic practice in Bollywood films.

Fourth, formal democracy has generated multiple forms of social mobilization and organization, from campaigns against corruption (Jenkins and Goetz 1999), to environmental movements around big dams (Baviskar and Sundar 2008), to movements against child and bonded labour (Weiner 1991). A number of scholars are now focusing on the growing role played by NGOs in India – grassroots non-profit organizations and international organizations – in processes of social development (e.g., Kamat 2002; Mehta 2007; Lerche 2008). For Mehta (2007), these organizations represent a type of 'post-democracy', since they are unaccountable to the people they serve. NGOs, especially proselytizing organizations, may be divisive or else depoliticize society (see Lerche 2008). But there is also good evidence that some NGOs, collaborating in particular ways with state agencies, can foster inclusive social development (Appadurai 2002; Manor 2010b; see also discussion in chapter 11 of this volume).

Fifth, democracy may have been important in preventing famine in India. In authoritarian China, a series of famines killed between 23 and 30 million people in 1958–61. Drèze and Sen argue that the famines could not have occurred in India because the Indian government would have been compelled to answer questions from opposition parties, the media and the public at large. Drèze and Sen also argue that many of the coercive measures introduced by the Chinese government since the early 1960s, including the One Child Policy, would not have been tolerated in democratic India. Whatever the flaws in India's democracy, there are important reasons for stressing the value of formal democracy over authoritarian rule.

7.3   Substantive Democratization?

1947–1990

Substantive democracy is conventionally imagined to require three elements (cf. Huber et al. 1997). First, individuals should be able to participate in political life in a meaningful way, for example, by being able to play fulfilling roles on local government councils or petition authorities for help through reference to their rights. Where they feel aggrieved, citizens should be able to complain and see their complaints heeded. Second, a country is a substantive democracy where social inequalities that impede political participation are addressed and where social policy is broadly inclusive and progressive. If people lack food, shelter and education, or depend on powerful brokers for basic needs, effective political participation is unlikely. Third, a positive feeling of involvement in democratic and political life is a prerequisite of substantive democracy.

For heuristic purposes, it is useful to consider the success of the Indian government in promoting substantive democratization with reference to two periods: 1947–90, and the early 1990s to the present. In the first period, the state's record in generating participatory, inclusive democracy is unimpressive. During the 1950s and 1960s, the Congress Party enhanced the power of the already dominant middle and upper castes in local arenas. Elites were able to control the votes of the poor (Shukla 1992; Singh 1992; Lerche 1995, 1999). Dominant castes could also manipulate policy directives to prevent the implementation of radical measures, such as land reform and agricultural taxation.

The Congress system of 'patronage democracy' also limited opportunities for the poor to complain about government services or become involved in politics at the local level. Frederick Bailey's research in Orissa (1963) and Anthony Carter's (1974) account of elite politics in Maharashtra showed that locally dominant intermediaries often blocked lines of communication between senior political figures and the masses in the 1950s and 1960s. The lowest tier of government, the local, village-level councils (*panchayats*), also tended to be controlled by Congress bigwigs. The poor had strong reasons to avoid becoming involved in democratic politics. The patron–client system was systemically corrupt and crime-ridden. Those attempting to reform it at the local level would face censure and reprisals. Moreover, even those who entered the fray would have required money to acquire posts. A certain level of 'corruption' was a prerequisite for obtaining local power.

These problems of democratic participation were exacerbated by ordinary people's illiteracy and, perhaps also, their lack of basic understanding about democracy and citizenship. According to Sudipta Kaviraj

(1991), most Indians in 1947 did not understand the principles of impersonal government enshrined in the Constitution because they believed primarily in other ideas of authority, for example, based around family and caste. Kaviraj suggests that the poor lacked not only the institutional strength required to influence government practice, but also the sense of citizenship rights that is a necessary foundation for democratic protest (see also Chatterjee 2004; and chapter 11 of this volume).

The decline of the Congress Party dominance in the late 1960s created some new opportunities for upper sections of the OBCs and middle castes to participate in politics (see Robinson 1988; Breman 1993; Corbridge and Harriss 2000). There is considerable evidence that this first democratic upsurge generated a novel sense of entitlement (cf. Kaviraj 1991), and maybe in some areas of India a new belief in the capacity of democracy to deliver on its promises. There was a slight relaxation in patron–client relations in many areas, as a result of social measures introduced by Indira Gandhi alongside a broader improvement in off-farm employment opportunities for labourers (see Robinson 1988; Breman 1993; Lerche 1999). In addition, Indira Gandhi's populist rhetoric served to politicize the issue of poverty, putting the question of economic inequality on to the agenda (Kohli 2001).

But Indira Gandhi's shift to dismantle the Congress Party and opt for populist messages was also associated with costs from the point of view of grassroots democratization. Indira Gandhi's decision to delink Lok Sabha elections and Assembly elections, and the general increase in electoral volatility, encouraged a type of narrow gamesmanship among political leaders (Rudolph and Rudolph 1987). A system took root – Rudolph and Rudolph (1987) call it 'demand politics' – in which parties made promises to selected sections of the electorate in return for votes. The political scientist Kanchan Chandra (2004) has analysed this process in considerable depth. She makes the persuasive argument that both political leaders and people on the ground lack the ability to be able to identify specific class or sectional interests. In general, politicians in India do not appeal to 'the middle classes', as they do in the USA, or 'working classes', as is common in some parts of Europe, because these social categories have little meaning on the ground. Instead, political parties use caste as a type of signal for mobilizing votes. For example, villagers voting for a Jat politician would expect the elected official to subsequently enact pro-Jat policies and channel resources to the Jats and castes of a similar standing.

From the perspective of politicking at the regional and local levels, the 1970s and 1980s were associated with the further criminalization and debasement of democratic practice in most parts of India. One type of corrupt politics – organized patronage systems orchestrated by the Congress Party – was replaced by another variation of this system, wherein politicians lavished support on key voters, which they recouped after victory through tapping state bureaucracies and black markets for funds. Elections are expensive in India. Politicians need to recover the money they spend getting elected, and they do so through pressing top officials in different government bureaucracies to collect illegal 'side incomes'. These senior state functionaries make money by exerting pressure, in turn, on subordinates within government bureaucracies, who accumulate money through a range of corrupt dealings, for example, by charging the public for services that are officially free. This system exists not only for many public bureaucracies, such as irrigation (see Wade 1985, 1988), but also within the police. The police acquire illegal incomes through bribes, extortion and payoffs. Some of this they keep themselves and the rest is passed on upwards through the police system, via IAS officers, to senior politicians (see Jeffrey 2000, 2001). Such corruption has doubly negative implications for the poor, compelling them to pay money for services that should be free and increasing their exposure to theft and violence.

Alongside growing bureaucratic corruption and police malfeasance, routine access to justice became increasingly difficult for ordinary people in India in the 1970s and 1980s. During this period, India's federal judicial system developed a huge backlog of cases. Thousands of prisoners were left in limbo awaiting trial, and the average time it took to get a judgment increased dramatically. Drèze and Sen (2002) note that 30 million people had pending legal cases in India in 2000, and 250,000 prisoners were awaiting trial. In the early 1990s, Atul Kohli (1990) warned that intensified political competition in India and attendant forms of corruption and state inefficiency had created a 'crisis of governability' in many states (see also Bonner 1990).

In sum, India did not experience rapid substantive democratization in the period between 1947 and 1990, if we define substantive democracy in terms of broad-based participation in everyday local politics, ordinary citizens' capacity to complain to local bureaucracies and the democratic distribution of resources. There was a complex geography to this general picture, since the nature of people's participation in politics varied between states (see Kohli 1990; Harriss 2003b) and more locally (e.g., Corbridge et al. 2005). Reflecting its distinctive history, the state of Kerala, in particular, bucked the national trend (Heller 2009). In Kerala, the struggle against British rule took the form of a broad-based lower-class movement. In the post-colonial period, the communist state government built on this legacy, mobilizing against upper castes (Heller 2000: 234). The degree and scope of public legality, integration of subordinate groups into public politics, effective mobilization, and large networks of cooperative societies all marked Kerala out from other states of India in the period between 1947 and 1990, throwing India's general 'crisis of governmentality' into stark relief.

1990–present

Geography is also important in order to understand the relationship between changes in the nature of formal democracy – for example, the rise of low-caste political parties – and substantive democratization in India since 1990. A comparison of Uttar Pradesh, Tamil Nadu and Madhya Pradesh is especially fruitful.

The rise of low-caste politics has been especially dramatic in Uttar Pradesh, and there are some reasons for optimism with respect to the question of substantive democracy in this State. Under Mayawati, the BSP tried to raise the political, economic and social standing of Dalits, especially members of the Chamar caste. The BSP transferred Dalits into key positions within government and improved Dalits' access to reserved positions in government training and professional courses (Duncan 1997, 1999; Frøystad 2005: 230). Mayawati also tried to create a 'climate of fear' among government bureaucrats through implementing a measure that made discrimination against Dalits punishable with imprisonment (Jaffrelot 2003). She extended efforts to target development resources towards villages with large Dalit populations, especially via an 'Ambedkar Village Scheme' (see Pai 2002). In addition, Mayawati embarked on an ambitious symbolic programme, establishing parks, statues and libraries dedicated to Dr Bhim Rao Ambedkar and other Dalit heroes.

The BSP improved Dalits' access to development schemes, at least during the 1990s (Pai 2002). It has also raised the confidence of Dalits in Uttar Pradesh (Pai 2002; Jeffrey et al. 2008; Jaoul 2010). Sudha Pai (2002) notes the rise in the 1990s and early 2000s of a new generation of educated Dalit young men who questioned established relationships of dominance in rural western Uttar Pradesh, especially through celebrating Dalit pride and the possibility of social improvement via education. Pai also emphasizes the practical importance of these men, who represented Dalit interests within local government *panchayats*, acted as intermediaries between their community and the state, and organized social mobilization (see also Jaoul 2009).

The rise of the BSP – and of its competitor, the Samajwadi Party, which represents OBCs in Uttar Pradesh – has also been accompanied by an influx into the formal electoral realm of new beliefs not shaped by the high ideology of Western-style liberal democracy (see Alam 2004; Michelutti 2007). For example, Lucia Michelutti (2007) describes how

Yadav leaders within the Samajwadi Party portrayed democracy as a distinctively 'Yadav' achievement – an 'ancient quality' passed down to the Yadav community from their ancestor-god Krishna. Such examples amount to what Michelutti terms the 'vernacularization of democracy'.

But substantive democratization in Uttar Pradesh has been partial at best. There remain widespread problems of bureaucratic inefficiency, corruption and maladministration that have generated a fiscal crisis at the state level and numerous difficulties for ordinary people in Uttar Pradesh, especially the poor, women, low castes and Muslims. Local government *panchayats* remain ineffective as instruments of mobilization and complaint. In many rural areas, men dominate women within these councils (Ciotti 2010), and higher castes exploit lower castes and Muslims (Lieten 1996; Lerche 1999). The judicial system in Uttar Pradesh is inefficient and mired by personal favouritism (Madsen 1998). Citizens often see little point in complaining to officials and have low levels of trust in formal accountability programs (Brass 1997; Jeffrey et al. 2008). Moreover, the criminalization of politics has deepened in the context of the rise of the BSP because of a general inflation in the competitiveness of politics and a continued increase in the financial rewards attached to office (see Brass 2011). The inability of the BSP to address the concerns of marginalized people in Uttar Pradesh has become more rather than less evident since its dramatic victory in 2007. Mayawati has de-emphasized Dalit empowerment, directing energies instead into cultivating a support based among upper castes and glorifying her own power. This shift in tactics, coming as it does on top of the BSP's already variable record in terms of ensuring broad-based participation and addressing social inequalities, is leading to considerable disquiet among Dalits. Dalits continue to vote for Mayawati, but the bulk of the Dalit population have little interest in political participation beyond the ballot box and a certain weary cynicism is taking hold (Jeffrey and Young, in press).

Noting the common failure of the democratic upsurge to seed widespread, equitable democratization in north India, Gail Omvedt (2003) advised commentators to 'look south', especially to Tamil Nadu. At first blush, Tamil Nadu appears to have been more successful in linking formal to substantive democratization. Tamil Nadu has a recent history of local Dalit mobilization. It also possesses a party with an ideological commitment to addressing caste-based social injustices. But Dalits in Tamil Nadu continue to face widespread discrimination and limited opportunities for mobility. They remain somewhat dependent on higher castes in many parts of the state (e.g., Anandhi et al. 2002; Gorringe 2010; Harriss et al. 2010).

Consideration of a Dalit political movement, the Dalit Panther Iyakkam (DPI), in Tamil Nadu provides a further basis for thinking about the gap between formal and substantive democracy. Hugo Gorringe (2010) notes the importance of the DPI in demanding rights, resources and power for Dalits in the 1990s. By mobilizing outside mainstream institutions and applying pressure on existing political parties, the DPI, as well as other Dalit movements, challenged higher-caste hegemony and spread new ideologies of equality and practical democracy. But Gorringe also notes the failure of the DPI and other Dalit social movements to press for better working conditions, fairer access to key services or comprehensive social support for the very poor. He also observes that many Dalits in Chidambaram district of Tamil Nadu lack access to food, secure dwellings and effective police assistance. In this context, many of the poor in the areas where Gorringe has worked argue that they have 'no democracy' (see Gorringe 2010).

The recent entry of the Dalit panthers into electoral politics has created further contradictions between formal and substantive democratization in Tamil Nadu. The DPI's new avatar – the Viduthalai Ciruthaigal Katchi (VCK) (Liberation Panther Party) – contested the 1999 Lok Sabha elections. In 2009, the VCK had one MP and one MLA (Wyatt 2009). The Dalit panthers have become much more prominent in the media since their entry into party politics. But the VCK has had to water down its radical agenda in the context of coalition politics, and there are currently numerous allegations that circulate regarding corruption and profiteering within the VCK. Dalit activists at the local level feel betrayed, and some are now turning to other parties (Gorringe 2010). Moreover, the Dalit movement in Tamil Nadu remains divided by caste: Paraiyars, Pallars and Chakkiliyars mobilize along distinct lines.

There are important differences between politics in Tamil Nadu and Uttar Pradesh. The Dalit panthers in Tamil Nadu, to a greater extent than the BSP in Uttar Pradesh, have a strong party and movement-based organizational structure that can act as a check on political leaders. On the other hand, the VCK – and other parties in Tamil Nadu representing low castes – is not as electorally strong as its north Indian counterpart. There are also similarities between Uttar Pradesh and Tamil Nadu, however. In both states, as in many regions of India (Mosse 2010), the 'second democratic upsurge' of Dalits within electoral politics has to a considerable extent deradicalized low-caste assertion and failed to generate sustained inclusive social policies. Dalits are drawn into alliances with higher castes that do not share their ideological drive. These coalitions then prove too feeble and fissiparous to address issues such as land redistribution or minimum wages. Low-caste party political leaders often respond by playing up questions of personality as a cover for a lack of action on issues that affect the poor (Currie 1998; see also Mosse 2010). In many instances, occupying power becomes an end in itself. Moreover, internal party organization is often weak or non-democratic; the BJP is probably a more disciplined party than either the BSP or VCK, and the Hindu right has arguably been better at coordinating between its electoral and movement-based wings (see chapter 9). In addition, low-caste political parties tend only to represent particular castes (*jatis*) among Dalits, and they enrol richer male Dalits to a greater extent than others. It is important to note that low-caste political parties have rarely found common cause with Muslims.

A rather different possibility for formal democracy to trigger substantive democratization emerges from Madhya Pradesh, where it is the Congress Party that has been most active in trying to foster poor people's empowerment. In Madhya Pradesh, in the 1970s and 1980s, the Congress tried to integrate the concerns of poor people, including Dalits, into its policies and functioning (Manor 2010b; Pai 2010). A further drive towards substantive democracy occurred with Digvijay Singh's assumption of the Chief Ministership in 1993. Singh increased funding to local-level *panchayats*, reformed how his party and the bureaucracy functioned, and introduced a successful Education Guarantee Scheme in 1997 (Manor 2010b). He also strengthened the accountability of government, through holding discussions with key civil servants about governance issues and by reaching out to downtrodden sections of society. This reform programme culminated in the 'Bhopal Conference' of January 2002, which focused on 'transforming India through a Dalit paradigm' and involved 250 academics, professionals and activists. The conference led, in turn, to a 'Bhopal Declaration' which outlined a programme for enhancing Dalits' control over economic and political processes.

James Manor (2010b) argues that this visible success of the Congress Party in Madhya Pradesh, in the period between 1993 and 2003, helped pave the way for the Congress Party's resurgence at the national level between 2004 and 2009 and thus for more progressive social policies at the centre. The Congress at the centre has tapped into the frustrations of the poor and lower middle class regarding the social distribution of the benefits of India's economic reforms, and its success in the 2004 Lok Sabha election campaign perhaps owed something to this fact. Between 2004 and 2009, the Congress mobilized lower classes fairly effectively (see Yadav and Palshikar 2009), having implemented some potentially far-reaching welfare policies, especially the National Rural Employment Guarantee (NREGS – see chapter 5). It also introduced the Right to Information (RTI) Act in 2005. This Act not only emphasized freedom of expression and addressed official censorship, in the US right to information tradition: it was also geared to improving government transparency and changing how bureaucracies work. RTI has been effective in curbing corruption within NREGS and the government's midday meals scheme in some parts of India (Jha 2009). The Congress should not take too much credit for these initiatives, which emerged out of prolonged public campaigns. But the recent success of the Congress provides some indication of a scaling-up of Madhya Pradesh's 1990s experience of democratization to the national level.

The extent to which Digvijay Singh and his Congress Party were able to foster grassroots democratization in Madhya Pradesh is open to question, however. Sudha Pai (2010) praises the Congress Party for recognizing a need to engage with Dalits and tribals in the state. But she claims that the Congress Party was only partly successful in empowering Dalits. Pai focuses on two of the major programmes that emerged out of the Dalit Agenda produced as part of the Bhopal Conference: a land distribution initiative and a project designed to ensure that companies source key services from Dalits, a scheme termed 'supplier diversity'. The land distribution for Dalits encountered strong resistance from local elites, who would lose out as a result of the reforms. Supplier diversity was more successful. But even this initiative was undermined by poor infrastructure, caste-based discrimination and corruption. While careful to acknowledge the increasing confidence of the poor in Madhya Pradesh, Pai concludes that the actual benefits to Dalits and tribals of Digvijay Singh's reforms were rather limited. Paralleling the situation in Uttar Pradesh and Tamil Nadu, dominant castes in Madhya Pradesh continued to obtain privileged access to the state at the local level, because they were better able to navigate corrupt networks, had superior access to channels of complaint, and could make more effective use of the disciplinary and judicial arms of the state. In Pai's view, Digvijay Singh's reforms lacked traction because he did not politicize marginalized communities or anticipate ground-level resistance. For example, the Bhopal Declaration was largely formulated by intellectuals from outside the state, showed a lack of understanding of the basic struggles in which Dalits are engaged, and offered nothing to dominant castes, who were always likely to oppose measures that trespassed on their privileges.

Madhya Pradesh therefore complements the Uttar Pradesh and Tamil Nadu cases. In the 1990s and 2000s, Uttar Pradesh and Tamil Nadu had powerful currents of grassroots mobilization. But the social movements that resulted in the formation of the BSP and VCK do not appear to have created parties capable of strong leadership on key issues affecting the poor. Madhya Pradesh had strong leadership. But it lacked a corresponding grassroots movement able to see through radical changes introduced by the government. In neither the instance of bottom-up assertion (Uttar Pradesh, Tamil Nadu) nor 'top-down' transformation (Madhya Pradesh) has formal political change been greatly effective in improving people's everyday capacity to participate equitably in politics and obtain vital resources.

7.4   Conclusions

India's democracy has been a success. Elections occur regularly, democratic institutions are strong, people are free to protest and civil rights are guaranteed. The media is lively and social movements are tolerated by the state. Formal democracy has also led to some substantive democratization. People have begun to participate more actively in forms of politics outside the ballot box. The masses feel more involved in politics and are articulating their own understanding of what democracy means. Broad-based rights movements have become a prominent feature of the political landscape. Read alongside the work of the doomsayers of the 1950s and 1960s – and studies of democracy's fragility in Latin America (Whitehead 2001) – India's achievements are remarkable. They are also noteworthy when compared with the political experiences of Pakistan and Sri Lanka (Adeney and Wyatt 2004).

Set against this picture must be the persistence of bureaucratic corruption, police harassment, an ineffective local and regional judiciary, and elite capture of local government councils. Some of the factors that allowed India to consolidate itself as a formal democracy – an expansive network of patronage founded on caste and class inequalities – are precisely those that impede substantive democratization. The result in most parts of contemporary India is a mismatch between the rising aspirations of the masses and real possibilities for transformation.

8

Is Government in India Becoming More Responsive?

8.1 Introduction

Government in India presents a number of striking paradoxes. India is – as we discussed in the last chapter – both the largest and one of the more robust parliamentary democracies in the world. Political participation, as given by such indicators as turnout rates in elections at different levels of government, compares favourably with those in most other democracies, and in some parts of the country at least, and, at some times, the turnout is inversely related to measures of socio-economic status (Alam 2004: chapter 2). This is to say that India is unique amongst parliamentary democracies in that poorer, more disadvantaged people often seem more likely to turn out to vote than their wealthier and more highly educated neighbours. Both state-level and national elections in India have more often than not been characterized by 'anti-incumbency' – incumbent governments have tended to be turfed out of office by voters, even if they have had a reasonable record of public service. Survey evidence shows that Indians generally still expect their state to supply solutions to common public problems, such as those of access to electricity and to water, to sanitation or to decent roads, to health care and to education (see Chandhoke 2005, citing data from a survey in Delhi). And yet the quality of service delivery, across the country, is very often abysmal. Studies show, for example, that although the country has a well-designed system of public health care, staffed by quite well-trained and technically competent personnel, which can provide care more cheaply than private medical practitioners, the public system is widely distrusted by people.

People, even very poor people, prefer to seek health care from private providers, even though (research shows) the private practitioners whom they seek out may be technically less competent than those in the public system, as well as costing more. An important part of the reason for this is the fact of very high levels of absenteeism that prevail amongst doctors and nurses, so that people cannot rely on local health centres being open when they should be, or on actually having access to a doctor when they go to higher-level primary health-care centres. Research has shown that absenteeism may be institutionalized, with health service managers actually conniving with junior staff to sanction and so to perpetuate absenteeism (Banerjee and Duflo 2009). How and why is it possible that voters should be ready to tolerate such failure? How is it possible that they should tolerate a public education system that fails to teach very large numbers of children to read even a very simple text, or to perform the most basic arithmetic, after several years of schooling (Banerjee et al. 2008)? Why are even poor people ready to pay for private schooling, rather than exercising their voice to demand a better public service (Jeffrey et al. 2008)? Why do voters apparently tolerate high levels of corruption in these and other public services, and on the part of their politicians – quite a high proportion of whom have criminal records? In the first part of this chapter, we review explanations for the often egregious failures of government in India. Why isn't government more responsive? Why is it that, as we showed in chapter 5, the drive for progressive social legislation has come through judicial activism rather than through a political process? Why is India experiencing 'the judicialization of politics'?

We then go on to consider what is now being done in the country to improve the quality of 'governance'. This is a term that has come to be used very widely, partly in recognition of the fact that the effective management of public affairs must often involve other actors as well as 'the government'. It began to be used in the 1990s, with recognition that development strategy must concern more than just the selection of appropriate policies. There was, and there remains, of course, fierce debate over whether or not the sorts of policies that have been urged by the international finance institutions – the so-called 'Washington Consensus' – are or are not appropriate (on which see Stiglitz 2002). What came gradually to be recognized, however, partly as a result of the failures of these policies, was that policy choice is only a part of the battle for development, and that the problems of implementation – 'how' questions, rather than 'what' questions – matter as much.

Historically, the presumption has been that policy decisions, made by the executive of the state, whether it has a democratic or an authoritarian regime, are implemented by the state's administrative arm, the bureaucracy. Bureaucracies (according to the ideal type defined by the great sociologist Max Weber) should be bound by transparent, impersonal rules, applied universally; they should keep records (in the 'bureau') and be accountable; they should have clear lines of authority (it should be clear exactly where 'the buck stops'), which means that they have a well-defined hierarchy of roles; and entry into them, and then promotion through the hierarchy, should depend upon ability. Recruitment and career paths should be determined, in other words, meritocratically. Some recent research has shown that those developing countries that have such meritocratically recruited bureaucracies do tend to have better records of performance (Rauch and Evans 2000). India, famously, has a higher-level bureaucracy that is quite fiercely meritocratic in terms of recruitment, and has many senior officials of exceptionally high calibre, but career paths in the civil service are much less clearly determined in the same way. And the recruitment of the very large numbers of lower-level civil servants is rarely meritocratic, being subject to a great deal of personal and political discretion (Chandra 2004: chapter 6; Krishnan and Somanathan 2005).

The conventional approach to policy implementation has been that policy addresses a problem and a set of needs that have to be supplied through the instrument of the civil service, operating according to the principles of bureaucracy. But, as Lant Pritchett and Michael Woolcock have argued in a paper with the intriguing title 'Solutions When *The* Solution Is The Problem' (2004), the conventional bureaucratic approach (*the* solution) often does not work at all well. This is not only because actually existing bureaucracies, modelled on the Western ideal but implanted into very different social and cultural contexts, do not function according to the Weberian template, but also because bureaucracies – even those that approximate Weber's ideal type quite closely – may not be very good at dealing with certain types of problems. Pritchett and Woolcock distinguish between the many types of services for which governments are commonly held responsible, in terms both of the degree of discretionary decision-making that they involve, and of the numbers and frequency (the 'intensity') of transactions that they entail. Some functions of government involve a high level of discretionary decision-making – setting the interest rate, for example – but very few transactions. In this case a small number of experts can operate very effectively. On the other hand, there are services that can be highly routinized and so require very little in the way of discretionary decision-making, but that are 'transactions-intensive'. An example is that of an immunization programme. Such services can be supplied very well (though they aren't always, of course) by a centralized bureaucracy, supplying a top-down and uniform public service. The really difficult cases, however, are those of services – such as policing, teaching and providing medical care – that involve both a lot of discretionary decision-making and large numbers of transactions. The conventional bureaucratic approach very often fails in regard to services such as these – '*the* solution', as Pritchett and Woolcock put it, may then become part of the problem. Many of the innovations in government in India and in other countries are aimed at finding a solution to the problems of delivering such 'discretion-and-transactions-demanding' services by overcoming the limitations of the bureaucratic approach. This is what is described as 'new public management' (NPM), which can involve different elements. One approach is to resort to market solutions, by privatization (increasingly favoured in India, in practice, in regard to health and education, as we discuss in chapters 5 and 14), and through such means as the contracting out of services. But another is to involve members of local communities – through 'participation' – in the design, operation and monitoring of the delivery of public services. This approach should allow for the application of local knowledge and make the local agents of the bureaucracy ('street-level bureaucrats' as they have been called) more accountable to citizens. The decentralization of government is held to have the same advantages and should encourage the participation of citizens in the management of their own public affairs. In the second part of this chapter, we consider India's experiences with decentralization and 'participation', in particular, from amongst the approaches of the NPM.

8.2 'Patronage Democracy' and the 'Flailing State'

India is of course a long way from being a 'failing state', and in regard to many of its functions the Indian state performs very well indeed. What Devesh Kapur (2010) refers to as the 'macro-state', responsible for the major instruments of economic policy, has generally done very well indeed even in the period of low rates of economic growth when India at least avoided the disasters of high rates of inflation that so badly affected other 'developing' economies. This is the sphere of the often highly competent upper echelons of the Indian Administrative Service. India does well, too, in regard to indicators of democracy. But the Indian government, as we have pointed out, actually performs very badly in regard to the delivery of services, even by comparison with its poorer and economically less dynamic neighbours. The 'Failed States Index' for 2010 shows Pakistan at tenth (i.e., there are only nine countries that do worse on this Index), Bangladesh at twenty-fourth, Sri Lanka at twenty-fifth and Nepal at twenty-sixth, while India is ranked eighty-seventh. In regard to the criterion (included in the Index) of 'progressive deterioration of public services', however, India does little better (with a score of 7.2, where 10 would mean complete breakdown) than its neighbours Pakistan (7.3) and Nepal (7.6), and worse than Sri Lanka (6.4) (see *Foreign Policy* August 2010). The 'micro-state' has, for example, launched a long series of programmes to address different dimensions of poverty, but with very little to show for most of them (Kapur 2010; and for a penetrating account of how benefits from poverty programmes leak upwards, see Guhan 1980). These characteristics of the Indian state – high levels of competence and performance at the centre, but a distressing inability to deliver programmes and services to the mass of the people – have led Lant Pritchett to describe it as a 'flailing state' (by analogy with a flailing human body when the brain loses control of the limbs: see Pritchett 2009). What accounts for this state of affairs?

An answer to this critical question comes from work by Kanchan Chandra, who – as we explained in the last chapter – describes India as a patronage democracy. India is formally a democracy, with free and mostly reasonably fair elections under a universal franchise, in which the state monopolizes access to very substantial resources – the allocation of which is, however, subject to a high degree of individual discretion on the part of elected officers and officials. Though under the impact of policies of economic liberalism the growth of public-sector employment has been contained, there remain many jobs in the public services and they are still much sought after (as Jeffrey et al. have explained with regard to wealthier rural people in western Uttar Pradesh, 2008). The allocation of most of these jobs is subject to the discretion of individual bureaucrats, usually influenced by politicians. The state, through its street-level bureaucrats, continues to control access to important inputs for agriculture, such as water and public-sector credit, and to loans, rations of essential commodities (through the Public Distribution System), and to employment in public works (now through NREGA, described in chapter 5) – and the allocation of these resources, too, is subject to political discretion. Politicians are able to exercise power over bureaucrats – even sometimes those at the highest levels of the civil service – through the mechanism of transfers. Governments, and consequently politicians, have almost unfettered power to transfer a civil servant from one post to another, and to promote and to demote them (Krishnan and Somanathan 2005: 292–9). This opens up huge possibilities for securing rents, on the parts of both officials and especially of politicians (Wade 1982, 1985), as officials seek to avoid difficult postings and to secure ones in which there are significant opportunities for graft. It also means that even the most competent and uncorrupted officials – often especially them – are unlikely to remain in one position for very long. We have all met senior IAS officers who have seldom remained in a post for much more than a year, and there are notable cases where even, for instance, a Chief Secretary to a state government has been removed from his post quite arbitrarily when he stood in the way of senior politicians.

From the point of view of the politicians, being able to control selective benefits through patronage, using the resources of the state, seems a more reliable way of ensuring continued support – and of realizing rents for themselves, of course – than standing on a policy platform including promises about the delivery of *public* goods. Even where public spending has not been directed at the supply of individual benefits, it has been focused on delivering transfers to particular interest groups – as Pranab Bardhan has shown in the studies of the political economy of India that we refer to in chapter 6, describing how public resources have been massively frittered away in often unproductive transfers (Bardhan 1984). Notable recipients, as well as private business groups, have been those labelled as farmers who have been and continue to be the beneficiaries of public subsidies for fertilizers, irrigation water and electricity, and of subsidized prices for at least some of their output. It has been particularly the wealthier farmers who have benefited from such subsidies, and not so much the many poor peasants of the country. The benefits of subsidies on food and fertilizers (equivalent to about 1.25 per cent of GDP in the early twenty-first century) accrued mainly to surplus grain producers in Punjab, Haryana, western Uttar Pradesh and Andhra Pradesh (Kapur 2010: 449; and see chapter 4 of this volume, where it is argued that these subsidies may also bring about huge inefficiency). But there is still a puzzle as to why voters – who include large numbers of poor people, who would greatly benefit from better provision of public health, education and other services – do not hold politicians (and through them the street-level bureaucrats who are immediately responsible for service delivery) democratically accountable for poor public provisioning.

One answer to this question is that it is because of the lack of credibility of political promises to provide broad public goods. Keefer and Khemani attribute 'the differential credibility of promises related to public goods versus private transfers' (2004: 935) to three factors – the history of electoral competition, the extent of social fragmentation of voters and to the limited information among voters about the quality of services. The first of these points involves an argument about historical path-dependency. There are states – Keefer and Khemani give the familiar example of Kerala – where there is a history of governments being held to account because voters have been highly mobilized (in Kerala by the communist parties) over service issues. In the absence of such a history, as in Uttar Pradesh, it is difficult for any political leader or party to break from a path that has been determined by competition around selective benefits. The argument then shows up the significance of the second factor – that of social fragmentation. Public provisioning has generally been better in those states in which poorer people have been mobilized collectively, as by the communist parties in Kerala, or by the Dravidian parties in Tamil Nadu (see Harriss 2003b), or perhaps around solidaristic sentiments of sub-nationalism (as has been argued by Prerna Singh in as yet unpublished work). And this factor in turn ties up with the one to do with information. This argument is made by Tim Besley and Robin Burgess (2000), in studies of variations in government responsiveness across the major Indian states. They examined public food distribution and calamity relief expenditure as measures of government responsiveness, and showed that differences between states in their regard are only weakly related to variations in economic development, but that states with historically higher electoral turnouts and more competitive politics, and those with higher newspaper circulation, are distinctly more responsive than others. It seems clear that higher levels of information among voters and higher levels of collective political mobilization are mutually supportive and interrelated. The data that are given by Besley and Burgess show that the most 'responsive states', according to their measures, are Kerala, Maharashtra, Tamil Nadu and West Bengal, which are also the states with the highest newspaper circulation, and states in which the lower classes have historically been most highly mobilized politically.

Keefer and Khemani's argument, therefore, seems to point to the significance of long-run trends of political mobilization, and so it poses a further question: why is it that poorer people have not been mobilized collectively to any great extent around public provisioning in most Indian states? We turn back to Chandra's analysis. She asks how benefit-seeking voters in a patronage democracy like India select politicians to vote for, and how politicians on the other hand decide which groups of electors to pitch for. The decisions both of voters and of politicians are subject, she says, to severe information constraints, which 'force voters and politicians to favour co-ethnics in the delivery of benefits and votes [resulting in] a self-enforcing and reinforcing equilibrium of ethnic favouritism' (2004: 12). What matters to voters is not what a party or a political leader says, but *who* it, or she, is. The basis for such ethnic favouritism may be caste, language or religion, or a sense of a 'national'/regional identity that is perhaps only rather loosely linked to linguistic difference (as in the Telengana region of Andhra Pradesh), and it is always subject to reconstruction. This is the reason why, according to Chandra's analysis, ethnic voting does not lead to permanent electoral majorities, because rival politicians can reconstruct salient identities (as, for example, Rajput politicians in Gujarat – from a numerically small group – succeeded in extending the category of Kshatriya to a very wide group; see Chandra

2004: 289). Ethnic parties are likely to succeed when they have com-petitive rules for intra-party advancement, and so are open to elites from across the possible subdivisions of the ethnic category around which they are organized, and when voters from the target category are sufficiently numerous to take the party to a winning or at least to an influential posi-tion. Once the equilibrium of ethnic favouritism is established it is not easily broken down.

With the decline of the Congress Party as an encompassing interest, embracing many different actually or potentially self-conscious groups of people (on which see Corbridge and Harriss 2000: chapter 3–6), so Indian politics has become more of a field of contestation over ethnic identities – often involving claims about dignity or self-respect as well as over resources – which has reinforced government failure. As Abhijit Banerjee and Rohini Pande have shown in a test using data from Uttar Pradesh, if voters are concerned about the group identity of political candidates, then if this group has a majority in a particular political jurisdiction the quality of the candidates can be very poor and yet they will still win. In such circumstances, 'a strengthening of group identity on citizens' politi-cal preferences worsens the quality of political representation' (Banerjee and Pande 2009: 2). The two authors developed a data set, from a field survey covering a sample of 102 jurisdictions, on legislator corruption in Uttar Pradesh over the period 1980–96, when it is generally recognized that ethnic voting became increasingly significant (the standard source on this is Yadav 1996). They then demonstrate both that increased legisla-tor corruption over this period can be attributed to legislators from the party that shared the ethnic identity of the dominant population group in a jurisdiction (Congress or BJP for upper-caste voters, Samajwadi Party or Bahujan Samaj Party for lower-caste voters), and that increased cor-ruption was largely concentrated in those jurisdictions with substantial high- or low-caste domination. Jurisdictions with the more biased caste distributions showed the greatest increases in corruption.

Lucia Michelutti's rich ethnography (2008) of political leadership amongst the numerically powerful Yadavs of northern India, to which we referred in chapter 7, adds to this picture. Michelutti shows that Yadavs, building in part on the idea of their claimed Kshatriya, warrior heritage, commonly value qualities of physical strength and toughness in their leaders, and may even celebrate their violence and criminality (*goonda*-ism). Such cultural constructions influencing political leadership go to enhance the tendencies that are analysed by Banerjee and Pande. Political leaders like both Lalu Prasad Yadav, long-time Chief Minister of Bihar, and Mulayam Singh Yadav, several times Chief Minister of Uttar Pradesh, owe much of their sustained political support to their ability to represent themselves as fighting successfully on behalf of the dignity of 'their people' – and this has clearly outweighed the limitations of their governments in regard to development and service delivery. As Lalu Prasad has said on different occasions to two of us, 'What is this "development" that you people talk about? I want respect for my people.' In circumstances such as these, attempts at bringing about administrative reform as the way of improving the delivery of public services are likely to be set at nought. Only for so long can there be maintained a gap between the actions of politicians and those of administrators. As a distinguished senior civil servant, N. C. Saxena, once wrote, 'the model in which the politics will continue to be corrupt, casteist and will harbour criminals whereas civil servants continue to be efficient, responsive to public needs and change agents, cannot be sustained indefinitely' (cited by Pritchett 2008).

Another way of looking at these characteristics of the state and of Indian democracy is suggested by Pratap Mehta. In a highly unequal society, he argues, politics is likely to become a struggle for position, as people struggle to sustain their sense of self-worth; and rights claims are likely to be used by groups in order to gain access to power: 'Democracy in India has advanced through the competitive negotiation between groups, each competing for their interests, rather than by the diffusion of democratic norms . . . The purpose of political mobilization has not been to make the state more accountable but to get access to or to share in its power' (2011: 23). The Constitutional provisions regarding affirmative action have served to entrench such politics, and the result – tragically, in his view – has been to reduce 'justice to crude and limited measures of power-sharing' (ibid.: 29).

There are other factors, too, that make for India's character as a 'flailing state'. With regard to measures to reduce poverty, in particular, there is a problem of the proliferation of programmes. New administrations at the centre and in different states are eager to become identified with particular programmes (even if people, in the end, benefit from them through discretionary allocations), and this has contributed to proliferation. As new programmes are introduced, old ones – even if they had very similar objectives – are rarely if ever closed down. And there are now many schemes sponsored by central government, which makes grants for their implementation to the states – but, as Devesh Kapur says, 'Few states have the administrative capacity to access grants from 200 plus schemes, spend money as per each of its conditions, maintain separate accounts and submit individual reports' (2010: 453). This capacity is most limited where most needed – as one of us observed in the course of a distressing visit to mainly defunct and decaying health centres in Bihar some years ago, when he learnt that the state had simply not claimed many of the resources available from the central government for primary health care. Large amounts of budgeted central state expenditures actually go unspent – and not only in Bihar (Kapur 2010: 453). It is a somewhat ironic fact, too, that despite being over-bureaucratized in so many ways, the Indian state(s) are often chronically under-staffed in key departments.

The factors we have discussed here relate mainly to the supply side of public services. On the demand side, adding to the limitations that follow from the significance of clientelism in India's 'patronage democracy', there is the fact that middle-class people, usually those most capable of ensuring the accountability of politicians, have increasingly withdrawn from using public services at all – going to private clinics and hospitals and sending their children to private schools (see our discussion in chapter 14). They have little interest, as a result, in exercising their voice in the cause of improved public services. They may be withdrawing, too, from participation in electoral politics. Javeed Alam maintains that middle-class people are increasingly withdrawing from what he refers to as 'the politics of din' – as he puts it, 'the core of civil society has turned against democracy' (2004: 122ff.) But, as Alam also says, his assertion calls for careful interpretation. Many of the most articulate members of the Indian middle classes are deeply committed to democratic values, but find these are corrupted by the way democratic politics work in their country – and they have turned instead to activism in civil society. It is members of the middle classes – as we discussed in chapter 5 – who have brought about important innovations in government (through the Right to Information Act) and in social provisioning (notably through NREGA, and now through continuing activism over food security) through their campaigning and lobbying, sometimes through the legal instrument of public interest litigation. Such litigation has led the Supreme Court to order the government to act – as, for example, over the use of stocks of cereals in the granaries of the Food Corporation of India. There is a sense, then, in which there is a judicialization of politics taking place in India, with rather ambiguous implications for the functioning of India's democracy. It may mean that some of the negative implications of patronage democracy are overcome – as we perhaps see in the implementation of the Right to Education and of NREGA – but it can also mean that technocratic measures that are ultimately most favourable to middle- and upper-class interests are implemented, rather than democratic solutions being sought for public problems. It contributes to what is becoming recognized as a critical problem for the future of the Indian polity – that of the increasing powers of the Supreme Court, and the consequent tensions between the legislature and judiciary. The Court threatens to become an *'imperium in imperio* [an order within an order], the creation of which the drafters of the Constitution specifically wished to avoid' (Rajamani and Sengupta 2010: 93).

These, then, are some of the critical problems affecting governance in India. What is now being done about them? Is government becoming more responsive?

8.3   Are Decentralization and 'Participation' the Answer to the Problems of the Flailing State? Is There a 'Silent Revolution' Taking Place in India Today?

Of the different approaches to the problems in the delivery, especially, of what Pritchett and Woolcock describe as 'discretion-and-transactions-intensive services' where conventional bureaucratic approaches are particularly problematic, those that have been most prominently experimented with in India hitherto are decentralization and participation. The first of these is expected to make government more responsive, by bringing it closer to the people, improving information flow both ways (from government to people and people to government), and the second – related to it – to empower ordinary people in relation to the state so as to make it work better for them. Both fit, more or less comfortably, into policy ideas about governance that are associated with economic liberalism, because they represent alternatives to the centralized state (see Harriss 2002); but they are expected also to be an important means of building the more substantive democracy to which we referred in chapter 7.

Decentralization, legislated for in India through the 73rd and 74th Amendments to the Constitution of India that entered into effect in 1993, involving the delegation of some authority to local levels of rural and of urban government respectively, is expected to make critical decision-making better informed about local needs and circumstances, and to make both politicians and bureaucrats more directly answerable to the people. Local governments should be much better able than bureaucrats appointed by central government to monitor and control the delivery of discretion-and-transactions-intensive services. These arguments led senior policymakers in the later 1980s to look to revitalizing and strengthening the *panchayati raj* system of local government that had been initiated in the 1950s, partly in response to ideas of Gandhi's about village self-government that were enshrined in a Directive Principle of the Constitution of India. The new legislation requires state governments to: establish *panchayat*s at village, intermediate (block) and district levels; to hold direct elections to all the seats in these bodies every five years; to reserve seats for SC/ST according their share in the population; and to reserve a third of all seats for women. It also mandates state governments to reserve a third of the positions as chairs at all three levels for women, and for SC/ST in proportion to their shares in the state's population. It thus provides local government bodies with constitutional status. Other provisions in the legislation, however, are discretionary – that is, states are called upon, but *not* explicitly required to devolve powers and resources to local bodies so as to enable them to play a central role in the provision of public services and in the planning, as well as in the implementation, of development programmes and the securing of social justice. This means that the idea of local self-government may be severely circumscribed in its practice, and that state governments may actually continue to exercise considerable power in regard to the local bodies. In practice, in most states, district officials, magistrates or collectors, have the authority to interfere in the functioning of local government, and MPs and MLAs exercise a lot of influence in the workings of the second and third tiers (Chaudhuri 2007).

Research internationally suggests that for democratic decentralization (such as *panchayati raj* intends) to work well there are three essential conditions: (i) the elected bodies should have adequate powers; (ii) they should be provided with adequate resources; and (iii) they must be provided with adequate accountability mechanisms (so that bureaucrats are accountable to the elected representatives and the representatives to the people) (Manor 2010a). James Manor writes of his regret that most Indian states have failed to satisfy these conditions and that they have consequently lost significant opportunities – given that in so many other ways India is well prepared for decentralized government by comparison with many other countries (Manor 2010a).

There is, in fact, a great deal of variation between the states – because of what the legislation leaves to their discretion – in the way in which the 73rd (and, as we shall see, the 74th) Amendments have been implemented. Shubham Chaudhuri's detailed review (2007) showed that more than ten years after the passage of the 73rd Amendment, fewer than half of the major states had satisfied the mandate regarding the holding of regular elections, and that some had failed to meet the requirements regarding the representation of women and of members of the Scheduled Castes and Scheduled Tribes. The evidence then available also showed that very little progress had been made in regard to functional and financial devolution to the local bodies, which continued to be characterized by high levels of dependency for their revenues on the higher levels of government. Chaudhuri concludes that 'even when functions have been statutorily or even administratively transferred to *panchayats*, in most states the funds and personnel necessary for meaningfully carrying out the functions remain under the administrative control of the state-level bureaucracy' (ibid.: 177). Exceptions are Kerala and West

Bengal – which according to Chaudhuri's analysis are the only states in which there has been any significant devolution of powers – and, to some extent, Karnataka (the state which, along with West Bengal, had a functioning *panchayat* system before the passage of the new legislation in 1993), and Maharashtra. The only other states in which Chaudhuri found that progress with devolution of powers had been other than 'minimal' are Madhya Pradesh and Rajasthan.

Indian politicians have long resisted the transfer of resources and authority to local bodies, because of the loss that it would entail of some of their powers of patronage. The political changes of the last two decades, which have seen regional political parties acquiring much greater influence, have increased the powers of the states in relation to the central government and changed the character of Indian federalism (see Mitra and Pehl 2010; and our chapter 6), but they have certainly not increased the incentives for state politicians to decentralize. Indeed, if anything, the increasing volume of resources coming from the centre to state governments has increased the incentives for state politicians to control local administration (Kapur 2010: 454).

The story thus far, of democratic decentralization in India, does not encourage one to think that it can have had very much of an effect on the quality of administration or the delivery of services. There is no authoritative analysis of its impact across the country as a whole – and we have to rely on studies of particular states. Those by Bardhan and Mookherjee of the *panchayat* system in West Bengal show that there it has increased the voice of women and of Dalits and *adivasi*s – though they all still participate only at low levels – and increased their share of public resources. Bardhan and Mookherjee also find, however, that the inter-village allocation of resources is subject to high levels of discretion, and report that 'Villages with greater landlessness, land inequality, or low-caste status among the poor received substantially fewer resources as a whole. Anecdotes and case studies indicate that the allocation of benefits followed party lines. Those that do not belong to the party locally in power get severely discriminated against' (2007: 219). Somewhat similarly, Tim Besley and his co-researchers, in their study of *panchayats* drawing on a large sample from across the four southern states, found that having a reserved *panchayat* chairman does improve targeting towards SC/ST households, but expressed concern about bias in the allocation of resources to benefit chairmens' own villages. They also thought it possible, however, from their findings, that poorer people may participate actively in *gram sabhas*, and that this may have a positive influence on targeting towards the poor (Besley et al. 2007). Two other scholars, Crook and Sverrisson, having studied analyses of decentralized government in several countries, and in West Bengal, concluded that decentralization has been most successful in regard to poverty alleviation in the Indian state largely because, in this case, state-level politicians have intervened at local levels in support of poorer people against local power-holders (Crook and Sverrisson 2003). Clearly – as was often the case in India's earlier experiments with local government through *panchayat*s – democratic decentralization may easily go to enhance the opportunities of those who are already locally powerful, and work against the interests of the poor and the excluded. There is indeed a paradox of decentralization – which is that effective decentralized government may actually require those in power at the centre to intervene *more* than before at local levels, against the manipulations of those who are locally powerful. This argument emerges very clearly from Judith Tendler's studies in her book *Good Government in the Tropics* (1997), about the state of Ceara in Northeastern Brazil.

The same point has been made by Patrick Heller (2011) in regard to decentralization in Madhya Pradesh during the government of the Congress Chief Minister Digvijay Singh (between 1993 and 2003). In this state, decentralization has had most effect in the sphere of primary education, through the Education Guarantee Scheme (EGS) established under Digvijay Singh's government. The EGS empowered any *panchayat* that did not have a school within one kilometre to demand one from the state government and mandated the latter to respond within ninety days. In turn, the *panchayat* had to identify a teacher from within the community and to establish a parent-teacher association to monitor the performance of the school. The goal of the EGS was 'to provide community-centred, rights-based primary education to all children in a quick and time-bound manner' (Anderson, quoted by Heller 2011: 167). By 2001, the primary education system in the state was entirely decentralized, with the *panchayat*s charged with recruiting and monitoring teachers – and, it appears, with very positive outcomes, for a nationwide study found teacher absenteeism in Madhya Pradesh to be well below the national average, while the 2001 census showed that literacy levels had been remarkably improved. The Singh administration worked quite like the progressive administrations of Ceara in Brazil, described by Tendler, devolving resources in such a way as to bypass the patronage channels of local bosses; and Singh relied significantly for the implementation of this, and other programmes, on a cadre of talented bureaucrats whom he kept in post and insulated from the pressures of patronage politics through the setting up of special delivery mechanisms called 'Rajiv Gandhi Missions'. In order to build and maintain political support, Digvijay Singh sought to break with his party's reliance on upper castes and local bosses, reaching out to the historically marginalized Dalits and *adivasis*. As we argued in chapter 7, however, the limits of this top-down process of reform have to be recognized, and the dangers of elite capture remain acute. In Madhya Pradesh, indeed, Digvijay Singh finally lost power, in spite of the successes of his administration in regard to the delivery of some public services, substantially because of losing the support of local elites and of information from them (Manor 2010a: 69–70).

Still, the story of the relative success of the Education Guarantee Scheme in Madhya Pradesh and, even more so, that of the People's Campaign for Decentralized Planning in Kerala, encourages Heller to argue that *panchayati raj* is bringing about a 'silent revolution' in India. As we have seen, Kerala is one of just two states (the other being West Bengal) in which, according to Chaudhuri's analysis, there has been significant devolution of authority, though the state was a relatively late entrant into the renewed experiment with democratic decentralization in India. The People's Campaign was supported only by a reformist fraction within the CPI(M) in Kerala, that has for long alternated in office in the state with Congress-led coalitions. This faction, inspired by arguments put forward by the legendary former leader of the Kerala Party, the late E. M. S. Namboodirapad, and under the leadership of Thomas Isaac, originally an academic economist and development studies scholar, launched the People's Campaign when the party regained office in 1996. Heller describes it, rightly, as 'the most ambitious decentralization initiative' yet to have been attempted in India. It involves a much greater level of fiscal decentralization – about 30 per cent of all state plan expenditures – than in any other state in India (while, according to the World Bank, in regard to fiscal decentralization Kerala is second in the world only to Colombia); and full devolution of functions in the context of 'the creation of a comprehensive, nested, participatory structure of integrated planning and budgeting' (Heller 2011: 164 – the planning and budgeting system is fully described and analysed by its architect, Thomas Isaac, with Richard Franke 2000). The system starts with meetings of *gram sabhas* – formal village assemblies – in which research by Heller and his co-researchers shows that women and SCs/STs participate somewhat disproportionately. Their research also shows that decentralized planning, through the *panchayats*, has had positive outcomes, especially in regard to the provision of roads, housing and child services. As one scholar from Kerala whom they quote – K. P. Kannan – who had been distinctly sceptical about the People's Campaign, has written, it has in the end been successful in establishing 'a public platform for a vigilant civil society' (Heller, Harilal and Chaudhuri 2007).

So, for Heller, *panchayati raj* appears to be effecting a 'silent revolution' in India, in spite of the severe limits thus far on its implementation, with little having happened at all in so many states. But the histories of Kerala and Madhya Pradesh, and perhaps those of West Bengal and of Karnataka, have shown that 'Ordinary citizens have been afforded opportunities to engage with public authority in ways that simply did not exist before' (2011: 169). As the authors of the book *Seeing the State: Governance and Governmentality in India* (Corbridge et al. 2005) have argued, based on research in part on the much less propitious terrain of Bihar and Jharkhand, the very language of participation 'resonates with popular aspirations and can readily be turned against a non-performing state' (Heller 2011: 169). Support for this positive view of the potentials that have been opened up, both for the deepening of democracy in India and for making the state more accountable to the people, comes from the mounting evidence – to some of which we have referred in the last chapter (and see also chapter 13) – about the changing social character of political participation in the country, as members of lower castes and classes, and women too, have begun to take part more actively at all levels of politics.

Other scholars, including one of us, are less sanguine about the prospects of this 'silent revolution'. Abhijit Banerjee and his co-researchers, for example, reach pessimistic conclusions from their study of participatory initiatives in regard to primary education in Uttar Pradesh. In this state, as in others, Village Education Committees (VEC) have been set up – or are supposed to have been set up. These bodies, in Uttar Pradesh, formed by headteachers together with the heads of local government (usually *panchayat* chairmen) and three parents, are expected to improve the functioning of schools through the involvement (or 'participation') of 'beneficiaries' (here children and their parents). The researchers' baseline surveys, however, showed both that parents were unaware of the existence of the committees and that VEC members were unaware of their powers. They then experimented with three different innovations designed to enhance participation in this case, but found – sadly – that none of them had a positive impact on community involvement in schools, or on teacher effort, or on learning outcomes. The one innovation that did have an impact was that of setting up reading camps, which both showed that parents are interested in their children's education and had some success in teaching reading. The researchers concluded that 'citizens face substantial constraints in participating to improve the public education system, even when they care about education and are willing to do something to improve it' (Banerjee et al. 2008: 1). The research in part brings out the familiar problems of collective action (on which see Olson 1965): in this case, parents' involvement in their children's schooling certainly can have positive outcomes, but how and why – under what conditions – should people get involved? The fact that there can be benefits from participation in bodies like VECs doesn't automatically mean that people will get involved in them – because participation also entails costs, not least in terms of time.

Studies of democratic decentralization in India's cities, following from the 74th Amendment, or Nagarpalika Act, (which, we know, was added almost as an afterthought by the architects of *panchayati raj*), and of other participatory initiatives in the cities, have shown that while the state encourages these endeavours rhetorically and to an extent in practice, in others of its measures it has made it possible increasingly for powerful people to bypass democratic processes over the vital matter of control of urban space. Solomon Benjamin, an urban planner and activist, argues that India's great cities are divided between what he refers to as the 'local economies', in which the mass of the people dwell, very often in circumstances of insecure tenure, and in which they try to secure their livelihoods, mostly through insecure, informal employment – and, on the other hand, the 'corporate economies' (Benjamin 2000). These are the city spaces that are controlled by industrial, bureaucratic and IT sector elites, which increasingly are demarcated physically from the geographical areas of the local economies. These elites operate through their political connections with politicians at levels beyond the immediate locality, and through mega-projects and the 'Master Planning' of Urban Development Authorities, and by these means have managed to achieve 'hegemony in the shaping of urban form that is quite unprecedented' (Nair 2005: 340, writing about Bangalore). Urban development authorities are empowered to exercise control over urban real estate in a way that bypasses elected local bodies, so that the urban poor, enormous in their numbers though they are, have little influence over the allocation even of the most minimal living space (see Roy 2006, writing on Ahmedabad; and Ghosh 2005, about the activities of the Bangalore Agenda Task Force). The facts that the provisions of the 74th Amendment have been implemented to a lesser extent even than those of the 73rd, or that the Jawaharlal Nehru Urban Renewal Mission (JNNURM) set up by the United Progressive Alliance government in 2005, for all its reference to the needs of the urban poor, should focus mainly on infrastructure and provisioning of the IT and service sectors, are hardly surprising in this context (see Mukhopadhyay 2006, and Gooptu 2011, on the JNNURM; and Harriss 2010b).

A good deal is expected, too, of the role of civil society organizations in India's metropolitan cities. Urban authorities in both Delhi and Mumbai have sought to establish partnerships with civil society groups – to bring about 'collaborative change', in the words of the Delhi government website, 'for the development of the city', through its *Bhagidari* Scheme; or in Mumbai through 'Advanced Locality Management Units' that were instituted first in 1997. The *Bhagidari* Scheme involves 'partnerships' between the Delhi government and local Residents' Welfare Associations (RWAs), and the Mumbai set-up, too, involves partnerships between residents/citizens and the municipal administration (Zerah 2007). In both cities, it is clear that the residents who are involved are generally those from middle-class areas where people have security of tenure for their homes. *Bhagidari* has hardly been extended into the massive areas of (officially) 'unauthorized' development in Delhi, or to the *jhuggi jhopris* (the slums). In other Indian cities, as well, RWAs are largely confined to middle-class areas, and there are many cases of political and legal action being sought by these groups to exclude poor people physically from their neighbourhoods (see Bhan 2009) – sometimes using the instrument of public interest litigation (which, as we have pointed out, has been used in other cases – as in that of food security – to advance socially progressive objectives). The whole sphere of formal association in civil society, indeed, involving a wide range of local associations, advocacy groups and service-delivery NGOs, is mainly the preserve of the middle classes. The consequence may be that, as Harriss argues, 'Civil society activism has opened up new opportunities for representation . . . but such opportunities hardly extend to the informal working class . . . the paradox that increasing opportunities for participation may actually go to increase political inequality stands against the claims of protagonists of 'new politics' [supposedly grounded in associational activism]' (Harriss 2007: 2721; and see chapter 11 of this book). Evidence of this kind adds to the doubts about the practical possibilities of participation that are expressed by Banerjee and his co-researchers, suggesting that there are ways in which the language and practice of participation and even of democratic decentralization can serve specifically middle- and upper-class interests, and in a way that complements the agenda of neoliberal economic policy.

This is not to say that members of the massive informal working class of India's cities do not organize themselves – and there are significant organizations of slum-dwellers, some of them led by women, as well as of groups of informal workers. These, like the women's rights movement, slum-dwellers' rights movement, and the Unorganised Workers Federation that Harriss describes from Chennai, may have been launched by left-wing middle-class activists, but they are movements *of* the working poor, rather than having been set up – like so many service-delivery NGOs – to deliver 'benefits' *to* them. But it is still the case that the mass of urban poor people depend substantially on the intermediation of their local leaders – those referred to in Delhi as *pradhans* – with both bureaucrats and politicians, when they try to tackle problems of access to public services (those that, according to Chandhoke's research to which we referred at the beginning of this chapter, they mostly do expect the state to supply; and see also Harriss 2006). Saumitra Jha and her co-authors have observed the significance of the role of the *pradhans* as intermediaries in their studies of Delhi slums (2007), and they argue that through these local leaders poor people enjoy good access to politicians and to the state. They suggest, therefore, that 'urbanization . . . (is) . . . providing the poor with greater voice in democratic discourse' (2007: 244). We question this conclusion: how so, we ask, when the 'participation' of poor people in the city is mediated by dependence upon particular gatekeepers?

Our conclusion, then, is that while decentralization and other ways of organizing participation can, in principle, serve both the cause of democratic deepening and that of improving the responsiveness of government in India so that public services are delivered more efficiently and more equitably, their practical achievements thus far are quite limited, certainly outside two or three states. Beyond this factual conclusion, we recognize that there is continuing debate between those scholars like Patrick Heller and others who believe that there is reason for thinking that a 'silent revolution' is taking place, as the language and practice of democratic decentralization increase the capacities of poor people to express themselves and their grievances, and, on the other hand, sceptics who find in the actual practices of participation vehicles for the interests of the dominant and middle classes of India that leave largely undisturbed the dependence of the labouring classes upon locally powerful intermediaries, so allowing the reproduction of patronage democracy.

9

Has the Rise of Hindu Nationalism Halted?

9.1 Introduction

In January 2004, the Bharatiya Janata Party (BJP) seemed to be riding high. The party had been in office in India's central government, albeit in coalition with other political parties in the National Democratic Alliance (NDA), for over four years, following an earlier short-lived coalition government that it had led in 1998–9. This in itself was a remarkable achievement for a party that had held only two seats in the Lok Sabha, following general elections as recent as those of 1984. In December 2003, the party had won elections to the state assemblies of Madhya Pradesh, Rajasthan and Chhattisgarh, overturning what had seemed successful Congress regimes. India's economic growth had recently started to accelerate. In this apparently favourable context, the BJP leader and Prime Minister, Atal Bihari Vajpayee, called fresh general elections for April–May 2004. The party set out to fight those elections on the strength of Mr Vajpayee's own credibility as a proven, respected Prime Minister, and on the platform of 'India Shining' – the idea of India as a now successful country taking its rightful place as one of the leaders amongst the nations of the world.

The hubris of Indian Shining was soon to be exposed. In the general election of 2004, the BJP lost to a Congress-led coalition that came to call itself the United Progressive Alliance (UPA). This defeat came about not, as some commentators thought at the time, because of a kind of electoral revolt on the part of poor rural people for whom India was definitely not 'shining', but because the Congress Party nationally had at last learnt the ropes of coalition arithmetic (Manor 2011b). As political analysts showed, the election was lost to the BJP not because of any great shifts

Table 9.1: BJP and Congress in electoral competition

Election	Vote (%) BJP	Vote (%) Congress	Seats BJP	Seats Congress
1991	20.04	35.66	120	244
1996	20.29	28.80	161	140
1998	25.59	25.82	182	141
1999	23.75	28.30	182	114
2004	22.16	26.53	138	145
2009	18.80	28.55	116	206

in national politics, but because of the outcomes of the different contests in the various major states. Still, the vote share of the BJP declined again nationally (see table 9.1), from the peak of more than 25 per cent of the electorate as a whole that it had achieved in 1998; and the party's vote share declined even further in the next general election of 2009, to less than 19 per cent of the electorate. In these elections, to the surprise of many, the Congress succeeded in increasing its number of seats quite dramatically, if not its share of the popular vote, and in securing a strong position for the United Progressive Alliance in the new Parliament. The remarkable rise of the BJP – the party political member of the *Sangh parivar,* the 'family' of organizations inspired by the Rashtriya Swayamsevak Sangh (RSS) which is dedicated to the realization of the aspirations of Hindu nationalism – appeared to have been checked.

But did this – does this – mean that the rise of Hindu nationalism has been halted? We believe that the failure of the BJP to extend the kind of ascendancy that it seemed to have around the turn of the twentieth century does not necessarily mean that the rise of Hindu nationalism has been halted. In part, we think, this is because of the ways in which India is becoming, remarkably perhaps, 'more Hindu'. As one writer has put it recently, in the title of a book, 'globalization is making India more Hindu' (Nanda 2009). Hindu religiosity is becoming increasingly publicly apparent, through temple construction and renovation – some of it involving Non-Resident Indians, mostly from North America; through the renewal and the invention of ritual; and through the actions and the followings of new religious leaders or 'gurus'. Any semblance of separation between religion and the state has long gone, and there is now – Nanda suggests – a 'state-temple-corporate complex' that has rendered Hindu nationalism banal: 'The banal, everyday Hindu religiosity is simultaneously breeding a banal, everyday kind of Hindu nationalism' (Nanda 2009: 140). This is the kind of banal nationalism that, for instance, leads mostly young men to attack other young people who want to celebrate Valentine's Day – something that has taken off in India in recent years substantially because of the huge success of a leading manufacturer of greetings cards in selling Valentine cards – or to try to stop young middle-class women from behaving in ways that they consider 'un-Hindu'.

But it is not only everyday Hindu nationalism that flourishes in spite of the political defeats of the BJP. There is also an often violent edge to Hindu nationalism which shows no sign of decline, and which deserves to be analysed in the comparative context of the religious violence occurring in other societies as well. At the time we first sat down to write this chapter, in the summer of 2010, the trial was taking place in India of several avowed Hindu nationalists who are suspected of having been responsible for carrying out a number of terror attacks in western India. At the same time the BJP Chief Minister of the state of Gujarat, Narendra Modi, was confronting investigations concerning his role in the orchestrated attacks on Muslims in his state in 2002 – violence in which there is strong evidence of the connivance of the state and of BJP politicians, but from which it seems, in view of the party's subsequent electoral successes, the BJP has gained significantly. The third part of this chapter concerns religious violence and the recent history of 'communalism' and of aggression between religious communities.

9.2   The BJP, the RSS, and the Struggle for Hindutva

Hindu nationalism began to develop alongside and even before 'secular' Indian nationalism. It has its origins in movements for religious revival and reform in the nineteenth century that responded to colonialism and to Christianity in a way that was both oppositional and emulative. They sought to create the community of Hindus without, initially, invoking hostility to those of other faiths – though such 'othering' followed soon after. John Zavos, in his study of this early history (2000), argues that at this time there came together with religion a recognition of the need for 'organization' as an essential facet of modernity – Indians had to be better organized if they were to contend with colonial power. One important manifestation of this was in the formation of Hindu 'sabhas' – distinctly modern organizations of Hindus – in different parts of the country, and the establishment in 1915 of the All India Hindu Sabha as a representative body for them. It was this body that became active as the Hindu Mahasabha in the 1920s, when Vinayak Damodar Savarkar became one of its leaders.

It was Savarkar who formulated the idea of *Hindutva* in a book with this title, written in English and so clearly intended for a middle-class readership, first published in 1923. Both orthodox and reformist Brahmin intellectuals had by that time sought to find 'an internal principle of unity' in religion, but Savarkar tailored this 'to emphasize territorial origin and broad cultural commonalities' (Khilnani 1997: 159–60). He effectively translated upper-caste ideology – Kshatriya as much as Brahmin, given its emphasis on militancy and political power – into a decidedly modern conception of ethnic nationalism. *Hindutva* is taken to mean 'Hindu-ness', but it is said most emphatically not to be equated with Hinduism. It is an idea, rather, of a political community united by geographical origin, racial connection and a shared culture based on Sanskritic languages and 'common laws and rites' (ibid.: 161). Savarkar writes:

> A Hindu then is he who feels attachment to the land that extends from Sindhu to Sindhu as the land of his forefathers – as his Fatherland; who inherits the blood of the great race whose first and discernible source could be traced from the Himalayan altitudes . . . and who . . . has inherited and claims as his own the Hindu Sanskriti, the Hindu civilization. (Savarkar 1923: 100)

Hindutva is, as the BJP now argues on its website – though without referring explicitly to Savarkar – 'a nationalist and not a religious or theocratic concept', and it describes the idea as one of 'cultural nationalism'. Savarkar evidently intended to emphasize the unity of Hindus, irrespective of caste and other distinctions (which had cut across the endeavours of the early Hindu nationalists), while at the same explicitly 'othering' Muslims and Christians, who 'cannot be recognized as Hindus; as since their adoption of the new cult they had ceased to own Hindu civilization as a whole' (1923: 100–1). Savarkar's primary concern, no doubt, was with the organization of Hindus, but hostility to Islam and to Christianity was the inevitable corollary. It has continued to be part of the double-speak of Hindu nationalists, however, including that of the leaders of the BJP, that they should claim to adhere to religious pluralism while in other statements they reflect anti-Muslim or anti-Christian sentiments. Some, notably those associated with the publishing house Voice of India, who accuse even the RSS of being 'soft', contrast the 'intolerance' of the monotheistic religions with the 'tolerance' of Hinduism. Yet within this, they find reason for wishing to suppress these other religions and to propagate what is in effect a theology of hatred – without perceiving in the least the bitter irony in their practice (Nanda 2009: 160–8).

Hindutva ideas have animated the RSS from its foundation by Dr Keshav Baliram Hedgewar in 1925. Since that time, the *Sangh* has always sought to bring about a kind of a social revolution from below, not through taking over state power, but through the establishment of a highly disciplined organization, and the disciplining (through exercise) of the bodies of young men in the daily meetings of its local cells, or *shakhas* – of what has been called 'the brotherhood in saffron' – capable of spreading and inculcating into people the *Hindutva* idea of the nation. It has recognized the importance of basic education – in remarkable contrast with the egregious failures of the Indian state in this regard. The Indian state, rather strangely by comparison with many others, has not sought to promote Indian nationalism through basic education nearly as much as it might have done, had education been made more of a priority (though, as Véronique Bénéï explains, there certainly is a lot of attention given to 'nation-building' for those who do go to school (Bénéï: 2001, 2008)). The RSS, however, because it has played a significant part in the shaping of modern Hindi, has ensured that 'moralizing within a [Hindu] revivalist world view became entrenched in school text-books' (Kumar 1993: 544). There are now as many as 70,000 schools across the country that are under its management (Panikkar 2001), and ethnographic research by Peggy Froerer has shown how successful these can be in inculcating the ideas and values of *Hindutva* specifically in rural, *adivasi* areas, and in opposition to the work of Christian missions and their schools (Froerer 2007). To further its aims, the RSS has also built up its 'family' of organizations, the *Sangh parivar*, which now includes most notably, as well as the BJP, the Vishwa Hindu Parishad (VHP, 'World Hindu Council'), an organization of Hindu religious leaders, founded in 1964 specifically to confront the perceived threat from Christianity, and the Bajrang Dal, a youth movement set up by the VHP in 1984, and that has sometimes supplied its 'shock troops' for attacks on minorities. It includes as well organizations for women, for education and social service and for cultural activities. Closely associated with the *Sangh parivar* is the Shiv Sena, a political party formed in Mumbai (then called Bombay) in 1966, and which emerged from a 'sons of the soil' movement that claimed the state of Maharashtra should belong to Marathis. In the 1980s, Shiv Sena turned to a distinctively rabid Hindu communal rhetoric – sometimes embarrassing the BJP, with which it has, however, fought elections, and governed Maharashtra between 1995 and 1999 (see Hansen 2002, on Shiv Sena).

For all the considerable strengths of the *Sangh parivar,* however, the success that it has had over the last two decades in bringing about a significant shift in India's political culture, such that *Hindutva* has claimed the imaginations of an important share of India's elites to an extent that was not true before, is due as much or more, to the failures of the Congress Party. In spite of its electoral strength in the early 1980s, the Congress lost direction, especially in the time of Rajiv Gandhi's prime ministership, leaving a kind of vacuum in Indian politics and creating a space for the rise of Hindu nationalist politics, articulated by the BJP but with the vigorous support of other members of the *parivar*. This culminated, at last, in 1998, in the electoral success of the BJP (Corbridge and Harriss 2000: chapter 5). A critical event in this history was the destruction of the Babri Masjid at Ayodhya in December 1992, subtly orchestrated by leaders of the BJP (as the official commission of enquiry, the Liberhan Committee, finally reported to Parliament in 2009), which marked the high point of Hindu nationalist agitation, and tested the Indian polity as never before. But by this time, too, the weaknesses of the Congress Party organization and of the governments of India since the mid-1980s had led a good many senior ex-officials and servicemen, and members of the upper middle classes more generally, to look to the BJP as capable of supplying stronger, less corrupt government, that would enable India to attain the more significant place in the world to which many of them believed their country was entitled by virtue of its size and history. The message of *Hindutva*, mediated by the BJP, seemed to promise that India would take its 'rightful' place amongst the nations of the world only if Indians were truly 'themselves' – that is 'Hindu' – rather than trying to emulate the West (Hansen 1996c). The widespread euphoria in India over the testing of a nuclear bomb in 1998, shortly after the BJP took over leadership of the Government of India for the first time, clearly reflected these sentiments.

In the 1996 general election, the BJP had won most seats in an inconclusive election, in spite of securing a much smaller share of the vote than the Congress (see table 9.1). Vajpayee, the leader of the BJP, was invited by the President to form a government, but this lasted only thirteen days before being defeated in a vote of confidence. This experience led the party to recognize the compulsions of power, the need to build an electoral coalition with other parties, and that for this to be possible it had to be ready to soften its stance on some issues – notably those critical matters having to do with building a temple at Ayodhya, with the civil code, and with the question of Article 370 of the Constitution concerning the status of Kashmir. Further elections in February 1998 – when the party won the highest share of the national vote that it has yet achieved – finally brought the BJP into office, in a coalition government, but it was brought down by the defection of a coalition partner after little more than a year. At last, in September–October 1999, the party, at the head of a coalition with thirteen other partners, won a majority that enabled it to govern for a full term. What did the BJP do with the political power that it had won, to advance *Hindutva*?

9.3   The RSS, and the BJP, In and Then Out of Office

From the first, the party was subjected to severe criticism by the RSS. The RSS initiated a series of conclaves of the *parivar*, with the stated objective of advancing *Hindutva*, not long after the Vajpayee government took office in 1998. These were actually occasions for criticism of the actions of the government, and it was Prime Minister Vajpayee who often came in for particular criticism. Indeed, it was usual at that time in the regular press for him to be described as presenting the 'moderate' or soft face of Hindu nationalism, while Lal Krishna Advani, the number two in the party and in the government, was represented as a hard-liner. Whether there was any such distinction to be made is certainly questionable. In 1999, for instance, at the height of an unprecedented wave of attacks on churches in Gujarat, Vajpayee, rather than insisting on tough measures to restore law and order, called for debate on the issue of religious conversion. It was generally his tactic, in such situations, to deflect attention away from the responsibility of members of the *parivar* for communal violence. Still, by the time of the RSS conclave of October 2000, attended by 50,000 delegates, the leader of the movement (the *sarsanghachalak*), K. S. Sudarshan, expressed concern over their pursuit of individual power by BJP leaders, as well as calling for Christians and Muslims to 'Indianize' themselves if they were not to be a threat to national security. Christianity, he argued, is more about politics than religion; and it is no accident that in recent years it has been Christians rather than Muslims who have often borne the brunt of communal aggression (as in the Kandhamal district of Orissa in 2008: Subrahmaniam 2010). The problem of religious conversions, which has become a major concern for Hindu religious leaders associated with the VHP, and strongly condemned by them, now refers mainly to the activities of some Christian sects and missions. Sudarshan went on to express concern over the dilution by the BJP of the campaign for the construction of a Hindu temple on the site of Babri Masjid in Ayodhya, and over Article 370 on the special status of Kashmir, but said nonetheless, that 'the party can do much to advance the nationalist cause' – and it seemed that the real purpose of the exercise was to warn Vajpayee not to go too far. As it was, though the conclave repeated the call for a *swadeshi* pattern of development – a pattern of autonomous development rather than one that opened up the Indian economy to trade and foreign investment – the BJP-led government was already embarking on what it called 'second generation' economic reforms. The demand of the trade union affiliate of the *Sangh parivar,* the Bharatiya Mazdur Sangh, for withdrawal from liberalization, was quietly ignored, both then and later (Ramakrishnan 2000). The

BJP was allowed (our choice of this word reflects our understanding of the tutelary relationship between the RSS and the party) to pursue economic policies entirely in line with those that had been pursued by the Congress government, while being subjected to criticism for its failures in regard to the critical cultural issues.

The most strident critics of all came from the VHP, which regularly activated its campaign for the construction of the Ram temple at Ayodhya to the more or less evident discomfiture of the BJP leadership. By 2003, when the BJP had been in power for five years, Vajpayee himself was described by Acharya Giraj Kishore, Vice-President of the VHP, as a 'pseudo-Hindu' – because of what was held to be his 'revisionist' explanation of the idea of *Hindutva,* which ceded too much independent space for the religious minorities (Venkatesan 2003b). This is, in fact, the idea of Hindu cultural nationalism that is now reflected on the English language website of the BJP – and it can almost be read as a restatement of the Nehruvian idea of Indian nationalism. In 2003, however, commentators spoke of schism in the *Sangh parivar* over the matter of the Ram temple in particular, and it was reported that Sudarshan, the RSS leader, had to intervene to maintain some semblance of unity in the ranks of the Hindu nationalists (Muralidharan 2003).

The difficulties that the BJP confronted in advancing *Hindutva* were shown up in the responses of its coalition partners in the National Democratic Alliance to the moves that it did make to advance the cause, through education policy. The officers of key bodies, the National Council on Educational Research and Training (NCERT), the Indian Council of Social Science Research (ICSSR) and the Indian Council of Historical Research (ICHR), were all replaced by individuals known to be sympathetic to Hindu nationalism. Shortly afterwards, the ICHR sought to withdraw from the press two volumes that had been written for the long-running 'Towards Freedom' project of the Council, intended to document the history of India's struggle for freedom from colonial rule. The case made to justify this action by the ICHR was essentially a procedural one, but a subsequent official inquiry has shown that it was motivated ideologically, and especially by the interest, eventually, of discrediting the role of the Communist Party of India (Rajalakshmi 2005). The teaching of history, in particular, became a field of controversy in a more general attempt to 'Indianise, nationalise and spiritualise' education (*Seminar* 2003). This included moves made by the University Grants Commission (UGC) in 2001 to introduce university courses in Vedic studies, astrology, palmistry and Hindu rituals – all in the name of restoring 'indigenous knowledge', which for the *Sangh parivar*, evidently, meant 'Hindu knowledge' (critiqued by Nandini Sundar 2002). Moves such as these were unwelcome to most of the BJP's coalition partners, who claimed in their home states to be upholders of secularism.

As it turned out, the most significant advance made by the forces of Hindu nationalism during the period of the BJP-led government came about not because of any actions on the part of the central government but because of those of a state government – that of Gujarat. On 27 February 2002, one of the carriages of a train carrying *kar sevaks* (volunteers) from Ayodhya was set on fire by a mob, reportedly of Muslims, in the railway station of the town of Godhra, killing fifty-nine people. In the immediate aftermath there was an orgy of violence against Muslims across the northern and central parts of the state (the geography of violence is significant, as we will explain), with the evident connivance and even encouragement of the forces of the state. The events were described as a pogrom. There were some incidents in which large numbers of Muslims were burnt alive – the most notorious case being that at the Gulmarg Society in Ahmedabad, where a Muslim former Congress MP was killed in this way along with many others. A Muslim judge of the high court was compelled to leave his residence and to take refuge. Muslim businesses as well as homes were quite systematically destroyed, and reports showed that members of the middle and upper classes of Gujarati society, as well as lumpens, were involved in the looting of them. The attacks were not confined to the towns and cities, and *adivasis* in particular joined in attacks in rural areas – reflecting in part the success of the educational work described by Froerer, Sundar and others. Hindu spiritual leaders of Gujarat remained silent. Not only were politicians and the state involved in the perpetration of violence, but the government of Gujarat has been quite blatantly partisan in its subsequent response, in the provision of relief to victims and in blocking efforts to secure justice for them (Chandhoke 2009; Yagnik and Sheth 2005: chapter 11; and Chandhoke et al. 2007).

It might have been thought that these horrific events, condemned by the BJP leaders at the centre, albeit with riders about the responsibility of Muslims themselves for what had happened, would have given rise to revulsion against the politicians who had been implicated in them and reinforced the voice of the secular opponents of communalism. In the state elections that followed not long afterwards, however, in December 2002, the BJP – led by Narendra Modi, who conducted a vicious campaign, making many stridently anti-Muslim statements – swept to a third consecutive victory (almost unprecedented in the see-saw world of Indian state politics over the last forty years). The National Executive of the party claimed that 'The people of Gujarat endorsed our commitment to cultural nationalism and voted us back for a third time in a row'. But what was so striking about the election results was that the BJP 'won

52 of the 65 violence-affected Assembly constituencies on the basis of a twelve percentage point swing . . . [while] . . . elsewhere in the State, where the impact of violence was muted or weak, the contest was more normal and the BJP suffered setbacks' ('Editorial' 2002). The constituencies in which the BJP was particularly successful were also those that had previously been held by Congress – so the victories seem clearly to have signalled 'that Hindutva mobilization through communal riots was successful' (Yagnik and Sheth 2005: 285). Gujarat was described by the BJP as 'the laboratory for *Hindutva*', and as shown by the verdict of the 2002 elections – repeated in 2007 – the state has become the bastion of Hindu nationalism (though in recent years Narendra Modi has played down *Hindutva* in favour of encouraging economic development, and has incurred the wrath of the VHP: see Spodek 2010). The success of the BJP in the state has been long prepared and has its roots especially in the reaction of upper-caste and educated middle-class Hindus to the successful mobilization by the Congress of an electoral combine of Muslims, lower castes and *adivasis* in the state elections of 1980. 'The upper castes in the state, particularly Patidars, felt humiliated and perceived a political and economic threat to their domination' (Yagnik and Sheth 2005: 255). They turned to *Hindutva*, and in the aftermath the *Sangh parivar* successfully penetrated local power structures across Gujarat, building an enduring power base against which the divided Congress Party of the state has been able only to scrabble (at least until its modest successes in the general election of 2009).

So the BJP, as the political wing of the *Sangh parivar*, has strength in Gujarat and in some other states – notably in the neighbouring states of Madhya Pradesh and Chhattisgarh, and in Rajasthan, in Himachal Pradesh in the north, and in the south, in Karnataka (where the party won office for the first time in 2008). These strengths were insufficient, however, to enable the party to retain office in 2004, when the Congress Party at last succeeded in putting together a more effective coalition, or again in 2009. In these general elections, commentators generally reckoned that the BJP fought a better campaign than the Congress, but the party lost crucial allies – and lost the aura that it had a decade before of being a party with a difference, offering competent government. Its decline seemed to be marked by its further losses in elections to the Maharashtra state assembly later in 2009.

Following its defeat in 2004, the BJP became the object of more open attacks from the RSS and other members of the *Sangh parivar*, with some (mainly from the VHP) arguing 'that the BJP was irredeemable and that the *Sangh parivar* should form a new Hindutva party under a new leadership' – though this line was rejected by the leadership of the RSS, even while it sought reforms in the party (Ramakrishnan 2005).

The party itself has undergone a series of convulsions, marked in part by changes of party president, and by resignations of senior leaders or, in some cases (like that, notably, of the former Foreign then Finance Minister, Jaswant Singh), their expulsion from the party (at least for a time). The tension between the injunction of the other members of *parivar* to uphold the primacy of *Hindutva*, and the politicians' speaking in different voices, at times proclaiming a hard line, at others protesting a commitment to something akin to Nehruvian pluralism, in order to secure wider support, shows no sign of resolution. It is a particular mani- festation of a general problem in the relationships of political movements and the parties to which they may give rise: the politicians must often trim in order to cope with political pressures, thus incurring the wrath of the ideologues of the movement from which they have come (Jaffrelot 2010). The political limitations of the BJP have not stood in the way, however, of 'the saffronization of the state and society in the last fifteen years. The Hindu rashtra is in the making along the societal lines the RSS has always valued' (Jaffrelot, cited by Noorani 2009). We go on to explain why.

9.4   Temples, Gods and Gurus: Banal Hinduism, Banal *Hindutva*

God is Back is the title of a recent book by two writers for *The Economist* (Micklethwait and Wooldridge 2009), who document the resurgence of religion very widely across the contemporary world, and its implications; and, as the sociologist Peter Berger puts it, 'not only is our world religious, it is religious in the old fashioned supernaturalistic way' (cited by Nanda 2009: 188). It might be thought that an argument about the resurgence of religion does not apply to India, for it is part of many Indians' own self-perception as well as of that of outsiders, that theirs has always been, and remains, a distinctly religious and deeply spiritual society (as Gandhi, indeed, argued). It may or may not be true that Indian society is especially religious – for people in other societies, even in some of those of Western Europe, are actually very much more religious than figures such as those on church attendance appear to suggest. But, even if it is true, there is still abundant evidence of the resurgence of popular Hinduism in recent years. 'God is Back' was also the title of the cover feature of the Indian news magazine *Outlook* in its issue for 21 August 2000; and it was a striking finding of the State of the Nation Survey, conducted by the Delhi-based Centre for Study of Developing Societies in 2007, that urban, educated Indians are more religious than their rural and illiterate counterparts. The conviction of modernization theorists that industrialization must inevitably bring about secularization, both in the sense that individuals no longer experience the need for belief in the supernatural, and in that of the separation of state and religion – which becomes restricted to the private sphere – is clearly confounded by contemporary changes, in India as elsewhere in the world (Nanda 2009: chapter 5).

Research on the religious beliefs and practices of owners and managers of big companies in the south Indian city of Chennai provides some insights into the processes of modernization in Indian society. The anthropologist Milton Singer published in 1972 an influential book, entitled *When a Great Tradition Modernizes*, and its 'capstone' (as one reviewer put it) was a long essay about 'industrial leaders' based mainly on interviews conducted in Madras (as the city was then called) in 1964. Singer was especially interested in big business people because he thought they were the ones at the cutting edge of modernization, so it would be through them that he could best study Indian modernity. For similar reasons, John Harriss chose to study people of the same social class but in the context of globalization, in a study that substantially replicated Singer's, carried out nearly four decades later (Harriss 2003a).

Singer found that, contrary to what he believed Weber had argued in his comparative research on different religious traditions, there is in Hinduism a set of beliefs quite comparable with those that Weber (in *The Protestant Ethic and the Spirit of Capitalism*) had identified in Calvinism and thought conducive to the development of capitalism. The interpretations of the scriptural text the *Bhagavad Gita* that were current amongst business people in the 1960s – and are still – offer striking parallels with Calvinism (as well as tying in closely with a burgeoning self-improvement literature in contemporary India). There was, Singer argued, an 'industrial theodicy', representing the 'modernization' of Hinduism without secularization. For the industrial leaders of Madras:

> 'the essentials of Hinduism' consist more in a set of beliefs and a code of ethical conduct than in a set of ritual observances. In this sense, the effect of industry is to change the traditional conception of the essentials of Hinduism from an emphasis on the correct ritual observances and family disciplines to an emphasis on philosophical principles, devotional faith, and right conduct. (Singer 1972: 342)

John Harriss observed, however, in his later study of big business people in Chennai, that – though one or two amongst them expressed themselves as being uninterested in religion – most showed a great deal of interest in and involvement with temple-going and public worship, following 'god-men' and gurus, and in the miraculous and ecstatic religion, as well as in the philosophical principles of what is called (by some of them) 'the Vedic Heritage'. The largest Chennai business group, for example, TVS, invests substantial resources in the restoration of eleven important temples, associated with Vaishnavism (though TVS was already doing this in the 1960s). One of the leaders of the group, a very prominent businessman indeed, says that a temple which is 'radiant' has a tremendous impact on people, whereas one that is dilapidated reflects a community that is disintegrating, and he is concerned for the maintenance of tradition, and of spirituality in the face of growing materialism. Several of the other big business houses of the city support the work of a particular religious teacher, or guru, Swami Dayananda Saraswathi (of whom more later), who operates in both the United States and India, teaches in English – in Chennai to packed middle-class audiences – and is active in the VHP. The foundation that is associated with him, funded by some of the business houses, produces a 'Vedic Heritage' teaching kit, directed at the education of middle-class children in India and in North America. Others of the 'industrial leaders' of present-day Chennai who are active followers of more traditional religious teachers – as were some of their predecessors in the 1960s – spoke freely of their experiences of the miraculous. The Chennai suburb of Nanganallur, where some IT companies are located, has seen a wave of construction of new temples – one of them the site of a massive idol of Hanuman, the monkey god of the *Ramayana,* who is increasingly the object of middle-class devotion – and is the home of a 'god-man' followed by some of the IT entrepreneurs, with whom, too, miracles are associated. The notion of the clear separation of religion and business affairs, which Singer referred to as 'compartmentalization' – an idea familiar to at least one of the businessmen, who has read Singer's work – is flatly rejected by Chennai's contemporary industrial leaders.

Religious activities of these kinds, and the frank religiosity that is shown by many big businessmen in Chennai, are shared very widely amongst members of India's 'new middle class', and across the country as a whole. Temple-building and restoration, the popularity of the invented tradition of what are actually new religious rituals, and the large followings of gurus and religious teachers who appeal to middle-class professionals, some of them by claiming that modern science has only rediscovered ideas and principles that are to be found in ancient Sanskrit texts, are widespread (as Meera Nanda's account shows: 2009). In Chennai, at least, all of this may not be quite as new as the comparison of Harriss's account with Singer's might suggest, for Singer's fieldwork notes (found in an archive in the Regenstein Library of the University of Chicago) show that he too encountered ideas and practices in 1964 not unlike those found commonly in 2000. That he set these observations

aside in his published work and rather emphasized the 'industrial theodicy' was probably a reflection, at least in part, of the concern of the
businessmen themselves in 1964 to project an image of being 'modern'
citizens of the secular Nehruvian state. Their successors, however, no
longer feel any such inhibitions, and some of them quite clearly express
the idea, dear to the *Sangh parivar*, that in order to be strong India must
be 'Hindu'.

That 'God is Back' – or at least that religiosity should now be more
freely and publicly expressed than was the case in the earlier years of the
Indian republic – was explained by *Outlook* in these terms:

> the religion that has been revived is . . . very needs-based . . . it caters to
> one's craving for security, peace, even belief . . . The new spirituality is
> just as much about material well-being as it is about spiritual health. It
> promises to endow its followers with inner peace, satisfaction, harmonious
> relationships in the private and public spheres and good health. (*Outlook*
> 21 August 2000)

The argument anticipates those of social scientists who have sought
to explain the resurgence of 'old-fashioned, supernaturalistic' religion across the world. Pippa Norris and Ronald Inglehart (2004), in
research drawing on large-scale public opinion surveys, have proposed,
influentially, what they refer to as 'the existential security hypothesis'.
They argue that religious enthusiasm is driven by the human need for
security, safety and predictability – which are found in religion (though
this is a proposition that would be challenged by many scholars of
religion). Economic development may well deliver existential security,
which is why there has been quite a strong positive connection historically between modernization and secularization – but the trend is not
inevitable. That 'religion remains far more robust in the U.S. than, say, in
Western Europe, [may be] because existential security dilemmas remain
much more prevalent in American society' (Bellin 2008: 332, referring to
Norris and Inglehart).

The argument might seem to apply well to Indian society now – exactly
as *Outlook* suggested – and, amongst other observations, to account for
the survey finding that urban and educated people are generally more religious than their less well-educated rural peers (though we do not know
whether this is a recent development or not; the finding is surprising only
because of the presumption of theorists of modernization that urbanization and the spread of education must inevitably lead to secularization).
Members of the 'new middle class' of India are often afflicted, some scholars suggest, with particular status anxiety (Fernandes 2006), and one has
argued specifically that 'globalization has made individuals and groups

more ontologically insecure and existentially uncertain – an uncertainty many people try to reduce by searching for new secure self-identities', and often to find them in religion (Kinnvall 2006: i). Such arguments are found wanting, however, in a study by Maya Warrier of the urban, educated, middle-class followers of Mata Amritanandamayi, probably the fastest-rising guru-saint in India today (Warrier 2003, 2005). She finds, rather, that such middle-class people are drawn to modern gurus because of the religious context that they establish, which offers 'immense choice, possibility and potential to individuals seeking to negotiate their religious lives in diverse ways' (2003: 247). The 'existential insecurity hypothesis' is plausible mainly because of an unquestioning acceptance of the propositions of modernization theory. Another factor, in India as elsewhere, is the search for meaning amidst material prosperity – as, again, was reflected in the ideas of the member of the TVS family of whom we spoke, and amongst the followers of Mata Amritanandamayi. Both poverty and prosperity may lead people to religion, and it is perfectly possible for people to be adepts of science and technology and yet to have recourse to belief in the supernatural – indeed, it is perfectly normal outside modern Western Europe (and certainly in the United States). Hindu nationalist thinking plays on this possibility.

The Indian state has long intervened extensively in religious affairs. Any semblance of separation between state and religion has long gone (see Fuller 2003). Legislation regarding the administration of temple affairs was initiated in the colonial period, but taken over and extended after Independence. The state has intervened – and continues to do so – to try to ensure that Dalits are able to enter temples from which they have historically been forbidden entry. The state governments of Kerala and of Tamil Nadu are very actively involved in temple management, and in the case of Tamil Nadu now also deeply involved in the training of temple priests. It is ironic, for example, that the two principal political parties in the state of Tamil Nadu, both of them owing their origins to the Dravidian movement that was founded by a self-proclaimed rationalist and strong critic of religion, E. V. Ramaswamy Naicker, should now compete with each other over which has done more to support rituals for the rededication of temples, and for the training of temple priests. The regular appearance of political leaders and politicians, and of senior civil servants, at temple functions contributes to the impression that in practice the state really is identified with Hinduism. And, in these days of public–private partnership, it is wholly unsurprising that there should be collaboration between the state and the corporate sector in support of religion – in 'the state-temple-corporate complex'. Some of the most senior Indian businessmen appear alongside the politicians at temple functions.

Actions of this kind, and the way in which, as Véronique Bénéï has shown in an ethnographic study, Hindu symbols and ideas are woven into the everyday routines of physical exercise and recitation in schools, immediately directed at building national consciousness, actually inculcate 'banal Hinduism' – that is, familiar, unquestioned, everyday religious practice. Bénéï found that teachers who were not at all sympathetic to militant Hindu nationalism saw nothing wrong 'with Hinduism being taught in school as part of "Hindu culture"', just as, these days, there is nothing at all questionable for most people about the association of politicians and of the state with religious observance. As Bénéï goes on to say:

> many people – even those not belonging to the Hindu fold – conceive of Indian culture and the Indian nation as essentially Hindu, without this conception *necessarily* being accompanied by any communalist claim or politically militant Hindu identity. Such is the ambiguity of Hinduism as both culture *and* religion. It is on this very ambiguity that militant religious nationalists play. (2001: 212, emphasis in the original)

There is a certain ambiguity, too, in the teachings of some of the gurus to whom middle-class Indians are attracted. Swami Dayananda Saraswathi, for example, argues that Hinduism is not *a* religion, but simply 'religion', and that it encompasses diversity. It actually embraces all the ideas that are found in Islam or in Christianity in a way that is much more cogent than are these 'founder religions'. But at the same time Saraswathi wittily belittles these other religious traditions, asserting the greatness of Hinduism, and decrying religious conversions as a kind of violence. His arguments may not be intended to justify religious violence in response, but they can certainly be taken as having that implication. He ended one of his sermons with the words: 'Strength is being what you are. You are a nobody if you don't know that. It is in this sense that Hindus must be strong.' Everyday religiosity, 'banal Hinduism', which has been increasing in contemporary India, can easily slip into acceptance of Hindu nationalist ideas. They too become familiar, accepted, everyday – 'banal *Hindutva*'. This is the way in which the 'saffronization' of state and society detected by Jaffrelot is taking place, whether the BJP is in power, or not.

Hindu nationalism has become part of the everyday common sense of many Indians, but it is not always 'banal'. As Steven Wilkinson has noted, though there were serious communal riots in the 1960s and 1970s, there was no sense then that the integrity of the nation was under any threat from religious polarization and violence. This changed in the succeeding decades, substantially if not entirely because of Hindu nationalist agitation (Wilkinson 2005: 1–3), as was brought out in Asghar Ali Engineer's documentation and analysis of riots from the early 1980s (Engineer 1984). And Paul Brass concludes from his detailed studies of the city over many years that 'though many communal riots in Aligarh and elsewhere in India have involved persons and parties not part of the *Sangh parivar*, militant Hindus have played a central role in every large-scale riot in Aligarh at least since 1961, however electorally weak or strong they were' (2003b). We will conclude our discussion of Hindu nationalism by examining explanations of why India is subject to incidents of communal violence (or what is referred to in the wider literature as 'ethnic violence'), when people from different religious communities kill, maim or humiliate each other.

9.5   Hindu Nationalism and Communal Violence

Michael Billig, who invented the idea of 'banal nationalism', associates it with 'the flag hanging unnoticed on a public building' (cited by Nanda 2009: 140). Hindu nationalist ideas have penetrated the public discourse in India in such a way that they too are almost unnoticed for much of the time. But flags are sometimes waved with passion, as Billig also says, and so too is *Hindutva* associated with popular passion, as was seen so strikingly in the destruction of the Babri Masjid in 1992 and in the many riots around the national *yatras* (processions across the country) that preceded it. But does Hindu nationalism bear a major responsibility for communal violence? Or should *Hindutva* be seen – as Hindu nationalists themselves argue – as being rather a rational political *response* to popular sentiments that sometimes erupt into appalling violence between Hindus and their Muslim or Christian or on one notorious occasion, in Delhi in 1984, following the assassination of Mrs Gandhi, their Sikh neighbours? There clearly is justification for the latter view, given that some incidents of communal violence have occurred at times and in contexts where there is no indication of the active involvement of politicians or others associated in any way with the *Sangh parivar*. Hindu nationalists argued, too, that the decline in the frequency of outbreaks of communal violence at the time of the BJP government – at least until Godhra – showed that they were better than the Congress at holding violence in check.

One major analysis of the causes of communal violence in India that makes very little reference at all to the possible role of the *Sangh parivar* is that of Ashutosh Varshney (2002), which takes off from the striking observation that the extent and frequency of occurrence of conflicts involving Hindus and Muslims vary enormously among Indian cities (which is where the overwhelming majority of incidents of communal violence occur – it is an urban phenomenon). Varshney therefore studied three pairs of cities, the two cities in each pair having important features in common, but very different histories of communal conflict. From his analysis, he concluded that the crucial factor is that of 'civic engagement': it is the varying extent of inter-community civic, associational life (what Robert Putnam, influentially, refers to as 'bridging social capital': e.g., Putnam 2000) that is most important in accounting for differences in the history of violence between the cities (in turn explained to a large extent by different patterns in the Gandhian popular political mobilizations in the 1920s and 1930s – so there is an important argument here about path-dependency). Varshney refers, too, to recent cases in which the actions of particular officials in some cities have encouraged the development of inter-community associational activism, where it was largely absent before, with positive results in reducing violence.

This 'civic engagement' thesis has been extremely controversial, especially because of its neglect of the possible significance of the activities of Hindu nationalists (Brass 2003a, 2003b; and Chandhoke 2009, who is strongly critical of Varshney's arguments about civil society). There are also methodological questions about Varshney's work, however, some of which he himself recognizes. One is that of 'the possible endogeneity of civic engagement to other factors. In other words, are successful inter-ethnic associations really a cause of peace so much as its effect?' (Wilkinson 2005: 12). There is a lack of longitudinal data that would make it possible to test the direction of causality. And, in the cases of apparent success in coping with violence through the building of inter-community ties, there are questions both because of the recurrence of violence in some of them, and because the officials involved in them also improved policing. 'So, was it increased civic engagement or better law enforcement that prevented the riots? A plausible case could be made for both, and in the absence of clear data on each over time the answer must remain open to debate' (Wilkinson 2005: 12).

But ethnographic research lends some support to Varshney's argument, while also extending it. Philippa Williams was doing fieldwork in Varanasi (Benares) in north India at the time of a terrorist attack in March 2006, when bombs were exploded at the Sankat Mocha temple, killing twenty-one people, and two more people were killed a little later in further blasts at a railway station. The city had not previously been immune from communal clashes and it was feared that tensions would erupt in violence again as a result of the bombs. That they did not has understandably quite complex and very particular causes, according to Williams's analysis (2007), but the factor of civic engagement – or, in this case, rather the fact that Hindus and Muslims were united by a shared belief in their 'brotherhood' as participants in the distinctive urban culture of Varanasi – certainly played a part. Williams, however, highlights the significance of the agency of particular individuals, and it appears from her account that the determination of the chief priest (*mahant*) of the Sankat Mocha temple that radical Hindu politics must be kept out of the religious space of the temple played an especially important part. The *mahant* successfully foiled attempts by a BJP leader to exploit the attack for political ends.

The agency of individuals, and in the case of Aligarh quite certainly that of militant Hindus, is also a major theme of Paul Brass's analysis of the way in which religious violence is produced in that city and elsewhere by 'a network of actors, groups and connections . . . whose effect is to keep a town or city in a permanent state of awareness of Hindu–Muslim relationships'. What he calls the 'institutionalized riot systems' (Brass 1997: 284) that are created by these networks produce violence (there is an explicit imagery of theatre here). It is hard to say, however, whether such systems exist generally, and Williams's ethnography suggests the likely importance of particular contingent and conjunctural factors (see also Tatsumi 2009). Of course, each individual case of the outbreak of ethnic violence has its own particular explanation. But Brass's argument, and even more that of Steven Wilkinson in his attempt to develop a general explanation for communal violence, emphasizes the overarching importance of the response of the state. Brass says: 'where the policy of a state government is decisively opposed to communal riots . . . riots will be either prevented or contained' (2003b); while Wilkinson states, as emphatically: 'state-level patterns of law enforcement dominate local factors – state law enforcement can prevent violence even in so-called riot-prone towns and facilitate it even in towns with no previous history of riots' (2004: 17). There are many local reasons for the occurrence of inter-community tensions that can give rise to violence, but whether they do or not depends heavily upon how governments act.

Then the question arises of what factors account for differences in governments' responses, and Wilkinson's answer, based on careful statistical and historical analysis of rioting in different Indian states and in several other countries, is that much depends on the extent and nature of electoral competition. His key finding is that politicians in highly fractionalized political systems have incentives to provide security to minorities 'in order to retain their electoral support today and the option of forming coalitions with minority supported parties tomorrow' (2004: 237). In these circumstances, even anti-minority politicians may be constrained to prevent ethnic violence – as happened in some Indian states in 2002 after the Godhra incident. At that time, BJP politicians in Gujarat, a state with a low level of party competition and one where they did not have to depend on any support from the Muslim minority, accurately calculated that they could reap political dividends from the violence. Meanwhile other state governments, in more competitive electoral environments, or those in which the ruling party depended on Muslim support, prevented riots (Wilkinson 2004: 154–60). Political competition, then, forces compromises – of the kind that the BJP has been constrained to make in order to win, to retain, and now to regain power. The culpability of militant Hindu nationalists, however, for many incidents of communal violence, in circumstances where they are not subject to such political constraints, is quite plain. Now there is strong evidence, too (see Ramakrishnan 2010a), of the existence of Hindu terrorism, not sanctioned formally by the leadership of the *Sangh parivar*, but clearly inspired by their ideas.

9.6   Conclusion

So has the rise of Hindu nationalism halted? It certainly is the case that the ascendancy of the BJP – the party political arm of the movement for Hindu nationalism – has faltered, even though the failures of the Congress-led government elected into office in 2009 (marked by the corruption scandals that have afflicted it in 2010–11) may mean that the BJP will again have the opportunity to govern the country. There is every indication, however, that the compulsions of politics will ensure the BJP continues to trim its attempts to pursue the *Hindutva* agenda, as it had to while in office until 2004. But both 'banal *Hindutva*' and its more extreme and violent forms are here to stay in the context of sharpened ethnic, religious identity in India today.

10

Rural Dislocations: Why Has Maoism Become Such a Force in India?

10.1 Introduction

In the early months of 2010, India was rocked time and again by attacks involving those described by the government and the press as Maoist rebels, or sometimes as Naxalites. In February, twenty-four members of the security forces were killed in an attack on a camp at Silda in West Bengal; on 4 April, the BBC reported that 'Suspected Maoist rebels have killed at least ten policemen in a landmine attack in the eastern state of Orissa'; just two days later, seventy-six paramilitaries of the Central Reserve Police Force were killed in a major attack in the Chhattisgarh district of Dantewada; on 17 May, in the same district, a mine detonated under a bus carrying both civilians and Special Police Officers, and killed forty-four; on 28 May, the derailment of an express train in West Bengal, killing about 150 people, was blamed on the Maoists, though denied by them; then, on 29 June, a further twenty-six of the Central Reserve Police Force were killed in Narayanapur in Chhattisgarh. These were only the more notable events that were widely reported internationally. The Indian press, meanwhile, recorded many more minor incidents almost every day across the states of Andhra Pradesh, Bihar, Chhattisgarh, Jharkhand, Orissa, Maharashtra, Uttar Pradesh and West Bengal (incidents are recorded by the South Asia Terrorist Portal: <http://www.satp.org>). The frequency, intensity and geographical spread of the Maoist insurgency explain the Prime Minister's earlier description of it, in 2006, as the most serious internal security threat that India has ever faced.

India's Maoist insurgency may be seen as part of a much wider phenomenon. The high incidence of civil war and of rural guerrilla warfare (that is, of 'insurgency') across much of the world over the last twenty years has attracted the attention of a number of scholars. For some time, it was thought that such conflicts arise principally because of ethnic grievances, or grievances relating to economic inequality or political oppression, but tests by James Fearon and David Laitin (2003), and by Paul Collier and Anke Hoeffler (2004, and with Rohner 2009), each using data relating to large samples of civil wars for, respectively, 1945–99 and 1960–2004, have led to the rejection of this thesis. Rather than 'grievance', it was argued by Collier and Hoeffler (2004), the possibilities of financial predation – securing loot – especially from valuable natural resources, supply a more powerful drive. 'Greed', rather than 'grievance', appeared to them a more powerful predictor of conflict. More recently, however, they – like Fearon and Laitin, though for somewhat different reasons – have come to the conclusion that the causes of civil war and insurgency have to do more with feasibility than with either greed or grievance. The existence of valuable natural resources that insurgents can control makes rebellion financially feasible. And the presence in a population of large numbers of young men (between the ages of fifteen and twenty-nine) is a further significant factor. Fearon and Laitin, however, find that insurgency is favoured especially by state weakness. Weak government, they argue, renders insurgency more feasible and more attractive, due to weak local policing or inept and corrupt counter-insurgency practices – which 'often include a propensity for brutal and indiscriminate retaliation that helps drive non-combatant locals into rebel forces' (Fearon and Laitin 2003: 76). Both they, and Collier and Hoeffler, find that insurgency is favoured by rough and mountainous terrain. Fearon and Laitin conclude:

> If, under the right environmental conditions, just 500–2000 active guerillas can make for a long-running, destructive internal war, then the average level of grievance in a group may not matter that much. What matters is whether active rebels can hide from government forces and whether economic opportunities are so poor that the life of a rebel is attractive . . . all guerrillas really need is superior local knowledge which enables them to threaten reprisal for denunciation. (2003: 88)

In this chapter, we will examine how far these rather bleak findings explain the resurgence of India's Maoists, in the context of an analysis of the wider problems of agrarian social change, of struggles in some areas over land, and of the turmoil that pervades large parts of the Indian countryside. We find that while there is no simple connection between accumulated grievance and political mobilization, or between the pursuit of economic liberalism and insurgency, there is substantial evidence showing that Maoists have built support by addressing the structural violence to which tribal people, Dalits and poor rural people more generally are subjected. This is in spite of the fact that the movement is marked by caste tensions and a gap between the social status of leaders and that of the youthful rank-and-file; and in spite of the close relations that can exist between the Maoists and local elites (Bhatia 2005a; Jaoul 2009; Shah 2010b). At the same time, all the conditions that are emphasized in the 'feasibility' thesis are in place: weak states, with ineffective though violent and oppressive police forces; rough country; lots of young people, men and women, with little other opportunity and little to lose (see also Gayer and Jaffrelot 2009: 5–9); and ample possibilities of raising resources through sale of protection and 'taxation' in resource-rich lands. The tragedy of the movement is that it is embedded in a spiral of violence, and that its support for the least privileged members of Indian society cannot finally be reconciled with its ambition of overthrowing the current Indian state. The result is that it endangers the lives of many of those whom it seeks to represent.

10.2   Maoism in India

'Maoism' is not a new phenomenon in India. The movement has its origins in fierce debates that took place amongst Indian communists and that culminated in the 1960s. The Communist Party of India split in 1964 when those who rejected what they saw as the 'reformism' of the leadership – and its readiness to compromise with the ruling Congress Party – broke away to form the Communist Party of India (Marxist) (CPI(M)). A small group of young Bengali communists, however, took up a more emphatically revolutionary line, rejecting both mass organization and democratic participation. Inspired by the example of the Chinese communists under Mao Zedong, and starting at Naxalbari in northern West Bengal, they launched an armed uprising of peasants against local landlords. Their action spread quite quickly into parts of Bihar, the Srikakulam district of Andhra Pradesh, Koraput in Orissa, and some other areas, where guerrilla squads of poor and landless peasants drove out landlords. In some cases, however, action degenerated into indiscriminate violence following from the injunction of Charu Mazumdar, who had emerged as the movement's leader, to undertake 'annihilation of class enemies'. Mazumdar once wrote that the battle cry of the movement should be: 'He who has not dipped his hand in the blood of class enemies can hardly be called a communist' (cited by Simeon 2010). The Naxalites, as they came to be called, won a lot of support amongst young Bengalis, especially in Kolkata and other towns, but these young people were quite ruthlessly suppressed by the Congress-led state government in the early 1970s (see Banerjee 1980 and 2009; and Ray 1988, on the history of the movement; and Bose (ed.) 2010b for a view from the CPI(M)).

By 1969, there were in the country (according to the current General Secretary of the Maoists' party: see Ganapathy 2007), two organized groups, one the Communist Party of India (Marxist-Leninist) (CPI(ML)) – Mazumdar's group – and the other, at that time more supportive of mass organization, which came later to call itself the Maoist Communist Centre (MCC). By the time that Charu Mazumdar died in police custody, in 1972, the movement as a whole appeared to have been very largely defeated by the state security forces. Repression was apparently effective, perhaps because of the lack of a mass base for the movement – and their defeats brought about rethinking amongst the surviving revolutionaries. One group, Liberation, began organizing mass fronts and later started participating in parliamentary politics. Others remained underground but began mass organizing amongst the poorest agricultural labourers and peasants, Dalits and tribal people, in northern Andhra Pradesh and in Bihar (including what is now Jharkhand). The movement, never entirely unified, fragmented even further, and Bela Bhatia – who is one of the very small number of scholars to have carried out systematic field research amongst the revolutionaries – records that there were as many as seventeen different groups active in central Bihar in the mid-1990s, divided by their varying commitments to parliamentary politics, to mass organization and to armed guerrilla struggle (Bhatia 2005a). Both Bhatia and George Kunnath, who has also done ethnographic research in central Bihar (Kunnath 2006, 2009; see also Jaoul 2009), show that there could be both complementarity and tension between mass organizing and guerrilla struggle. The two modes of action might be supportive of each other, and perceived as such by village people, but the demands of armed struggle for secrecy and authority could also come into conflict with the democratic principles of the mass organizations.

By the end of the century, a process of fusion had at last begun amongst the principal groups. The CPI(ML) People's War Group, which had formed in Andhra Pradesh in 1980, joined in 1998 with CPI(ML) Party Unity, formed in Bihar in 1976, to establish CPI(ML) People's War, operating in Andhra, Orissa, Chhattisgarh, Madhya Pradesh and Maharashtra. The Maoist Communist Centre, together with the Revolutionary Communist Centre of India (Maoist) of Punjab, formed the Maoist Communist Centre of India in 2003, operating in Bihar and Jharkhand. It was the coming together of the latter, MCCI with CPI(ML) People's War, in September 2004, that established the unified Communist Party of India (Maoist), and provided a large swathe of mainly hilly, forested country in the east and centre of India –

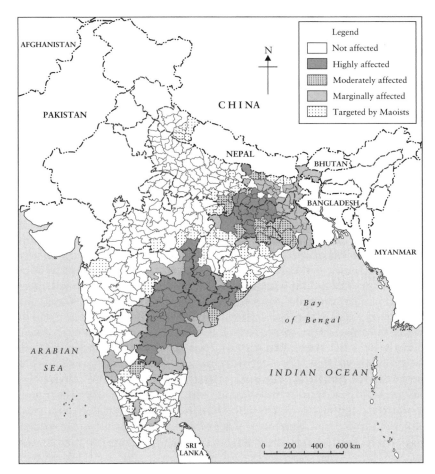

Figure 10.1: India's 'red corridor'.

Source: Derived from P. V. Ramana, *The Naxal Challenge* (New Delhi: Pearson Longman 2008, p.210); Map by Lee Li Kheng, National University of Singapore, for Robin Jeffrey, Ronojoy Sen and Pratima Singh (eds), *More Than Maoism* (New Delhi: Manohar for Institute of South Asian Studies, 2012).

terrain that favours guerrilla insurgency – within which the Maoists are able to move without the problems of coordination that afflict the different state police forces (Ramakrishnan 2009; Myrdal and Navlakha 2010). This is what has come to be known as 'the red corridor', stretching south from the borders of Nepal as far as northern Tamil Nadu, and across the centre of the country into Maharashtra and parts of Gujarat (see figure 10.1). Whereas in 2004 it was thought that fifty-five districts in nine states of India were 'Maoist affected', by 2010 about a third of the country – 223 districts in twenty states – had a Maoist presence (*The Economist* 27 February 2010). This corridor is twice the geographical size of the other two insurgency-affected areas of India, in the North East and in Kashmir, while the numbers of armed cadres mobilized by the Maoists – some estimates suggest perhaps as many as 20,000 men and women, though these figures may well be inflated by the security forces – are also greater than the numbers of insurgents elsewhere in the country. All accounts show them to be mostly young men and women, some of whom have been recruited while still very young indeed (see, for example, Roy 2010). *Adivasis* – tribal people – are now most numerous amongst the foot-soldiers of the movement, though the leaders are generally people of higher castes, many of them it seems from Andhra Pradesh. There are some parts of Chhattisgarh and of Jharkhand that are now effectively controlled by the Maoists. These are their 'guerrilla zones' – that may become 'base areas' (with no state presence at all).

Since 2004, the Maoists have grown in strength, and the frequency and intensity of confrontations between them and the security forces, and of their attacks on state structures – notably the railways, and schools (when they are, or might be used as bases by the security forces) – have increased in this time. The CPI(Maoist) was formally banned by the Government of India as a terrorist organization, under Section 41 of the Unlawful Activities (Prevention) Act, on 22 June 2009. Thereafter, the central government has sought to intensify counter-insurgency operations, summed up in the words 'clear, hold and build'. As an official explained to Ramakrishnan, 'It is a comprehensive operational strategy that would first seek to clear an area of Maoists, occupy it militarily, and follow up with socio-economic development activity.' This strategy, that has come to be known as 'Operation Green Hunt', has been questioned both by security experts, who argue that the police forces lack the numbers, the intelligence, the coordination and the organization to make it work, and by Congress leaders – notably by the former Chief Minister of Madhya Pradesh, Digvijay Singh – who do not believe this 'security-centric' approach is the right one to pursue. They argue that the prior concern should be to tackle the problems of rights and livelihoods – 'grievances', in the wider literature to which we referred earlier – that lead people to support the Maoists in the first place (Ramakrishnan 2010b). Repression worked against the Naxalites in the early 1970s, when the activists eschewed mass mobilization. But can it work now if – as seems likely – the Maoists have built mass support, partly by addressing problems of social justice amongst very poor people, and are integrated into the fabric of local society?

10.3   Class, Caste and Production in Rural India

Analysis of agrarian class relations, in order to identify the likely friends and enemies of revolutionary transformation, has been of great importance to Marxists since the work of Lenin and later of Mao Zedong (see Alavi 1965) – and it is so for India's Maoists. They have always argued that India is, in the words of its current *Party Programme* (which can be read at <http://www.satp.org>), 'a semi-colonial and semi-feudal country'. The 'principal contradiction' in India, however, still is that 'between feudalism and the broad masses of the people'. The central class contradiction in India, they are saying, that has to be resolved in order to bring about progressive social change, beneficial to the majority, is that between landlords – the owners of large estates – and the mass of the peasantry. In support of this argument, the *Programme* advances the following:

> Despite the hoax of all land reforms, 30% of the total land is concentrated in the hands of landlords, who constitute only 5% of the population, while middle peasantry constitute about 20% of the rural population, whereas rich peasantry constitutes 10%. 65% of the total peasantry are landless and poor peasants, who own either no land at all or meager land. Extreme forms of semi-feudal exploitation are still prevalent in the countryside. The major prevailing forms of such exploitation are extortion of their produce through share-cropping, which is robbing them of their produce up to 50%, bonded labour, usurious and merchant capital and other forms of extra-economic coercion. The most vicious form of extracting surplus through extra-economic coercion was through the caste system . . . The scheduled castes continued to be treated as near slaves.

The Indian countryside is dominated, they say, 'by landlords, usurers, merchants and religious institutions', who are politically reactionary and supportive of the continuing influence of imperialism. The main force that will overthrow these groups is said to be the peasantry, and centrally the landless poor peasants and agricultural workers, in a 'democratic revolution carried out under the leadership of the proletariat', though to advance this revolution it will be necessary to build a 'four class united front – the working class, the peasantry, petty bourgeoisie and national bourgeoisie'. Consequently, one of the primary tasks of the new people's democratic state, established by the revolution, will be to 'confiscate all land belonging to the landlords and religious institutions and (to) redistribute it among the landless poor peasants and agricultural labourers on the slogan of "land to the tillers"'.

This is not at all an exceptional analysis of the problems of rural India, or of what to do about them. As we observed earlier (in chapter

4), there has been a marginal increase in the recent past in the concentration both of ownership and of operational landholdings across India as a whole, and there has been a resurgence of private moneylending in rural India at usurious rates of interest, following the financial sector reforms of the 1990s. And there are a good many independent scholars who have analysed India's agrarian problems and come up with comparable arguments to those of the Maoists. Much of their analysis was anticipated in the early 1950s by the American scholar Daniel Thorner, when he argued famously that Indian agriculture and the rural economy as a whole are subject to what he called 'the depressor' – by which he meant the 'complex of legal, economic and social relations uniquely typical of the Indian countryside', that made it pay for landlords to live by appropriating rents, usurious interest and speculative trading profits from the impoverished mass of the peasantry, rather than by investing in productivity-enhancing innovations (Thorner 1956 [1976]: 16).

An analysis of the agrarian problems of India comparable with that of Maoists now, with recommendations for the implementation of redistributive land reform – for 'land to the tiller' – was actually advanced within the Congress in the course of the Freedom Struggle, and then by the party in the period of its hegemony in the 1950s. Land reform legislation was enacted, to varying but always very modest effect in different states, in the early decades after India's Independence. Now it is being given up and even reversed in some areas, in order to facilitate the acquisition of land by large owners and by corporations, in the interests – supposedly – of encouraging high-value commercial agriculture (see chapter 4). In response to these moves, the Communist Party of India (Marxist)(CPI(M)), the most significant organized left-wing political party in the country – to which the Maoists are very hostile – argues in its current programme that the first task of a People's Democratic government in regard to agriculture is still to 'Abolish landlordism by implementing radical land reforms and give land free of cost to the agricultural labourers and poor peasants'.

So, as Tilak Gupta has put it, the programme of the CPI(Maoist), and the analysis on which it is based, are ones with which 'a large chunk of the Indian political class should have nothing to quarrel about' (Gupta 2006: 3172). But there is little sign these days of there being very much pressure from below in the major agricultural regions of the country for redistributive land reform, which has only had any success at all in the country in Kerala and West Bengal, the states where the CPI(M) has had real strength. The mainstream left parties have either not chosen or have been unable to concentrate attention on marginal areas where the land issue still is alive, and the Maoist/Naxalite organizations have filled the gap. Gupta argues that 'the major Naxalite contribution to

Indian politics is that they have kept alive the agrarian demands of the rural poor through persistent but not always successful struggles' (Gupta 2006: 3173).

We will examine Gupta's claim later in this chapter. First, we want to consider whether the analysis of agrarian class struggles of the left, including that of the Maoists, remains as powerful today as it was in the middle and later twentieth century. Thinkers associated with the CPI(M) are surely right when they argue that the Maoists' analysis seriously underestimates the extent of the development of capitalist relations of production in agriculture (Grewal 2010: 30–3). Other researchers argue that the importance of land as the basis both of livelihood and of social dominance is decreasing, as the main locus of economic activity has shifted away from the village (Singh 2005), or, like the sociologist Dipankar Gupta, that 'The village is shrinking as a sociological reality, though it still exists as a space' (Gupta 2005: 752). Statements of this kind reflect the fact that even in the most important agricultural regions of India people have come to depend less exclusively on agriculture and agricultural-related activities – though they may still have an important foothold in the agricultural economy and be recorded in the Census as agricultural workers. It is very widely the case that work outside the village, whether locally and on a daily basis, or at a considerable distance, on the basis of circular migration, to construction sites in big cities or to brickfields just outside them (to give two significant examples), is now very important, and that it has changed both the basis of livelihoods and social and political relationships in the villages. As Dalits' and others' absolute dependence upon landowners for their livelihoods has declined, so has their willingness to submit to the forms of social oppression to which they were subjected historically (though this is not to say that such oppression does not persist, as reports even from what are generally considered to be socially progressive states, such as Tamil Nadu, clearly demonstrate: see, for example, Harriss et al. 2010). At the same time, as we explained in chapter 4, the so-called 'farmers' movements' to which the extensive commercialization of agriculture gave rise, following upon the Green Revolution of the 1970s, have declined in power and influence over the last decade. The political mobilizations driven by these movements appear to have been supplanted by greater individualism, with rural people increasingly 'looking after themselves', as Jonathan Pattenden has argued (2005). Collective action of any kind, leave alone the sort of revolutionary collective action sought by the Maoists, has become more difficult in the major agricultural regions of India. There is little sign of movement from below for the sort of agrarian radicalism propounded by the Maoists in the *Party Programme*, outside a very few pockets.

10.4   Struggles Against Enclosures

What has become a striking feature of contemporary, liberalizing India, on the other hand, has been the rise in the frequency and intensity of mobilizations of people against their dispossession and displacement for development projects such as dams, for mining ventures, in the interests of commercial forest management or of wildlife conservation, or most recently for the establishment of Special Economic Zones (SEZs) – regions, that is, with distinctive governance regimes and favourable taxation, and that are expected to have high-quality infrastructure, all intended to provide incentives for investment, to promote exports and generate employment. The widespread dispossession of peasant proprietors and the privatization of what have hitherto been common resources, especially affecting some of the poorest and most marginalized people in the country, but to the benefit of capital accumulation, is a process rather like that of the enclosure movements in early modern England, considered by Marx as an instance of 'primitive accumulation'. It is an example of what David Harvey (2003: chapter 4) analyses as 'accumulation by dispossession', and comparable with the even more extensive and often violent evictions of peasants from their lands, to make way for industrial projects and for property development, taking place in China (Harvey 2005: chapter 5; Yang Lian 2005). But the people, in India as in China, are not giving up without a fight – and their struggles in central and eastern India provide a terrain that is sympathetic to the Maoists.

For a long time, the Government of India had no figures for the numbers of people displaced by dams (once described by Nehru as the 'temples of the modern India'), or other projects (Roy 2001). This seems remarkable, but it is a fair reflection of the almost complete disregard on the part of the state historically for those displaced from their homes and livelihoods by 'the march of progress'. Their misfortune was held to be a price well worth paying for the common good of irrigation water and power generation. Now 'reliable' estimates of the numbers of people displaced in India since Independence vary quite widely between 20 and 38 million (Whitehead 2003), and N. C. Saxena, then Secretary to the Planning Commission, was reported as having said in a private lecture that he thought the number was in the region of 50 million, equivalent to the population of a substantial state. Walter Fernandes (n.d) places the figures as high as 60 million. What is certain is that members of the Scheduled Tribes – 'tribals', or *adivasis* – who make up only about 8 per cent of the population of the country, are quite disproportionately represented amongst those who have been displaced, with Dalits disproportionately represented amongst the remainder. What is also certain is that only a very small minority of those displaced have been at all adequately compensated, and most states still do not have resettlement and rehabilitation policies.

The greatest and now most notorious of India's major dam projects is the Sardar Sarovar Project (SSP), part of a gigantic scheme to build more than 3,000 dams along the length of the river Narmada, in western India, in Madhya Pradesh, touching Maharashtra, and in Gujarat, for irrigation, drinking water supply, and power generation. It is expected to become the largest irrigation project in the world, but SSP alone is also reckoned to be displacing 200–250,000, or even as many as 500,000 people, 60–70 per cent of them tribals. It was concern on the part of civil society groups – brought together under the banner of the Narmada Bachao Andolan – about the extent of the benefits from the scheme, and to whom they would accrue (disproportionately to agro-industrial elites), as well as about the sheer impossibility that the Narmada projects could be implemented in such a way as to provide full resettlement and reha- bilitation to all those ousted, that led to the very effective mobilization of opposition to the completion of the project. In the end, the Narmada Bachao Andolan (NBA) lost its fight to prevent completion, when judges of the Supreme Court finally found against it in 2000, in the case that it had brought against the Government of India. But NBA has had an indel- ible influence on public opinion about the rights of those displaced by projects. The judges ruled, for example, in 2003 – in regard to the Tehri dam in Uttarakhand – that the overall project benefits from the dam could not be used as an excuse to deprive those ousted of their fundamen- tal rights, the reverse of the Supreme Court judgment of 2000. Appeal to the 'common good', in other words, does not cancel out fundamental human rights (a key part of the discourse of the NBA, see Nilsen 2010). The NBA has played a significant role, too, in mobilizing a wider social movement – through the National Alliance of People's Movements – 'to struggle for a development process that empowers people against the hegemonic, exploitative culture associated with the terms "privatization" and "liberalization"' (in the words of its mission statement).

The people who have been most affected by displacement have been members of the Scheduled Tribes – those people from what were thought of as backward, tribal areas who were 'scheduled' for particular protec- tion under the Constitution of India – living in the forested hilly tracts of eastern and central India (Guha 2007a). These *adivasis* include many different tribes but they have in common a way of life, bound up with the forest, and ritual and religion centred around village gods and spirits. *Adivasis* also have in common their exceptional disadvantage in regard to all the key indicators of social welfare, even by comparison with members of the Scheduled Castes: a literacy rate, for example, of 23.8

per cent, as compared with 30.1 per cent amongst the Dalits; 28.9 per cent have no access to doctors and clinics, while for Dalits the percentage is 15.6 per cent; 49.5 per cent of *adivasis* live below the official poverty line, while 'only' 41.5 per cent of Dalits do so. Unlike the Dalits, too, they have till now been unable to constitute themselves as an interest group in national politics (Guha 2007a).

Adivasis have suffered in particular from the forest policies of successive governments. There has been marked continuity between colonial and post-colonial forest policy, and the historian Ramachandra Guha thinks that in spite of the changing interests involved, 'In both cases the successful implementation of policy has been only achieved at the expense of the forest communities and their life-support systems. The communities, thus deprived, have characteristically responded through different forms of protest' (Guha 1983: 1893). The Forest (Conservation) Act of 1980 continued the pressures on those it defined as 'encroachers' upon officially designated 'forest' land – though figures released by the Ministry of Environment and Forests in 2005, while a new forest Bill was under discussion, showed that the area supposedly encroached was only a little greater than the area of forest land that had been released by the Ministry for various mining and industrial development projects. The state has often preferred to champion capitalist interests in the forests of India, as against the needs and interests of those who have historically been forest-dwellers. Recently, too, to the pressures upon the *adivasis* from the Forest Department and from the alienation of forest tracts for mining and industrial projects, have been added demands from wildlife conservation. The demarcation of Protected Areas, under the Wildlife Protection Act, for the conservation of particular species, resulted in the dispossession and threatened displacement of three to four million more people (Kothari 2007). The Draft National Tribal Policy of 2006 recognized that 'Alienation of tribal land is the single most important cause of pauperization of tribals'; and in the same year the historical marginalization of the tribal people of India was at least partially reversed, in the face of opposition from some conservationists, in the Scheduled Tribes and Other Traditional Forest Dwellers (Recognition of Forest Rights) Bill (of December 2006, implemented from the beginning of 2008), which at last vested in forest-dwellers inheritable rights in land, which were not alienable or transferable (Bhatia 2005b; 'Editorial' 2007; Prasad 2007).

The pressures upon the forests and the lands of tribal people remain intense, however, across large parts of central and eastern India, because of the escalating demand for the resources of the region, which include most of India's reserves of coal, iron ore, bauxite and other minerals. The state of Orissa is said now to be the object of a kind of latter-day gold rush (Misra 2010), as Indian and international companies contend for rights to exploit the rich mineral resources of the state (and much the same might be said of both Jharkhand and Chhattisgarh). By January 2006, when fourteen *adivasis* who were struggling against the taking of their land to make way for a Tata steel plant were killed by police firing at Kalinga Nagar in Orissa, the government of the state had already signed forty-three memoranda of understanding for steel plants and three for aluminium refineries (Das 2006). The *adivasis'* struggle in Kalinga Nagar was not crushed, however, and the firing incident lent strength to the Visthapan Virodhi Janmanch, a popular movement against displacement, and sparked tribal agitations in other parts of the state. Struggle in Kalinga Nagar goes on ('Tension in Kalinga Nagar Steel Hub', *The Hindu* 20 January 2010), as it has done against other major projects that threaten the rights and livelihoods of tribal people, notably the South Korean steel firm POSCO's project to mine iron ore and build a new steel plant and port facilities near Paradeep; the London-based Vedanta company's alumina refinery at Lajgarh; and the same company's plans to clear a huge site for a private university campus. Vedanta's projects have been stopped, the first as a result of the recommendations of an official panel chaired by N. C. Saxena (*Business Line*, 25 August 2010); and the second by the High Court of Orissa (*The Hindu* 17 November 2010). These moves are indicative of the increasing concern that has been mobilized by civil society groups over the dispossession of *adivasis*. Competition continues, however, between Orissa and Jharkhand for mining projects.

Several of the contested sites in Orissa were approved as Special Economic Zones (SEZs), following the passage of the Special Economic Zone Act in 2005 (see Jenkins 2011). Altogether, almost 600 SEZs had been approved across India by July 2009, most of them located in areas that were already highly developed, and the majority for IT and IT Enabled Services (and so probably not generating very much employment). Though it was stated repeatedly by Congress leaders that prime agricultural land cannot be taken over for SEZs, this unquestionably has happened in some cases, and has given rise to massive protests. An early report said that 'Lakhs of people from States as far-flung as Haryana, Orissa and Maharashtra are engaged in sustained agitation against the "unjust" acquisition of their land for many SEZ projects. These agitations focus attention on the potential massive displacement of people from agricultural areas' (Ramakrishnan 2006: 4). Later, in 2007, grassroots opposition to SEZs became most visible at Nandigram in West Bengal, where the CPI(M)-led state government sought to take over land for a chemical complex that would be developed by the Salim Group of Indonesia (Chattopadhyay 2007). Local opposition was met in March 2007 with police action, and at least fourteen people were killed. Subsequently the attempt, also by the government of West Bengal to take over land (though not formally in an SEZ) at Singur for the establishment by the Tata Company of a plant to manufacture its new Nano motor car was met with comparably fierce opposition, causing the company to withdraw the project in October 2008 (Chattopadhyay 2008). In both cases, the protests became highly politicized and seem to have been used very successfully by the opposition Trinamool Congress to mobilize support against the ruling CPI(M), and there has been a great deal of controversy over who was to blame for the deaths at Nandigram. Opposition to SEZs has been broad-based, however. On the one hand, a leading industrialist, Rahul Bajaj, speaking in the Rajya Sabha, argued that real-estate developers were using SEZs, with the connivance of government, to perpetrate major land-scams. On the other, the CPI(Maoist) has decided, in the words of General Secretary Ganapathy, 'to take up struggles against the SEZs which are nothing but neo-colonial enclaves on Indian territory' (Ganapathy 2007). The National Alliance of People's Movements has campaigned all over the country, in the frame of a National People's Audit of SEZs. It has marshalled evidence from these inquiries in support of its case that 'SEZs across the country have entailed serious violations of the constitution, laws, and procedures laid down by the government itself, and of people's rights', and argues 'All SEZs entail dispossession and displacement' (NAPM 2010). There has been at least one success for farmers in a fight over land acquisitions for an SEZ, at Raigad in Maharashtra, in 2009 (Bavadam 2009).

The 'new enclosure movement' has met with fierce local resistance, therefore, as in the Narmada Valley, at Kalinga Nagar and elsewhere in Orissa, or in Raigad, at Nandigram and Singur. There is widespread dislocation and turmoil in rural India. How have the Maoists acted in relation to these struggles? How far can the power they have developed early in the twenty-first century be accounted for as being the outcome of their responses to the class tensions of rural India?

10.5 The Maoists and Rural Struggles

Studies of the ways in which Maoist groups acted in the agricultural region of central Bihar show them as having initially built a social base amongst landless and small and marginal peasants of lower and intermediate castes – though there were some supporters also from amongst higher castes and classes, whose presence was felt quite strongly in the leadership. Their mobilizations of Dalits, especially, against higher-caste landowners established land rights for some, raised wages in areas of struggle and, most important of all, inspired poor people to assert themselves as human beings and to claim their social and political rights. But George Kunnath found from his conversations with a friend whom he calls Rajubhai, a landless Dalit who had been the leader of a *dasta* (one of the Maoists' underground squads, of six to ten members, carrying on armed struggle), the relationships between landless Dalits and the Maoists changed over time. Rajubhai told him that:

> When the *sanghathan* [the term he uses to refer to the Maoists' organizations] came here, it began among the mazdoor varg [working class]. The cadres used to sleep and eat in the mud houses of the *mazdoor*. It fought for the issues of the working classes – land and wages, as well as against social abuses, exploitation and sexual abuse of women. But now that the *sanghathan* has got a foothold here, its ambition has grown into one of capturing state power. So they have started taking in people from dominant castes, against whom we fought previously. As a result of the entry of the landowning castes into the *sanghathan*, it is hesitant to raise the issues of land and wages. For the last twenty years, wages have remained the same: three kilos of paddy for a day's work. The working class is no longer a priority for the *sanghathan*. (Kunnath 2006: 110)

Rajubhai's disaffection from the *sanghathan* was completed by the fact that landless *dalits* in the *dastas*, despite having died or suffered physically the most, received less compensation for these hardships than did the middle-caste members. The Maoist movement is far from being immune against caste tensions (and see Gayer and Jaffrelot 2009: 4).

A human rights activist from Andhra Pradesh, K. Balagopal, tells a quite similar story in regard to that state. In the 1970s, the Naxalites fought fairly successfully, in spite of police actions, against landlordism (including the practice of *begar*, or bonded labour), and then encouraged tribals to cut down reserve forests for cultivation. This was by 'far and away the most successful land struggle of the Naxalites' (though later, in the mid-1990s – changing their policy in the light of changed circumstances – they were quite successful in imposing a ban on forest cutting). Balagopal argues that:

> the main reason for the wide popularity of the Naxalites in the entire forest region abutting the Godaveri river in Telengana, Vidarbha and Chhattisgarh is the protection they gave to the forest dwellers for cultivation in reserve forests, the substantial increase they achieved in the payment for picking tendu leaf, and the end they put to the oppressive domination of the headmen and *patwaris*. (Balagopal 2006a: 2185)

This account is confirmed in the story recounted by a Maoist leader from the Bastar region of Chhattisgarh, that in the early years there they found the first problem that had to be tackled was that of the conflict between the *adivasi* population and the Forest Department (Navlakha 2010). Both in Bastar, and in the northern Telengana region of Andhra Pradesh, to begin with the Naxalites spread mainly through mass organizations of agricultural labourers, students and youth, but thereafter heavy repression on the part of government forces brought an increased reliance on armed squads:

> The immediate economic and social problems of the masses took a back seat and the battle for supremacy with the state became the central instance of struggle . . . This requires a range of acts of violence, which have no direct relation to the immediate realization of any rights for the masses, though the resulting repression invariably hits at the masses. (Balagopal 2006b: 3185)

Unsurprisingly, this led to questioning amongst people as to whether they hadn't been made into 'guinea pigs of revolution'. New generations, though they may have benefited from the earlier actions of the Maoists, are less sympathetic to them than were people of their parents' generation, while at the same time the tactics employed by the state in Andhra Pradesh in recent years have seriously weakened them. These tactics included the creation of special police forces – the 'Greyhounds' – that live and operate like the Naxalites' own squads and are 'bound by no known law, including the Constitution of India' (Balagopal 2006b: 3185).

These histories show that there is a justification for Tilak Gupta's claim that the Maoists have 'kept alive the agrarian demands of the rural poor' and that they have articulated the struggles of poor people against exploitation and oppression. They have a history of supporting common people in struggles over the conditions of their everyday lives and, in the areas in which they have been able to establish control (as in their *Jantanam Sarkar*, or 'people's government' in the Bastar region of Chhattisgarh), of projecting an alternative vision of how society can be organized (Navlakha 2010). But the stories of Maoism in Bihar, or Andhra, or Bastar also bring out the tensions within Maoism, and the problem of revolutionary violence. Even sympathetic observers recognize the problem of the spiral of violence: armed attacks, whether by revolutionaries against landlords, or by state security forces against them, invite a violent response, and in these circumstances suspicions of others, of informing or even just of being sympathetic to the other side, easily lead to violence against individuals, inviting retaliation (Alpa Shah explains the personal dilemmas, born of the uncertainty surrounding their social relationships, of those living in an area in which Maoism is part of the fabric of local society: Shah 2009). Maoists themselves are extremely sensitive, it seems from interviews with their leaders and with individual cadres, about accusations that they are engaged in unconstrained violence. Gautam Navlakha is one who has questioned the Maoists he has travelled amongst in Bastar about this: 'They said that they did not kill everyone who was considered an enemy and the party stopped its members from killing informers. It was only when they did not mend their ways despite repeated warnings that such persons were killed . . . [and] . . . They insisted that the party acted rather firmly against those responsible for acts of indiscipline or reckless violence' (Navlakha 2010: 39–40; and see also Shah 2010a). And indeed, Navlakha's account, or that of Arundhati Roy on 'Walking with the comrades' in Dantewada (2010), show the cadres of the CPI(Maoist), very many of them young women, as being a highly disciplined force. The General Secretary of the Party, Ganapathy, can well claim that the party has been 'compelled to take up arms and not out of any romantic notion' (Ganapathy 2007), when it confronts the security machinery of a state that is responsible for all manner of violence against its own people. The Indian police forces, after all, according to Human Rights Watch, 'have largely failed to evolve from the ruler-supportive, repressive forces they were designed to be under Britain's colonial rule', habitually using abuse and threats as a primary means of crime investigation and of law enforcement (Human Rights Watch 2009). But then the state necessarily defends itself against the threats to its authority from a party that is committed to its overthrow.

There is an irreconcilable contradiction in the actions of the Maoists, and in the end it does appear to be the case, as Nirmalangshu Mukherji has argued, that the real material benefits to *adivasis* and others in Maoist-dominated areas are very small, and that poor people's welfare is sacrificed to the demands of military strategy (Mukherji 2010). There is also, as Nicolas Jaoul suggests, a permanent temptation, where the Maoists are well entrenched, for them 'to reach arrangements with dominant interests' (2009: 35). Quite clearly, it can happen that ordinary *adivasis* and others are caught in the crossfire between the revolutionaries and the forces of the state and that the kind of gap between party and masses that both Kunnath and Balagopal identify, opens up. The party is then exposed to the criticism that it is led by middle-class ideologues who, 'claiming "correct knowledge", take it upon themselves to lead "the people", treat *adivasis* as people who cannot represent themselves, and actually end up using *adivasis* to play out their own revolutionary fantasies' (Nigam 2010; and see also Simeon 2010).

Many, perhaps most movements of organized resistance to the new enclosures – movements such as Visthapan Virodhi Janmanch at

Kalinga Nagar, or the Bastar Sambhag Kisan Sangharsh Samiti (BSKSS), in Chhattisgarh, that opposes displacement to make way for the construction of the Bodh Ghat dam, and the privatization of mines and river water resources (Navlakha and Gupta 2009) – are branded by the authorities and a pliant media as 'Naxalite' or Maoist. Independent evidence suggests it is most unlikely that they really are, but equally that there is a recognition on the part of those involved that the Maoists are on their side. Of movements in Orissa it is said that they are based on 'an aggregation of different political faiths' (Misra 2010), while a rally of the BSKSS in 2009 was observed to have been addressed from across 'the entire political spectrum from the right to the left, including sadhus/mendicants', and from communists to former members of the RSS. None spoke against the Maoists, however, while all spoke critically of the government that had unleashed the Salwa Judum against them, and of the corporate houses that threatened their environment and their livelihoods (Navlakha and Gupta 2009). The Salwa Judum – meaning, in one translation, 'purification hunt' – is an independent militia, originally set up at the instigation of a sometime communist, later Congress MLA, with a criminal record. Framed by him as a popular and 'Gandhian' movement of tribal people against the Naxalites, in practice there is strong evidence of the responsibility of the Salwa Judum, with Special Police Officers, for the use of considerable violence in forcing large-scale displacements of tribal people to roadside camps in the Bastar region, and for the destruction of villages; and it is reportedly no longer entirely under the control of the authorities, though it may be used by companies in order to try to gain control of land (Miklian 2009; and Sundar 2006).

There is not always, or necessarily, the kind of disconnect between the Maoists and people that writers such as Aditya Nigam (2010) think exists. At the same time, it is equally important to recognize that poor peasants, Dalits and tribal people are not inherently or naturally 'revolutionaries', but rather possessed of practical common sense (just as Ben Kiernan argues of the Cambodian peasantry in the period of the Khmer Rouge: Kiernan 1996: 210–15). Bela Bhatia makes these points very strongly from her ethnographic researches in central Bihar in the 1990s (Bhatia 2005a). Both she and George Kunnath (2006, 2009) show that there was a perception amongst poorer people that Naxalites were 'good people', who were opposed to their oppressors and who supported them in a struggle for their basic rights (exactly as was observed at the rally of the BSKSS in Bastar in 2009). But, according to Bhatia, people understood the objective of the movement as being 'change', not 'revolution'. They supported it because they felt that the Naxalites shared their sense of injustice, rather than for any ideological reasons. The appeal of 'class struggle' was as a means of securing needs – for higher wages, land redistribution and freedom from harassment. Bhatia notes that people petitioned the Maoists for exactly the same things for which they also petitioned government. Smita Gupta reports in a somewhat similar vein from a visit to Bastar in the early months of 2010, though her point is that the *adivasis* there are caught between government and Maoists. Both sides want the world outside to believe the *adivasis* are all committed Maoists. This helps the Maoists to project an impression of power, and to build the atmosphere of fear through which they really can exercise power; on the side of the government, it provides an excuse for not delivering basic services, and it justifies the use of force in support of companies that are seeking to exploit the mineral resources of the area. The people, however, are said to want the civil administration back, being in desperate need of basic services. The Maoists score over the government in just one respect – they are regarded as being more 'trustworthy' and as providing some sort of justice in an area where the government has been seen as an oppressor (Gupta 2010). There are, therefore, good reasons for thinking that the many movements of resistance to the new enclosure movement generally aren't 'Maoist', though they welcome support from the Maoists, and – up to a point, but only up to a point – support them in turn. It is not surprising if on their part the Maoists should have begun to focus more on fighting against SEZs and the corporate takeover of land – against the effects of liberalization and globalization – rather than on 'anti-feudal' struggles (as a well-informed human rights activist from Andhra Pradesh informed one of us in March 2010; see also Shah 2010a).

10.6   So Why Has Maoism Become Such a Force?

There are immediate, pragmatic reasons for the way in which the Maoists have gathered strength in the first decade of the twenty-first century. The coming together of the major groups in 2004 opened up, as we said, a huge swathe of favourable terrain where they have significant military advantages, and they do not confront the same problems of coordination as the police forces. They have benefited in some ways, no doubt, from the spectacular maladministration of the new states of Jharkhand and Chhattisgarh in particular, and from political corruption. In Jharkhand, we know from work by the anthropologist Alpa Shah how at an earlier stage the MCC and the local state functioned in tandem, and had a kind of symbiotic relationship with each other, both materially and symbolically (Shah 2006a, and 2010b: chapter 6). In the region that Shah studied, the MCC spread in the first place not by mobilizing poor tribal peasants but rather amongst the rural elite, including non-tribal people from intermediate castes, by supplying protection and facilitating their acquisition of lucrative contracts for local government projects. This is an important reminder that we must not assume there is a simple or an unmediated connection between the grievances of poor rural people and their mobilization against the state – and also that insurgent movements, like the state, require resources, and may obtain them from supplying protection in exchange for taxation, just like the state. Alpa Shah asked Gopalji, the spokesperson from Jharkhand whom she interviewed, 'It is widely reported that you finance yourself through the black economy of development schemes coming in through the state. How do you justify participation in the very systems of corruption that you oppose?' Gopalji answered, 'This is not corruption. This is taxation . . . We are not simply collecting money for private gain.' Resources raised from the supply of protection are used, Gopalji claims, 'for the service of the toiling masses' (Shah 2010a: 27). The tropes of 'greed' and 'grievance' are blunt instruments for capturing the complexities of the Maoists' mobilizations.

The Government of India recognizes its own responsibility when it narrates the reasons for the spread of the Maoist insurgency. An expert group set up by the Planning Commission in May 2006 argued in its report to government, entitled *Development Challenges in Extremist Affected Areas* (published in March 2008), that the failures of the state through denial of basic rights to the poor, bureaucratic corruption, and its complicity in police violence, very largely explain the extent of popular support for the Maoists (labelled as 'extremists'). This support comes mainly, the group argued, from the tribals and Dalits who together make up about a quarter of the population of the country because they are the ones who have most suffered from the neglect of the state and from the violence for which it has been responsible. The report stressed 'the structural violence which is implicit in the social and economic system', and drew attention to the ways in which the shift towards liberal economic policies has hurt poor people (Banerjee 2008; 'Editorial' 2009a). Subsequently, the Prime Minister has spoken in a similar vein, for example, at a meeting of chief ministers in November 2009, when he said that 'systemic exploitation and social and economic abuse of our tribal communities can no longer be tolerated'. The government has not been ready, however, to follow the advice of the expert group, which was that it should pursue 'an ameliorative approach with emphasis on a negotiated solution' rather than resorting to 'security-centric' measures. Thus far, all reports suggest that the implementation of the Forest Rights Act of 2006 has been desultory (as of November 2009, Bihar and Orissa had not distributed a single title). The overwhelming emphasis in the government response has been, as we mentioned earlier, on the use of force to eliminate the Maoists, even while it has continued to pay lip service to the importance of 'ameliorative' measures. Yet, as commentators have said, this has been tried before, but the revolutionary movement has sprung back time and again ('Editorial' 2009b). The use of force, especially when it is poorly disciplined, is liable to be counterproductive. There is good reason, for example, to believe that the actions of Salwa Judum in Chhattisgarh have driven more *adivasis* there to support the Maoists (exactly as Fearon and Laitin argued is commonly the case in insurgencies: 2003).

Even though there is no simple connection between accumulated grievance and political mobilization, or between the pursuit of economic liberalization in India and the Maoist insurgency, there is substantial evidence that the Maoists have built support by addressing the grievances of tribal people, Dalits and rural poor people. The expert group of the Planning Commission noted the extent to which the Maoists in Bihar and in the forest areas of Andhra, Chhattisgarh, the Vidharbha region of Maharashtra, Jharkhand and Orissa have been effective, for example, in redistributing land to poor people when the state itself has failed so egregiously to do so, in spite of its own laws. Long-running grievances over land and access to forest resources are being significantly exacerbated by the impacts of liberal economic policies. In many cases, it does seem that the voracious drive to acquire resources that lie in tribal areas has triggered movements of resistance – movements which have not been organized by the Maoists but which are sympathetic towards them, because they are perceived as being more 'trustworthy' than government. One implication is that the Maoist insurgency will not easily be crushed. But it is the tragedy of the politics of armed struggle that it is a response to the appalling structural violence that has been perpetrated historically, and that continues to be perpetrated by elites, supported by the state, against landless and poor peasants, Dalits and *adivasis,* and yet it leads to a spiral of violence in which the same people become trapped. In the end, armed struggle against the state cannot be reconciled with a mass movement of the least privileged.

PART III
SOCIETY

11
Does India Have a Civil Society?

11.1 Introduction

'Civil society' is a notoriously difficult term. The concept was once used in a manner quite different from the way in which it is employed today. Influential commentators in the seventeenth and eighteenth centuries in Britain imagined civil society not as an alternative to the state – as in today's definition – but rather as a social order shaped by government and the law. Civil society referred to a set of state institutions exercising authority over a given national community and was counterposed to an anarchic 'state of nature'. In nineteenth-century Germany a different vision of civil society emerged. Departing from convention, Georg Hegel presented civil society as a sphere of social action separate from government and outside the immediate influence of the state. Hegel also linked civil society to a particular type of sociability. He argued that civil society involved people meeting as autonomous individuals blind to differences of background and status. Ferdinand Tonnies (1955) distinguishes between *gemeinschaft* – affective forms of sociality founded on feelings of family spirit – and *gesellschaft*: disinterested social relations conducted without reference to family, caste and creed. For Hegel, civil society was founded on *gesellschaft* sociality.

In early twentieth-century Britain, the rise of the modern state encouraged the adoption of this Hegelian vision of civil society. Theorists came to believe that the greatest threat to individual rights came not from anarchy, as earlier generations of British commentators had feared, but from governments interfering too much with people's lives (see Harris 2003: 31f). Scholars such as Harold Laski (1921) stressed the importance of social associations – what he termed 'multicellular group life' – as a counterweight to the overweening power of the state. In mid-century Germany, some scholars began to deploy a similar vision of civil society in order to critique a decline in the quality of public associational life. Jurgen Habermas (1965), especially, argued for the role of a public sphere – comprised of cultural societies, reading groups and clubs, for example – in promoting healthy democratic practice and the transition to modern, urban life in Europe.

Writing on civil society flourished in the 1980s, 1990s and 2000s. The fall of the Berlin Wall in 1989 led scholars to reflect on the role of civil society in nurturing democracy in post-Soviet states: civic associations could act as a bulwark against a return to Leninism (see Taylor 1990). Another strand of scholarship has considered how civil society might trigger democratization in the wake of sectarian strife, for example, in the Balkans (see A. Jeffrey 2008) or Africa (see Ferguson 2006); or how it may prevent communal and ethnic violence in the first place (Varshney 2001). Still other commentators have reflected on the role played by civil society organizations in economic development. A strong associational life may be a type of resource that can be leveraged for economic growth, as Putnam et al. (1993) have argued in work on 'social capital' (see Harriss 2002 for a critique). In all this writing, civil society is imagined as a sphere founded on relatively impersonal social relations, *gesellschaft* rather than *gemeinschaft*. Scholars have also tended to fasten upon local, grassroots organizations as examples of civil society.

The tendency for scholars since the 1980s to define civil society as a realm of impersonal contact, and primarily with reference to 'local' organizations, raises two points of conceptual confusion (see also Ferguson 2006). First, it is far from clear at present whether civil society must, by definition, be founded on the forms of sociality that Tonnies describes as *gesellschaft*. Can kin-based or caste institutions be included in the sphere of 'civil society'? Second, it is not clear to what extent vertical organizational structures, for example where international institutions work alongside small-scale NGOs, are usefully described as forms of civil society: can civil society be detached from its now familiar mooring in 'local society' to be something international?

These questions take on a particular pertinence in literature on civil society outside the West. Considerable writing has focused on Africa. A dominant line of argument, emerging out of the work of Jean-François Bayart (1993) and Mahmood Mamdani (1996), in particular, is that Africa does not possess a civil society in the Hegelian sense. Bayart argues that people simply lack the organizational skill and motivation to aggregate into the type of public associations that are typically imagined as characteristic of civil society. Mamdani makes the parallel argument that throughout colonial Africa majority rural populations were governed through indigenous chiefs and 'customary law', under a regime of 'decentralized despotism'. They were consequently ill prepared to participate as citizens in modern post-colonial states. These arguments seem to apply if we adopt the strict Hegelian definition of civil society based upon *gesellschaft*-type social relations. If we relax the definition of civil society to encompass organizations that critique the state on the basis of *gemeinschaft* forms of sociality, a whole range of forms of civil society in Africa hove into view: Christian missionary organizations (Ferguson 2006), Islamic societies (see Turner 2009), kinship networks (Mains 2007), to name but a few. If we also look beyond local, grassroots forms of civil society, it is evident that international development and other forms of globalization have spawned a range of forms of what is now often termed 'global civil society' in Africa: South African 'community organizations' bankrolled by USAID, for example, or European church groups in Zimbabwe.

This chapter reflects on the usefulness of the term 'civil society' in describing contemporary political and social life in India. We begin by discussing examples of upper-middle-class civil society in India, which was stronger than it was in Africa during the colonial and post-colonial periods, using Partha Chatterjee's work on civil society and political society as a starting point. We then engage with the question of whether India's masses exhibit the characteristics of civil society. In contrast to Chatterjee, we argue that the poor are often engaged in civil society, and we emphasize a need to move beyond strict European definitions of civil society in studying these practices.

11.2   Upper-Middle-Class Civil Society?

The prospects for civil society in India were considerably better than they were in Africa during the period of decolonization. India was the venue for a nationalist movement in the early twentieth century that was founded precisely on imitating the civil society organizations of the West. To a greater extent than in most African states, people in post-colonial India had a strong sense of nationalism, which as J. S. Mill pointed out long ago can provide a basis for the emergence of civic consciousness. The British encouraged upper sections of Indian society to absorb Western liberal traditions of civic consciousness, for example, by founding schools dedicated to the production of an Indian elite (see Srivastava 1998; Watt 2005). Sociological work points to multiple forms of elite civil society among Indians in the colonial period. For example, Sanjay Joshi (2001) charts the rise of a colonial middle class which consolidated its power precisely through building civic associations: schools, reading groups, libraries and organizations dedicated to social service. Likewise, Carey Watt (2005) foregrounds the role of voluntary Hindu societies in the emergence of Indian nationalism. Paralleling the work of Joshi and Watt in key respects, Partha Chatterjee (1993) describes a type of 'civil society' in colonial Calcutta. Chatterjee draws out especially the gendered nature of this sphere: a male space of civic associations existed alongside a more intimate, female space of family relations.

Chatterjee has also constructed a larger pan-Indian theory of civil society, building on his own substantive work and that of others. He argues that in the post-colonial period the upper middle classes have consolidated their hold on power. The urban rich have seized land from the poor, dominated lucrative work, and controlled access to social networks and education. But Chatterjee also points to the risks inherent in upper-middle-class accumulation strategies. Unlike in Europe during the Industrial Revolution, those dispossessed from the land cannot find work in manufacturing industry in India, and therefore constitute a major threat to upper middle classes and the state. Moreover, India's formal subscription to a democracy creates expectations of progress in the minds of downtrodden classes. In Chatterjee's view, the state manages this potential powder keg through instigating what Antonio Gramsci (1971) called a 'passive revolution'. The rich extend certain minimal rights to the poor and allow marginalized groups to bargain for a share of state resources. This entails upper middle classes and the state encouraging the poor to imagine themselves as people in a process of 'development'. It also involves the production of categories – such as 'Other Backward Class' and 'Below the Poverty Line' – that provide subordinated communities with a basis for staking claims to government largesse. In practical terms, the poor receive some benefits, such as loans, places in schools, scholarships and, in some cases, positions in government service. But this strategy also allows the rich and their allies in the state effectively to neutralize social threats.

Chatterjee argues that the passive revolution has been associated with the emergence of two distinct forms of politics that are mapped into the class position of Indian subjects. The rich occupy civil society. Chatterjee defines civil society in Hegelian terms as, 'Those characteristic institutions of modern associational life originating in Western societies that are based on equality, autonomy, freedom of entry and exit, contract, [and] deliberative procedures of decision making' (Chatterjee 1998: 234). The poor occupy a more obviously 'political sphere' in which they form into specific groups on an ad hoc basis in order to try to bid for government resources and help. Chatterjee calls this 'political society'. Chatterjee argues that the occupants of political society 'Make their claims on government, and in turn are governed, not within the framework of stable constitutionally defined rights and laws, but rather through temporary, contextual and unstable arrangements arrived at through direct political negotiations' (ibid.). These 'temporary, contextual and unstable arrangements' are often illegal, regularly unruly and sometimes bloody. Chatterjee (2004: 74) writes that 'Political society will bring into the hallways and corridors of power some of the squalor, ugliness and violence of popular life.' The people occupying political society rarely use the language of abstract rights and norms of impartial solidarity (*gesellschaft*). Rather, they petition the state through reference to kinship, caste and religion (*gemeinschaft*). Moreover, whereas those in civil society typically congregate within formally recognized horizontal associations, the poor are compelled to mobilize through powerful patrons and brokers. In many situations, the poor become dependent on these local bigwigs and have to pay them large sums of money in order to obtain social goods.

There are a number of studies that support Chatterjee's writing on upper-middle-class civil society. Building on research in Chennai, John Harriss (2006) has identified a divide between upper-middle-class and working-class practices that mirrors the distinction made by Chatterjee between civil society and political society. Upper middle classes in Chennai have developed a range of civil society institutions to bolster their power, including bodies that are registered as Non-Governmental Organizations (NGOs). These organizations are formally committed to the notions of abstract citizenship associated with the European model of civil society. As Chatterjee's writing would lead us to expect, these NGOs work with the state to offer poor people certain minimum goods, such as micro-credit loans, while preventing marginalized communities from launching critiques of established power structures. The rich use their NGOs to put forward technocratic solutions to problems of poverty, governance and city infrastructure. Harriss emphasizes that the NGOs representing the upper middle classes are highly professionalized, such that they have become key players in processes of urban governance and planning; for example, many upper-middle-class NGOs garner support from international funding bodies. At the same time, the rich have removed themselves from electoral politics, which they regard as corrupt and ineffective. This leads Harriss to describe upper-middle-class mobilization as a 'new politics' distinct from the 'old politics' of seeking electoral power and directly bargaining with state representatives. By contrast, the working classes in Chennai are much more engaged with representative politics. Their demands centre on the provision of basic services, and tend to involve direct protest or more everyday politicking via patrons and brokers. The division Harriss identifies between upper-middle-class civil society and working-class politics also has a strong geographical dimension. Middle-class civil society tends to occur in city spaces distinct from those of working-class mobilization.

Chatterjee's writing on upper-middle-class civil society, and Harriss's development of his ideas in a Chennai context, highlight three important themes in the emerging literature on upper-middle-class politics and society in India. First, Chatterjee demonstrates the capacity of the rich to build durable institutions within urban areas that serve to defend their interests. Residents' associations are a common topic in the wider literature. For example, Leela Fernandes (2006) has described neighbourhood associations and Resident Welfare Associations (RWAs) in Mumbai that police their gated communities, build parks adjoining their homes and celebrate religious festivals. RWAs also aim to intervene in the life of the city by improving governance, contributing to urban planning and fostering certain forms of 'development'. Such associations are not limited to metropolitan regions of India. Janaki Abraham (personal communication) has described upper-middle-class associations in the relatively small town of Bikaner, Rajasthan, which aim to improve the town's infrastructure while also offering the urban poor certain social goods, such as access to books via a mobile library. Nor are upper-middle-class efforts to build durable civil society institutions a function only of urban life. Roger Jeffery et al. (2006) describe how upper middle classes in a rural part of western Uttar Pradesh have reproduced their privilege in part by establishing educational NGOs. These bodies offer schooling to lower-middle-class and some poor children in the region, without substantially altering patterns of social reproduction. Moreover, by controlling private educational opportunities, upper middle classes are able to inculcate norms of good behaviour and discipline in poorer people – and they make considerable money from schooling.

Recent qualitative research in India also provides a basis for qualifying some of Chatterjee's arguments with respect to middle-class civil society. It is important to acknowledge that there are gradations within India's urban middle classes. Lalita Kamath and M. Vijayabaskar (2009) analyse differences between upper middle classes and less wealthy fractions of the middle classes in Bangalore. They found that upper-middle-class RWAs tended to focus on organizing cultural and religious events reflecting their own interests. Since their access to most government services was secure they found little need to mobilize in pursuit of development resources or seek legal help. By contrast, lower fractions among middle classes in Bangalore were much more concerned about obtaining government resources, participated to a greater extent in electoral politics and were more likely to use law courts in pursuit of their goals. Upper middle classes and less wealthy middle classes also came into conflict.

For example, the elite supported a Bangalore metro project, while less rich middle-class traders were opposed to the scheme, which threatened their livelihoods. Chatterjee tends to imagine the middle class as a single 'bloc'; Kamath and Vijayabaskar's (2009) work provides an important corrective.

It is also important to recognize that many of the institutions run by upper middle classes are not always based on the forms of impartial sociability that Tonnies (1955) referred to as *gesellschaft*. Upper middle classes also create forms of civil society that operate along the lines of religion, caste and family (*gemeinschaft*). The rise of Hindu nationalism in India has been founded on the emergence of a vast 'civil society' rooted in a particular vision of politicized Hinduism (Hansen 1996a; and see chapter 9 of this volume). In addition, much middle-class activism in urban areas, especially within small-town India, is founded on caste solidarities rather than norms of liberal democracy and civic association. For example, caste associations are prominent in many Indian cities and towns and typically defend the interests of members of particular castes or subcastes (see Jeffrey 1999).

A second theme in Chatterjee's and Harriss's work that is reflected in broader literature is that of the increasingly globalized and professionalized nature of upper-middle-class organizations. The urban rich in India are enmeshed in global flows of money, know-how and cultural capital that are redefining how civil society works (e.g., Ellis 2010). For example, the business and industrial elites in metropolitan areas have often used funds from international organizations to establish NGOs. With assistance from organizations such as the World Bank, they extend micro-credit to poor families, conduct health 'camps', provide tuition or scholarships and educate the poor with respect to issues of public health, for example (Roy 2009). At the same time as engaging with these international organizations, elite civil society organizations increasingly 'partner' with central or state governments in urban planning, governance and anti-corruption initiatives. Such civil society/state initiatives are prominent themes of recent research based in Chennai (Harriss 2006; Ellis 2010), Delhi (Webb 2010) and Mumbai (McFarlane 2009).

Contrary to the impression given by Chatterjee that upper middle classes rarely lobby government, recent research describes them engaging in this type of politicking. Karen Coelho and Venkat (2009) describe how electoral activism and negotiations with state politicians were key strategies for the upper-middle-class members of the RWAs they studied in Chennai. Amita Baviskar (2007) makes a similar point with reference to upper middle classes' involvement in legal campaigns in the Indian capital. The rich in Delhi have successfully pursued their goal of 'beautifying' the city through a multi-pronged strategy. They have petitioned the courts to shut down industries allegedly responsible for pollution and filed public interest litigation aimed at cleaning up the city.

Much of the urban middle classes' professed love of the law is a sham, however – and here is another point at which it is important to qualify Chatterjee's writing on middle-class civil society (see also Baviskar and Sundar 2008). Legality is a key axis of difference in Chatterjee's model. He views the rich as legal and the poor as prone to 'para-legal' or 'illegal' practice. This distinction ignores the many ways in which upper middle classes break the law: for example, through seizing the property of sub-ordinated sections of society (Roy 2009), engaging in corruption (Jeffrey 2002, 2008; Harriss-White 2003) or colluding in the false registration of land (Coelho and Venkat 2009; Brass 2011). Solomon Benjamin (2000) offers an especially fine-grained account of the manner in which local elites collude with senior politicians and bureaucrats in his discussion of urban planning in Bangalore. Truelove and Mawdsley's (2010) study of the politics of water in Delhi is similarly detailed, highlighting how the Delhi rich invest in illegal water pumps and routinely bribe engineers, water sellers, meter readers and officials. Such elite informality is by no means only a metropolitan or even urban phenomenon. Barbara Harriss-White (2003) has documented the ways in which rich merchants and prosperous farmers in small-town and village south India break the law to defend their social position.

A third theme in Chatterjee's work is of upper middle classes' exploitation and marginalization of the poor. This is a topic that emerges in recent research on the 'new politics' of upper-middle-class NGOs, which present themselves as agents of social development while effectively neutralizing political threats from the poor. Harriss (2010b) argues that, by bidding successfully for grants and tenders offered by the state and international organizations, elite civil society organizations often 'crowd out' opportunities for other sections of urban society to become more involved in participatory governance. Furthermore, urban civil society often promotes social projects that have the effect of further marginalizing and disciplining the urban poor. Many civil society organizations currently focus on making loans to poor women through micro-credit schemes. These schemes provide some economic and social opportunities. But they may also have negative effects, making women feel responsible for their own relative poverty, drawing poor people more tightly into patronage networks, and inculcating forms of economic discipline (see also Corbridge et al. 2005; Coelho and Venkat 2009; Young 2010).

The experience of the anti-corruption movement led by the social activist 'Anna' Hazare in 2011 complements this critique of upper-middle-class civil society. Hazare launched a hunger strike in April 2011 in Delhi demanding that the state establish a new ombudsman – the

Lokpal – to deal with corruption at high levels of the legislature, judiciary and executive. Well-financed volunteer organizations, prominent Indian intellectuals and legal activists quickly weighed in, and a coordinated 'Anna movement' unfolded through direct urban protest and use of social media (see Jayal 2011). When Hazare went on hunger strike again, the movement was finally successful in forcing the government to change proposed legislation regarding the powers of the *Lokpal*. A popular guru, Swami Ramdev, has been similarly active in this sphere, hitching his demand for a cleaner state to the need to build a strong spiritual (Hindu) 'Bharat'. The Anna movement, and Ramdev's similar mobilization, has been primarily driven by upper and middling sections of the urban middle class. It does not include a critique of corporate lobbying and tends to stylize the state as inherently corrupt, repressive and 'dirty'. As Bardhan (2011) argues for middle-class voluntary organizations more broadly, the earnestness of the Anna movement tends to act as a substitute for deliberative reflection. And the constant disparagement of representative government may weaken the democratic process.

Urban middle classes, too, are often proactively involved in marginalizing and exploiting the poor through their actions in 'civil society'. In research in New York, Katharyne Mitchell (2003) and Neil Smith (1996) have described a process of 'urban revanchism' wherein middle classes seek to 'cleanse' the city of poor populations to reflect their own desire for comfortable housing, leisure facilities and consumption opportunities. Building on this literature, Nandini Gooptu (2011) argues that urban revanchism in India takes three particular forms: a righteous opposition to the supposed lawlessness of the poor; perceptions of the poor as a threat due to their growing electoral influence; and opposition to collective mobilization by the working classes. Consistent with this analysis, an upper middle class hankering after improved housing and modern sites of recreation in Delhi has led them to use public interest litigation to 'clean up' the capital. At the same time, the rich often try to redefine 'the public interest' with reference to their own narrow goals (Bhan 2009). Asher Ghertner (2010) has charted a key shift in dominant strategies in Delhi. The Delhi government was once required to document the technical rationale for clearing away poor people's houses. But the state and its civil society allies are increasingly able to tear down slums by simply referring to a need to 'beautify' the capital.

Another aspect of elite civil society's marginalization of the poor is the manner in which they denigrate India's downtrodden classes (see also Legg 2006). In Britain in the eighteenth century, the rich contrasted their own civic sense with 'the rude pleasures of country talk' (Harris 2003: 123). A more sinister reenactment of these discourses currently characterizes elite public culture in India. For example, Sanjay Srivastava

(2007) has conducted ethnographic work on RWA meetings in Delhi that demonstrates an elite obsession with the threat posed by subaltern people to the security of middle-class homes. Coelho and Venkat (2009) and Baviskar (2007) have made similar points in their ethnographic research in metropolitan India. Upper-middle-class prejudices undermine any prospect of the rich engaging in cross-class mobilization and thus deepen the gap between civil society and political society.

In sum, upper-middle-class civil society in India is vibrant, but it is neither particularly 'civil' nor especially 'social' (Harriss-White 2003). In conceptual terms, Chatterjee (2004) offers a valuable heuristic for understanding upper-middle-class civil society. He usefully stresses the importance of civil society organizations for this class stratum, the increasingly professionalized nature of these institutions and the manner in which the urban rich marginalize the poor – all key themes in the wider literature. But recent social research points to a need to enter several caveats: there are gradations within the upper middle classes; there are institutions run by the rich that are not based on the principles of impartiality and rational talk; the upper middle classes have not removed themselves from lobbying political figures; and the rich are often involved in illegal activity. Moreover, governmentality as a strategy of rule may be giving way in certain areas to more naked forms of primitive accumulation justified with reference to international 'norms' around aesthetics.

11.3   Subaltern Civility

A further problem with Chatterjee's analysis is that it exaggerates the divide between civil society and political society. One reason for this, perhaps, is that he often focuses on social extremes: the very rich and very poor. Lemanski and Lama-Rewal (2010) have conducted research with people living in unauthorized colonies (UCs) in Delhi, who they term the 'real middle class'. UC residents lie between the upper middle classes and very poor in terms of their income, and they also occupy an intermediate position with respect to the legal status of their housing – more secure than those living in slums but much less secure than Delhi's rich. Lemanski and Lama-Rewal (2010: 13) argue that the UC residents employ strategies reminiscent of both civil society and political society.

> [UC residents] successfully employ discourses and strategies that are typically perceived as methods of the poor, for example engagement with political parties and claiming a basic human right to services; in addition to reliance on typically 'elite' discourses and mobilization strategies, for

example claiming respectability based on tax-paying and 'good' citizenship, forming neighborhood associations and blaming the state rather than self-interest for their predicament.

Lemanski and Lama-Rewal make the persuasive case that the boundary between civil society and political society is 'porous'. Jeffrey (2002) makes parallel observations with respect to the politics of prosperous Jat farmers in rural western Uttar Pradesh, who both engage in civil society organizations and participate in everyday 'hustle' to improve their access to land and agricultural marketing opportunities.

Another reason why Chatterjee perhaps overplays the distinction between civil society and political society is that he overlooks the extent to which the social practices associated with civil society characterize subaltern politics. In his defence, Chatterjee does sometimes acknowledge instances in which civil and political society interlink. For example, he draws on Bhattacharya's (2001) work on the social activism of middle-class teachers in West Bengal to demonstrate the effectiveness of cross-class mobilization and the interpenetration of the 'civil' and 'political' spheres. But Chatterjee emphasizes the gap between the two arenas and he seems fairly pessimistic at many points in his writing about the possibility for political society to morph into more durable, deliberative, civil forms of public assertion. In contrast, Corbridge et al. (2005) have used extensive social research in Bihar and West Bengal to stress how political society may offer the basis for the creation of civic practices and institutions (see also Harriss 2010b). Corbridge et al. provide numerous examples: village brokers who improve the access of the poor to the state, village meetings in which notions of civic responsibility are nurtured, and the sometimes positive impact of the Communist Party India (Marxist) on development programmes targeted at the rural poor.

Such interlinked action within political society and civil society can have lasting effects, as evident in the example of a grassroots anti-corruption organization – the Mazdur Kisan Shakti Sangathan (MKSS) (Jenkins and Goetz 1999). The MKSS was formally established in 1980 with the goal of allowing poor populations to demand accountability from the state. In this part of Rajasthan, government officials routinely embezzled money earmarked for public-works projects and development schemes. The MKSS adopted a multi-pronged approach to countering government corruption. At the local level, poor people mobilized via large public meetings to demand the right to access and photocopy state documents, and to deliberate on strategy, priority and dilemmas. Unlike the Hazare movement, the MKKS was centrally driven in large part by ordinary, ground-level reformers and activists. At the same time upper middle classes in urban areas – sympathetic former IAS officers, lawyers and politicians, for example – helped to coordinate MKSS activities and lobbied for legislative reforms that would improve public access to government records in the long term. In Chatterjee's terms, the MKSS therefore combined the direct confrontational approach of subaltern 'political society' with the institution-building and legal expertise associated with 'civil society'. This collaboration helped to reshape public debate within India on issues of transparency, corruption and the law.

Corbridge et al. (2005) and Jenkins and Goetz (1999) both refer to the potential for cultural organizations to bridge the boundary between civil society and political society. This theme is taken up by Da Costa (2008) in her study of the radical theatre organization Jana Sanskriti (see also Ganguly 2010). Jana Sanskriti was established in 1985 with the goal of effecting positive social change via the use of participatory performance techniques. Its thirty teams of actors tour rural West Bengal, provoking critical reflection among rural audiences by inviting them to become involved in the drama they witness. Audiences are encouraged to come on to the stage and take on the personas of the various figures being depicted – landlords, labourers, corrupt politicians and local bureaucrats, for example. Jana Sanskriti straddles rich and poor: its performers are mostly women from poor households, but the organization also has considerable support from West Bengal's urban upper middle classes. Jana Sanskriti also bridges civil society and political society. Its concern around 'rights' – and determination to look beyond caste and class difference – marks Jana Sanskriti out as a form of 'civil society'. But it also has the spontaneous, improvised, mischievous qualities that Chatterjee views as characteristics of political society, and Jana Sanskriti is engaged in lobbying government officials and intervening in electoral politics.

Youth politics may be a particularly important site for cross-class collaboration in India, as age and generation 'over-trump' other particularistic identities (cf. Mannheim 1972). Craig Jeffrey's (2010) research in Uttar Pradesh develops this point, while also showing how civil society and political society come to be blurred in practice. A decline in the quality of higher education combined with rising unemployment has sparked a series of protests among young male students in western Uttar Pradesh. Jeffrey uses ethnographic research to show that these protests typically occur across caste, religious and class lines; students voice their demands in the abstract language of their 'rights' as youth and students, and they typically overlook class, caste and religious difference during their mobilization. Moreover, the students are usually concerned to ensure that their protests are legal and civilized, and they have tried to institutionalize their assertion via the founding of student associations. In all these respects, the student mobilization is analogous to civil society. But student protests tend to be reactive rather than proactive – responding to specific incidents rather than building durable strategies. Moreover, the protests are highly irreverent and frequently involve students in using local patronage networks and links with politicians to try to secure short-term gains. Jeffrey's work therefore offers another example of how civil society and political society may combine and how in specific conjunctures people may come together across class boundaries to engage in progressive action.

It is important to stress the fragility of these forms of cross-class mobilization. For example, Da Costa (2010) argues that rural political theatre in West Bengal never operates as a pure space of social critique. Divisions based, for example, on caste, background and generation fracture performances, sometimes creating powerful divides among participants. Similarly, Jeffrey (2010) argues that where an inter-caste sexual relationship comes to light the carefully orchestrated cross-caste, cross-class protests of students quickly fragment along caste lines. This theme of the reassertion of hierarchy within subaltern civil society is also prominent in Martin Webb's (2010) study of public activism in Delhi. Webb worked with 'citizen activists' involved in campaigns around social justice and corruption in the Indian capital. He describes a wide range of activist types: individual 'crusaders' operating in cyberspace, members of local and national volunteer groups, working-class *karyakarte* (social workers), NGO employees, journalists, lawyers and academics. Webb shows that these diverse social constituencies are sometimes able to coordinate one with another in order to mount successful campaigns, for example, with respect to the Right to Information (RTI) Act. But Webb enters two important cautionary notes. First, he points to how class and gender undermine collective action. Rich activists have the social connections and knowledge (*jankaari*) required to pursue their everyday politics successfully and build political careers. In contrast, poor activists often find themselves marginalized within political circles. Similarly, Webb shows that female activists – unlike men – often face opposition from family members when they enter politics; some are even regarded as having 'shamed' their kin. Second, Webb argues that many of the forms of civil society action promoted by local activists are short term and piecemeal. For example, activists often file an RTI request in order to jolt government officials into action on a particular issue, but once it is resolved they do not generally follow up on their case.

Webb's points about the contradictions of cross-class mobilization therefore seem to take us back to the arguments that Chatterjee makes about the distinctive nature of the politics of the rich and the poor. In India, the political strategies pursued by urban upper middle classes are often quite markedly different from those of subalterns. Where cross-class mobilization takes place – and varied styles of politicking are brought together – this is often a short-term achievement. This is also a theme of literature on cross-class mobilization in Africa (see Ferguson 2006), but the manner in which caste overlaps with class means that collective assertion in India is often especially fragile.

Notwithstanding these points, however, social research is exposing an increasing number of situations in India, as well as in Africa (see Ferguson 2006), in which the rich and poor, urban and rural, and well-educated and illiterate work together to try to tackle problems of poverty and governance, and they typically do so in ways that blend political society and civil society. In specific places and at certain times, counterintuitive political practices flicker into life.

11.4   Rethinking Civil Society: *Gemeinschaft* and Globalization

Two further questions about subaltern civil society in India merit attention. First, can family, caste and religion act as foundations for civil society? Jenkins and Goetz, Da Costa, Jeffrey, and Webb point to associational action which traverses family and communal ties, and which is thus broadly in the *gesellschaft* tradition. But there are also many examples in contemporary India of something approximating 'civil society' founded on particularistic identities, especially caste and religion (*gemeinschaft*). In the late nineteenth and early twentieth centuries, the Arya Samaj – an ostensibly religious, anti-Brahmin movement – played a crucial role in strengthening civic life in India (Jones 1966). The Arya Samaj built numerous schools, libraries and cultural associations across north India, especially in the four decades prior to Independence. More recently, a shared sense of low-caste identity has often provided the basis for forms of civil society. For example, in many parts of Uttar Pradesh, Dalits have come together to establish libraries, schools, rotating credit associations, and other social and economic organizations (Pai 2002; Jaffrelot 2003). These institutions tend to cater only for low castes, but they draw together urban Dalit elites and the very poor, creating meaningful and lasting forms of cross-class collaboration analogous to those discussed by Jenkins and Goetz (1999) and Da Costa (2010). There are also many examples of Muslim organizations in India that simultaneously communicate religious ideas while also providing opportunities for some of India's poorest people to acquire schooling, credit and basic health care (Engineer 2004).

As Kaviraj (2001) points out, principles of *gesellschaft* and *gemeinschaft* may be combined within some forms of associational action.

The Bharatiya Kisan Union (BKU) farmers' movement in western Uttar Pradesh offers one example. It began as a movement aimed at galvanizing the rural public across the lines of caste, religion and class (see Bentall 1995; Bentall and Corbridge 1996). During the 1990s, the BKU increasingly lost its character as a broad movement of the rural poor and began to resemble more closely a political organization representing the interests of members of the middle-ranking Jat caste. But even when primarily reflecting Jat interests, the BKU continued to demonstrate a commitment to critiquing the state on behalf of the rural masses as a whole, and it also maintained its tradition of deliberative reflection (see Madsen and Lindberg 2003).

Some may object to a characterization of the Arya Samaj, Dalit associations and the BKU as examples of civil society (see Kaviraj 2001). Where communal or caste-based organizations critique the state effectively, their victory often comes at the cost of entrenching particularistic principles. There is also the problem that many associations misrepresent their core aims. For example, the caste associations (*mahasabhas*) across India typically downplay their role in consolidating the power of urban elites, preferring to stress their work on behalf of the poor. And even caste *panchayats*, which typically engage in more aggressive forms of reactionary social practice such as punishing people for marrying across caste lines (see Kaur 2010), sometimes claim to be part of 'civil society' (see Chowdhry 2009). Nevertheless, there is no necessary contradiction between caste and communal projects, on the one hand, and deliberative critique, on the other. Indeed, Kaviraj (2001) argues that efforts to encourage 'civil society' in India might actually work with rather than against social formations representing caste and religious goals.

A second issue is whether international organizations and networks can contribute to effective civil society in India. Webb (2010) is pessimistic on this point. He argues that foreign donors have become involved in trying to sponsor particular community activists in Delhi. Institutions such as the Association for India's Development in the US offer activists fellowships and stipends. But this sponsorship comes at a price. Money and influence become concentrated in the hands of a few prominent activists at the expense of more democratic group-based forms of civic activism. At the same time, those who do obtain foreign funding increasingly imagine their work less in terms of community service and more as a form of 'social entrepreneurship' that can contribute to their curriculum vitae.

There are parallels between Webb's account and Jens Lerche's (2008) research on the involvement of international organizations in low-caste (Dalit) activism in north India. Foreign organizations claiming to represent Dalits' rights have become an increasingly prominent feature of civil society in India. Lerche focuses on the efforts of the International Dalit Solidarity Network [IDSN] to draw Dalit activists together around the quest for a certain form of 'empowerment'. IDSN tends to only work with the Dalit elite, however, and it downplays issues of caste oppression and exploitation in favour of a focus on affirmative action and diversity issues. In Lerche's view, global civil society in India remains a chimera.

Arjun Appadurai (2002) offers a different vision of the potential for transnational organizations and advocacy to foster grassroots civil society in India. He focuses on the activities of the Society for the Promotion of Area Resource Centres (SPARC), an NGO with strong international links which seeks to improve sanitation and housing facilities for slum-dwellers in Mumbai. In Appadurai's view, SPARC has been highly successful in fostering a sense of civic consciousness among poor populations in the city and has also helped slum-dwellers to obtain practical assistance from the state. Appadurai concentrates not on unruly acts of defiance and illegality to explain this success, but refers instead to how poor people, working with middle-class SPARC activists, have used the legal system and peaceful demonstrations to negotiate with a previously obdurate state bureaucracy. For example, SPARC and the poor in Mumbai have been effective in archiving their actions. This chronicling of political efforts provides the legal basis for a strategy of 'precedent setting' wherein former victories are mobilized in future struggles. Appadurai's emphasis is very much on the long-term nature of this politicking within urban civil society – he refers to it as a 'politics of patience'. He also argues that an allegiance to the law underpins subaltern mobilization.

It is also possible that SPARC has done more to prevent than encourage radical critique in Mumbai. For Ananya Roy (2009), SPARC is an example of conservative middle-class activism, putatively espousing the case of the poor while simultaneously pacifying the subaltern population and paving the way for foreign capital. But Colin McFarlane's (2008) work on transnational self-help housing schemes in western India supports Appadurai's writing in certain respects. Focusing on the activities of 'the Alliance', a set of different NGOs including SPARC, McFarlane documents the emergence of a form of global civil society oriented around improving urban living conditions and involving the urban poor in Africa, Latin America and Asia in periodic conferences and other exchanges of knowledge. Through networking with the poor in cities such as São Paolo and Johannesburg, sharing ideas and offering solidarity, sections of the poor in Mumbai gain confidence, know-how and a certain training in the deliberative discussion historically associated with civil society.

The poor may also make effective use of global media contacts in their campaigns. Liza Weinstein (2009) documents the attempts of a private developer, Mukesh Mehta, to convert the Dharavi slum in Mumbai into lucrative real estate for upper middle classes. Weinstein emphasizes the capacity of the Dharavi poor, with assistance from sympathetic international organizations and the global media, to negotiate with the state and Mehta over the nature of urban redevelopment. Urban activists and poor communities used the local and global media to publicize instances in which the state and Mehta reneged on promises or obtained the signatures of poor people under false pretences. One result of these efforts was that Mehta and the Maharashtra government were forced to change their plans for Dharavi significantly. Weinstein's work therefore provides another example of how global and local political effort can be harnessed to advance the interests of subalterns and to ameliorate the accumulative cruelty of the state.

11.5   Conclusions

Partha Chatterjee's account of colonial and post-colonial Indian politics makes the important point that civil society – in its Hegelian (European) guise – was largely restricted to upper middle classes in the colonial period and much of the post-colonial era. The poor in India have typically mobilized in different ways, for example, via short-term protests aimed at capturing a share of government resources. Chatterjee's recent writing also has the merit of critiquing many of the activities of upper-middle-class civil society, which often marginalize and oppress the poor.

But there is no longer – if there ever was – a sharp divide in India between an upper class of urbanites well-versed in liberal democratic traditions and a public engaged only in barracking the local state in search of short-term gains, violently and in an unruly manner. Poor people increasingly imagine themselves as citizens capable of critiquing the state, and much of their mobilization occurs via legal channels, and with reference to abstract notions of rights, which they understand and embrace. To make these points is to expose the inadequacy of Chatterjee's vision of civil society and political society as a model for understanding the political sociology of contemporary India. It is also to answer the question posed as a title in the affirmative: India has a large and effective civil society, albeit civic action that often takes a markedly different form from those associated with the European experience of democracy. In this respect, India stands out as something of a success with respect to large parts of Africa and some of its South Asian neighbours. Crucial questions for further research include the particular conditions in which cross-class collaboration becomes possible in Indian civil society, caste and religion as bases for progressive associational action, and the role of globalization in reshaping civic life. Added to this list might be the pressing need for further investigation of small-town and rural civil society and the political life of India's 'real middle class': the multitude of 'middling sorts' who neither grapple with enduring poverty nor occupy the upper echelons of society.

12
Does Caste Still Matter in India?

12.1   Introduction

Addressing this question involves engaging with a series of querulous debates: how to define caste, the role of caste in politics, and how positive discrimination has changed society, to name but a few. The contentious nature of these debates partly reflects disagreement about the meaning of the word 'caste'. There is no direct translation for 'caste' in India; it comes from the Portuguese word *casta*, meaning 'pure breed'. 'Caste' most closely approximates two terms: *varna* or *jati*. *Varna* refers to the four subdivisions of the traditional Hindu hierarchy: Brahmins, who were traditionally priests; Kshtariyas (warriors); Vaishyas (merchants); and Sudras, who performed a broad range of other tasks. The Brahmins, Kshatriyas and Vaishyas together comprise the 'twice-born' castes in which male adolescents undergo a second, spiritual birth. These three *varnas* are also known as the Forward Castes, in contrast to Sudras, termed the Backward Castes. Scheduled Castes (SCs) or 'Dalits' lie outside the *varna* hierarchy altogether and tended to be confined to work that other castes imagine as demeaning. It is difficult to estimate the population of each *varna* because figures on caste have not been included in the census since 1931. But numbers of SCs are recorded: they constituted 16 per cent of the Indian population in 2001.

Each *varna* is comprised of thousands of *jatis*: endogamous caste 'groups' that were until recently linked to a specialist occupation. Members of each *jati* usually have a good idea about where they are placed with respect to the *varna* hierarchy. But the relationship between *jati* and *varna* is not fixed (e.g., Béteille 1992, 2001). M. N. Srinivas (1989) argued that in certain circumstances *jatis* may try to move up within the fourfold *varna* classification, a process he termed 'sanskritization'. It is also possible for *jatis* to move in the other direction, for example, where a Forward Caste tries to establish a Backward status in order to obtain government reservations for Sudras in public-sector employment (Jeffrey et al. 2008).

There are marked variations in how caste becomes manifest in north and central India, on the one hand, and the four main linguistic regions of the south. As Manor (2011a) reminds us, there are few indigenous Kshatriyas and Vaishyas in the south, and thus the Sudra category is far larger there than elsewhere. Moreover, *jatis* in the south – unlike their counterparts elsewhere – were split historically between right-hand and left-hand divisions, which derive from religious ritual and shape social relations (e.g., Mines 2006). It should also be noted that there are castes among Christians, Sikhs and Muslims in India (see Srinivas 1996). People's identities are multiple and flexible, and many Muslims, for example, are able to simultaneously adhere to normative aspects of Islam regarding equality while also espousing notions of caste hierarchy (see Jamous 1996).

Reflecting the complexity of the issues involved, the answer to the question posed as the title of this chapter is both 'no' and 'yes'. On the one hand, caste hierarchies have become less important over the past sixty years. Few people think or talk about *varna* in twenty-first-century India. On the other hand, *jati* identities remain significant in the fields of politics, education, work and marriage. Caste has moved to some extent from being a hierarchical system to a horizontal assortment of competing interest groups (see Harriss 1982: chapter 6), even while some elements of hierarchy remain important. This 'shift' is part of longer-term processes of change involving the interaction of principles of hierarchy and counter-currents from within India's religious traditions.

12.2   Caste Dominance in Mid-Twentieth Century India

Although there is a long history of writing on caste and its salience in India (see Quigley 1993 for a review), much of our knowledge about caste and the caste system emerged through the work of Indian and foreign anthropologists in the 1950s and 1960s. The French anthropologist Louis Dumont was a pre-eminent theorist of caste in that period. Dumont (1970) used ancient Hindu texts and a broad range of ethnographic village studies to argue that the Hindu caste system is oriented around the principles of purity and pollution. He maintained that Brahmins are at the top of the resulting hierarchy and untouchables at the bottom, and that all castes are linked together via a complex system of ritual acts that confirm and reproduce conceptions of purity and pollution. Dumont insisted that caste was not based upon power, status or authority, as is the case for Western structures of stratification, but on the purity embodied by the Brahmin.

Dumont's ideas have been roundly critiqued, as misinterpretations of Hindu texts, overly reliant on written sources and reflecting Brahmin ideology (see Fuller 1996: 3ff. for a review). Other scholars in the 1950s and 1960s focused on how caste is lived and practised on the ground (e.g., Srinivas 1955; Mayer 1996) – providing a 'field view' to complement Dumont's 'book view' (Béteille 1991). These scholars usually imagined caste society at the village level as a type of 'jajmani system', a term originally associated with the work of William Wiser (1936) in southern Uttar Pradesh. In the jajmani system, as described by anthropologists of the 1950s and 1960s, a powerful caste – or 'patron' (jajman) – made payments (dan) to a range of clients (kameen), usually in kind. The patrons' power was derived in part from their control over local social and economic assets. The patron was the major landowner, usually lived in the largest house and typically possessed the most extensive contacts outside the village. Each dominant caste was governed by a decision-making body (panchayat) composed of elder caste members whose purpose was to establish and sanction caste-wide standards of conduct. Patrons were usually from a relatively high jati within the varna hierarchy and they commonly dominated the ritual life of the village. But patrons were not usually Brahmins. One of the most important empirical studies of the jajmani system, by Gloria Raheja (1988), focuses on Gujars, a caste of only middling status within the varna hierarchy. Raheja concentrates on symbolic aspects of the relationship between dominant Gujars and other service castes, especially Brahmins. Through giving prestations (dan) to Brahmin priests, the Gujars marked their own power as a dominant caste and confirmed their auspiciousness and well-being. The protection of the family and village through the giving of dan operated, Raheja argues, as the 'ideological core' of Gujar dominance.

The 'jajmani system', as described by scholars such as Raheja, could only capture certain elements of what was inevitably a much more complex social reality. It should also be noted that the various 'caste systems' described – such as they were – never reached a fully fledged form or became wholly taken for granted, partly because large sections of the rural economy were already integrated into the capitalist economy in the 1950s and 1960s. For example, Scarlett Epstein (1973) notes that in the two villages she studied in the 1960s jajmani systems were well developed but coexisted with a cash economy. Many anthropologists have also pointed out that there was no pan-Indian *jajmani* arrangement, but multiple different systems.

But there were certain common features to caste in the 1950s and 1960s that together suggest the existence of durable structured inequalities. It is possible to identify five key features of these hierarchies. First, *jatis* tended to specialize occupationally. The functions performed by particular castes within the *jajmani* system tended to be fairly stable over time and passed on inter-generationally within the family. Thus, particular *jatis* came to be associated with specific hereditary trades. For example, in large parts of Uttar Pradesh, the Dhimmars served the function of carrying water, the Chamars were leatherworkers or shoe-makers, and the Dhobis washed clothes. It would be mistaken to imagine that all members of these castes performed these tasks – as early as the 1890s, in Uttar Pradesh, many Chamars worked in agricultural labour in western Uttar Pradesh, for example (see Nevill 1922). Yet occupational categories were often indicative of people's work in the 1950s and 1960s.

A second key feature of caste was its reproduction through rules about the sharing of food, bodily contact and other interpersonal relations. These norms covered everything from who could officiate at marriage ceremonies, where people should sit at village feasts, and who could attend the birth of a child, among any other aspects of everyday village life at the time (see Mandelbaum 1970). Low-caste inequality had a marked spatial aspect, too: Dalits were forced to live in specific parts of the village away from higher castes; they were often refused entry to temples and schools; and they were banned from using the water pumps of the rich, for example (see Srinivas 1955; Béteille 1965; Mayer 1996). Contraventions of these norms often led to violent higher-caste retribution and reprisals.

Third, caste shaped marriage practices. Most castes practised endogamy. Many had further rules about marriage, for example, that a member of a specific sub-caste could not marry within their own sub-caste or that of their paternal and maternal grandparents, to take the case of the Jats of western Uttar Pradesh (Pradhan 1966). Within the caste-based arranged marriage system other norms applied, too: for example, in many parts of the plains of north India, it was usual for a woman's family to pay a dowry to a husband's family.

Fourth, notions of caste hierarchy had achieved a degree of acceptance in rural areas. We need to enter some caveats here. Low-caste political movements aimed at raising the standing of Dalits were active in parts of India in the late nineteenth and twentieth century (e.g., Gooptu 2001; Rawat 2011). In some parts of the country, Dalits effectively questioned dominant caste power (e.g., Lerche 1999). Moreover, even in the areas where Dalits were not engaged in forms of social mobilization, they had not wholly internalized the notion of themselves as defiled (see Berreman 1960: 127). But the weight of evidence from village ethnographies suggests that in the 1950s and 1960s higher castes had little compunction about using the language of caste to explain and justify their elevated position. As Dalit biographies and autobiographies also show (Ilaiah 1991), low castes had often internalized social subordination; low self-esteem came to be reflected in their demeanour, confidence and sense of self.

Fifth, higher castes were often able to translate their local economic and political power into a wider dominance over state bureaucracies, representative government and local electoral outcomes. Marguerite Robinson (1988) points to how dominant castes in Andhra Pradesh in the 1950s and 1960s were able to influence the votes of lower castes, such that rural elites were able to deliver 'vote-banks' to political parties. Pradhan (1966) analyses the capacity of dominant-caste Jats to control village government through the use of traditional caste councils in Uttar Pradesh. Brass (1965) demonstrates that higher castes monopolized key posts in the district offices of the ruling Congress Party in the 1950s and 1960s (Brass 1965). Dominant castes also predominated within state legislative assemblies and the Lok Sabha (Jaffrelot and Kumar 2009).

Studies of these five dimensions of dominance in mid-twentieth-century India cannot be read as wholly accurate reflections of village power structures at the time, tainted as they undoubtedly were by a tendency to ignore women's social practices and overplay caste to the detriment of analysis of other axes of differentiation. It is also important to note a relative lack of material on caste in urban India (see Vatuk 1972; Gooptu 2001). But the work of scholars of the 1950s and 1960s suggests that fairly rigid and stable caste hierarchies existed in India during this period. Higher castes benefited from mutually reinforcing modes of power and their dominance tended to be reproduced inter-generationally in predictable ways.

12.3   The Decline of Caste Hierarchies

In the late 1960s there was a shift in scholarly approaches to Indian anthropology (Singer and Cohn 1968). An old idea of the subcontinent as timeless gave way slowly over the 1970s and early 1980s to understandings of India – and caste within it – as a product of history and changing experience (see Corbridge 1988; and Clark-Decès 2011, for a review). This shift spurred academics to reconsider caste in pre-Independence India. To rework the question posed as the title: *did* caste matter, for example, before the British arrived? Some argued that the British effectively invented the Indian caste system, because of the manner in which they ruled and because they were influenced by Orientalist fantasies about India's innate 'irrationality' (e.g., Inden 1990; cf. Dirks 2001). The British certainly consolidated aspects of caste difference and power, for example, by including caste on the Census and inducting dominant castes into the lower reaches of the colonial administration. Stuart Corbridge (1988) has traced this process in Jharkhand, India, showing how in the second half of the nineteenth century the British imposed rigid caste and tribe labels on populations that were fluid and internally differentiated. In the early twentieth century, the British policy of divide and rule meant that tribes were increasingly hived off from castes, and in the post-colonial era political parties have found it expedient to persist with the 'ST' nomenclature, in spite of its faulty sociological logic. David Washbrook (1988: 83) therefore has a point when he notes that 'much of India's ancient past may have been made in the second quarter of the nineteenth century'. But the British did not conjure caste difference from the ether. Peabody (2001) argues that pre-British rulers also used caste-wise tabulations to enumerate subjects and that the British were encouraged by sections of Indian society to continue this practice. Certainly, elements of a *jajmani* 'system' and accompanying notions of hierarchy existed long before the British extended administrative control over India in the eighteenth and nineteenth centuries (see Bayly 2001).

The question that more directly occupies us here is: does caste still matter today in such a rapidly growing and increasingly urban society, in which the state has sought for many years to compensate for the disabilities that have been inflicted upon some social groups through affirmative action policies? Dipankar Gupta (2005) makes a strong case that caste became much less important in the period between the 1960s and early 2000s in India. First, a former tendency for caste to reflect occupation has declined. Growing urbanization and commercialization, as well as rapid economic growth in some parts of India, has allowed people from many caste backgrounds to find off-farm work or incomes (see chapter 4). This has had the wider effect of undermining the *jajmani* system (Gupta 2005). People formerly dependent on local landowners have been able to migrate to other parts of India or even abroad to work. Some studies emphasize the capacity of lower castes to travel every day to local urban areas to find jobs (e.g., Anandhi et al. 2002), or else move within India on a seasonal basis (Shah 2006b). Surinder Jodhka (2008) describes the rapid growth of a wide range of Dalit enterprises in western Uttar Pradesh and Haryana in the 1990s and early 2000s, which have elevated individual entrepreneurs out of poverty while also providing jobs for others. Others, Osella and Osella (2000) among them, describe the movement of low castes to the Middle East for work.

Oliver Mendelsohn's (1993) research draws out these processes of change especially clearly. Building on fieldwork in Behror village, northern Rajasthan, Mendelsohn maintains that, by the late 1980s, the traditional system of *jajmani* relations in Behror had become marginal to the overall economy of the village. There appears to have been a parallel decline in awareness of caste as a religiously sanctioned institution and of traditional councils dominated by a single caste claiming authority over other villagers. Mendelsohn links the decline of the *jajmani* system and traditional councils not only to a sharp rise in rural people's economic activity outside the village, but also to increased economic differentiation amongst Ahirs, the erstwhile 'dominant caste'. Economic differentiation had eroded a sense of collective interest among Ahirs, such that caste solidarity had been replaced by 'pragmatic individualism or at least family-centredness' (Mendelsohn 1993: 824–5).

Reservations have also played a prominent role in delinking caste from occupation. Positive caste-based discrimination in India can be traced to the 1930s, when the British created lists of formerly Untouchable castes and tribes deemed eligible for special state assistance: 'Scheduled Castes' (SCs) and 'Scheduled Tribes' (STs). The 1950 Indian Constitution offered SCs and STs legal equality and reserved places in public-sector employment, educational institutions and government representative bodies (Galanter 1984). Shortly after Independence, Nehru established a Backward Classes Commission to investigate the condition of castes for- mally above the SCs but nonetheless suffering from social and economic disadvantages. This Commission reported in 1956 with a list of 2,399 Backward Caste *jatis* and suggested measures to improve their position. Nehru believed it politically impossible to implement this recommenda- tion. But the issue of reservations for these 'Other Backward Classes' (OBCs) – as they came to be labelled – emerged again in 1977 when the Janata Party pledged to establish a new investigative body. The result- ing Commission under the chairmanship of B. P. Mandal reported in 1980, recommending the extension of positive discrimination to OBCs. The Mandal Report was set aside for the next ten years, but V. P. Singh promised to implement its major recommendations during electoral hus- tings in Autumn 1989, and made the actual decision to institute reforms in August 1990 (Dirks 2001: 284–5). This provoked a fierce higher-caste backlash, especially among students (Balagopal 1991).

In most parts of India, the effect of OBC reservations was more symbolic than substantive. When reservations were introduced for Backward Castes, competition for positions in government employment was intense. It was typically only households who could afford to pay a bribe and had the right social contacts – a 'creamy layer' of relatively rich OBCs from comparatively well-placed *jatis* – who obtained quota positions (Michelutti 2007).

Similarly, a few Dalit *jatis* have tended to dominate access to reserved jobs. In addition, wealthier Dalits and those already possessing good links in government service have often monopolized access to public-sector jobs, becoming in some places a self-reproducing clique. Béteille (1992) notes other problems with SC reservations: since those in government employment are legally debarred from participating in politics, positive discrimination deprives low-caste communities of potential political representatives. Moreover, many SCs move out of their villages and urban neighbourhoods to work in government, thus robbing communities of talented individuals. Government-employed Dalits may withdraw psychologically from their origins or even refuse to acknowledge their caste peers as they become assimilated into an urban middle class. But Parry (1999) points out that for every one SC who enters government employment many others in the immediate and extended family will benefit. Moreover, the entry of SCs into government employment plays an important symbolic role, instilling a measure of confidence and pride in low-caste communities. Parry contests the notion that low castes in government service disown their caste peers: they often play important roles in caste associations, social organizations and cultural festivals. Parry concludes that SC reservations have led to greater churning in local patterns of caste and class reproduction and contribute to a diminution in caste hierarchies, even while they have failed to transform society.

Corbridge's (2000) account of the cultural politics and substantive effects of Scheduled Tribe (ST) reservations in the Jharkhand parallels Parry's analysis in several key respects. Corbridge shows that reservations have been important in the creation of an ST middle class in Jharkhand. Most members of this ST petty bourgeoisie now live in urban areas and come from established tribal elites. But some tribals from non-elite backgrounds have been able to take advantage of reservations. Moreover, reservations have worked in part to 'crystallize a conception of *adivasi* [tribal] identity that recognizes the exploitation/marginalization of many tribal communities and which demands compensation from the authorities' (ibid.: 65).

Beyond reservations, the proliferation of government programmes catering for disadvantaged groups has contributed to a decline in low castes' dependence on higher castes (see chapter 5 of this volume; Manor 2011a). During Indira Gandhi's period of rule in the 1970s, a wide range of initiatives emerged, often specifically directed towards low castes, which provided small amounts of land, grants to purchase livestock or housing, and cheap credit for the poor. Such programmes frequently offered a bulwark against the most extreme forms of poverty and dependence (Krishna 2002). Since 2004, the Indian state has rapidly expanded the range, scope and size of such development efforts, which are likely to further accelerate the diminution of caste and class hierarchies in rural India (Manor 2011a). For example, Craig Jeffrey revisited a village in rural Bijnor district in 2010 that he had studied in 2000–2. He found that the new range of government programmes in the village are enhancing low castes' standing in the village: schemes to provide the poor with permanent Class IV jobs, small initiatives to expand sports' provision and grants to encourage girls to attend school – for example – are moderating class and caste dominance.

Across India, education has been crucially important in challenging hierarchical ideas of caste. Dalit enrolment in education improved in many areas in the 1980s, 1990s and 2000s, especially among boys (e.g., Mendelsohn and Vicziany 1998; Gorringe 2010). Basic education provides Dalits with the numeracy and literacy skills required to manage businesses, navigate urban society, and negotiate legal and government bureaucracies. It improves Dalits' ability to manage their own health and reduces their dependence on higher castes (Sen 1999). Formal education also often increases Dalits' self-confidence and sense of entitlement to equal treatment by the law and government (Wadley 1994: 222f), especially where rising education is wedded to a strong Dalit movement for social empowerment (Gorringe 2010). In Uttar Pradesh, educated Dalits commonly argue that people should be judged and valued on their behaviour, not according to their caste, and they claim that education has instilled in them confidence, civility and self-belief (Jeffrey et al. 2008: chapter 3). Rising education, combined with the growing influence of the media, have also influenced the thinking of middle and upper castes in India, many of whom no longer believe in hierarchical ideas of caste (cf. Béteille 1991). Moreover, education has been important in precipitating a public culture in India in which it is no longer acceptable to speak of caste in hierarchical terms.

Education, growing urbanization, the expansion of the media and the spread of ideas of democracy across India have also had the cumulative effect of altering what is considered acceptable in terms of the everyday practice of caste. There are many examples of different castes socializing together, often in intimate ways, in even some of India's more remote rural locations. Of course, this is not wholly new. Adrian Mayer (1996) points out how Rajputs in the village in which he studied in the 1960s sometimes dropped restrictions on sharing food with lower castes in order to seek their political support. But what is striking about contemporary rural India is the ubiquity of less strategic forms of everyday intimate interaction across caste lines. Even the briefest visit to an Indian village would yield numerous examples: higher castes buying snacks from a Muslim vendor, schoolchildren squabbling over sweets and people from a wide variety of castes pushing each other on to the bus. Inter-caste sociality is a theme that emerges, too, in several ethnographies. Sarah Pinto (2008) records numerous examples of cross-caste friendship and mutual understanding in her ethnography of birth practices in rural eastern Uttar Pradesh. Da Costa (2010) offers a similarly rich picture of inter-caste collaboration in her study of rural theatre in West Bengal. And Nisbett (2007) refers to college students from different castes openly sharing snacks and cigarettes in south India. Reading ethnographies of the 2000s against those of the 1950s and 1960s is to appreciate the scale of change in people's mindsets and practices with respect to caste.

Politics has also changed dramatically in the sense that higher castes have been unable to maintain their monopoly over political institutions. Jaffrelot and Kumar's (2009) analysis of the changing caste profiles of Members of Legislative Assemblies (MLAs) across sixteen states of India brings out regional variations in the extent and nature of change. Jaffrelot and Kumar argue that the Deccan (Maharashtra, Karnataka and Andhra Pradesh) and communist states (Kerala and West Bengal) remain dominated by upper castes. But in the Hindi belt (Uttar Pradesh, Madhya Pradesh and Bihar) and north-west (Punjab, Rajasthan and Gujarat), an upper-caste majority gave way to OBC (Hindi belt) or middle-caste (north-west) administrations in the early 1990s (see also chapter 6 of this book).

Politics at the village level has also been transformed. In sixty plus years since Independence, Dalits and other lower castes have increasingly challenged the notion that higher castes are their natural superiors. Marguerite Robinson (1988) describes how the rise of political parties and other institutions representing the interests of the poor, and growing political awareness as a result of media expansion and education, loosened the control of higher castes over vote-banks and lessened Dalits' dependence on village notables in Andhra Pradesh. In a similar vein, rising education and political consciousness has allowed Dalits in western India to bypass established patron–client networks and set themselves up as social reformers operating between poor people and the state (Krishna 2002). Moreover, the 93rd Amendment Act to the Indian Constitution, passed in 1994, introduced reserved seats for Dalits in village-level *panchayats*. The degree to which this has empowered SCs varies geographically (compare Lieten 1996 with Ciotti 2006), but Dalits have benefited to a significant degree from this legislation, and some Dalit women have come to hold significant power (Ciotti 2006).

In sum, four of the five important features of caste that we identified as characterizing the ethnographic work of the 1950s and 1960s are no longer markedly apparent in many parts of rural India. The link between occupation and caste has been broken, rules around commensality have been relaxed, the taken-for-granted nature of caste is less evident and upper-caste dominance of politics has declined in some regions.

12.4   Caste, Identity and Politics

As early as 1957, M. N. Srinivas noted that, as caste was declining as a hierarchical 'system', it was simultaneously being reinvented and redeployed as an identity in the sphere of modern competitive politics. This is a theme that has been developed in a wide range of works (e.g., Kothari 1970; Jaffrelot 2003). In a recent review article on caste and politics, James Manor (2011a: 26) uses an analysis of National Election Survey (NES) data to argue that caste continues to influence voting behaviour in India, if not at the all-India level, then certainly in many states. Manor argues that individual *jatis* are less important as political actors than *jati*-clusters comprised often of castes that have roughly similar standing with respect to the *varna* hierarchy. He also emphasizes the frequently localized nature of these caste effects: it is often within specific regions at the sub-state level that influence of *jati* cluster over voting behaviour becomes apparent.

Of course, caste is only one among many bases upon which people may vote. Drawing on a survey of people's voting behaviour in three states, Dipankar Gupta (2000) claims that people's individual choices at elections are a great deal more idiosyncratic than most commentators would lead us to believe. Factors other than caste – economic interest, personal links with a local politician, party loyalty, for example – are often as or more important than people's *jati* or *jati*-cluster in governing voting behavior. But, as Kanchan Chandra (2004) points out, voters often use politicians' pronouncements regarding caste as a short-cut means of guessing what their policies and priorities will be when in office (see also chapter 8). In the absence of detailed information about a party's intentions, people imagine the *jati* of a politician and his or her lieutenants as a condensed symbol of their sympathies.

What is abundantly clear is that, whether people ultimately vote by caste or not – and the evidence is mixed and complicated (Yadav and Palshikar 2009; Manor 2011a) – caste provides a powerful vocabulary for politicians and political parties to utilize in the quest for power (e.g., Kothari 1970; Chandra 2004). That politicians and newspaper columnists put so much emphasis on caste as a means of manipulating electoral outcomes has its own sociological effects: strengthening caste identities, heightening people's suspicion of other castes, and encouraging people to consult with each other in *jati* meetings in the period running up to elections. In the 1960s, OBC and middle-caste mobilization was most evident. For example, in Uttar Pradesh in the 1960s and 1970s, Chaudhury Charan Singh, a member of the middle-ranking Jat caste, developed an alliance of Ahirs, Jats, Gujars and Rajputs (AJGAR) that served as a durable support base. Dipankar Gupta (2000: 143ff.) argues that AJGAR was a community of rich peasants rather than a caste-based coalition. But fears about Dalit assertion certainly contributed to AJGAR solidarity. In the late 1980s, the Mandal issue heightened the connection between caste and politics. The OBC reservations issue polarized opinion and encouraged people to link their future prosperity to collective caste 'interests'. The political landscape changed again in the 1990s, and again caste came to the fore. During that decade and the following one, the BJP defended higher castes' economic and cultural-political goals while strategically cultivating support among sections of the lower castes that had not been mobilized by other groups, such as the so-called Most Backward Castes (MBCs) – the poorest among those in the OBC category – and poorer Dalit *jatis*.

The importance of caste in processes of political mobilization spreads well beyond central and state-level elections to influence almost all processes of competitive election in India's vast democracy: union ballots, district board elections, even appointments to neighbourhood associations and voluntary groups. For example, in the period before a *panchayat*, election village homes are typically abuzz with calculations regarding how different castes are going to vote and what this means for the eventual outcome (Lieten 1996). Similarly, caste is also crucial in student politics in many parts of provincial India. Young people often hold *jati* meetings to decide on how to vote, and candidates often recruit statistically minded peers to compute how caste might shape the election (Jeffrey 2010).

Caste has been given a fresh salience, too, by the rise of parties associated with the cultures of specific *jatis*, such as Mulayam Singh Yadav's Samajwadi Party (SP), and Lalu Prasad Yadav's Rashtriya Janata Dal (RJD) party in Bihar. These politicians garnered support through promoting Yadav and Backward Class interests, while at the same time making links with Muslims and some other castes. As Michelutti (2008) avers, the SP played on notions of Yadavs as people with a democratic tradition, and used symbols of Yadav identity in its campaigns. This encouraged the emergence of Yadav social associations and cultural practices. Similarly, the Bahujan Samaj Party (BSP) in Uttar Pradesh made explicit efforts to court the votes of Dalits, especially the most important Dalit *jati* in Uttar Pradesh: the Chamars. Since the 1990s there has been a huge effervescence of 'mytho-histories' of Dalit achievement circulated by educated politicos with links to the BSP (Narayan 2008).

The decline of caste as a hierarchical system has therefore been accompanied by the cultural production of caste and caste-cluster identities in the field of Indian electoral politics. Castes are arranged 'horizontally' – separated from each other on the basis of their different identities and myths – rather than 'vertically' along the lines of purity and pollution.

12.5 Caste as Habitus: Hierarchy Revisited

Yet caste hierarchies continue to have some importance in many parts of India. This is a point that comes out especially strongly in analyses of schooling, work and marriage. Dalits remain well behind upper castes and OBCs in terms of their access to education (see Ramachandran 2004; Shah et al. 2006: 46). In most parts of India, higher castes enter school at an earlier age, obtain admission in better institutions, follow more prestigious routes through education and acquire relatively marketable qualifications. The main difficulty for Dalits is not access to primary school, but remaining in education in the context of discrimination, poverty and a lack of obvious incentives to study (cf. chapter 14). According to one estimate, of every hundred Dalits who enter primary education in India, four reach Class 12 (Shah et al. 2006: 47), and the dropout rate for girls is especially high. None of this is to diminish education's empowering effects, but it illustrates the importance of examining low-caste education in relation to that of higher castes.

Educational inequalities have knock-on effects in terms of Dalits' and other low castes' capacities to compete for secure and well-paid work. For example, dominant castes' monopoly over the credentials and forms of comportment that confer advantage in social settings has allowed them to dominate access to secure salaried work in rural western Uttar Pradesh (Jeffrey et al. 2008). This is all the more surprising since western Uttar Pradesh has been an area in which low castes have achieved new forms of political representation through the rise of the BSP. Jeffrey et al. (2008) show that higher castes are able to draw upon local and regional stocks of social and cultural resources, as well as their formidable economic advantage, to 'counter-resist' low-caste political assertion. This is a point that also emerges from research among Dalits in Tamil Nadu (Gorringe 2010), where low-caste political mobilization has a longer history but where there are similar barriers to rapid low-caste mobility. Caste hierarchies are often fairly persistent even in a political context conducive to change.

A similar picture emerges in small towns and big cities. Dalits and MBCs are less successful at finding secure salaried work, and establishing successful businesses, than are higher castes in urban India. Thorat and Newman (2007) provide quantitative evidence of discrimination in hiring, wages, working conditions and patterns of upward mobility within urban labour markets in India. Thorat and Newman (2010) sent mock applications for private-sector service jobs in India, using identical CVs but two sets of names, one high caste and one Dalit or Muslim. Their experiment showed that Dalit and Muslim applicants face significant discrimination in the white-collar job market. The odds of a Dalit applicant receiving a follow-up call were 67 per cent of a high-caste Hindu applicant with the same CV. Research on Delhi students' experiences of seeking white-collar work provides comparable evidence (Deshpande and Newman 2010). Dalit students were much more likely to experience searching interviews, and these often entailed being quizzed on their caste, views on reservation and family background. Deshpande and Newman (2010) conclude that recruitment to private-sector jobs is often 'rigged' in India in favour of higher castes.

Harriss-White (2003) makes similar points on the basis of long-term research in the small town of Arni, Tamil Nadu. Arni experienced rapid economic change during the 1980s and 1990s, in part through the rise of new forms of commodity production. But caste continues to shape people's capacity to participate in relatively secure and lucrative sections of the economy. Moreover, caste interests strongly influence the activities of the institutions, such as trade associations, that have emerged to adjudicate on wages, working hours and employment disputes in the town. Harriss-White and Vidyarthee (2010) use economic census data to tease out how discrimination against SCs and STs in different parts of India shapes their participation in various forms of business. Summarizing the data, they note that:

> SCs have entered mining, quarrying and construction and are most consistently prevented from entering trade, transport, hospitality and service sectors [. . .] STs have a relative disadvantage in all sectors of the non-agricultural economy but have been able, with the help of improvements in literacy, to move into services – though, it is likely, at the low end. (Harriss-White and Vidyarthee 2010: 332)

Read together, the work of Jeffrey et al. (2008), Thorat and Newman (2010), Harriss-White (2003) and Harriss-White and Vidyarthee (2010) challenge predictions that modernization and democratization would decouple caste from the market.

In metropolitan India caste inequalities also come to the fore. Fuller and Narasimhan (2007) show in their research on the IT sector in Chennai that the great majority of people in skilled jobs are from urban, upper-middle-class, Brahmin backgrounds. In her work in Bangalore, Carol Upadhya (2008) makes similar points. Higher castes are more likely to possess the money, social links, education and other types of cultural capital to acquire relatively good jobs in India's new economy (cf. Nisbett 2007). Upadhya also explains the dominance of upper castes in Bangalore's IT sector with reference to the caste-bias of engineering colleges and the industry's recruitment process, which place explicit emphasis on cultural markers of distinction. The IT leaders to whom Upadhya spoke denied their complicity in perpetuating caste disparities. They claimed to be engaged in countering caste discrimination and they strongly contested any notion that caste reservations should be introduced in the private sector. But reading the studies of Fuller and Narasimhan (2008) and Upadhya (2008) alongside the work of Thorat and Newman (2007) and Harriss-White (2003) is to recognize the force of continued caste inequalities, even in some of India's most 'modern' arenas.

The marked over-representation of Brahmins in the IT sector does not necessarily imply that recruitment markets and the wider economy are caste discriminatory, however. John Harriss's (2003c) examination of trust in Indian business practices points to ways in which people's attitudes to caste are changing in urban India. Drawing on research conducted in 2000 within firms in Ahmedabad, Gujarat and Chennai, Tamil Nadu, Harriss shows that, in small- and medium-sized companies, people's assessment of whom to trust is based primarily on their own personal history of conducting transactions, not on their caste, class and other aspects of their background. Harriss points to a general move towards more 'modern' forms of business organization, for example, through the restructuring of family business and inter-caste marriage.

The point remains, however, that caste continues to shape people's access to secure and well-paid employment, partly because of the manner in which caste and class overlap but also because of continued caste prejudices among many people in Indian society. Moreover, it is by no means certain that caste discrimination and inequality will gradually decline. It is possible to discern from the existing scholarly literature three negative feedback loops operating in contemporary India. First, higher-caste discrimination prevents low castes from obtaining high-status positions in the modern economy. This, in turn, discourages inter-caste mixing and militates against the emergence of new attitudes. Second, low castes' efforts to accumulate economic, social and cultural capital tend to reinforce 'the rules of the game', as set by dominant castes (Bourdieu 1984). Third, low castes' relative exclusion from lucrative sectors of the modern economy prevents them from acquiring knowledge and the sense of entitlement that comes with inherited caste and class privilege. Higher castes monopolize the information and embodied assurance that comes with success, while low castes commonly come to experience feelings of embarrassment and awkwardness – precisely the type of qualities that higher castes view as markers of a low-caste status.

Marriage is another sphere in which ideas of caste hierarchy remain important in contemporary India. Many commentators predicted that the spread of ideas of individual choice and romantic love through the global media would lead to a shift to Western-style marriages in India wherein young people would arrange marriages themselves, based on their own preferences and independent of caste (see Clark-Decès 2011 for a critical review). Recent scholarship on middle-class urbanites provides some support for this idea. Donner (2002) has written on the rise of inter-caste love marriages in urban India, and Fuller and Narasimhan (2008) have discussed similar marriages among upper castes in Chennai, for example (see also Harriss 2003a). But most studies suggest that a widespread move away from a system of caste-based arranged marriages has not taken place. What appears to have emerged instead in many areas of provincial India, including among low castes in rural areas (e.g., Roulet 1996; Biao 2005), is some version of a 'dowry system' with four key characteristics: senior kin arrange the union; marriages are usually caste endogamous; socio-economic considerations are primary in the choice of partner; and dowry is used as a bargaining tool in families' efforts to secure a groom with valued qualities, such as secure work.

There are certain circumstances in which caste remains explicit within this dowry system. Advertisements for brides and grooms in newspapers and on websites are often organized by *jati* or *varna*. But euphemism is much more common. A vocabulary of code words has emerged that serves the function of signalling caste without making it explicit. People refer to the importance of finding a match for their son or daughter who is of the right 'community' (*biradiri*) or has the right 'culture'. Without mentioning caste, people often speculate about the negotiations and misunderstandings that may ensue if two people from different *jatis* marry: whether to celebrate particular festivals, when to fast and which deities to worship, for example (see Jehan 2009). In other circumstances, class differences act as a relatively safe idiom for talking about caste. For example, people refer to the importance of spouses' compatibility at the level of 'lifestyle'. It is tempting to view these examples as providing more evidence of caste's modern incarnation as a horizontal identity. But veiled discussions of caste in marriage have a hierarchical element. For higher-caste parents, the variations between Brahmin habits and

Kshatriya ones can be a matter of somewhat light-hearted reflection, in a way that the differences between Brahmin and Dalit cultures cannot.

Nowhere is this residual importance of caste difference and caste hierarchy in marriage arrangements better illustrated than in the caste *panchayats* that continue to adjudicate on situations in which people have contravened marriage norms in many parts of north India, especially among the Jats of Haryana and western Uttar Pradesh (Chowdhry 2009; Kaur 2010). The caste *panchayats* increasingly enroll younger men as well as elders, and they often spend a significant portion of their time meting out punishments to people perceived to have endangered caste honour. Situations in which a Dalit man elopes with a Jat woman arouse the fiercest reprisals, because of the large gap between the hierarchical standing of the two young people and the anxieties it produces about low castes 'stealing' (and polluting) dominant-caste women. Ravinder Kaur's (2010) analysis of Haryanyi Jats' practices highlights the idiosyncratic manner in which norms of caste purity are invoked. Her informants make great play of abiding by caste rules but are also increasingly importing non-Jat brides from Orissa, Kerala and Assam.

What is partly interesting about how caste resurfaces in spheres such as marriage is its tendency to operate on the unconscious levels of presupposition and taste. To adopt one of Bourdieu's (1984) terms, caste is imbued in the 'habitus': an embodied system of dispositions durably inscribed in people's reflexes, movements and desires. In an illuminating passage, Bourdieu (2001: 216) describes the habitus as something that is 'deposited like a spring at the deepest level of the body' – a conceptualization that is especially useful in thinking about caste. Students in Uttar Pradesh told Jeffrey (2010) that they are often unaware of their classmate's caste when they make friends or start a relationship. If the person turns out to be from the same caste, students said that they experience a 'strange feeling of happiness welling up from within' – it is precisely at the level of pre-conscious, embodied feeling that young people experience caste most viscerally. That they refer to the feeling as 'strange' is notable. Bourdieu argues that in certain moments or conjunctures people can become aware of their inherited habitus and problematize embodied dispositions. Students were conscious that favouring a person – in a sexual relationship or friendship – on the grounds that they are from the same caste is somehow not acceptable in modern India. At the same time, they felt helpless in the face of embodied emotion.

Such embodied feelings are linked to practices of untouchability. There are some seasoned commentators in India who argue that untouchability has entirely vanished from the subcontinent. For example, Dipankar Gupta (2005) draws on research in villages in Punjab and Haryana to assert that 'untouchability has disappeared from India' (see also Deliege

1999). Shah et al. (2006) conducted a survey of 565 villages across eleven states of India to test the merits of such assertions. They found that, in over half the villages they studied, Dalits were still denied entry into non-Dalit houses and prohibited from sharing food with higher castes. In over a quarter of the villages, Dalits were forced to stand before upper-caste men and refused employment in house construction. Practices of untouchability also mark the activities of the state. Shah et al. found that Dalits were prevented from entering police stations and ration shops in over a quarter of the villages they surveyed, and excluded from electoral booths in 12 per cent. This depressing picture is broadly supported by intensive ethnographic research in different parts of rural India. Gorringe (2010) notes continuing practices of untouchability in Tamil Nadu, as does Dube (1998) in research in Uttar Pradesh, and Da Costa (2010) in work in West Bengal. As Harriss (1982: 298) presciently argued with respect to social change in rural Tamil Nadu, 'Although the restrictions on commensality and interaction between castes have largely broken down, they are still maintained in relation to untouchables.'

The denigration of low castes continues in part because of how it is embedded in the higher-caste habitus. For example, higher castes across large parts of north India use the phrase 'Chamari-si' to refer to embarrassing and uncouth behaviour (Chamar is the name of a Dalit caste). Similarly, rural women who hitch their saris up when passing through Dalit parts of villages in western Uttar Pradesh do so unconsciously, almost out of habit (see Jeffrey et al. 2008). When this continuing embodied caste prejudice interacts with low-caste self-assurance violence often results (e.g., Brass 1997). If there is a theme of contemporary caste-based violence, it is of Dalits contravening partially forgotten norms around caste, and their trespass on higher-caste sensibilities then triggering fierce reprisals. The resulting atrocities, in turn, become a focus of further caste-based tension and conflict, as Dalits and higher castes compete for political assistance, legal support and public sympathy.

12.6   Conclusions

There is no longer anything like a caste system in India. The relatively closed economies of the 1950s and 1960s, in which caste formed an interrelated sociological organism, have crumbled away. They have been replaced by a situation more complex, fluid and indeterminate, one in which castes are more commonly jostling up against each other – literally and figuratively – than marking hierarchical difference. At the same time, forms of caste hierarchy continue to haunt India, as reflected at the level of everyday practice. What is also clear is that caste often intersects in important ways with other axes of social difference – especially class and gender – to privilege some and markedly disadvantage many others.

The collective significance of these points is at least twofold. First, it is evident that how one assesses the question 'does caste matter?' depends in part on one's temporal frame of reference. We have mainly compared the 1950s and 1960s, on the one hand, with the 1990s and 2000s, on the other. There is logic to this comparison, since it covers a key period in India's history. But there are many other ways that the argument might have been set up. For example, Michelutti (2008) has recently written of the growing importance of caste in politics and society in Uttar Pradesh, adopting the decade of the 2000s as her historical stage. We might have answered the question posed as a title differently had we adopted this horizon, or compared, for example, the early eighteenth century with the present. A still broader historical sweep might have revealed hierarchy and difference as competing principles of caste that have varied in their prominence over time. For instance, Metcalf and Metcalf (2006) suggest that there are other periods in Indian history when ideas of caste as hierarchy have tended to move towards more horizontal conceptualizations. Second, it is important to note that one's answer to the question posed as a title depends to a significant extent on one's standpoint. This is true of scholars: their experience of caste and of specific places in India influence their conclusions. It is also true of people in India. The notion that 'caste does not matter any more' is endlessly repeated in the living rooms of India's middle classes. But it has little meaning for Dalit labourers, whose lives continue to be shaped by discrimination.

13

How Much Have Things Changed for Indian Women?

13.1 Introduction

Feminist scholars have done a great deal to make us understand that women and men make their way in the world differently. Women shoulder a double burden of paid and unpaid work and family maintenance that men for the most part do not. Women also continue to face problems in getting their voices heard in public. In a small number of countries they are denied equal voting rights with men. In almost all countries, women constitute a minority among elected representatives or members of the executive branch of government. Struggles for equal pay continue to be fought even in countries with very good Gender Related Development Index (GDI) and Gender Empowerment Measure (GEM) scores, as defined and calculated by the United Nations Development Programme (UNDP). Female literacy rates across the developing world are generally much lower than are those for males, as indeed are labour-force participation and wage rates in the formal sector. The gap between women and men along many dimensions of welfare is very often as significant, and in some cases more significant, than are the welfare gaps between ethnic groups, urban and rural populations, or social classes. Older women, disabled women and widows tend to fare worst of all.

Feminists also remind us that female identities, just like male or transgender identities, are never closed or singular (Butler 1990). There are women and women, men and men, and it is a category error to assume that well-to-do metropolitan women see the world in the same way as female agricultural labourers. People construct their lives with reference to multiple identities and points of view – sexuality, class, ethnicity, religion and so on – and it is a crude form of social science which essentializes any one of these identities or which fails to explore areas of overlap and tension between them (Kabeer 1994). Some women, for example, become de facto heads of household when male family members migrate elsewhere for work. In other cases, households migrate en masse and deal with their new employers on a more collective basis. Bargaining relationships between household members take shape in different contexts, and this complexity is multiplied when extra-household bargains are struck between members of different religious or ethnic groups (Folbre 1986).

So, why a chapter on women? We have two motivations. First, there are powerful reasons for believing that large numbers of women – and girls – in India suffer significant disadvantage because of their sex, or, more precisely, because of the way that local gender relations are constructed. Women's struggles against disempowerment need to be understood alongside other forms of politics, of course, including those centred upon class, caste, religion or age, but the gender gap in India is considerable.

Second, the Government of India has increasingly recognized the country's gender development and empowerment gaps, and has taken more and less effective measures to deal with them. Highlighting the importance of female education, for example, has been a major aim of the government's planning machinery since at least the Sixth Plan period (1980–5). The reservation of positions for women in *panchayati raj* institutions has likewise become mandatory since the time of the 73rd and 74th Amendments to the Constitution of India. More recently, the government has responded to the UNDP's construction of gender development and empowerment measures by providing indices of its own that aim to 'recast GDI and GEM to make them meaningful for India within the limits of data availability' (Government of India, Ministry of Women and Child Development 2009a: 2). The GDI is a version of the Human Development Index. It adjusts for disparities between men and women in relation to life expectancy at birth and measures of 'knowledge' and 'decent living standards'. The Government of India uses the infant mortality rate and life expectancy at age one to proxy for 'a long and healthy life', the seven-plus literacy rate and mean years of education as an index for 'knowledge', and estimated earned income per capita per annum to measure 'a decent standard of living'. GEM parameters are made up of political participation and decision-making scores, and measures of economic participation and decision-making power, and power over economic resources. The Government of India includes representation in local government as well as share of parliamentary seats in its political score, while its preferred measure for decision-making power includes representation in the Indian Administrative, Police and Forest Services. The Government of India estimates that overall GDI scores increased from 0.514 in 1996 to 0.590 in 2006 – scores that are almost twice as high as the UNDP's scores for India – while the GEM measure moved up from 0.416 to 0.497 over the same period. Significantly, too, the Government of India continues to insist on special waiting lines for women in some public places (not to mention special carriages on the Delhi Metro), and it provides benefits that are targeted only to females. In short, an increasing number of the machineries of rule that provide governance in India – nationally, at the state level, and locally – work through socio-legal categories that assume the unity of women. And even where this is not the case – where, for example, rules governing property inheritance or divorce are specific to religious communities – an underlying assumption remains in place about the importance of attending to the claims that women can make on the developmental state.

Mainstream economic and political theory inclines us to think that the position of women in India must have improved significantly over the past few decades, and will be better than in many countries with similar per capita income levels. The intuitions that inform these thoughts are as follows: (a) processes of economic growth and development – what used to be called modernization – generally expand the public sphere, lead to higher literacy rates and create new opportunities for paid employment; (b) democratic deepening for the most part encourages citizen voice and perhaps even cultures of complaint and protest, including a greater range of exit options; (c) affirmative action has since the early/mid-1990s provided routes for women in India to engage a rapidly growing number of spaces for representative and participatory politics – from membership of *panchayati raj* institutions to work for joint forest management committees; and (d) greater awareness of gender issues can be expected to feed into public spending decisions that attend more directly to women's needs or revealed preferences. Set against these intuitions, feminist scholars point out that female control over immovable assets like land or housing, or indeed over the bodies of women themselves, does not always increase in tandem with improvements in real household incomes. Indeed, there are notable reversals, including in India worsening sex ratios in some relatively affluent north-western states. A considerable body of work also exists on the feminization of poverty – not least in rural India, which itself has become considerably more female over the past few decades.

In this chapter, we examine *some* of these intuitions and counter-claims. We cannot hope to be comprehensive. There are ever present dangers in generalizing about women, as we have indicated, and these are compounded by huge variations in the position of women across India's constituent states. For the most part, women have fared better in south

India than in north India, although the north–south gap is now closing in key respects. Unsurprisingly, GDI scores for women are lowest in India's poorest states. We also face difficulties in knowing what has happened over time. Credible panel data exist on literacy rates and maternal health, of course, as well as on voting rates for women and men in national and state elections. But longitudinal comparisons are hampered by the cross-sectional nature of most ethnographic work, including, for example, on whether women *pradhans* are proxies for male household members. Our own take on what has been happening to India's women is probably also not helped by the fact that all three of us are white, Western males.

We begin with female bodies, which are themselves a major focus for governmental technologies of registration, surveillance and public action. We consider the changing capabilities of women in different parts of India in terms, for example, of sex ratios, nutritional status, literacy rates and control over key life-cycle events. Next, we examine violence against women, which Bina Agarwal, in particular, has linked to women's lack of command over property resources and other assets. We also comment briefly on the sectoral composition of India's female labour force and real wage rates, as well as on women's access to state officials. Lastly, we consider issues of voice, political selection and the exercise of power. We ask whether and by how much women are now benefiting from repeat plays in democratic games, both as political representatives and as beneficiaries of government spending. It goes without saying that all three of these topics overlap with each other. We separate them here for convenience of treatment.

13.2   Bodies and Capabilities

Trying to measure how much autonomy a person has, or how much command an Indian woman might have over her own body, is not straightforward (Jejeebhoy 2001). An obvious danger is that conceptions of autonomy and command are defined in universal terms, or without proper regard for local conceptions of acceptable behaviour (Madhok 2007). *Purdah*, for example, or the strict separation of the (female) realm of the home and the (male) realm of the public sphere, is common among some Muslim and Hindu communities in north India but is less often found in *adivasi* communities. Dowries, meanwhile, have historically been more common in north India than in south India, where bride price was the norm in some regions, but recent work suggests this is changing: dowries are becoming common in the south as well (Bloch and Rao 2002).

The fact that social arrangements are in flux suggests it is a mistake to privilege ideas of local cultural stability too strongly, or in a manner which ignores the asymmetries of power that produce gendered divisions of labour or forms of social performance. Patriarchal power relations take many forms but they always work to circumscribe female life chances in the name of certain 'biological facts'. Feminism's greatest achievement has been to unpack a naturalistic fallacy that suggests women can't do various things that men can do *because of their sex*. In fact, it's men who can't do something that women around the world do every minute: give birth. Women's movements have worked hard to argue that the narrowing of female life chances has always been constructed politically. It is not the biology of the female body that determines that fewer women become leading scientists or politicians than do men. Rather, the disadvantaged female body is produced at the end of a long set of decisions which seek the domestication of girls and women and which have worked to ensure their relative powerlessness. This is the work that patriarchy strives to perform. Its success, moreover, is greatest where women govern themselves in accordance with gender ideologies that acquiesce in stereotypes of male superiority and privilege.

Sex ratios and marriage patterns

Consider, in this regard, the extraordinary and deeply saddening fact that there are over 30 million missing women in India. Amartya Sen reminds us that, 'At birth, boys outnumber girls everywhere in the world, by much the same proportion – there are around 105 or 106 male children for every 100 female children' (1990: 1). Women, however, tend to 'be more resistant to disease and in general hardier than men' (ibid.). Initial sex disparities thus come to be offset in most parts of the world. In Europe, Japan and the US 'women outnumber men substantially' (ibid.), while in sub-Saharan Africa the ratio of women to men is around 1.02. In South and West Asia and China, however, there are only 0.94 women to men, a deficit of 6 per cent when measured against an even distribution of the sexes. This figure worsens to 11 per cent if these regions are compared with countries where women and men receive similar levels of health care and medical attention, in which cases the female to male ratio rises to 1.05. All told, Sen concludes, about 100 million women are missing in the world today: about 50 million in China and significantly more than half of the rest from India.

There is precious little evidence that bias against girl children is lessening across India. The British passed an Infanticide Act in 1870 with the particular aim of making female infanticide illegal. The colonial authorities were thus surprised when the census of 1881 revealed

Table 13.1: Sex ratios in India, 1901–2011

Census Year	Sex Ratio (Females per 1,000 Males)
1901	972
1911	964
1921	955
1931	950
1941	945
1951	946
1961	941
1971	930
1981	934
1991	927
2001	933
2011	940

'a significantly abnormal sex ratio of 940 women to 100 men (Patel, nd: 2) – a pattern very much at odds with what was being observed at the same time in the UK, where women slightly outnumbered men. Later and more accurate census surveys through the twentieth century revealed all-India sex ratios of around 970–930 women for every 1,000 men. The 1991 census, indeed, showed a worsening in the ratio to 927 after a very slight upturn in the 1981 census. The census of 2001 returned a ratio of 933 women for every 1,000 males (table 13.1) – another hugely dispiriting figure, especially if we bear in mind that many other indicators of female welfare report marked improvements since Independence. (The 2011 Census offered better news.)

No one imagines this holocaust of females is caused mainly by infanticide: this is extremely uncommon and probably always was (though see Miller 1981; and Sudha and Rajan 1999). Girls lose out because of neglect. They suffer from malnutrition and from untreated illnesses, including from conditions like dysentery, diarrhoea and measles which should not be life threatening (Kishor 1993). Sex-selective abortion, however, or female feticide, did become a problem in the last quarter of the twentieth century, and perhaps especially so after the 1971 Medical Termination of Pregnancy Act. The *Washington Times* reported in 2007 that, 'According to a UNICEF report released in December 2006, about 7,000 fewer girls than expected are born daily in India, and about 10 million fewer girls than expected were born in the past 20 years' (5 March). This was so notwithstanding the passing in 1994 of a Prenatal Determination Act which supposedly 'bans the use of technologies such as ultrasounds and sonograms for the purpose of sex-selective abortion' (ibid.).

The flouting of laws meant to protect the unborn female child, or indeed the welfare needs of young girls, has historically been much less evident in India's southern states than in the north of the country. In Kerala, uniquely among major Indian states, the female/male ratio in 2001 was above parity at 1,058: 1,000. It is widely believed that the better achievements of south Indian states have something to do with the historic dominance there of wet-rice cultivation, which makes significant demands of female labour, as well as longstanding resistance to deeply conservative forms of Brahminical Hinduism. Amartya Sen also maintains that investments in female education in Travancore and Cochin since the early 1800s have played a key role in improving the economic worth of women in that region, while in some parts of what is now Kerala 'property is usually inherited through the female line' (1990: 5; see also Harriss and Watson 1987). More recent scholarship supports the thesis that government investment in education, as also in irrigation, electrification and family health clinics, helps to empower women and is associated at a lag with higher female wage rates (Murthi, Guio and Drèze 1995). This in turn increases the ability of women to engage more forcefully in household decision-making about the health and education of their children.

Unhappily, recent scholarship also suggests that the sex ratio in Kerala might 'no longer be favourable to women, if adjusted [for] large-scale male migration' (Srinivasan 2009: 23; see also Mukhopadhyay 2007), and this is certainly the case if we look at the ratio for children under six (987 girls per 1,000 boys in 2001). In part, this is because marriage patterns in south India have become more like those in north India over the past thirty years, with the result that longstanding ideas about the cultural bases of 'greater female autonomy' in the south need to be re-evaluated. Rahman and Rao (2004) have challenged a seminal paper by Dyson and Moore (1983) which sought to explain higher levels of female autonomy in south India, relative to north India, mainly in terms of the prevalence in south India of endogamous marital relations between close kin. Dyson and Moore argued that 'a wife's lifelong access to the kinship network of her birth' (Rahman and Rao 2004: 239) was associated with a local preference for the payment of a bride price. This in turn helped to explain why 'daughters were more highly prized, and fertility rates were lower than in the North' (ibid.: 240). Rahman and Rao carried out comparative empirical work in 1995 in five districts in Karnataka and five districts in Uttar Pradesh. They discovered that village exogamy was the norm in both states, and that dowry payments, and distances between the home of the bride and her parents, were on average about the same in the Karnataka and Uttar Pradesh field sites. '[C]onditions have changed considerably since Dyson and Moore's study with regard to village exogamy, which today is far and away the norm throughout India' (ibid.: 247). Rahman and Rao found that women in Uttar Pradesh were more likely to face restrictions on their personal mobility than women in Karnataka, *purdah* being twice as common in the Uttar Pradesh field sites. However, when it came to intra-household decision-making, both Hindu and Muslim women in Uttar Pradesh exercised greater agency than their Karnataka counterparts.

Rahman and Rao conclude that north–south differentials in the welfare and autonomy of Indian women are less significant today than they were a generation or two ago (see also Caldwell, Reddy and Caldwell 1988). Some convergence is apparent, at least in regions that have not been cut off from broader processes of economic modernization and integration. This does not mean, however, that we should assume that the position of women in contemporary India is entirely consistent with more general maps of poverty or plenty. Nor is it sensible to define the welfare of women (or men) entirely in terms of one variable (income) or even one composite variable (HDI or GDI). We need to underscore the fact that women in India are still missing most of all from some of India's richest states, notably Haryana, Delhi and Punjab, and that things are not getting much better (Raju et al. 1999). There is some evidence to suggest that the mechanization of key agricultural tasks in India's Green Revolution heartlands has removed women from the fields and returned them to the family home (Chowdhury 1994; see also Jeffery and Jeffery 1997). Development as modernization has not improved the perceived economic value of women in this part of India. In urban India, too, a sense that paid female work is undignified, or even shaming, has kept many well-qualified women out of the labour force.

Capabilities

Rising household incomes in states like Punjab and Haryana have also been associated with a decline in the incidence of malnutrition among women, as well as among local male populations. According to data from the National Family Health Survey-3, just under 19 per cent of women in Punjab suffered from Chronic Energy Deficiency (CED) in 2005–6, and just over 8 per cent from CED and anaemia. CED, or chronic under-nutrition, occurs when a person's Body Mass Index, itself a measure of weight to squared height, is below 18.5. 'Iron deficiency anaemia, one of the most widespread forms of women's under-nutrition in developing countries, is indicated usually by 11.9 grams/decilitre of haemoglobin in the blood. Haemoglobin below 9.0 and 7.0 grams/decilitre denotes moderate and severe anaemia, respectively' (Jose and Navaneetham 2008: 62). Only Kerala had a lower incidence of CED and anaemia in 2005–6,

Table 13.2: Women's malnutrition across major states in India, 2005–6

	BMI		Anaemia		CED and Anaemia	
	CED	Overweight or Obese	Moderate or Severe	Any	Both	Either
Kerala	18.0	28.1	7.1	32.8	7.6	35.5
Punjab	18.9	29.9	11.8	38.0	8.1	40.6
Tamil Nadu	28.4	20.9	15.8	53.2	16.7	47.9
Uttaranchal	30.0	12.8	14.8	55.2	18.1	48.7
Haryana	31.3	17.4	18.5	56.1	18.5	49.6
Andhra Pradesh	33.5	15.6	23.9	62.9	22.5	51.3
Karnataka	33.5	15.3	17.1	51.5	19.8	46.9
Uttar Pradesh	36.0	9.2	14.7	49.9	18.9	47.6
Maharashtra	36.2	14.5	15.6	48.4	19.0	46.1
Gujarat	36.3	16.7	19.1	55.3	22.8	45.5
Assam	36.5	7.8	24.7	69.5	26.2	53.3
Rajasthan	36.7	8.9	17.9	53.1	20.2	48.5
West Bengal	39.1	11.3	17.4	63.2	27.1	48.2
Orissa	41.4	6.6	16.3	61.2	27.5	47.2
Madhya Pradesh	41.7	7.6	15.1	56.0	25.2	47.0
Jharkhand	43.0	5.3	19.9	69.4	31.2	50.1
Chhattisgarh	43.4	5.6	17.6	57.5	26.5	47.3
Bihar	45.1	4.6	16.9	67.4	31.7	49.5
India	35.6	12.6	16.8	55.3	21.6	47.5

Source: After Jose and Navaneetham (2008).

while scores in Haryana were among the best third of India's major states (see table 13.2).

Elsewhere in India the story is a dismal one. More than a third of the country's women were still suffering from CED in the mid-2000s, down only slightly from 1998–9 (NFHS-2 data), while the percentage of women suffering from some form of anaemia *increased* from 51.8 per cent in 1998–9 to 55.3 per cent in 2005–6. (By way of comparison, male CED and anaemia rates were 28 per cent and 24.3 per cent in 2005–6.) Obesity among urban women also jumped sharply through this period, presaging no doubt higher rates of heart disease and diabetes among India's middle-class females (and indeed males). Bodies that suffer from CED or persistent anaemia are generally not best suited to sustained hard work – although such work is unavoidable for most rural and urban day labourers – or indeed for reflective learning at school or later in life (Bentley and Griffiths 2003; Unni 2009).

Girls across India are now going to primary school in much greater numbers than in 1990 or in 1970, and this is hugely to be welcomed.

Table 13.3: School enrolment and literacy rates by gender, 1970–2005/8

Year	Primary (I–V)			Middle/upper primary (VI–VIII)			Higher/secondary (IX–XII)		
	Boys	Girls	Total	Boys	Girls	Total	Boys	Girls	Total
1970/71	35.7	21.3	57.0	9.4	3.9	13.3	5.7	1.9	7.6
1980/81	45.3	28.5	73.8	13.9	6.8	20.7	7.6	3.4	11.0
1990/91	57.0	40.4	97.4	21.5	12.5	34.0	12.8	6.3	19.1
2000/2001	64.0	49.8	113.8	25.3	22.0	42.8	16.9	10.7	27.6
2007/2008	71.5	64.8	136.3	30.7	26.1	56.8	15.9	12.3	28.2

Literacy rates by gender (%), 1971–2005

Year	Literacy		
	Boys	Girls	Total
1971	46.0	22.0	34.5
1981	56.4	29.8	43.6
1991	64.1	39.3	52.2
2001	75.3	54.2	64.8
2005	77.0	57.0	57.0

Source: Selected Educational Statistics (2008). Ministry of Human Resource Development, Department of Education, Planning, Monitoring and Statistics Division, Government of India; World Development Indicators, World Bank (2011).

Female literacy rates increased sharply from just 8.86 per cent in 1950–1 to 54.16 per cent in 2000–1, with a particular jump upwards occurring in the 1990s (see also table 13.3). It is still the case, however, that female literacy rates lagged behind those of males by over 20 per-centage points in 2000–1, and that only just over 10 per cent of India's girls made it into higher or secondary education at the start of the new millennium. Given that India's definition of 'literacy' barely goes beyond the ability to write one's name and read a few sentences, it is unwise to write too positively about improvements in female education in India. Strong incentives continue to exist for officials to over-report school attendance and achievements. It also needs to be recognized that, while almost half of all girls in India are clinically underweight, many of them suffering from growth retardation, more than 70 per cent of *adivasi* (ST) girls, and fully 90 per cent of *adivasi* (ST) girls from among the poorest quintile of households in rural areas, are similarly afflicted (see figure 13.1, taken from Gragnolati et al. 2005). We also know that a higher percentage of girls were recorded as literate in Maharashtra (67.51 per cent) in 2001 than were boys in Bihar (60.31 per cent), and that in some states the Hindu–Muslim literacy gap is greater than the

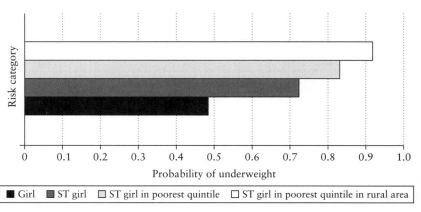

Figure 13.1: Probability of being underweight: all girls and ST girls.

Source: Calculated from NFHS II data; World Bank (2006).

male–female gap (29.4 per cent versus 22.9 per cent in Haryana, for example). Gender is not the only determinant of deprivation (see also Bose 2007).

Persistent under-investment in public education provision in India's poorest states has damaged employment opportunities for girls and boys alike. In the longer run, it will also damage India's rate of GDP growth. Interestingly, however, new evidence has emerged over the past two decades that suggests female illiteracy has not held back India's fertility transition in the way that once was expected (Dyson 2010). According to data from the country's Sample Registration System (SRS), India's 'crude birth rate (per 1,000 population) and total fertility rate (TFR) declined from 31 and 4.0, respectively, in 1991, to 24 and 2.6, respectively, in 2004. [Furthermore] the bulk of fertility decline in India is now occurring among women without education and this transition is being driven in a major way by increasing contraceptive prevalence rates among uneducated women' (Arokiasamy 2009: 55, citing also Bhat 2002 and McNay et al. 2003; see also Bhattacharya 2006). India is fast catching up with Bangladesh in this regard, and the positive conclusion that might be drawn from these new trends is that some of India's poorest and least conventionally capable women are now able to exercise significant control over their reproductive cycles. This, together with the fact that the age of marriage is rising for many Indian women (on average it is now close to seventeen years, still a year below the legal minimum age: Mathur 2008: 55), and with it, perhaps more importantly, the age at first pregnancy, means that India's women have less to fear than a generation ago from childbirth itself. We know, too, that neonatal mortality rates (children aged zero to twenty-eight days) decline significantly in developing countries where succeeding children are spaced further apart.

International comparisons

Welcome as these improvements are, India is still performing poorly in global health league tables. A recent paper in *The Lancet* reports that 'more than 10 million children [under five] die each year, most from preventable causes' (Black, Morris and Bryce 2003: 2226), of which fully 2.4 million deaths are in India. Further, while India's infant mortality rate (deaths in the first year of life per 1,000 live births) came down from almost 130 in 1971 to under eighty by 2001, deaths in the first week of life (the perinatal mortality rate) stayed stubbornly close to fifty throughout this thirty-year period. Delivery conditions remain poor in many parts of India and for many poor people (Radkar and Parasuraman 2007). Infant mortality rates in India are no better than in Togo or Central African Republic, and considerably worse than in the Philippines or Vietnam. Within India, moreover, 'the 1998–99 national family health survey found that mortality rates for children younger than 5 years varied from 18.8 per 1000 births in Kerala to 137.6 per 1000 in Madhya Pradesh' (ibid.: 2227). Meanwhile, in 2000, over 130,000 women in India died at childbirth – about 26 per cent of the total of such deaths worldwide.

The welfare of women in India *has* been improving in many respects since Independence, and indeed since *c.*1990. It clearly matters that female literacy rates have increased from under 9 per cent in 1951 to over 54 per cent in 2001. It also matters that average female life expectancy at birth in 2000–1 was 66.9 years, while in 1950–1 it was only 31.7 years. Relative to Indian men, however (save for in this one respect: life expectancy at birth), or many women elsewhere in the developing world, the ability of poor women in India to shape their own lives or even to control their own bodies remains depressingly low. We have several times drawn comparisons in this book between India and China, both from 1947–9 and from *c.*1978–80, roughly the time of new economic policies. In regard to the changing position of women in the two countries – putting to one side questions of political participation and representation – it should be noted that the male to female ratio for children under six is even worse in China (1.19) than in India (1.08) (Bardhan 2010: 100). Women's control over their bodies has been severely compromised by China's one-child-per-family policy. Set against this, India's adult female illiteracy rate of more than 50 per cent compares unfavourably with a figure close to 10 per cent in China, and the incidence of CED in China is less than 15 per cent across the country (see Popkin et al. 2001). Large numbers of women in rural India suffer as well from respiratory illnesses brought about by cooking indoors with traditional stoves and fuels, a technology that has been replaced now in most parts of China (Duflo, Greenstone and Hanna 2008). Female labour-force participation rates are also much higher in China than in India, something we consider further in the next section.

Finally, the idea that India might be on a par with its three BRIC counterparts is far from self-evident when it comes to some well-known measures of female development. Table 13.4 pulls together some key indicators of female well-being and capabilities for the BRIC countries from 1950 to 2010. It displays, as far as is possible, data for male–female sex ratios, female literacy rates, female CED scores, female labour-force participation rates, and the UNDP's GDI score. The sex ratio aside, women as a whole are living longer and are better educated in India than twenty, forty or sixty years ago. Compared to Indian men, however, as we have seen, and compared to women in Brazil, Russia and China, the position of most women in India leaves much to be desired.

13.3 Violence, Assets, Work and the State

Thus far, we have not mentioned violence against women. It would be wrong to suggest that women never act violently against men. Or, indeed, that highly educated women in affluent Indian households are on average as exposed to male violence as are poorer and less well-educated women, or any more, perhaps, than their counterparts in Western societies, including Latin America, or Japan (Chant 2007). A significant number of women in India enjoy much greater control over their working lives and sexual choices than their mothers enjoyed a generation ago (Parry 2001; Shah 2006b). In a landmark judgment in July 2009, the Delhi High Court decriminalized homosexuality in India's capital city, overturning a colonial law dating from 1861. (The case is now before the Supreme Court. Several religious bodies have opposed the Delhi judgement.) At the same time, there is an accumulating body of work which documents the scale and nature of violence against more vulnerable women in India, including within the marital home. Pradeep Panda and Bina Agarwal have drawn on the former's household survey work in Kerala – the state in India, presumably, where we might expect the lowest levels of male violence against women – to argue that:

Table 13.4: Women in the BRICS

Indicator	Country	1980/1	1985/6	1990/1	1995/6	2000/1	2005/6	2009/10
Sex ratio (males per 100 females)	Brazil	99.6	99.2	98.7	98.2	97.7	97.3	97.0
	Russian Federation	85.4	86.6	88.0	88.2	87.7	86.5	85.8
	India	108.5	108.3	108.2	108.0	107.6	107.7	106.8
	China	106.3	106.4	106.6	107.0	107.4	107.7	107.9
Female literacy rates (% age 15+)	Brazil	72.9				86.5	89.9	90.2
	Russian Federation			96.8		99.2		99.4
	India	29.8		39.4		54.2		65.4
	China	51.1		68.1		86.5		90.0
Female labour force participation rates (%)	Brazil	38.2	41.3	44.7	53.6	54.7	58.5	
	Russian Federation	63.0	62.0	60.0	54.6	53.9	55.5	
	India	32.6	33.2	34.0	34.5	33.0	32.4	
	China	71.0	71.6	73.0	72.3	70.9	68.5	
GDI score	Brazil				0.709	0.736	0.786	0.810
	Russian Federation				0.822	0.769	–	0.816
	India				0.401	0.545	0.586	0.594
	China				0.578	0.700	0.754	0.770

Source: World Bank Data 2009, UNDP Human Development Reports 1980–2009, United Nations Population Division.

> Marital violence against women ruptures the myth of the home as a protective space, exposing it as a chamber of horrors. . . . Violence during pregnancy is associated with miscarriages, low birth weight infants, maternal morbidity, and even foetal and maternal deaths. Children witnessing domestic violence tend to suffer from higher emotional and behavioural problems than do other children. Overall, marital violence has high human, social and economic costs. (Panda and Agarwal 2005: 824)

Estimating the extent of male or husband violence against women or wives is never easy. Panda and Agarwal join with other scholars in insisting that male violence can take the form of physical abuse (thought to affect 10–50 per cent of wives worldwide, ibid.: 824), sexual abuse and psychological violence. In Kerala, fully 41 per cent of women in Panda and Agarwal's rural survey households, and 27 per cent in the urban sample, reported 'at least one incident of physical violence by their husbands after marriage' (ibid.: 829). And this is in a state where the claims of daughters to property are better established than elsewhere in India, and where some girls do still marry within the support systems of their natal villages. Worse, 'of the women reporting long-term physical violence, most had experienced various forms in combination: sixty-one percent of the 179 women who reported being hit, kicked, slapped or beaten by their spouses, had experienced all four types of violence, and 90 per cent had suffered at least three types' (ibid.). Interestingly, and again unexpectedly, data reported to the National Crime Records Bureau (NCRB) on Crimes Against Women (CAW), including 'dowry deaths, rape, molestation, sexual harassment, cruelty by husband and his relatives, and kidnapping and abduction of women and girls' (Rustagi 2004: 330), place Kerala seventh worst among twenty-five Indian states in 1999 in terms of crime rates against women. The reported figure, however, of 153 crimes per 1 million persons, while significantly below rates of 231 and 206 respectively in Rajasthan and Madhya Pradesh, is absurdly on the low side, doubtless reflecting the fact that most women victims of crime are unwilling to report violence against them to the police. Doubtless, too, the NCRB count of 17,936 'accidental deaths by fire' of women in 2000 – against 7,531 male deaths – is far below the true number of women killed in this gruesome fashion.

Martha Nussbaum maintains that important new steps are being taken in India to protect women against rape and other violent crimes. Nussbaum points out that her own country, the USA, could learn from recent landmark judgements of the Supreme Court of India (which notably declared in 2000 that 'Rape is a crime not just against the person of a women, it is a crime against the entire society . . . It is a crime against basic human rights' [Nussbaum 2002: 96]), and from the Government of India's efforts to provide reserved seats for women and, a point made separately by Panda and Agarwal (2005: 846), All Women Police Stations. Struggles to secure legal protection for India's women, however, while extraordinarily valuable, and the result of tremendous political mobilizations, are effective only to the extent that new laws are widely understood across India, acted upon, and actively policed. Put another way, efforts to provide women with legal protections have to go hand in hand with broader struggles to increase the perceived value of females in India. As things stand, a large number of women are counted as burdens upon their families. When they marry, their families are expected to provide the groom's family with a dowry. When they enter the work-force, moreover, it is often as providers of household or agricultural labour (not always paid), or as low-waged and highly flexible contributors to India's urban economies (as we argued with regard to changes in labour-force participation in chapter 4; and see Gill 2010).

Underlying these patterns of workforce and marital engagement, some aspects of which we come back to shortly, is the continuing weak asset base of women in India. An old feminist saying holds that 'women make up half of the world's population [just under half, sadly], do at least two-thirds of the world's work, and own just one percent of the world's property'. Matters are not quite this bleak in India, but Bina Agarwal has established over the course of many research projects that the vulnerability of many women in India follows on quite directly from the fact that few of them both own and control immovable property: land and/or a house (see especially Agarwal 1994). Lacking such property, many women are also deprived of banking services, not least in rural areas (Chavan 2008).

The combination of ownership and control is what is critical here. Agarwal has argued that the Constitution of India and the Hindu Succession Act (HSA) of 1956 'embodied [a] notable shift in the vision of gender equality in Indian society' (2002: 1; see also Agarwal 1998). Prior to the HSA 'the majority of Hindu women could only inherit their fathers' (or husbands') property after four generations of agnatic males, and even then only as a limited interest. . . . [In contrast] the HSA gave them rights of inheritance on par with brothers (or sons) in relation to most property' (ibid.). In practice, though, while the 'HSA of 1956 constituted a substantial move forward' (ibid.: 7), the Act 'exempts from its purview significant interests in agricultural land' (ibid.). Tenurial rights in land remained a states subject, and in India's north-western states male lineal descendants took priority over female descendants. Where women did inherit tenurial rights over land they generally lost it upon remarriage, in the case of widows, or where land lay uncultivated for a year or two. In this part of India, too, the continued existence of joint family property – governed under provisions of the *Mitaksara* property rights code – conferred a significant advantage upon male heirs that in practice still often continues. Significantly, in most of India's southern states, and indeed in Maharashtra since 1976, amendments to the HSA were passed which either abolished joint family property altogether (Kerala) or which included daughters as coparceners (Andhra Pradesh, Karnataka, Tamil Nadu and Maharashtra: Agarwal 2002: 8). Agarwal herself, it should be noted, spearheaded a campaign which finally secured an end to legal provisions in six states – Delhi, Haryana, Himachal Pradesh, Jammu and Kashmir, Punjab and Uttar Pradesh – which treated inheritance in highly gender-unequal ways (see interview with Bina Agarwal in *The Indian Express*, 13 September 2005).

Agarwal recognizes that it will take time before the key provisions of the Hindu Succession Amendment Act of 2005 are enforced effectively in rural India (see also Yadav 2009 on the continuing power of male-dominated *khap* (lineage) *panchayats* in Haryana). Ironically, perhaps, it is the growing feminization of the countryside – as males move in large numbers to India's towns and cities – that might allow more women to exercise greater de facto rights over the fields they work in. 'Today, 53 percent of all male workers, 75 percent of all female workers, and 85 percent of all *rural* female workers, are in agriculture. And, for women, this percentage has declined less than four points since 1972–73' (Agarwal 2003: 192, emphasis in the original). Because of widowhood, marital breakdown or male outmigration, an estimated 20–35 per cent of India's rural households are now de facto female-headed (ibid.: 193, citing studies by Buvinic and Youssef 1978; and Government of India 1988).

At the same time, as Agarwal goes on to report, and as several distinguished studies have shown (Government of India 2009b; Breman 2010b), even in agriculture the casualization of work has been more apparent for women than for men, and real wage rates for women continue throughout India to be lower than those for men doing similar tasks (see also table 13.5). While matters can be expected to improve for India's women, including widows, following the passing of the 2005 Hindu Succession Amendment Act, such survey evidence as we have confirms that few women as yet are both inheriting and controlling land. Agarwal cites an important study by the development sociologist, Marty Chen:

In Chen's [1991] sample of rural widows across seven states, only 13 per cent of the 470 women with land-owning fathers inherited any land as daughters (the figure being 18 per cent for South India and 8 per cent for North India. This means that 87 per cent of the surveyed women did not

Table 13.5: Average daily wage rates by sex, October–December 2007

Occupation	Daily wage (Rs.)	
	Male	Female
Ploughing	91.86	51.80
Sowing	79.85	56.46
Weeding	68.84	57.18
Harvesting	75.48	61.86
Threshing	73.25	59.00
Herding	47.96	42.38
Well digging	110.12	56.29
Cane crushing	77.64	52.28
Sweeper	64.11	59.43
Unskilled labour	74.31	55.05

Source: Occupational Wage Survey Sixth Round, 2008; Ministry of Labour, Government of India.

receive their due as daughters. Among widows, of the 280 whose deceased husbands owned land, 51 per cent inherited some, but this still means that half the widows with claims did not inherit anything. And of those that did, typically their shares were not entered formally in the village land records. (Agarwal 2003: 202, also citing Chen 1998)

Agarwal insists that women will continue to be at the mercy of violent male kin, including their husbands, until they take effective possession of land and housing – the latter not least as a safe space. Panda and Agarwal conclude that women are most at risk of marital violence where their husbands are poor, out of work, and have been brought up in violent households, and where the women themselves are property-less and removed from their families. Interestingly, Panda and Agarwal find that 'the woman's own employment status does not appear to matter [in explaining marital violence], except if she has a regular job: this lowers the risk of long-term physical violence. But seasonal/irregular work makes no significant difference' (2005: 842). They also report that the frequency of physical violence against women is greater in rural than in urban areas, even when controlling for other factors.

In the longer run, it is to be hoped that women will come to escape male violence as new property laws are enforced and as women participate more in regular, paid employment. A study conducted in Delhi in 2006 by Sudarshan and Bhattacharya suggests that National Sample Survey data on female workforce participation may not be fully capturing women's growing involvement in urban labour markets, where unmarried women in particular, at least in the nation's capital, provide employers with low-waged, 'flexible' bodies for hire (Sudarshan and Bhattacharya 2009). As of 2010, however, there are few signs that any but the most well-educated of India's females – mainly young women, it should be said, not least in the 'new service economy' (Lukose 2010) – are joining its urban workforces on equal terms with their male counterparts. Generally, female work participation (by Usual and Principal Subsidiary Status (UPSS)) appears to fluctuate significantly, increasing in periods of greater economic stress (chapter 4; and Himanshu 2011).

Nor, unhappily, is it yet the case that many women feel comfortable approaching state officials or politicians directly for help, even in cases that involve problems with the receipt of statutory benefits or marital violence (Visaria 2008). Most of the limited studies that we have on the gendered nature of state–society exchanges suggest that women are kept waiting longer than men to see public officials, experience corruption differently from men (partly as a result of having to wait, partly on account of sexual harassment, and undoubtedly because fewer women than men are the beneficiaries of corruption: Corbridge 2011), and very often meet government officers in the company of male relatives (Corbridge et al. 2005; see also Tambiah 2002). Women are, of course, receiving various benefits from the state in India, including from National Rural Employment Guarantee scheme (see chapter 5), but, just as with control over land, it has only been of late that struggles for control over India's political and bureaucratic systems have begun to deliver new and increased spending on issues that matter greatly for India's women. The United Progressive Alliance government did introduce Gender Budget Statements into the Union budget from 2005–6, but as yet there is little evidence that extra funds are flowing to the Ministry of Women and Child Development (MWCD) which it created in 2006 and which took the place of an earlier government department. Indeed, Mishra and Jhamb (2009: 61) report a '42 per cent decline in allocations for schemes meant for women's welfare under the MWCD in the union budget 2009–10'.

13.4   Voice, Agency and Power

Women were strongly involved in the struggle for Independence, but as late as 1946 it was uncertain that women in post-colonial India would be given voting rights on the same basis as men (Forbes 1996). Indira Gandhi, as is well known, became India's third Prime Minister following the death of her father Jawarharlal Nehru in 1964, and after the unexpected demise of Lal Bahadur Shastri in 1966. She remains India's second longest-serving

Table 13.6: Women's representation in Parliament (Lok Sabha), 1952–2009

Year	Turnout Differential between men and women (per cent)	Per cent women in the Lok Sabha
1952	–	4.4
1957	–	5.4
1962	17	6.7
1967	11	5.9
1971	21	4.2
1977	11	3.4
1980	9	5.1
1984	10	7.9
1989	9	5.3
1991	10	7.9
1996	9	7.3
1998	8	2.9
1999	8	8.8
2004	12	8.3
2009	9	10.9

Source: Statistical Reports on General Election to the Lok Sabha 1952–2009; Election Commission of India. New Delhi; Chibber (2003).

Prime Minister. During the time that Mrs Gandhi led India (1966–77 and 1980–4), however, the proportion of women voting in parliamentary elections consistently lagged behind men by between 9 and 21 percentage points, while the proportion of women serving as MPs in the Lok Sabhas that were dominated by Nehru's daughter never reached 6 per cent (see table 13.6). More recently, the turnout differential between women and men has reduced to single figures, albeit the percentage of women serving as MPs has struggled to reach 11 per cent (10.9 per cent in 2009). As Chibber (2003) reports, too, the percentage of women holding seats in State Legislatures either side of 2000 was above 10 per cent only in Delhi (13 per cent following the 1998 elections) and Tamil Nadu (11 per cent from 2001). Close to two thirds of India's women are now voting in India's parliamentary and Assembly elections, but the election of female MPs and MLAs on an equal basis with males remains a long way off.

How unusual is this state of affairs, and how and why does it matter? The UNDP's Human Development Report of 2008 placed India in a broad band of Median Human Development countries and ranked it 128th out of 177 countries in terms of its Gender Empowerment Measure (GEM). In terms of other South Asian countries, the 9 per cent of parliamentary seats occupied by women in India in the mid-2000s compared with 20.4 per cent in Pakistan, 15.1 per cent in Bangladesh,

17.3 per cent in Nepal, and 4.9 per cent in Sri Lanka. Unfortunately, the UNDP does not report scores for India for two other components of the GEM, the percentage of female legislators, senior officials and managers and the percentage of female professional and technical workers. It does, however, report estimated female to male earned income in India at 0.31, compared to 0.29 in Pakistan, 0.46 in Bangladesh, 0.50 in Nepal and 0.41 in Sri Lanka. All of these figures need to be taken with a grain of salt, and cross-sectional data tell us little about what is happening over time. Compared to its South Asian neighbours, however, let alone Brazil, China and Russia, India is not doing terribly well. In China, which ranks 81st in the UNDP's GEM league table, 20.3 per cent of parliamentary seats were occupied by women in the mid-2000s, while the female–male earnings ratio was 0.64. The corresponding paired figures for Brazil were 9.3 per cent and 0.58 (rank 70), and for the Russian Federation 8 per cent and 0.62 (rank 67).

There are a number of reasons why women in India are not winning positions of power in higher-level elected assemblies. Party discrimination is clearly part of the story. Voter perception that female politicians might be less able or weaker than their male counterparts is another, not least among male voters. Before we consider these reasons, however, and recent attempts by the Government of India to ameliorate their effects, it is worth underlining the fact that women in India have been major players in non-parliamentary forms of politics. Uma Bharati and Sadhvi Rithambara were at the centre of some of the most militant forms of Hindu nationalism in the 1980s and 1990s, including at Ayodhya in 1992, where they drew on very gendered ideas of loathing and desire to suggest that *Bharat Mata* (mother India) was under threat from an alien Islam (Corbridge 2002). At about the same time, the Chipko movements in Uttarakhand, while they were never as female-dominated as Vandana Shiva (1988) made out (compare Guha 1989 and Rangan 2000), and while they mobilized ideas about effective forest management that moved beyond simplistic ideas about women being in tune with nature (see Jackson 1993; and Jewitt 2000 for critiques), involved women very strongly from the outset, as indeed has the Slum Dwellers' Rights Movement. Poor women have played an active part in the struggles of unorganized workers – such as the Unorganised Workers' Federation – and in campaigns for women's rights specifically, as, for example, in the Penn Urimai Iyakkam (Women's Rights Movement) in Tamil Nadu (see Harriss 2007). Very often, as Janaki Nair points out, the leadership of poor women's organizations will be made up in part of liberal middle-class female activists – this has been the case, for instance, in the right-to-information movement in Rajasthan, where Aruna Roy has been one of the most prominent and effective leaders of the hugely influential

Mazdur Kisan Shakti Sanghatan (Jenkins and Goetz 1999) – while on other occasions middle-class Indian women pursue forms of politics that are meaningful to them in less solidaristic terms. 'Roads, rather than public transport . . . mosquitoes and public toilets rather than public health', is how Nair (2005: 336) puts it.

India's right-to-information and environmental movements have each contributed to what Heller (2001) has called the increased surface area of the state. Buoyed in part by ideas emerging from the new public administration (see Brett 2009), and mindful of social activism in favour of the merits of greater citizenship participation, the Government of India moved at the end of the 1980s and into the 1990s to create new forms of user group that would shorten the accountability mechanisms that link citizens to the state. Village education committees and joint forest management (JFM) protection committees, for example, were set up to cut out the middleman: be it a teaching trade union, the forest bureaucracy, or even some local politicians – and provisions were also put in place to involve women in these new institutions. (For a review of the effectiveness of women in green governance institutions in India and Nepal, see Agarwal 2010.)

With the passing into law in 1993 of the 73rd and 74th Constitutional Amendment Acts, the representation of women in the three tiers of rural India's local governance institutions, and in urban municipal councils, was raised to a minimum level of 33 per cent. This level is much higher than the normal presence of women in user-group committees. As we write (in 2010 but with no signs of further progress by September 2011), the Rajya Sabha has been debating whether a similar percentage of seats should be reserved for women in India's Parliament and State Assemblies (Diwarkar 2009; Bose 2010a). Significantly, Mayawati and Lalu Prasad Yadav have been active in leading opposition to the Bill that went to the upper house in Parliament in March 2010. They objected that reservation of seats for women would weaken the representation of India's Backward Classes in New Delhi. In effect, gender would trump class (or caste). Reservation of seats for women would lead to the recolonization of the Lok Sabha by India's Forward Castes or classes, this time fronted by well-to-do Indian females.

In raising these concerns, Mayawati and Lalu Yadav put their fingers on a number of issues that are now occupying a new generation of political scientists and economists. Consider, for example, the questions of whether and by how much the representation of women in India's *panchayati raj* institutions (PRIs) has gone beyond 33 per cent since the mid-1990s, and whether the reservations of seats for women in PRIs has changed perceptions among men and women in India about the 'aptitude' of women for public-service positions. India is now one of more than 100 countries that have introduced affirmative action policies to overcome 'voter and party bias in favour of male politicians' (Beaman et al. 2008: 1). In India, however, the random rotation of village council leader positions has allowed social scientists to test in a rigorous fashion whether greater exposure to women politicians changes voter attitudes over time towards women leaders.

Using Implicit Association Tests – a technique used in social psychology to examine how respondents pair concepts: for example, male and female names against leadership or domestic tasks – Beaman and her colleagues found in their study, conducted in Birbhum district, West Bengal, that villagers' 'distaste for female leaders is not ameliorated by exposure' (ibid.: 19) over the course of a first electoral cycle. In part, this bias reflects the fact that male respondents were twice as likely as females to know their current *pradhan's* name, a gap that would be even wider in some other parts of India, while men were four times as likely as females (53 per cent to 13 per cent) to have approached a *pradhan* 'about their needs or village issues' (ibid.: 18), and almost five times more likely than local women (34 per cent against 7 per cent) to have attended a village meeting (*gram sabha*). Men are used to seeing men in positions of power.

Beaman and her colleagues note that results like this offer scant comfort to those who wish to believe that 'affirmative action can, in the short to medium run, alter voter preferences' (ibid.). It also helps us to understand why leading political parties in India have generally been reluctant to field more than 10–15 per cent female candidates in elections which they contest: outside West Bengal, Kerala and Tripura this means the Lok Sabha and State Assembly elections, but not usually local government (where independent candidates generally stand: Basu 2010). As in most countries around the world, political parties don't trust voters to be gender blind when they vote, while their selection policies have until recently strongly reinforced existing gender stereotypes. The result is that women made up more than 40 per cent of local government representatives in very few of India's states before 2005, although there have been positive changes to report since then, especially outside the north-west of the country (table 13.7). Nor is there yet clear evidence that fifteen plus years of affirmative action in local government bodies has led to many more women receiving party 'tickets' for winnable seats in parliamentary or Assembly elections (table 13.8). India's gender democratic deficit remains very wide: hence the new proposals to extend affirmative action or compensatory discrimination to the Lok Sabha itself.

Interestingly, though, when Beaman and colleagues tested the effectiveness of female *pradhans* in West Bengal they found that 'women leaders provide more public goods, of equal quality, at a lower effective

Table 13.7: Percentage of elected women members, three-tier
Panchayati Raj, 1999–2007

	Year		
State	1999	2002	2006
Andhra Pradesh	34	33	33
Arunachal Pradesh	–	–	40
Assam	30	34	38
Bihar	–	–	55
Chhattisgarh	–	34	43
Goa	37	32	53
Gujarat	33	33	44
Haryana	33	34	44
Himachal Pradesh	33	37	45
Jharkhand	–	–	–
Jammu & Kashmir	–	–	–
Karnataka	44	45	73
Kerala	38	36	71
Madhya Pradesh	33	34	63
Maharashtra	33	33	42
Manipur	37	36	56
Meghalaya	–	–	–
Mizoram	–	–	–
Nagaland	–	–	–
Orissa	35	36	38
Punjab	30	36	63
Rajasthan	33	35	35
Sikkim	1	36	41
Tamil Nadu	34	27	51
Tripura	33	33	49
Uttar Pradesh	25	–	73
Uttaranchal	–	–	9
West Bengal	35	22	45
Total	32	34	48

Source: Annual Reports, Ministry of Panchayati Raj, Government of India.

price [than male leaders in unreserved *gram panchayats*]' (ibid.: 25).
Initially, as we have seen, this didn't seem to change the attitudes of
male voters to their female leaders. Even though female *pradhans* were
outperforming local male counterparts, they earned significantly lower
satisfaction ratings. Over time, however, as a second cohort of female
leaders came on the scene, male reported bias against female leaders
disappeared or became statistically insignificant.

Table 13.8: Percentage of female MLAs elected in State Assembly elections, 2002–2008

Election Year	State	Elected female MLAs (%)
2002	Jammu and Kashmir	2
2003	Chhatisgarh	6
	Delhi	10
	Madhya Pradesh	8
	Mizoram	0
	Rajasthan	6
2004	Andhra Pradesh	9
	Arunchal Pradesh	0
	Karnataka	3
	Maharashtra	4
	Orissa	7
	Sikkim	9
2005	Bihar	10
	Haryana	12
	Jharkhand	4
2006	Assam	10
	Kerala	5
	Pondicherry	0
	Tamil Nadu	9
	West Bengal	13
2007	Goa	3
	Gujarat	9
	Himachal Pradesh	7
	Manipur	0
	Punjab	6
	Uttar Pradesh	6
	Uttarakhand	6
2008	Meghalaya	2
	Nagaland	0
	Tripura	5

Source: Statistical Reports on General Election to the Legislative Assemblies 2002–8; Election Commission of India, New Delhi.

In other words, it is possible that affirmative action might lead to more gender-neutral voting behaviour over time, so long as women in public offices perform particularly well. It is possible, too, that voters pay fewer bribes in villages with women leaders (Duflo and Topolova 2004). But just why women should perform better than men – controlling for other variables, such as education levels, which we might expect to affect the quality of the political agent selected by voters (Pande 2003; Besley, Pande, Rahman and Rao 2004) – is as yet not clearly understood, even if we assume it can be locally true. (One area where women leaders are still at a disadvantage to male leaders – predictably enough – is in terms of their 'interaction with higher-level officials' (Ban and Rao 2008: 526).) One hypothesis, which has been advanced by Swamy, Knack, Young and Azfar (2000), is that women are less willing to condone corruption than are men. However, this seems unlikely to be true over a longish period of time, or as women learn to take advantage of new opportunities for corruption (see also Dollar, Fisman and Gatti 2001). Another hypothesis, which seems to be confirmed by further work in West Bengal and in Rajasthan by Chattopadhyay and Duflo, is that women in power are simply more likely than men to be responsive to locally voiced needs for public goods provision (2004: 1411).

Of course, this doesn't help us to understand why men warm to competent female *pradhans* over time – unless we assume that men value competency in general rather than in gender-specific terms. But experimental work of the type that Chattopadhyay and Duflo have pioneered, for all that it operates with a binary model of male/female support for some public goods rather than others, and for all that it allocates greater powers to *pradhans* than we would usually recognize, does give us some basis for being optimistic about the effectiveness, and indeed the independence, of elected female leaders in reserved political constituencies. Most ethnographic studies of female *pradhans* have tended to report their lack of autonomy from male kith and kin, husbands most of all. In quite a few cases – and this has been commonly noted in Madhya Pradesh (Srivastava forthcoming; see also Singh 2005) – elected women leaders can be found who live in local towns while their husbands serve as de facto village leaders, just as many women *pradhans* can be identified who carry out the instructions of locally resident male family members. Work carried out by the broad Beaman collective, however – Beaman, Pande, Topolova, Chattopdahyay and Duflo – does suggest for West Bengal both that more women are now getting elected to unreserved *gram panchayats* (in 2008 as compared to 2003), and that, 'contrary to the popular claim that women *pradhans* simply function as "shadows" for their husbands (who are disqualified from running), very few women *pradhans* are spouses of former male pradhans' (Beaman et al. 2009: 1506; though see also Tiwari 2009). Their study adds to evidence collected from another arguably unusual state, Kerala, where Chaudhuri and Heller (2003: 8) discovered that participation in *gram panchayats* by SCs and STs, and by women, increased substantially over time, partly on account of mobilization work by local society organizations, including the Kerala Sashtra Sahitya Parishad (KSSP: the People's Science Movement).

13.5   Conclusion

It would be unwise on the basis of even very good academic studies from Kerala and West Bengal to conclude that a broad plurality of India's women is yet coming to think of themselves as active citizens in India's participatory democracy. Most of India's women, along with most of India's men, make their way in the clientelist and quasi-legal worlds of India's political society that have been described by Partha Chatterjee (2004). But the changes that Beaman and others describe should not be ignored; nor should we discount the very real improvements that can be discerned in the life expectancies and capabilities of many Indian women. It is reasonable to suggest that Indian women today typically enjoy at least some life opportunities that would have escaped their mothers and grandmothers; in some cases, many more opportunities. Dowries, and the size of dowries, are growing in significance, including in some *adivasi* communities in central India, but child marriages are increasingly a thing of the past (Fuller and Narasimhan 2008). Literacy rates are much higher than thirty or sixty years ago, even though they lag behind comparable rates for males and may not tell us terribly much about functional literacy. Likewise, maternal health indicators have improved over time, even though conditions for expectant women in India continue very often to be worse than in sub-Saharan Africa.

In short, things *have* improved for most women in India compared to a benchmark of a generation or two ago. This is true also in the political sphere. Some women have been 'returned' to *purdah* in north-west India following rapid agricultural growth there in the wake of the Green Revolution, but more widely across the country women are becoming more and not less active in formal politics. Even when it comes to marital violence against women there are reasons to believe that urbanization, along with better education levels for women and men, will slowly reduce present levels of men-on-women violence. All of these observations, in short, bear out our starting intuitions about the generally empowering effects for women of economic growth and an expanded public sphere, whether or not this is also inflated by affirmative action.

Rather like India's record on poverty reduction, however, improvements in female living standards in India have not lived up to expectations, whether these are political or theoretical. This is not just a case of India's worsening sex ratios, although these surely tell us something important about how women are valued across the country. Nor even is it a judgement that is linked in a singular fashion to indices of female undernutrition or weak high-school enrolment rates. The wider truth is that sustained economic growth and the deepening of democracy in India have not yet delivered sufficient power and resources to females that ordinary women can individually and collectively say they have command over (most) of their lives. Clearly, this judgement does not hold true for many young urban professional women, increasing numbers of whom are engaged in politics mainly around consumption and lifestyle choices. And it is a judgement whose force is lessening over time. As of 2011, however, it is a judgement that holds true for many women in India most of the time.

How much have things changed for Indian women? A huge amount when we look at life expectancies and female literacy scores. Quite a lot for many educated women, even compared to their parents and grandparents, albeit not always in one direction: dowries and female seclusion have been increasing in better-off households. Not so much for the increasing numbers of women left behind in rural India, or for illiterate women – fertility decisions clearly and importantly excepted. And perhaps least of all for widows without land or sons.

14

Can India Benefit From Its Demographic Dividend?

14.1 Introduction

On 31 March 2011, the Census of India announced a provisional total for the population of India of 1.21 billion. The Indian population had increased, therefore, by 181 million between 2001 and 2011 – at a slower rate than in the previous decade but still by numbers equivalent to the population of Brazil. Information for different age cohorts had not been released at the time of writing, but it is likely that the trend in previous decades towards an especially large population of relatively young adults (age fifteen to forty-four) will have continued. Can India benefit from this bulge?

Coale and Hoover (1958) and Enke (1971) argued that rapid demographic growth can discourage economic advance because of its negative effects on people's saving rates. For these critics, a shift from agriculture to manufacturing was necessary to reduce fertility rates and thus set poorer countries on the path to modernization. For neo-Malthusians like Paul Ehrlich and Anne Ehrlich (1970), sharp increases in population in the global South amounted to a wholesale development disaster.

Yet as early as the 1960s, scholars were also rehearsing the alternative argument that a large number of people can be a source of positive change (Boserup 1965; Simon 1977). For example, Esther Boserup (1965) argued that rising population density was historically significant in precipitating new innovations, such as the plough and crop rotations. This more optimistic vision of population growth has found a new incarnation in recent scholarship on 'the demographic dividend'.

Building on an analysis of East Asia in the 1980s and 1990s, Bloom and Williamson (1998) point out that the rapidity with which some countries are moving from a stage of high birth rates to one of much lower fertility results in the emergence of an unusually large young adult labour force. A country may pass through several decades in which both children and the elderly will be comparatively small proportions of the population. A relatively substantial population of young adults may trigger an increase in earnings, since a high proportion of the citizenry are in productive employment (Bloom et al. 2003). The state, in turn, has more resources to invest in economic development and welfare measures (see also Drèze and Sen 1995). At the same time, a substantial young adult population generates increased personal savings which, in turn, can lead to growth in per capita income. Moreover, the emergence of a low dependency ratio typically coincides with a period in which people are living longer (Bloom et al. 2003). This may encourage the adult population to engage in long-term planning, for example, in relation to their retirement and children's education. Furthermore, the rise of a young adult population with few children may foster investment in girls' education and boost female participation in the workforce (Nayab 2007: 6).

The analysis by Bloom and his colleagues suggests that for a country to take advantage of the demographic dividend two conditions must be met: first, there must be a 'youth bulge'; second, infrastructural and institutional conditions must be such that the young adult population can contribute positively to the economy and society. There is general agreement that in India the first condition is met. There has recently been a marked decline in fertility rates in India, caused in large part by shifting attitudes to family, rising education, urbanization and India's family planning programme. This has slowed the rate at which the Indian population is increasing. It has also brought about a change in India's population structure. In censuses up to 1981, roughly 40 per cent of the population was aged zero to fourteen. But this figure fell to about 37 per cent in 1991 and 35 per cent in 2001 (Registrar General, India 2006). The proportion of the relatively 'young' adult population is consequently rising – the percentage aged fifteen to forty-four increased from 43 to 51 between 1981 and 2001 – and is likely to continue to rise until the mid-2020s (Dyson 2010: 40).

There remain substantial regional differences in population dynamics in India. The north has relatively high levels of fertility and mortality. The four most populous north Indian states (Uttar Pradesh, Bihar, Rajasthan and Madhya Pradesh) were growing at an annual rate of 2 per cent between 1991 and 2001, compared to 1 per cent in Kerala and Tamil Nadu. In 2001, about 38 per cent of the population of Uttar Pradesh and Bihar was under fifteen, compared to roughly 26 per cent in Tamil Nadu and Kerala (Dyson 2010). The 'demographic dividend' effect will therefore be muted in the north of India over the next twenty years because of the relatively slow decline in fertility rates and therefore age dependency ratios. But some type of youth bulge will be evident throughout India over the 2010s and 2020s (Dyson 2010).

There is much less agreement about whether the second condition for the demographic dividend is met in India. The World Bank (2005: 10) claims that India 'has a critical mass of skilled English-speaking knowledge workers, especially in the sciences' and predicts that India will receive its anticipated 'dividend'. Nandan Nilekani is similarly upbeat in an article for *Outlook* (1 December 2008): 'A talented pool of workers, along with abundant capital and investment, presents us with immense opportunities for creativity and innovation.'

Others are less optimistic. K. S. James (2008) examines the relationship between India's changing age structure, household savings rate and female participation in the labour force. He finds some support for the claim that savings rates have increased. But there is not a clear positive correlation between the emergence of a young adult 'bulge' and increasing participation of women in the labour market. He concludes that there is a connection between demographic change and economic growth, but that it is more complex than assumed and depends on how changes to the age structure connect with a range of other factors, including public policy. James's work ties in with that of other authors who argue that India's demographic dividend is unlikely to be realized without greater investment in education, health and infrastructure (Mitra and Nagarajan 2005; Chandhrasekhar et al. 2006; Dyson 2010). Chandrasekhar et al. (2006) focus especially on educational under-investment and the apparent failure of liberalization to create jobs. Mitra and Nagarajan (2005) make the wider argument that the government must invest in infrastructure, education, health, gender equality and employment generation.

Read together, these recent critical studies point to the institutional and infrastructural barriers to productive young adult activity in India. In what follows, we reflect on the scale of the difficulty that India faces in realizing its demographic dividend through focusing particularly on India's record with respect to education and the growing problem of youth unemployment.

14.2   Education

Article 45 of the Indian Constitution directed the new post-colonial government to provide free and compulsory education to all children under fourteen within ten years. But the task of providing equitable access to formal education has been honoured only in the breach. It is true that primary school enrolment in India rose from 46 per cent in 1987 to 83 per cent in 2006, and gender, religious and caste-based gaps in enrolment have narrowed considerably (Huebler 2008). But formal enrolment does not often translate into regular attendance. Banerjee et al. (2007) found that children enrolled in school in villages in eastern Uttar Pradesh tended to attend haphazardly. Even when they attend, the standard of education is often poor, and children – especially low castes and girls – often leave school after just a few years. Many sections of the child population remain entirely excluded from formal education, especially in the north (see Drèze and Gazdar 1997; Ramachandhran 2004; Jeffery and Chopra 2005).

Educational under-investment is partly to blame for the state's failure to meet its Constitutional obligations. The state's investment in education since 1990 has hovered around 4 per cent of GDP: considerably less than the 6 per cent often mentioned as the desirable figure in planning reports and political speeches (Harriss 2011; and chapter 5 in this volume). Under-investment partly reflects a lack of public action on educational issues. People have not mobilized around the issue of education to the same extent as they have on food prices, employment reservations, subsidies and corruption. This may be beginning to change. There has recently been a mass campaign in India for primary education to be listed as a compulsory right, which culminated in the passing of the Right to Education Act in 2009 (see also chapter 5). But education still remains a relatively underdeveloped theme of elections and popular mobilization in India (see Majumdar and Mooij 2011).

The poor state of education in India also reflects the misallocation of educational expenditure. State money for education is channelled overwhelmingly into the payment of teachers' salaries. Schools are consequently starved of funds for educational facilities, curricular reform, and the monitoring and training of teachers (Probe Report 1999; Pritchett and Murgai 2007). Teacher absenteeism is a particular problem (as we also discuss in chapter 8). Muralidharan and Kremer (2006), in a large-scale study of teaching standards in Indian rural primary schools, found that teachers were absent from the schools in which they were registered in 25 per cent of cases. A recent report by the Central Advisory Board of Secondary Education (CABE) in India chronicled widespread infrastructural and curricular neglect within secondary schooling, and called for an urgent review of the funding and organization of schools (CABE 2004). Under-investment and misdirection of funds in the schooling sector is reflected in students' skill levels. An impressive rise in India's literacy rate – from 28 per cent to 65 per cent between the 1961 and 2001 censuses

(Kingdon 2007) – masks chronic problems of skill deprivation. Banerjee et al.'s (2005) nationwide survey of seven to fourteen year olds found that 35 per cent could not read a simple paragraph and 41 per cent could not do simple subtraction, including many formally listed as 'literate'.

Weaknesses in school governance exacerbate these problems. It is typically only the poor who use government schools, and this militates against effective campaigns to improve state provision – an 'account-ability deficit' (Majumdar and Mooij 2011). At the same time, influential private educational operators and politically minded schoolteachers are able to block reform that does not coincide with their interests (see Kingdon and Muzammil 2003; Kapur and Mehta 2007).

The state has engaged in repeated attempts to improve education. In the early 1990s, the Indian government partnered with international organizations to launch the District Primary Education Program (DPEP) aimed at boosting enrolment in primary school. In 2001, the government established a similarly large-scale development initiative, the 'Education for all programme' (Sarva Shiksha Abhiyan). These programmes have addressed some of the worst forms of gender and caste discrimination in schools. But they were much less effective in terms of school infra-structure and teaching standards (Das 2007). They have also done little to improve school governance in many areas. Under the DPEP, Village Education Committees (VECs) comprised of local community members were established to supervise education in local schools. Recent research in Uttar Pradesh shows that VECs are non-functional in parts of north India and do not address issues of access and social disadvantage (Banerjee et al. 2007).

There has been an increase in the amount of NGO activity aimed at improving the quality of government and private schools, enhancing school participation, and preventing children dropping out of school. Most notably, Pratham India Education Institute (Pratham), an NGO based in Mumbai, tries to improve educational governance and provide tutoring of at-risk children. Emerging studies suggest that Pratham has had limited effect on educational governance but more success in improving children's reading skills (Banerjee et al. 2007). Economists at MIT have used research with Pratham to help develop the Jameel Abdul Latif Poverty Action Lab (JPAL). JPAL has raised teacher attendance, enhanced tuition, and played an important role in monitoring educa-tion in several parts of India. The work of organizations like Pratham and JPAL must be read in context, however: on their own they can do little to address the widespread effects of state under-investment and mismanagement.

The government's neglect of the schooling sector has led to the rapid growth of private schools. These can be broadly grouped into two types.

First, a large number of privately managed schools function by receiving state aid. These 'private aided schools' typically cater for relatively poor and lower-middle-class households (Jeffery et al. 2005; Majumdar and Mooij 2011). Second, there are 'unaided' schools that are both managed and funded privately. This second category can itself be divided into two subcategories. In a tiny first tier, there are elite institutions such as Delhi Public School that cater for elites in India's largest cities. In the second tier, there are numerous unaided schools in rural and small-town India – many of them falsely claiming to be 'English-medium' – that provide for poor and lower-middle-class households. These households have the financial means to find alternatives to decrepit government/aided schools, but not the connections and large amounts of money required to enter Delhi Public School and its ilk (see Muralidharan and Kremer 2006).

The state's inability to increase its educational funding to reflect growing demand has often hit government and aided schools especially hard. Class sizes have often become very large in these schools – sometimes of over 100 children in Uttar Pradesh – as a result of a failure by the state to replace teachers who retire. Standards in second-tier schools within the unaided sector are often little better. Muralidhran and Kremer's (2006) survey of rural unaided schools showed that teacher absenteeism was over 20 per cent – only slightly better than in government and aided institutions. Facilities and educational standards were likewise only marginally better in unaided educational institutions in rural and small-town India than in government and aided schools (see also Majumdar and Mooij 2011).

Regardless of the type of school a child attends, they are increasingly likely to also obtain private tuitions. There is now a vast penumbra of educational advisors, tutors and coaches involved in education in India. Some of these institutions and individuals offer key skills to disadvantaged children. But others prey on poor people's lack of information and desire to pass examinations (see Faust and Nagar 2001; Kingdon 2007). Jeffery et al. (2005) record many instances in which teachers in western Uttar Pradesh in government and aided schools told pupils that they would not receive proper instruction during school time and should pay for extra-school tutorials, often run by the same teacher.

Another major problem with the privatization of education is that it has resulted in the proliferation of schools that advance particularistic religious or political agendas. The rise of educational institutions offering a militaristic education consonant with right-wing Hindu nationalist ideas has received considerable attention (see SAHMAT 2001, 2002a, 2002b, 2002c, 2003). In the 1990s, especially, Hindu nationalists used images of India being swamped by the modernizing forces of the West to emphasize the importance of 'value education' rooted in 'Hindu traditions' (e.g., Sundar 2004). This ideological programme came to be reflected in mainstream school curricula and also undergirded a programme of school foundation orchestrated by the Hindu right-wing Rashtriya Swayamsevak Sangh (e.g., Sarkar 1996). Véronique Bénéï (2008) has documented ethnographically the implications of this religious communalization for educational functioning, highlighting how Hindu nationalists in Maharashtra have influenced teaching practices within schools. She argues that there was no homogeneous 'hidden agenda' being played out in schools; teachers and children reworked the discourses and practices they encountered. But, through such strategies as venerating the seventeenth-century king Shivaji Maharaj, many schools inculcated aggressive, masculinized versions of Hindu nationalism (and see chapter 9).

One of the effects of the generally poor standard of educational provision in India and the politicization of schools has been to push young people out of formal education altogether (see Krishna 2002). While primary school attendance figures are impressive, primary school completion rates are much lower. National Family Health Survey data show that growth in school enrolment over the 1990s was much larger at six to ten years than at age eleven to fourteen years (Bhalotra and Zamora, 2006). Only 39 per cent of children in India attend secondary school (Joshi 2009). It is often the need to receive assistance from children in household or paid employment that forces parents to remove boys and girls from school, as Jane Dyson's (2008) ethnography of children's lives in the Indian Himalayas shows. In other cases, specific shocks – the death of a family member or an impending marriage – compels parents to take a child out of formal education (Krishna 2002; Alex 2008). The problem of high dropout rates is especially marked among girls, whose education is often devalued relative to that of boys and who are more likely to be withdrawn from school to assist with housework. Religious disparities are equally troubling. For example, Husain and Chatterjee (2009) note that primary school completion rates of Muslims in West Bengal are substantially lower than those of Hindus – indeed, their data suggest that the gap may have actually increased during the 2000s. Other studies show that SCs and STs are often especially likely to drop out of school (Shah et al. 2006).

Recent research on school dropouts also underlines the connection between educational malaise and problems in India's health sector (see especially Krishna 2002). The Expanded Programme of Immunization introduced in India in 1978 has gone a long way towards reducing child deaths from many major diseases. Moreover, the past fifty years has witnessed a considerable expansion of health facilities and some improvements in sanitation and water supply in most parts of India, especially the south. But health-care spending in India has remained under 1 per cent of GDP in spite of repeated calls for it to be raised to 2 per cent (Harriss 2011). Access to health care has become rapidly privatized since the early 1990s. In most parts of rural and small-town India, as well as in poorer areas of big cities, people are unable to acquire cheap and rapid access to medical facilities (Jeffery and Jeffery 2011). Health care is typically expensive, and acquiring the assistance of a nurse or doctor often involves the expenditure of money and time as well as the mobilization of social networks. There is also a pressing need for a review of the allocation of health spending. For example, in contemporary Uttar Pradesh, about 360,000 children die each year from diseases linked to poor sanitation and nutrition, such as fever and dehydration, compared to about 200 who die from polio. Yet 74 per cent of the state's health budget is earmarked for polio eradication (Jeffery and Jeffery 2010).

Negative experiences of education, interacting with health issues, do not affect the poor alone. Upper-middle-class children often suffer from the opposite problem of being the subjects of too much scrutiny. The spread of neoliberal ideas of success and rising competition for scarce credentials have further entrenched an entrepreneurial approach to education within large sections of India's middle classes. Parents and young people are typically less concerned with acquiring problem-solving and vocational skills than with moving quickly through school, excelling in examinations, and obtaining marks of cultural distinction (Fernandes 2004; Ganguly-Scrase and Scrase 2009). As Anagnost (2008) has noted in parallel work in China, the lives of many middle-class children in India have become thoroughly 'curricularized', as they are forced to follow a hectic daily schedule, alternating between tutorials, school and specialist classes – all the time subject to strict disciplinary regimes. In addition, many children are compelled to migrate for education: to an urban home, where they might live with a relative; to other parts of India; or abroad.

Exacerbating pressures on middle-class children still further is the shift occurring in the attitudes of many parents since the early 1990s. Whereas exam grades were once the key criterion of youth success, middle-class parents are increasingly pushing their offspring to acquire a range of other attributes, such as communication skills and other 'extracurricular' accomplishments. The cumulative impact of such hothousing results in widespread childhood stress, and there are increasing instances of suicide among middle-class children in India (see Pramanik 2007).

Another worrying dimension of how parents manage their children's futures, one especially evident among the middle class, is the rise of narratives of children as 'investments'. It is now common across India to hear middle-class parents discussing the 'returns' that they will receive after successfully educating and placing a child in work or marriage:

a son who will support them in old age and a daughter well set in an influential, high-status family. Donner (2006), for example, recalls the popular phrase 'a son is capital, a grandson is interest'. Such discourses are not new (see Vatuk 1972), but they have become more prominent since the early 1990s. At the everyday level, the added burden of parental expectations often gives rise to inter-, intra- and trans-generational conflict (Jeffrey et al. 2008).

Even where young people effectively negotiate primary and secondary school, they are often unable to acquire a good college or university education. Only about 9 per cent of men and 7 per cent of women in India attend higher education (Upadhyay 2007). But there has been a substantial increase in university and college education since the 1950s, and especially since the early 1990s. In 1950–1, India had 27 universities, 370 colleges for general education and 208 colleges for professional education (engineering, medicine, education). By the academic year of 2006–7, India had 369 universities and just over 18,000 colleges. The concentration of the population in lower age cohorts, allied to the demand for education, means that growth in the number of students in higher education has been rapid since 1990 – an average of about 5 per cent increase per year (Kapur and Mehta 2007). Higher education has also become outwardly more inclusive. The ratio of male to female students in higher education dropped from 8.3:1 in the 1950s to almost 1.5:1 by the late 1980s, and the ratio of general to SC/ST students has dropped from almost 12:1 in the late 1950s to just above 6:1 in 2004.

The majority of higher educational institutions in India are of poor quality. They lack good facilities and amenities. The curricula are outdated, and there is little continuous assessment or careers advice. Employers have come to distrust degrees from most small-town colleges and universities in India. Kapur and Mehta (2007) argue that the Indian state is caught between a 'half-baked socialism and half-baked capitalism'; an ideological commitment to equality and some form of 'socialism' prevents the state from mobilizing private money for higher education, but it is unwilling to invest the large sums required to improve higher education.

One result of this state under-investment has been to encourage elites in India to send their children abroad to acquire university degrees. Indian parents spend $3.7 billion annually educating their children abroad (Kapur and Mehta 2007). Another result of the Indian government's inability to fund higher education is privatization of colleges and universities. This privatization occurs in the absence of state oversight and programmes of pedagogic review. At the same time, there are numerous state functionaries and private brokers who extract money from the system of regulations imposed on higher education by the state and who therefore have an interest in the maintenance of the status quo (see Gould 1972; Jeffrey 2010).

Social inequalities are pronounced within higher education. SCs, STs, Muslims, and also OBCs, remain seriously under-represented in India's colleges and universities relative to their population share (Hasan and Mehta 2006). Casteism within higher education is also a problem. The death of Senthilkumar, a Dalit research scholar at the University of Hyderabad, early in 2008, led to the exposure of many examples of caste prejudice in colleges and universities (see Senthilkumar Solidarity Committee 2008). University education is also strongly gendered. For example, young women have historically been concentrated in non-professional courses that offer relatively few opportunities for lucrative employment (Chanana 2007).

In sum, India has been less effective than was China in the 1980s and 1990s in channelling resources into education and health (see Drèze and Sen 1995), and this militates against a demographic dividend effect. Kapil Sibal, the Minister of Human Resource Development in India, is currently seeking to improve poor people's access to schooling, pledging to double the percentage of Indians in higher education, bolster oversight of colleges and universities, and enhance quality and accountability in formal education. But these efforts are unlikely to change the mass education system sufficiently radically and quickly, and gender, caste and religious inequalities remain a major cause for concern.

14.3   Unemployment

Another major reason why India is unlikely to benefit quickly from its demographic dividend is the shortage of employment in the country for educated youth. It is true that a thin upper stratum of young people has moved quickly and successfully into well-paid, secure salaried work, often the IT sector and allied employment. But this elite is small and almost entirely from upper castes and classes. Fuller and Narasimhan (2007) have described how upper-middle-class youth in Chennai have used their social connections and cultural confidence to dominate access to IT jobs, and Carol Upadhya (2007) makes the same argument based on research in Bangalore (see also Nisbett 2007; and chapter 12).

Another much larger section of educated youth – those from lower-middle-class or poor backgrounds – has typically faced disappointing occupational outcomes. Educated unemployment is not new in India. The colonial state often encouraged large numbers of young people to enter formal education, and not all of these men acquired salaried work (see Coleman 1965). Complaints about 'semi-educated' young men 'hanging about' around government offices surface in the reports of colonial officials at least as far back as the mid-1850s in India (Dore 1976: 53). Moreover, Ronald Dore (1976) argued over thirty years ago that a combination of population growth, a lack of expansion in manufacturing and service industries, and increased enrolment in education had created a large cohort of unemployed young people in many parts of India.

Yet educated unemployment has become especially pronounced since the 1970s in India and in many other post-colonial settings, as well as in the West (see Kaplinsky 2005). Substantial numbers of people in India, especially those from lower middle classes and upwardly mobile formerly disadvantaged groups, have looked to formal schooling as a means of social mobility since 1970, and they have been exposed via this education, and media or development institutions, to images of progress through education and entry into white-collar work (e.g., Silberschmidt 2001). At the same time, global economic changes since 1970 have often failed to generate sufficient numbers of permanent white-collar jobs to meet this growing demand (and see chapter 4 regarding economic liberalization and employment generation in India). The result has been the emergence of a surplus population of people who, unlike those in the 'reserved army of labour' discussed by Marx in the nineteenth century, possess educational qualifications and are sometimes highly skilled (see Kaplinsky 2005). Indeed, many in this group perceive themselves to be 'under-employed' rather than wholly without work. They are dependent on involuntary part-time work, engaged in intermittent unemployment, and/or involved in poorly remunerated labour (Prause and Dooley 1997: 245). In many parts of India, educated unemployment bears most pressingly on men in their twenties or early thirties. But young women are also experiencing increased unemployment, and they are often exposed to reinforcing modes of subordination, as young people excluded by economic structures from salaried work and as women seeking to challenge entrenched gendered ideas (Miles 2002).

Educated young people are not only unable to acquire secure salaried work, but also commonly lack the skills, aptitudes and contacts required to migrate in search of work or establish successful businesses. This partly reflects the institutional environment in many parts of India, where high levels of crime, endemic corruption and the poor physical infrastructure act as blocks to new forms of entrepreneurship (see Harriss-White 2003). In addition, the school and university system ill-prepares young people for establishing new ventures: they typically lack the necessary skills and motivation. In a recent India-wide survey, young people listed 'unemployment' as the most important challenge facing the country (see de Souza et al. 2009).

Scholars employing ethnographic methods have started to uncover the anxieties of educated unemployed youth in the 1990s and 2000s in India. Jamie Cross (2009) focuses on lower-middle-class youth unable to acquire prestigious jobs in a Special Economic Zone (SEZ) in Andhra Pradesh. Cross tracks the fortunes of unemployed young people who entered 'fallback work' in a diamond manufacturing plant. The work in the plant offered a measure of respect and an income higher than manual wage labour. Yet it also locked young people into hierarchical relationships within the company and prevented them from achieving further upward mobility. Cross writes of a generalized atmosphere of 'blighted hope' among these youth. Cross's work is more broadly indicative of research with educated unemployed youth in India, who are often unable to marry (see Chowdhry 2009), find it difficult to leave home and purchase or rent independent living space, and are commonly dogged by a sense of not having achieved locally salient notions of gendered success (Osella and Osella 2000).

Economists writing on the demographic dividend stress the capacity of young people to invest judiciously in their families and futures. But educated unemployed youth often appear to occupy a type of limbo in which the whole issue of planning a 'future' is rendered open to doubt. Craig Jeffrey (2010) describes educated Jat young men in western Uttar Pradesh who have acquired prolonged formal education but have been unable to obtain secure salaried work. Many of these men have responded by remaining in education, where they imagine themselves as people 'just passing the time' (doing 'timepass'). Timepass simultaneously conveys young men's sense of being detached from their education, plagued by feelings of surplus time, and left behind by Indian modernity. Many young men told Jeffrey that they are just 'waiting for their lives to change'. This haunting vision of youth frustration is reflected, too, in other writing. The author Pankaj Mishra (2006) has discussed towns in north India where young people appear to be 'waiting', and his novel on youth politics in Benares is full of images of youth in limbo (Mishra 2004). Gerard Heuzé (1996) refers to a population of lower-middle-class young men who spent long periods in education but who were unable to acquire government work or marry, and spent most of their time simply 'hanging around' at major road intersections. He concludes that, 'waiting has become an art and may become a profession for the majority of India's youth' (Heuzé 1996: 105; see also Myrdal 1996).

The state aggravates problems of youth ennui. On the one hand, governmental agencies perceived jobless youth as threats to the state and civil society. In many places, the state has resorted to strong-arm tactics and intimidation to police the behaviour of educated unemployed young people, especially men (see Jeffrey 2010). On the other hand, the state and other powerful organizations often identify young people as sources of hope, and enjoin them to craft their own futures (see Gooptu 2007). The educated unemployed are 'responsibilized' – charged with finding their own, individual solutions to the problem of prolonged joblessness – at the same moment that they are denigrated and disciplined by sections of the state.

Among those facing educated unemployment in India, SCs and STs are often especially disadvantaged (see also chapter 12). Chakravarthy and Somanathan (2008) have used an analysis of the occupational outcomes for college-leavers in Ahmedabad, Gujarat, to demonstrate that graduates belonging to SCs or STs receive significantly lower wages than those in the general category. Likewise, Deshpande and Newman (2007) found that university-educated Dalits' relatively scarce social and cultural capital relative to higher castes places them at a marked disadvantage in markets for graduate-level private-sector jobs. Moodie's (2008) recent research with a small ST group in Rajasthan gives a sense of the challenges affecting many SCs and STs in an era of highly intense competition for white-collar work (see also Parry 1999). Moodie shows that Dhanka men in Jaipur City were able to use reservations to acquire government posts in the 1970s and 1980s. But the increasing privatization of utilities in the city means that younger men of the community are unable to obtain government positions.

Moodie also emphasizes the gendered nature of any upward mobility that has occurred: women and girls have rarely been encouraged to pursue education or employment via reservations in her Jaipur study area. There is a paucity of good recent research on young women's experience of educated unemployment, but the picture Moodie provides is likely to hold true for large sections of the youth population in provincial India, especially in the north. Educated unemployment among men may also have indirect negative effects on women's autonomy. For example, Chowdhry (2009) argues that parents' increased concern over young men's public behaviour in contemporary Haryana has sometimes led them to discipline young women more tightly within the household.

14.4   The Politics of Youth Unemployment

The emergence of a large cohort of frustrated educated unemployed youth in India raises pressing questions about the political future of the country. In the absence of a propitious institutional and infrastructural environment, the apparent advantage to a country of a large adult population may turn into a negative risk. A large unemployed youth population in post-colonial countries may lead to rising crime (e.g., Roitman 2004) and pose a security threat (Cincotta et al. 2003) – a 'demographic timebomb'. This is an argument that also comes across strongly in the recently published 2011 *World Development Report*. The World Bank (2011: 81) uses a selection of surveys to argue that the main motivations for young people to become rebels or gang members are unemployment rather than any type of ideological commitment. In an accompanying bar chart, the World Bank shows unemployment towering above two alternative motivations – 'revenge and a sense of injustice' or 'belief in the cause' – as triggers to violent gang activity and rebellion.

The problems with the World Bank's report are legion: it conflates gang and rebel activity with violence, fails to specify how different grievances such as unemployment and injustice can be teased apart in a survey, and does not examine how unemployment is shaping politics in regions not affected by widespread violence. But the timebomb thesis deserves careful scrutiny. There are several more serious and careful studies that emphasize the reactionary, self-serving nature of educated unemployed young people's mobilization. For example, Hansen (1996a) describes how widespread exclusion from secure employment led lower-middle-class young men in Bombay in the 1990s to develop identities as Hindu nationalist political bosses. These men reconstructed a sense of masculine prowess through assuming roles as brokers between the urban poor and government officials. They also acted as provocateurs during anti-Muslim agitations and as 'hard men' capable of intervening violently to assist their friends (see also Heuzé 1992; chapter 10). Paralleling Hansen's account, Prem Chowdhry (2009) has studied unemployed young men in Haryana, north India, who channelled frustration into work in all-male caste *panchāyats* (caste associations). These young men used the *panchayats* to engage in illegal reactionary political practices, for example, violently punishing those who marry across caste boundaries.

Yet there is now evidence from many parts of the world that unemployed youth may play a key role in progressive social and political change. Harriss (R. Harriss 2003), for example, has described the role of educated unemployed young men in democratic political demonstrations in Argentina in the early 2000s. In his account of 'pavement politics' in Cape Town in the mid-1980s, Bundy (1987) emphasizes the importance of unemployed youth in challenging apartheid. In Bundy's account, it was educated unemployed young men who possessed the time and motivation to work as provocateurs. More recently, the democratic uprisings across North Africa and the Middle East attest to the potential for educated unemployed youth to engage in positive democratic change. It was police intimidation of an educated under-employed fruit-seller that provided the trigger for a political uprising in Tunisia in December 2010. In Egypt, educated unemployed young people in their teens and twenties were at the forefront of protests in 2011. We need to tread carefully here: Mubarak presented the rebels as a 'youth movement' in order to denigrate and trivialize opposition to his power. The movements in the Arab World are youth movements in part simply because the population is young. But emerging reports from Egypt and neighbouring states suggest that young people in their late teens and twenties have often been in the vanguard of popular mobilization. For example, a report on Al Jazeera on 25 April 2011 identified educated unemployed youth in Morocco as central to unrest in the country (see <http://english.aljazeera.net>).

There is also some recent evidence of democratic activity among unemployed youth in India. Krishna (2002) argues that educated unemployed young people from lower-middle-class backgrounds in rural western India in the 1990s often used their schooling to assist impoverished villagers in their negotiations with the state, circulate political discourses and intercede in local disputes (see also Kamat 2002). In a similar vein, Gooptu (2007) has described relatively wealthy young men from families historically associated with organized labour in West Bengal who engaged in 'social service' (*samāj sewā*). Likewise, Jeffrey (2010) has discussed the rise of higher-caste and low-caste youth in western Uttar Pradesh who style themselves as 'social reformers'. In addition to assisting the poor in their dealings with the state, they are often concerned to change society for the better, for example, through campaigning on labour issues, dowry and education.

Another way in which unemployed or under-employed young people may contribute to wider society is via the role they commonly play as educators or advisors to children. Youth in India have often responded to joblessness by working as tutors or establishing private schools. Even where they do not act as educators, they may help younger children with homework, advise them on schooling decisions and guide them with regard to employment. The rapid pace of socio-economic change in many parts of India means that parents are sometimes poorly positioned with respect to advising children in these areas. Youth in their late teens, twenties and early thirties act as a type of 'interstitial generation', mentoring and guiding younger children. As Mannheim (1972) argued in his classic writing on generations, particular age cohorts, because they have experienced similar social forces at the same stages of life, may feel a sense of generational solidarity, and in certain circumstances they may act on these bonds to try to change society. This is a type of 'demographic dividend', if not the one anticipated by David Bloom and fellow economists.

14.5   Conclusions

Bloom et al. (2003) emphasize that the demographic dividend will only work in specific conditions and, because it passes fairly quickly, countries only have a short time to get things right: a demographic dividend may be 'utilized' or it may be 'squandered'. The reasons for India's failure to take more immediate advantage of the demographic dividend are multiple. Corruption, poor physical infrastructure, educational decay and inadequate health services are all well-known impediments to broad-based social development, as we have noted in other chapters of this book (see also Harriss-White 2003). In this chapter, we have focused on two of the most pressing difficulties that young people face in developing their own human capital: the poor quality of mass education in India and the absence of secure salaried jobs in many parts of the country.

China provides something of a counterpoint to India. China was able to take advantage of its demographic dividend in the 1980s and 1990s because it was relatively successful in ensuring that children receive a meaningful elementary education and in guaranteeing some degree of health care to the mass of the population (Drèze and Sen 1995). Compared to India's northern states, China had a relatively good infrastructure and lower levels of corruption.

There are nevertheless at least three signs of hope in India. First, the state is expending increasing effort on trying to improve the prospects of people in their late teens and twenties in the country. The recent pronouncements of Kapil Sibal on widening access to higher education are indicative of this trend, as is the rapid expansion of public development projects (see chapter 5). Second, NGO activity in the realms of education, and to a lesser extent unemployment, is burgeoning. Third, young people themselves, including the educated unemployed, are becoming involved in public action. As recent events in the Arab World attest, a youth generation hardened by dispiriting experiences may emerge as agents of change.

15

Afterword: India Today, and India in the World

In this book we have sought to explain the key aspects of what is happening in India today. It is, as we hope to have shown, a fascinating story – and fascinating partly because of its complexity. In some ways, India has witnessed quite remarkable change over the last decade. Less than ten years ago, India was still described by serious economic commentators, writing for such newspapers as the *The Economist*, as a 'caged tiger', and compared very unfavourably with China. These perceptions changed very rapidly in the course of the year 2003, as we recall from our reading of the *Financial Times* at the time. But even two years before that, Jim O'Neill, Chief Economist at Goldman Sachs, formulated the idea of the BRICs, through which he successfully drew attention to the great significance of the economic dynamism of Brazil, Russia, India and China (the BRICs), and pointed out the historic shift that, as he saw it, is inexorably taking place in the global economy (O'Neill 2001). For rather less than two centuries, the economic centre of gravity of the world has lain in 'the West', initially in Western Europe and then – and most comprehensively – in the United States. Now, however, that centre of gravity is shifting back to where it has lain for a much longer span of human history, in Asia. Even in 1820, according to the calculations of the economic historian Angus Maddison (1998: 40), China accounted for 32.4 per cent of world GDP, India for 15.7 per cent, and Europe for only 26.6 per cent; and only by much later in the nineteenth century did Europe overtake China and India. The balance of the world economy is now shifting back, in other words, to where it was. Recent estimates by Goldman Sachs's economists suggest that by 2050 the Chinese economy will be 75 per cent bigger than that of the United States, and it is possible that by that time – or even well before it according to some projections – the Indian economy will be as big or bigger than that of the USA, and will dwarf the historically powerful Western European economies (O'Neill and Stupnytska 2009). The Indian economy is already the fourth largest in the world, according to the Purchasing Power Parity way of comparing economies, after the US and China, and Japan; and for several years now it has been the second fastest-growing large economy. This is an extraordinary transformation, as we have explained, for a country that was characterized by the (very low) 'Hindu rate of growth', and taken as being pretty much the archetype of a poor, less-developed economy. It is a transformation, too, that defies easy explanation by any of the currently favoured general theories of economic growth (see chapter 2). Its origins lie, as we have shown in chapter 6 of this book, in the changing politics of the Indian state and in what Corbridge and Harriss earlier described as an 'elite revolt' (2000: chapter 6).

Alongside the phenomenon of this extraordinarily rapid rate of economic growth other historically massive changes are taking place. These are marked especially by the growth in the presence of India's middle classes and by the changes in lifestyles and (much less certainly, as we have argued in chapters 9 and 12) in values as well, that are driven by the middle classes. These are changes observed most of all in India's metropolitan cities – in Delhi, Mumbai, Chennai, Hyderabad, Bangalore and Kolkata, all of which aspire to be global cities – but increasingly in smaller towns and cities too (see chapter 11). Goldman Sachs anticipates that 'Millions in the BRICs [with India making a contribution second only to China] will Enter Middle Class Income Bracket by 2020, Far Surpassing the G7' (Goldman Sachs 2010). With this development, the expectations of Indians are changing rapidly, and these seem likely to bring about great changes in politics as well as in society. It is important, of course, not to read too much into particular events, but it is surely possible that the popular movement against corruption, sparked by the Gandhian activist Anna Hazare, which has been gathering strength in India as we have been writing this book (and to which we refer in chapter 11), will bring about far-reaching change. The Commonwealth Games held in Delhi in October 2010 may come to be seen in historical perspective as a moment of change (see articles in *Frontline* 27 (21), 22 October 2010). On the one hand, there was enormous pride in the historic achievements of Indian athletes, who have usually been notably absent from the podia at major international events, but, on the other, there was a sense of shame at the evidence of corruption and of the inefficiency of administration, obvious to the whole world, in the run up to the Games. This was followed, only shortly after, by the unfolding of the '2G' scandal, over the way in which telecommunications bandwidth had been sold. These events have given rise to massive middle-class protest against the ways in which politicians behave. It remains to be seen whether the effects of the actions of the Hazare movement will be to strengthen what we refer to in chapter 7 as 'substantive democracy' in India, or not.

India today is a scene of great change. But it is hard not to be struck as well by how much has *not* changed – perhaps above all by the enduring inequalities of Indian society, and by the continuing prevalence of great poverty, in spite of such successful economic growth (as we discuss in chapters 3 and 4). The persistence of the hierarchical values of Indian's *ancien régime*, and of patriarchy, are reflected most clearly in the disabilities – in spite of years of affirmative action – of the Scheduled Castes and the Scheduled Tribes who together make up more than a quarter of the population (see chapter 12), and in the continuing deep disadvantage of Indian women (chapter 13). Where multiple forms of inequalities intersect, individuals often find themselves doubly or triply disadvantaged, as recent research with Dalit young women, for example, has shown (chapter 14). It is hard to avoid the conclusion that underlying the persisting problems of the delivery of the critical social services of education and health (discussed in chapters 8 and 14) – that are in turn so much bound up with the persistence of poverty (as we have shown in chapter 3) – are hierarchical values that conflict with those of universal citizenship and of social justice. So many of the civil servants and politicians who are concerned in the delivery of these services still appear to lack commitment to social justice, exactly as Myron Weiner (1991) argued in regard to education in particular. Civil society organizations, even those that pursue objectives of social justice, are not notably democratic in themselves, as Jean Drèze, whom we quoted on this in chapter 5, says; and members of the middle classes use the instrument of public interest litigation to clear away the poor – who are disproportionately from the Scheduled Castes – from their neighbourhoods (as we have mentioned in chapter 11), even as others from these same social classes use this legal mechanism for the pursuit of social justice. Enduring inequality also accounts for the limitations of Indian democracy (see chapter 7). Democracy, in India, has encouraged competition between social groups for advantage in access to state resources, rather than for the accountability of the state to citizens. Politics, as Mehta says, is a struggle on the part of different groups for position, rather than for social transformation (Mehta 2011).

It remains to be seen whether these enduring characteristics of India's society and politics will come to limit India's economic growth and will ultimately falsify the bullish projections of Goldman Sachs and of those writing of India's 'demographic dividend' (chapter 14). A group of thinkers and administrators who have ventured to project that India can become an affluent society by 2039 cautions, nonetheless, that one of the fundamental challenges for India in realizing this objective is that of bringing about the transition from a poor to a cohesive as well as an affluent society. In tackling this challenge, it foresees 'dire implications' for the country if India fails to address 'issues related to structural inequalities' (Kohli and Sood 2010: 4) – those that we have drawn attention to in chapters 3, 4 and 14. The point is explained very effectively by Michael Walton, who emphasizes three intimately interconnected problems that must be addressed if India is not to go the way of major Latin American economies that have at one time or another experienced periods with very high rates of economic growth, but have then fallen back. He speaks of:

> the need to develop a competitive corporate sector with checks and balances against excessive market or political influence; tackling group-based inequalities but with more emphasis on reducing the politicization of such differences and the pursuit of universal citizenship, to complement explicit affirmative action; and the development of a more accountable state. (Walton 2010: 99)

The arguments of this book are entirely supportive of this position. The strength of the Maoist insurgency (that we discuss in chapter 10) – even if it does not seriously threaten the Indian state – is one marker of the significance of the last two of these problems, and even of the first. India's future place in the world will depend substantially on how these problems are dealt with.

Another of the challenges that India faces, according to the group that is looking to 'India 2039', is that of 'moving from a small player in global affairs to a responsible global citizen' (Kohli and Sood 2010: 4). This is perhaps a surprising statement given that none other than the President of the United States, Barack Obama, has described India as being an 'emerged' rather than an 'emerging' power, and that India has a long record of engagement with and of commitment to international law and institutions – with some very notable and deliberate exceptions amongst these. In particular, India maintains its opposition to the Comprehensive Test Ban Treaty and other instruments of the international nuclear nonproliferation regime, on the grounds that it enshrines a fundamentally unequal world order, that maintains the hegemony of the West. This position is entirely in line with the approach to international relations taken by Independent India from the outset. The Nehruvian state – which aimed, self-consciously, to be a good 'global citizen' – sought, of course, non-alignment, aiming to side with neither of the great powers of the Cold War era, and to pursue a line that, while being generally supportive of an international order secured by deliberation and negotiation rather than by force, also aimed to advance the interests of the erstwhile colonies of the imperial powers. Similar ideas, which correspond broadly with an 'idealist' position in international relations, continue to influence India's foreign policy. But the Indian foreign and defence policy establishments, including academics, advisers and journalists, as well politicians, diplomats and senior military officers, also include advocates of a harder line, reflecting the 'realist' position in international relations. This is the view that the international sphere is fundamentally anarchic; that within it states must pursue their interests and be ready to advance and defend them by force. The realists in the Indian policy establishment, or 'hyper-realists' as the international relations scholar Kanti Bajpai describes them (2010), would have India pursue a more aggressive line, for instance, in regard to Pakistan. These contending views will continue to influence India's policies in regard to Pakistan, China and the United States. So long as the 'idealist' voice is powerful, India will seek negotiated solutions to its relations with both Pakistan and China, but there can be no guarantee that the realists will not at some future point win out.

One very significant marker of the fact that India is no longer only a small player in world affairs is that the former President of the United States, George W. Bush, was ready to overturn the constraints of the non-proliferation treaties that successive US administrations had negotiated, in order to establish an effective alliance with India that is clearly, implicitly if never quite explicitly, intended to counterbalance the rise of China. The former editor of *The Economist*, Bill Emmott, has likened Bush's visit to India in 2006, in pursuit of his deal with India, to the celebrated visit of President Nixon to Beijing in 1972 (Emmott 2008). There can be no question but that the future of the world as a whole now depends quite significantly on the future development of relations between India and China. Will these be essentially cooperative – as those who have welcomed the development of trading relations between the two countries hope – or will they be more confrontational, as those who observe the developing naval competition between the two countries think is more likely? No doubt the answer to this question will not be at all clear-cut. But the way in which India's position in the world changes over the coming years will certainly be influenced quite fundamentally by the outcomes of the largely domestic trends of economic and political change, and of conflicts between social groups and classes with which this book has been concerned.

Glossary

adivasi	indigenous people; Scheduled Tribes
Bhagavad Gita	Hindu scriptural text (part of the *Mahabharata*); seen as a 'manual for mankind'
Bharat Mata	mother India
bustee	informal settlement
crore	10 million rupees
Dalit	'the downtrodden'; ex-untouchable caste groups; Scheduled Castes
dalitbahujan	the oppressed majority
dhanda	occupational trade
dharma	moral or religious duty or obligation
dharna	rally
dirigiste	strong state direction of the economy
garibi hatao	banish poverty; political slogan associated with Indira Gandhi
gram panchayat	local self-government institution at village or small-town level
gram sabha	formal village meeting provided by government statute
gram vikas	village development
Hindutva	'Hindu-ness' or Hindu cultural identity/ nationalism
Indira Awaas Yojana	government housing scheme for the rural poor
izzat	honour or dignity
jati	literally birth; subcaste (mainly by occupation)

Jawahar Rozgar Yojana	food for work scheme
kali yuga	'Age of Kali' in Hindu scripture; a 'dark age'
kar sevaks	volunteers (esp. Hindu nationalists)
khap	lineage
kisan	farmer
Lok Sabha	'House of the People'; Lower House of Parliament
Madrasah	Muslim school of learning, possibly attached to a mosque
Mahatma	great soul; appellation for Mohandas Gandhi
Mahabharata	Sanskrit religious epic
Mahant	chief temple priest
mandir	temple
Masjid	mosque
Mitaksara	property rights code (once) common in north-west India
Naxalites	Maoist guerrillas; originated in Naxalbari district, West Bengal
panchayat	'five-person' village council
pradhan	elected chairperson of a *gram panchayat*; term for local leader in Delhi slums
purdah	restriction of females to the home or domestic realm
raiyatwari	system of tenure where cultivators paid rent directly to government
Rajya Sabha	'Council of States'; Upper House of Parliament
Ramjanmabhoomi	movement to build a Ram temple
Rashtra	nation or homeland
Salwa Judum	'Purification Hunt'; state-sponsored vigilante groups in Chhattisgarh
samāj sewā	social service
Sangh parivar	family of Hindu nationalist organizations
Sarsanghachalak	leader of the RSS
Sarva Shiksha Abhiyan	'education for all' programme
satyagraha	non-violent resistance
sena	private army
swadeshi	national self-sufficiency
zamindari	system of land tenure administration where landlords (*zamindars*) collected rent from peasants and transferred revenue to government

Bibliography

There are a number of articles from *The Hindu* newspaper included in this bibliography, which may be accessed at the following website: <http://www.thehindu.com/navigation/?type=static&page=archive>. References for news items, as opposed to articles, are given by date in the text and are not included in the bibliography.

Acemoglu, Daron (2009), *Introduction to Modern Economic Growth* (Princeton, NJ: Princeton University Press).

Acemoglu, Daron, Simon Johnson and James Robinson (2001), 'The colonial origins of comparative development: an empirical investigation', *American Economic Review* 91(5): 1369–1401.

Acemoglu, Daron, Simon Johnson and James Robinson (2002), 'Reversal of fortune, geography and institutions in the making of modern world income distribution', *Quarterly Journal of Economics,* 117(4): 1231–94.

Adeney, Katharine and Andrew Wyatt (2004), 'Democracy in south Asia: getting beyond the structure-agency dichotomy', *Political Studies* 52(3): 1–18.

Agarwal, Bina (1994), *A Field of One's Own: Gender and Land Rights in South Asia* (Cambridge: Cambridge University Press).

Agarwal, Bina (1998), 'Widows versus daughters or widows as daughters? Property, land and economic security in rural India', *Modern Asian Studies* 32(10): 1–48.

Agarwal, Bina (2002), 'Bargaining' and legal change: toward gender equality in India's inheritance laws', *Working Paper no. 165*, Brighton: Institute of Development Studies.

Agarwal, Bina (2003), 'Gender and land rights revisited', *Journal of Agrarian Change* 3: 184–224.

Agarwal, Bina (2010), *Gender and Green Governance: The Political Economy of Women's Presence Within and Beyond Community Forestry* (Oxford: Oxford University Press).

Agarwal, Bina and Pradeep Panda (2007), 'Toward freedom from domestic violence: the neglected obvious', *Journal of Human Development,* 8(3): 359–88.

Agarwala, Rina (2006), 'From work to welfare: a new class movement in India', *Critical Asian Studies*, 38(4): 419–44.

Ahluwalia, Montek (1978), 'Rural poverty and agricultural performance in India', *Journal of Development Studies* 14(3): 298–323.

Ahluwalia, Montek (1994), 'India's quiet economic revolution', *Columbia Journal of World Business* 29(1): 6–12.

Ahluwalia, Montek (2002), 'Economic reforms in India since 1991: has gradualism worked?' *Journal of Economic Perspectives*, 16(3): 67–88.

Ahmed, Sadiq and Ashutosh Varshney (2008), 'Battles half won: the political economy of India's growth and economic policy since independence', *Working Paper No.1* (Washington, DC: Commission on Growth and Development).

Alam, Javeed (2004), *Who Wants Democracy?* (Delhi: Orient Longman).

Alavi, Hamza (1965), 'Peasants and revolution', *Socialist Register,* 2(1): 241–77

Alex, Gabriele (2008), 'Work versus education: children's everyday life in rural Tamil Nadu', in Deepak Behera (ed.), *Childhoods in South Asia* (Delhi: Pearson), 119–39.

Alfaro, Laura and Anusha Chari (2009), 'India transformed? Insights from the firm level, 1988–2005', *National Bureau of Economic Research*, Working Paper 15448.

Alkire, S. and E. Santos (2010), 'Acute multidimensional poverty: a new index for developing countries', *Working Paper* 38 (Oxford: Oxford University Poverty and Human Development Initiative).

Ambirajan, Srinivasa (1978), *Classical Political Economy and British Policy in India* (Cambridge: Cambridge University Press).

Amsden, Alice (1989), *Asia's Next Giant: South Korea and Late Industrialisation* (Oxford: Oxford University Press).

Anagnost, Ann (2008), 'Imagining global futures in China: The child as a sign of value', in Jennifer Cole and Deborah Durham (eds), *Figuring the Future: Globalization and the Temporalities of Children and Youth* (Santa Fe, NM: School for Advanced Research Press), 49–73.

Anand, Sudhir and Ravi Kanbur (1993), 'The Kuznets process and the inequality-development relationship', *Journal of Development Economics*, 40(1): 25–52.

Anandhi, S., J. Jeyaranjan and R. Krishnan (2002), 'Work, caste and competing masculinities: notes from a Tamil village', *Economic and Political Weekly* 37 (43): 4403–14.

Andersen, Steffan, Erwin Bulte, Uri Gneezy and John List (2008), 'Do women supply more public goods than men? Preliminary experimental evidence from matrilineal and patriarchal societies', *American Economic Review, Papers and Proceedings*, 98(2): 376–81.

Andersen, Walter K. and Shridhar D. Damle (1987), *The Brotherhood in Saffron: The Rashtriya Swayamsevak Sangh and Hindu Revivalism* (Delhi: Vistaar Publications).

Anderson, Benedict (1983), *Imagined Communities. The Origins and Spread of Nationalism* (London: Verso).

Appadurai, Arjun (2002), 'Deep democracy: urban governmentality and the horizon of politics', *Public Culture* 14(1): 21–47.

Appadurai, Arjun (2004), 'The capacity to aspire: culture and the terms of recognition', in V. Rao and M. Walton (eds.), *Culture and Public Action* (Stanford, CA: Stanford University Press), 59–84.

Arnold, David (1993), *Colonizing the Body: State Medicine and Epidemic Disease in Nineteenth Century India* (Berkeley, CA: University of California Press).

Arokiasamy, P. (2009), 'Fertility decline in India: contributions by uneducated women using contraception', *Economic and Political Weekly*, 44(30): 55–64.

Austin, Gareth (2008a), 'The "reversal of fortune" thesis and the compression of history: perspectives from African and comparative economic history', *Journal of International Development* 20(8): 996–1027.

Austin, Gareth (2008b), 'Resources, techniques, and strategies south of the Sahara: revising the factor endowments perspective on African economic development, 1500–2000', *Economic History Review* 61(3): 587–624.

Bailey, Frederick G. (1957), *Caste and the Economic Frontier: A Village in Highland Orissa* (Manchester: Manchester University Press).

Bailey, Frederick G. (1963), *Politics and Change: Orissa in 1959* (Berkeley, CA: University of California Press).

Bailey, Frederick G. (1996), *The Civility of Indifference: On Domesticating Ethnicity* (New York: Cornell University Press).

Bajpai, Kanti (2010), 'India and the World', in Niraja Gopal Jayal and Pratap Bhanu Mehta (eds), *The Oxford Companion to Politics in India* (Delhi: Oxford University Press), 521–41.

Balagopal, K. (1991), 'Post-Chundur and other Chundurs', *Economic and Political Weekly*, 26(42): 2399–2405.

Balagopal, K. (2006a), 'Physiognomy of violence', *Economic and Political Weekly*, 41(20): 2183–6.

Balagopal, K. (2006b), 'Maoist movement in Andhra Pradesh', *Economic and Political Weekly*, 41 (29): 3183–7.

Ban, Radu and Vijayendra Rao (2008), 'Tokenism or agency? The impact of women's reservations on village democracies in south India', *Economic Development and Cultural Change,* 56(3): 501–30.

Banerjee, Abhijit (ed.) (2007), *Making Aid Work* (Cambridge, MA: MIT Press).

Banerjee, Abhijit and Esther Duflo (2003), 'Inequality and growth: what can the data say?', *Journal of Economic Growth*, 8(3): 267–99.

Banerjee, Abhijit and Esther Duflo (2009), 'Improving health care delivery', Homepage of Abhijit Banerjee, Massachusetts Institute of Technology. Retrieved from: <http://econ-www.mit.edu/files/5172> (last accessed at July 2010).

Banerjee, Abhijit and Esther Duflo (2011), *Poor Economics: A Radical Rethinking of the Way to Fight Global Poverty* (Philadelphia, PA: Public Affairs).

Banerjee, Abhijit and Thomas Piketty (2005), 'Top Indian incomes: 1922–2000', *World Bank Economic Review*, 19(1): 1–20.

Banerjee, Abhijit and Rohini Pande (2009), 'Parochial politics, ethnic preferences and politician corruption', Homepage of Abhijit Banerjee, Massachusetts Institute of Technology. Retrieved from: <http://econ-www.mit.edu/files/3872> (last accessed July 2010).

Banerjee, Abhijit, Pranab Bardhan, Kaushik Basu, Mrinal Datta Chaudhuri, Maitreesh Ghatak, Ashok Sanjay Guha, Mukul Majumdar, Dilip Mookherjee and Debray Ray (2003), 'Strategy for economic reform in West Bengal', *Economic and Political Weekly*, 37(41): 4203–18.

Banerjee, Abhijit, Shawn Cole, Esther Duflo and Linden Leigh (2005), 'Remedying education: evidence from two randomized experiments in India', *NBER Working Paper No. 11904*. Retrieved from: <http://www.nber.org/papers/w11904> (last accessed May 6, 2011).

Banerjee, Abhijit, Rukmini Banerji, Esther Duflo, Rachel Glennerster, Danile Kennistion, Stuti Khemani and Marc Shotland (2007), 'Can information campaigns raise awareness and local participation in primary education?', *Economic and Political Weekly* 42(15): 1365–72.

Banerjee, Arpita and Saraswati Raju (2009), 'Gendered mobility: women migrants and work in urban India', *Economic and Political Weekly*, 44(28): 115–23.

Banerjee, Arpita, Rukmini Banerji, Esther Duflo, Rachel Glennerster and Stuti Khemani (2008), 'Pitfalls of participatory programmes: evidence from a randomized evaluation in education in India', *Working Paper No. 14311*, Cambridge, MA: National Bureau of Economic Research.

Banerjee, Sumanta (1980), *In the Wake of Naxalbari: A History of the Naxalite Movement in India* (Calcutta: Subarnrekha).

Banerjee, Sumanta (2008), 'On the Naxalite movement: a report with a differ-ence', *Economic and Political Weekly*, 43(21): 10–12.

Banerjee, Sumanta (2009), 'Reflections of a one-time Maoist activist', *Dialectical Anthropology*, 33 (3–4): 253–69.

Bardhan, Pranab (1984), *The Political Economy of Development in India* (Oxford: Oxford University Press); 2nd edn 1998.

Bardhan, Pranab (2009), 'Notes on the political economy of India's tortuous transition', *Economic and Political Weekly*, 44(49): 31–6.

Bardhan, Pranab (2010), *Awakening Giants, Feet of Clay: Assessing the Economic Rise of China and India* (Princeton, NJ: Princeton University Press).

Bardhan, Pranab (2011), 'Our self-righteous civil society', *Economic and Political Weekly*, 46(29): 16–18.

Bardhan, Pranab and Dilip Mookherjee (2007), 'Decentralization in West Bengal: origins, functioning and impact', in Pranab Bardhan and Dilip Mookherjee (eds), *Decentralization and Local Government in Developing Countries: A Comparative Perspective* (Delhi: Oxford University Press), 203–22.

Bardhan, Pranab and Isha Ray (2008), 'Methodological approaches to the ques-tion of the commons', in Pranab Bardhan and Isha Ray (eds), *The Contested Commons: Conversations between Economists and Anthropologists* (Oxford: Oxford University Press).

Baru, Sanjaya (2007), 'Strategic consequences of India's economic performance', in Baldev Raj Nayar (ed.), *Globalization and Politics in India* (New Delhi: Oxford University Press), 321–45.

Basu, Amrita (2010), 'Gender and politics', in Niraja Gopal Jayal and Pratap Bhanu Mehta (eds), *The Oxford Companion to Politics in India* (New Delhi: Oxford University Press), 168–80.

Basu, Kaushik and Annemie Maertens (2007), 'The pattern and causes of economic growth in India', *Oxford Review of Economic Policy* 23(2): 143–67.

Basu, Tapan, Pradip Datta, Sumit Sarkar, Tanika Sarkar and Sambuddha Sen (2003), *Khaki Shorts, Saffron Flags* (Delhi: Orient Longman).

Bates, Crispin (2007), *Subalterns and the Raj: South Asia since 1600* (London: Routledge).

Bavadam, Lyla (2009), 'Farmer's victory', *Frontline*, 26(13) (3 July): 119–21.

Baviskar, Amita (2007), 'Cows, Cars and Rickshaws: Bourgeois Environmentalists and the Battle for Delhi's Streets', unpublished ms.

Baviskar, Amita and Nandini Sundar (2008), 'Democracy versus economic transformation?: A response to Partha Chatterjee's democracy and economic transformation in India', *Economic and Political Weekly* 43(46): 87–9.

Bayart, Jean-François (1993), *The State in Africa: The Politics of the Belly* (London: Longman).

Bayly, Christopher (1998), *Origins of Nationality in South Asia: Patriotism and Ethical Government in the Making of Modern India* (New Delhi: Oxford University Press).

Bayly, Christopher (2004), *The Birth of the Modern World, 1780–1914* (Oxford: Blackwell).

Bayly, Susan (2001), *Caste, Society and Politics in India from the Eighteenth Century to the Modern Age* (Cambridge: Cambridge University Press).

Bayly, Susan (2007), *Asian Voices in a Postcolonial Age: Vietnam, India and Beyond* (Cambridge: Cambridge University Press).

Beaman, Lori, Raghabendra Chattopadhyay, Esther Duflo, Rohini Pande and Petia Topolova (2008), *Powerful Women: Does Exposure Reduce Bias?*, mimeo. Retrieved from: <http://cpe.ucsd.edu/assets/002/6984.pdf> (last accessed 1 June 2010).

Beaman, Lori, Raghabendra Chattopadhyay, Esther Duflo, Rohini Pande and Petia Topolova (2009), 'Powerful women: does exposure reduce bias?', *Quarterly Journal of Economics*, 124(4): 1497–1550.

Bellin, Eva (2008), 'Faith in politics: new trends in the study of religion and politics', *World Politics*, 60(2): 315–47.

Bénéï, Véronique (2001), 'Teaching nationalism in Maharashtra schools', in Christopher J. Fuller and Véronique Bénéï (eds), *The Everyday State and Society in Modern India* (Delhi: Social Science Press), 194–221.

Bénéï, Véronique (2008), *Schooling Passions: Nation, History and Language in Contemporary Western India* (Stanford, CA: Stanford University Press).

Benjamin, Solomon (2000), 'Governance, economic settings and poverty in Bangalore', *Environment and Urbanisation*, 12(1): 35–51.

Bentall, Jim (1995), '"Bharat versus India": peasant politics and urban–rural relations in north-west India', PhD dissertation (Cambridge: University of Cambridge).

Bentall, Jim and Stuart Corbridge (1996) 'Urban–rural relations, demand politics and the "new agrarianism" in north-west India: the Bharatiya Kisan Union', *Transactions of the Institute of British Geographers*, 2(1): 27–48.

Bentley, Margaret E. and Paula L. Griffiths (2003), 'The burden of anaemia among women in India', *European Journal of Clinical Nutrition*, 57(1): 52–60.

Bernstein, Henry (1977), 'Notes on capital and peasantry', *Review of African Political Economy*, 4(10): 60–73.

Berreman, Gerald D. (1960), 'Caste in India and the United States', *American Journal of Sociology* 66(2): 120–7.

Besley, Timothy and Robin Burgess (2000), 'The political economy of government responsiveness: theory and evidence from India', *STICERD Development Economics Discussion Paper Series Number 28*, London School of Economics.

Besley, Timothy and Robin Burgess (2004), 'Can regulation hinder economic performance? Evidence from India', *Quarterly Journal of Economics*, 119(1): 91–134.

Besley, Timothy, Robin Burgess and Berta Esteve-Volart (2007), 'The policy origins of poverty and growth in India', in Timothy Besley and Louise Cord (eds), *Delivering the Promise of Pro-poor Growth: Insights and Lessons from Country Experiences* (New York: World Bank), 59–78.

Besley, Timothy, Rohini Pande, Lupin Rahman and Vijayendra Rao (2004), 'The politics of public goods provision: evidence from Indian local governments', *Journal of the European Economics Association, Papers and Proceedings*, 2(2–3): 416–26.

Besley, Timothy, Rohini Pande and Vijayendra Rao (2007), 'Political economy of panchayats in south India', *Economic and Political Weekly*, 42(8): 661–6.

Béteille, André (1965), *Caste, Class and Power: Changing Patterns of Stratification in a Tanjore Village* (Berkeley, CA: California University Press).

Béteille, André (1991), *Society and Politics in India: Essays in a Comparative Perspective* (London: Athlone Press).

Béteille, André (1992), *The Backward Classes in Contemporary India* (Delhi: Oxford University Press).

Béteille, André (2001), 'Race and caste', *The Hindu* (10 March).

Bhaduri, Amit and Deepak Nayyar (1996), *An Intelligent Person's Guide to Liberalization* (New Delhi: Penguin).

Bhagwati, Jagdish (1993), *India in Transition: Freeing the Economy* (Oxford: Clarendon Press).

Bhagwati, Jagdish (2006), 'Keeper of the flame', *Hindustan Times* (20 December). {accessed at: http://www.hindustantimes.com/News-Feed/NM21/Keeper-of-the-flame/Article1-194907.aspx}

Bhagwati, Jagdish and Padma Desai (1970), *India: Planning for Industrialisation* (London: Oxford University Press).

Bhalla, G. S. and Gurmail Singh (2009), 'Economic liberalisation and Indian agriculture: a statewise analysis', *Economic and Political Weekly*, 44(52): 34–44.

Bhalla, Surjit (2002), *Imagine There's No Country: Poverty, Inequality and Growth in the Era of Globalisation* (Washington, DC: Institute for International Economics).

Bhalla, Surjit (2003a), 'Recounting the poor: poverty in India, 1983–99', *Economic and Political Weekly*, 38(4): 338–49.

Bhalla, Surjit (2003b), 'Crying wolf on poverty, or how the millennium development goal for poverty has already been reached', *Economic and Political Weekly*, 38(27): 2843–56.

Bhalotra, Sonia and Bernarda Zamora (2008), *Primary Education in India: Prospects of Meeting the MDG Target* (Bristol: Centre for Market and Public Organisation).

Bhan, Gautam (2009), '"This is no longer the city I once knew". Evictions, the urban poor and the right to the city in millennial Delhi', *Environment and Urbanization*, 21(1): 127–42.

Bhat, Mari (2002), 'Returning a favour: reciprocity between female education and fertility', *World Development*, 30(10): 1791–1803.

Bhattacharjea, A. (2009), 'The effects of employment legislation on Indian manufacturing', *Economic and Political Weekly*, 44(2): 55–62.

Bhattacharya, Debashish (2000), 'Globalising economy, localising labour', *Economic and Political Weekly*, 35(42): 244–63.

Bhattacharya, Dwaipayan (2001), 'Civic community and its margins: school teachers in West Bengal', *Economic and Political Weekly*, 38(8): 673–83.

Bhattacharya, Prabir (2006), 'Economic development, gender inequality, and demographic outcomes: evidence from India', *Population and Development Review*, 32(2): 263–91.

Bhattacharyya, Subhas (2007), 'Power sector reform in South Asia: why slow and limited so far?', *Energy Policy*, 35(1): 317–32.

Bhatia, Bela (2005a), 'The Naxalite movement in central Bihar', *Economic and Political Weekly*, 60(10): 1536–43.

Bhatia, Bela (2005b), 'Competing concerns', *Economic and Political Weekly*, 40(47): 4890–3.

Bhowmick, Sharit (1998), 'The labour movement in India: present problems and future perspectives', *Journal of Development Studies*, 30(2): 443–65.

Biao, Xiang (2005), 'Gender, dowry and the migration system of Indian information technology professionals', *Indian Journal of Gender Studies*, 12(2–3): 357–80.

Birchfield, Lauren and Jessica Corsi (2010), 'Between starvation and globalization: realizing the right to food in India', *Michigan Journal of International Law*, 31(1): 691–764.

Bird, Kate and Priya Deshingkar (2009), 'Circular migration in India', *ODI Policy Brief*, No.4 (London: Overseas Development Institute).

Black, Robert, Saul Morris and Jennifer Bryce (2003), 'Where and why are 10 million children dying every year?', *The Lancet*, 361(1): 2226–34.

Bloch, Francis and Vijayendra Rao (2002), 'Terror as a bargaining instrument: a case-study of dowry violence in rural India', *American Economic Review*, 92(4): 1029–43.

Bloom, David E. and Jeffrey G. Williamson (1998), 'Demographic transitions and economic miracles in emerging Asia', *World Bank Economic Review*, 12(3): 419–455.

Bloom, David, David Canning and Sevilla Jaypee (2003), *The Demographic Dividend: A New Perspective on the Economic Consequences of Population Change* (Santa Monica, CA: Rand)

Bonner, A. (1990), *Averting the Apocalypse: Social Movements in India Today* (Durham, NC: Duke University Press).

Bose, Ashish (2007), 'India's disturbing health card', *Economic and Political Weekly*, 42(50): 10–13.

Bose, Prasenjit (2010a), 'Women's reservation in legislatures: a defence', *Economic and Political Weekly*, 45(14): 10–12.

Bose, Prasenjit (ed.) (2010b), *Maoism: A Critique from the Left* (Delhi: LeftWord Books).

Boserup, Ester (1965), *The Conditions of Agricultural Growth: The Economics of Agrarian Change under Population Pressure* (Chicago, IL: Aldine).

Bosworth, Barry and Susan Collins (2007), 'Accounting for growth in China and India', *Working Paper 12943* (Cambridge, MA: National Bureau of Economic Research).

Bosworth, Barry, Susan Collins and Arvind Virmani (2007), 'Sources of growth in the Indian economy', *Working Paper 12901* (Cambridge, MA: National Bureau of Economic Research).

Bourdieu, Pierre (1984), *Distinction: A Social Critique of the Judgement of Taste* (London: Routledge and Kegan Paul).

Bourdieu, Pierre (2001), *Masculine Domination* (Stanford, CA: Stanford University Press).

Bourguignon, Francois (2003), 'The growth elasticity of poverty reduction: explaining heterogeneity across countries and time periods', in Theo Eicher and Stephen Turnovsky (eds), *Inequality and Growth: Theory and Policy Implications* (Cambridge, MA: MIT Press), 3–26.

Brass, Paul (1965), *Factional Politics in an Indian State: The Congress Party in Uttar Pradesh* (Berkeley, CA: University of California Press).

Brass, Paul (1974), *Language, Religion and Politics in North India* (London: Cambridge University Press).

Brass, Paul (1994), *The Politics of India Since Independence*, 2nd edn (Cambridge: Cambridge University Press).

Brass, Paul (1997), *Theft of an Idol: Text and Context in the Representation of Collective Violence* (Princeton, NJ: Princeton University Press).

Brass, Paul (2003a), *The Production of Hindu–Muslim Violence in Contemporary India* (Delhi: Oxford University Press).

Brass, Paul (2003b), 'Response to Ashutosh Varshney' (accessed at <http://www.mail-archive.com>, 4 September 2010).

Brass, Paul (2011) 'Development and the peasantry: land acquisition in Ghaziabad and the cultivators (1950–2009)', in *An Indian Political Life: Charan Singh and Congress Politics, 1937 to 1961*. Delhi: Sage, 133–53.

Breman, Jan (1993), *Beyond Patronage and Exploitation* (New Delhi: Oxford University Press).

Breman, Jan (2001), 'An informalized labour system', *Economic and Political Weekly*, 36(52): 4804–21.

Breman, Jan (2010a), 'India's social question in a state of denial', *Economic and Political Weekly*, 45(23): 42–6.

Breman, Jan (2010b), 'The political economy of agrarian change', in Paul Brass (ed.), *The Routledge Handbook of South Asian Politics* (London: Routledge), 321–36.

Breman, Jan (2010c), *Outcast Labour in Asia: Circulation and Informalisation of the Workforce at the Bottom of the Economy* (New Delhi: Oxford University Press).

Brenner, Robert (1977), 'The origins of capitalist development: a critique of neo-Smithian Marxism', *New Left Review*, 104(1): 25–92.

Brett, Edwin (2009), *Reconstructing Development Theory* (London: Palgrave).

Brosius, Christiane (2010), *India's Middle Class: New Forms of Urban Leisure, Consumption and Prosperity* (New Delhi: Routledge).

Bundy, Charles (1987), 'Street sociology and pavement politics: aspects of youth and student resistance in Cape Town 1985', *Journal of Southern African Studies*, 13(3): 303–30.

Burgess, Robin and Timothy Besley (2003), 'Halving global poverty', *Journal of Economic Perspectives*, 17(3): 3–22.

Butler, Judith (1990), *Gender Trouble* (London: Routledge).

Buvinic, Mayra and Nadia Youssef (1978), '*Women-headed Households: The Ignored Factor in Development Planning*', Report submitted to AID/WID (Washington, DC: International Centre for Research on Women).

CABE (2004), 'Report of the Central Advisory Board of Education'. Retrieved from: <http://www.education.nic.in/cabe/universalisation.pdf> (last accessed 22 January 2007).

Caldwell, John, Palli Hanumantha Reddy and Pat Caldwell (1988), 'The causes of marriage change', in John Caldwell, Pat Caldwell and Palli Hanumantha Reddy (eds), *The Causes of Demographic Change: Experimental Research in South India* (Madison, WI: University of Wisconsin Press), 80–107.

Carter, Anthony T. (1974), *Elite Politics in India: Political Stratification and Political Alliances in Western Maharashtra* (Cambridge: Cambridge University Press).

Castells, Manuel (1997), *The Rise of the Network Society* (Oxford: Blackwell).

Chakravarthy, Sujoy and E. Somanathan (2008), 'Discrimination in an elite labour market? Job placements at IIM-Ahmedabad', *Economic and Political Weekly*, 43(44): 45–50.

Chakravarti, Sudeep (2008), *Red Sun: Travels in Naxalite Country*, revised and updated version (Delhi: Penguin Books).

Chanana, Karuna (2007), 'Globalisation, higher education and gender, changing subject choices of Indian women', *Economic and Political Weekly*, 42(7): 590–8.

Chandhoke, Neera (2005), 'Seeing the state in India', *Economic and Political Weekly*, 40(11): 1033–40.

Chandhoke, Neera (2008), 'Globalization and the Indian state', unpublished mss.

Chandhoke, Neera (2009), 'Civil society in conflict cities', *Economic and Political Weekly*, 44(44): 99–108.

Chandhoke, Neera, Praveen Priyadarshi, Silky Tyagi and Neha Khanna (2007), 'The Displaced of Ahmedabad', *Economic and Political Weekly*, 42(43): 10–14.

Chandra, Kanchan (2004), *Why Ethnic Parties Succeed: Patronage and Ethnic Head Counts in India* (New York: Cambridge University Press).

Chandrasekhar, C. P. (2007), 'Progress of "reform" and retrogression of agriculture'. Retrieved from: <http://www.macroscan.org/anl/apr07/anl250407Agriculture.htm> (last accessed 21 June 2010).

Chandrasekhar, C. P. and Jayati Ghosh (2002), *The Market that Failed: A Decade of Neoliberal Economic Reforms in India* (New Delhi: Leftword).

Chandrasekhar, C. P. and Jayati Ghosh (2007), 'What explains the high GDP growth?', *Business Line* (11 September).

Chandrasekhar, C. P., Jayati Ghosh and A. Roychowdhury (2006), 'The demographic dividend and young India's economic future', *Economic and Political Weekly*, 41(49): 5055–64.

Chang, Ha-Joon (2010), *23 Things They Don't Tell You About Capitalism* (London: Penguin).

Chant, Sylvia (2007), *Gender, Generation and Poverty: Exploring the "Feminisation of Poverty" in Africa, Asia and Latin America* (Aldershot: Edward Elgar).

Chari, Anurekha (2009), 'Gendered citizenship and women's movement', *Economic and Political Weekly*, 44(17): 47–57.

Chatterjee, Partha (1986), *Nationalist Thought and the Colonial World: A Derivative Discourse* (London: Zed Books).

Chatterjee, Partha (1993), *The Nation and Its Fragments: Colonial and Postcolonial Histories* (Princeton, NJ: Princeton University Press).

Chatterjee, Partha (1997), *A Possible World: Essays in Political Criticism* (New Delhi: Oxford University Press).

Chatterjee, Partha (1998), 'Beyond the nation or within?', *Social Text* 56(3): 57–69.

Chatterjee, Partha (2004), *The Politics of the Governed: Reflections on Popular Politics in Most of the World* (New Delhi: Permanent Black).

Chatterjee, Partha (2008), 'Democracy and economic transformation in India', *Economic and Political Weekly*, 43(16): 53–62.

Chatterjee, Upamanyu (2000), *The Mammaries of the Welfare State* (New Delhi: Penguin).

Chattopadhyay, Raghabendra and Esther Duflo (2004), 'Women as policy makers: evidence from a randomized policy experiment in India', *Econometrica*, 72(5): 1409–33.

Chattopadhyay, Suhrid Sanka (2007), 'Another land row', *Frontline*, 24(1): 36–40.

Chattopadhyay, Suhrid Sanka (2008), '"Singur's loss"', *Frontline*, 25 (22): 37–40.

Chaudhuri, Shubham (2007), 'What difference does a constitutional amendment make? The 1994 Panchayati Raj Act and the attempt to revitalize local government in India', in Pranab Bardhan and Dilip Mookherjee (eds), *Decentralization and Local Government in Developing Countries: A Comparative Perspective* (Delhi: Oxford University Press), 153–202.

Chaudhuri, Shubham and Patrick Heller (2003), *The Plasticity of Participation: Evidence from a Participatory Governance Experiment*, mimeo (New York and Rhode Island: Columbia and Brown Universities).

Chaudhury, Nazmul, Jeffrey Hammer, Michael Kremer, Karthik Muralidharan and Halsey Rogers (2005), 'Teacher absence in India: a snapshot', *Journal of the European Economic Association*, 3(2–3): 658–67.

Chaudhury, Nazmul, Jeffrey Hammer, Michael Kremer, Karthik Muralidharan and Halsey Rogers (2006), 'Missing in action: teacher and health worker absence in developing countries', *Journal of Economic Perspectives*, 20(1): 91–116.

Chavan, Pallavi (2008), 'Gender inequality in banking services', *Economic and Political Weekly*, 43(47): 18–21.

Chen, Marty (ed.) (1998), *Widows in India: Social Neglect and Public Action* (New Delhi: Sage).

Chen, Shaohua and Martin Ravallion (2008), 'The developing world is poorer than we thought, but no less successful in the fight against poverty', *World Bank: Policy Research Working Paper 4703* (Washington, DC: World Bank).

Chenery, Hollis, Montek Ahluwalia, Clive Bell, John Duloy and Richard Jolly (1974), *Redistribution with Growth* (London: Oxford University Press and World Bank).

Chibber, Pradeep (2003), *Why Some Women are Politically Active: The Household, Public Space, and Political Participation in India*, mimeo. Retrieved from: <http://www.worldvaluesurvey.com/Upload/5_india-gender_2.pdf> (last accessed 14 May 2010).

Chibber, Vivek (2003), *Locked in Place: State-Building and Late-Industrialisation in India* (Princeton, NJ: Princeton University Press).

Chopra, Deepta (2011), 'Policy making in India: a dynamic process of statecraft', *Pacific Affairs,* 84(1): 89–107.

Chopra, Radhika and Patricia Jeffrey (2005), *Educational Regimes in Contemporary India* (Delhi: Sage).

Chopra, Surabhi (2009), 'Holding the state accountable for hunger', *Economic and Political Weekly*, 44(33): 8–12.

Chowdhry, Prem (1994), *The Veiled Woman: Shifting Gender Relations in Rural Haryana, 1880–1990* (New Delhi: Oxford University Press).

Chowdhry, Prem (1997), 'A matter of two shares: a daughter's claim to patrilineal property in rural north India', *Indian Economic and Social History Review*, 34(3): 289–311.

Chowdhry, Prem (2009) '"First our jobs then our girls": the dominant caste perception on the "rising" Dalits', *Modern Asian Studies* 43(2): 437–79.

Cincotta, Richard P., Robert Engelman and Danile Anastasion (2003), *The Security Demographic: Population and Civil Conflict after the Cold War* (Washington, DC: Population Action International).

Ciotti, Manuela (2006), '"In the past we were a bit 'Chamar'": education as a self- and community-engineering process in northern India', *The Journal of the Royal Anthropological Institute*, 12(4): 899–916.

Ciotti, Manuela (2010) 'Futurity in words: low-caste women political activists' self-representation and post-Dalit scenarios in north India', *Contemporary South Asia*, 18(1): 43–56.

Clark, Gregory and Susan Wolcott (2003), 'One polity, many countries: economic growth in India, 1873–2000', in Dani Rodrik (ed.), *In Search of Prosperity: Analytic Narratives on Economic Growth* (Princeton, NJ: Princeton University Press), 53–79.

Clark-Decès, Isabelle (2011), 'The decline of the Dravidian kinship in local perspectives', in Isabelle Clark-Decès (ed.), *A Companion to the Anthropology of India* (Oxford: Blackwell), 517–35.

Coale, Ansley J. and Edgar M. Hoover (1958), *Population Growth and Economic Development in Low Income Countries* (Princeton, NJ: Princeton University Press).

Coelho, Karen and T. Venkat (2009), 'The politics of civil society: neighbourhood associationism in Chennai', *Economic and Political Weekly*, 44(26–7): 358–67.

Cohn, Bernard (1961), 'From Indian status to British contact', *The Journal of Economic History*, 21(4): 613–28.

Coleman, James S. (1965), *Education and Political Development* (Princeton, NJ: Princeton University Press).

Collier, Paul (2007), *The Bottom Billion: Why the Poorest Countries are Failing and What Can Be Done about it* (Oxford: Oxford University Press).

Collier, Paul and Anke Hoeffler (2004), 'Greed and grievance in civil war', *Oxford Economic Papers,* 56(4): 563–95.

Collier, Paul, Anke Hoeffler and Dominic Rohner (2009), 'Beyond greed and grievance: feasibility and civil war', *Oxford Economic Papers*, 61(1): 1–27.

Connelly, Matthew (2007), *Fatal Misconception: The Struggle to Control World Population* (Cambridge, MA: Belknap-Harvard).

Corbridge, Stuart (1988), 'The ideology of tribal economy and society: politics in the Jharkhand, 1950–1980', *Modern Asian Studies*, 22(1): 1–42.

Corbridge, Stuart (1991), 'The poverty of planning or planning for poverty? An eye to economic liberalisation in India', *Progress in Human Geography*, 15(4): 467–76.

Corbridge, Stuart (2000) 'Competing inequalities: the scheduled tribes and the reservations system in India's Jharkhand', *Journal of Asian Studies*, 59(1): 63–85.

Corbridge, Stuart (2002), 'Cartographies of loathing and desire: the BJP, the bomb and the political spaces of Hindu nationalism', in Yale Ferguson and R. J. Barry Jones (eds), *Political Space: Frontiers of Change and Governance in a Globalizing World* (Albany, NY: State University of New York Press), 151–69.

Corbridge, Stuart (2010), 'The political economy of development in India since Independence', in Paul Brass (ed.), *The Routledge Handbook of South Asian Politics* (London: Routledge), 305–20.

Corbridge, Stuart (2011), 'The contested geographies of federalism in post-reform India', Chapter 5 in Sanjay Ruparelia, Sanjay Reddy, John Harriss and Stuart Corbridge (eds), *Understanding India's New Political Economy: A Great Transformation?* (London: Routledge), 66–80.

Corbridge, Stuart and John Harriss (2000), *Reinventing India: Economic Liberalization, Hindu Nationalism and Popular Democracy* (Cambridge: Polity).

Corbridge, Stuart, Glyn Williams, Manoj Srivastava and Réne Véron (2005), *Seeing the State: Governance and Governmentality in India* (Cambridge: Cambridge University Press).

Cox, Oliver (1948), *Caste, Class and Race* (New York: Doubleday).

Cramer, Christopher (2006), *Civil War is Not a Stupid Thing: Accounting for Violence in Developing Countries* (London: Hurst).

Crook, Richard C. and Alan Sverrisson (2003), 'Does decentralization contribute to poverty reduction?', in Peter Houtzager and Mick Moore (eds), *Changing Paths: International Development and the New Politics of Inclusion* (Ann Arbor, MI: University of Michigan Press), 233–59.

Cross, Jamie (2009), 'From dreams to discontent: educated young men and the politics of work at a special economic zone in Andhra Pradesh', *Contributions to Indian Sociology*, 43(3): 351–79.

Currie, Bob (1998), 'Public action and its limits: re-examining the politics of hunger alleviation in eastern India', *Third World Quarterly,* 19(5): 873–92.

Da Costa, Dia (2010), *Development Dramas: Reimagining Rural Political Action in Eastern India.* (London: Routledge).

Dahl, Robert (1961), *Who Governs? Democracy and Power in an American City* (New Haven, CT: Yale University Press).

Dandekar, V. M. and N. Rath (1971), 'Poverty in India: dimensions and trends', *Economic and Political Weekly*, 6(1): 25–48, and 6(2): 106–46.

Das, Amarendra (2007), 'How far have we come in Sarva Siksha Abhiyan', *Economic and Political Weekly*, 42(1): 21–3.

Das, Gurcharan (2002), *India Unbound: The Social and Economic Revolution from Independence to the Global Information Age* (New York: Anchor Books).

Das, Jishnu and Jeffrey Hammer (2004), 'Strained mercy: quality of medical care in Delhi', *Economic and Political Weekly*, 39(9): 951–64.

Das, Prafulla (2006), 'Churning in Orissa', *The Hindu* (13 January).

Das, Ritanjan (2012), 'The politics of industrial change in West Bengal, India', unpublished PhD thesis (London: London School of Economics).

Dasgupta, Jyotirindra (2001), 'India's federal design and multicultural national construction', in Atul Kohli (ed.), *The Success of India's Democracy* (Cambridge: Cambridge University Press), 49–77.

Datt, Gaurav (1999), 'Has poverty in India declined since the economic reforms?' *Economic and Political Weekly*, 34(50): 11–17.

Datt, Gaurav and Martin Ravallion (1998), 'Why have some Indian states done better than others at reducing rural poverty?', *Economica*, 65(257): 17–38.

Datt, Gaurav and Martin Ravallion (2002), 'Is India's economic growth leaving the poor behind', *Journal of Economic Perspectives*, 16(3): 89–108.

Datt, Gaurav and Martin Ravallion (2009), 'Has India's economic growth become more pro-poor in the wake of economic reforms?', *World Bank Policy Research Working Paper* 5103 (Washington, DC: World Bank).

Datt, Gaurav and Martin Ravallion (2010), 'Shining for the poor too?', *Economic and Political Weekly*, 65(7): 55–60.

Davis, Kingsley (1951), *The Population of India and Pakistan* (Princeton, NJ: Princeton University Press).

Davis, Mike (2001), *Late Victorian Holocausts: El Niño Famines and the Making of the Third World* (London: Verso).

Davis, Mike (2006), *Planet of Slums* (London: Verso).

Deaton, Angus (2003), 'Health, inequality, and economic development', *Journal of Economic Literature*, 41: 113–58.

Deaton, Angus and Valerie Kozel (2005), 'Data and dogma: the great Indian poverty debate', *World Bank Research Observer*, 20(2): 177–99.

Debroy, Bibek, Shubhashis Gangopadhyay and Laveesh Bhandari (2004), 'An Economic Freedom Index for India's states', in Bibkek Dubroy (ed.), *Agenda for Improving Governance* (New Delhi: Academic Foundation with Rajiv Gandhi Institute for Contemporary Studies), 611–41.

Deliège, Robert (1999), *The Untouchables of India* (Oxford: Berg).

De Long, Brad (2003), 'India since Independence: an analytic growth narrative', in Dani Rodrik (ed.), *In Search of Prosperity: Analytic Narratives on Economic Growth* (Princeton, NJ: Princeton University Press), 184–204.

Denoon, David B. (1998), 'Cycles in Indian economic liberalization, 1966–96', *Comparative Politics*, 31(1): 43–60.

Deshingkar, Priya and John Farrington (eds) (2009), *Circular Migration and Multilocational Livelihood Strategies in Rural India* (Delhi: Oxford University Press).

Deshpande, Ashwini (2010), 'Women in the labour force', in Kaushik Basu and Annemie Maertens (eds), *The Concise Oxford Companion to Economics in India* (New Delhi: Oxford University Press), 460–4.

Deshpande, Ashwini and Katherine Newman (2007), 'Where the path leads: the role of caste in post-university employment expectations', *Economic and Political Weekly* 42 (41): 4133-4140

Deshpande, Ashwini and Katherine Newman (2010), 'Where the path leads: the role of caste in post-university employment expectations', in Sukhadeo Thorat and Katherine S. Newman (eds), *Blocked by Caste: Economic Discrimination in Modern India* (New Delhi: Oxford University Press), 88–122.

De Souza, Peter R., Sanjay Kumar and Sandeep Shastri (2009), *Indian Youth in a Transforming World* (New Delhi: Sage).

Dev, Mahendra S. (2008), *Inclusive Growth in India: Agriculture, Poverty and Human Development* (Delhi: Oxford University Press).

Di John, Jonathan (2009), *From Windfall to Curse? Oil and Industrialization in Venezuela, 1920 to the Present* (College Station: Penn State Press).

Dirks, Nicholas (2001), *Castes of Mind: Colonialism and the Making of Modern India* (Princeton, NJ: Princeton University Press).

Diwarkar, Vaishali (2009), '*Maya machhindra* and *amar jyoti*: reaffirmation of the normative', *Economic and Political Weekly*, 44(17): 75–84.

Dobb, Maurice (1963), *Economic Growth and Underdeveloped Countries* (London: Lawrence and Wishart).

Dollar, David and Aart Kraay (2002), 'Growth is good for the poor', *Journal of Economic Growth*, 7(3): 195–202.

Dollar, David, Raymond Fisman and Roberta Gatti (2001), 'Are women really the "fairer" sex? Corruption and women in government', *Journal of Economic Behavior and Organisation*, 46(4): 423–9.

Donaldson, John (2008), 'Growth is good for whom, when, how? Economic growth and poverty reduction in exceptional cases', *World Development* 36(11): 2127–43.

Dong, Xiao-yuan, Paul Bowles and Hongqin Chang (2010), 'Managing liberalization and globalization in rural China: trends in rural labour allocation, income and inequality', *Global Labour Journal*, 1(1): 31–55.

Donner, Henrike (2002), 'One's own marriage: love marriages in a Calcutta neighbourhood,' *South Asia Research,* 22(1): 79–94.

Donner, Henrike (2006), 'Committed mothers and well-adjusted children: privatisation, early-years education and motherhood in Calcutta', *Modern Asian Studies*, 40: 371–95.

Dore, Robert (1976), *The Diploma Disease: Education, Qualification and Development* (Berkeley, CA: University of California Press).

Doron, Assa (2010), 'Caste away: subaltern engagement with the modern Indian state', *Modern Asian Studies* , 44(4): 753–83.

Drèze, Jean (2002), 'Democratic practice and social inequality in India', *Journal of Asian and African Studies,* 37(2): 6–37.

Drèze, Jean (2004), 'An unconventional convention', *Frontline*, 21(14): 124–8.

Drèze, Jean (2010), 'Employment guarantee and the right to work', in Niraja Gopal Jayal and Pratap Bhanu Mehta (eds), *The Oxford Companion to Politics in India* (Delhi: Oxford University Press), 510–18.

Drèze, Jean (2011), 'A notional advisory council?', *The Hindu* (10 January).

Drèze, Jean and Haris Gazdar (1997) 'Uttar Pradesh: the burden of inertia', in Jean Drèze and Amartya Sen (eds), *Indian Development: Selected Regional Perspectives* (New Delhi: Oxford University Press), 33–128.

Drèze, Jean and Reetika Khera (2009), 'The battle for employment guarantee', *Frontline*, 26(1): 4–26.

Drèze, Jean and Amartya Sen (1995), *India: Economic Development and Social Opportunity* (Oxford and New Delhi: Oxford University Press).

Drèze, Jean and Amartya Sen (2002), 'Democratic practice and social inequality in India', *Journal of Asian and African Studies*, 37(2): 6–37.

Dube, Siddarth (1998), *In the Land of Poverty: Memoirs of an Indian Family 1947–1997* (London: Zed Books).

Duflo, Esther and Petia Topolova (2004), 'Unappreciated service: performance, perceptions and women leaders in India (unpublished)', mimeo. Retrieved from: <http://www.povertyactionlab.org/sites/default/files/publications/66_Duflo_Topolova_Unappreciated_Service.pdf> (last accessed 20 July 2010).

Duflo, Esther, Michael Greenstone and Rema Hanna (2008), 'Cooking stoves, indoor air pollution and respiratory health in rural Orissa', *Economic and Political Weekly*, 43(32): 71–6.

Dumont, Louis (1970), *Homo Hierarchicus: The Caste System and Its Implications* (London: Weidenfeld and Nicolson).

Duncan, Iain (1997), 'Agricultural innovation and political change in north India: the Lok Dal in Uttar Pradesh', *Journal of Peasant Studies*, 24(4): 246–68.

Duncan, Iain (1999), 'Dalits and politics in rural north India: the Bahujan Samaj Party in Uttar Pradesh', *Journal of Peasant Studies*, 27(1): 35–60.

Dyson, Jane (2008), 'Harvesting identities: youth, work and gender in the Indian Himalayas', *Annals of the Association of American Geographers*, 98(1): 160–79.

Dyson, Tim (2010), 'Growing regional variation: demographic change and its implications', in Anthony Heath and Roger Jeffery (eds), *Diversity and Change in Modern India: Economic, Social and Political Approaches* (Oxford: Oxford University Press and The British Academy), 19–46.

Dyson, Tim and Mick Moore (1983), 'On kinship structure, female autonomy and demographic behaviour in India', *Population and Development Review*, 9(1): 35–60.

Easterly, William (2009), 'The anarchy of success', *New York Review of Books*, 56(15) (8 October).

Easterly, William and Levine, Robert (2003), 'Tropics, germs and crops: how endowments influence economic development', *Journal of Monetary Economics,* 50(1): 3–39.

The Economist (2010), 'Crop Circles', *The Economist* (13 March), Leader article.

'Editorial' (2002), *Frontline*, 19 (26). Retrieved from: <http://www.flonetcom.com> (last accessed 27 August 2010).

'Editorial' (2007), 'Restoring rights', *Economic and Political Weekly*, 42(1) (6 January): 4–5.

'Editorial' (2009a), 'Beyond the Security-Centric Approach', *Economic and Political Weekly*, 44(8): 6.

'Editorial' (2009b), 'Under the shadow of the gun', *Economic and Political Weekly*, 44(46): 6.

'Editorial' (2010a), 'Jobless growth', *Economic and Political Weekly*, 45(39): 7–8.

'Editorial' (2010b), 'Trivialising food security', *Economic and Political Weekly*, 45(16): 7–8.

Ehrlich, Paul R. and Anne H. Ehrlich (1970), *Population, Resources, Environment: Issues in Human Ecology* (San Francisco, CA: Freeman).

Ellis, Rowan (2010), 'Civil society, savage space: spaces of urban governance in Chennai, India', unpublished PhD dissertation (Washington, DC: University of Washington, Department of Geography).

Emmott, Bill (2008), *Rivals: How the Power Struggle between China, India and Japan Will Shape Our Next Decade* (London: Allen Lane).

Engerman, Stanley and Kenneth Sokoloff (1997), 'Factor endowments, institutions, and differential paths of growth among New World economies: a view from economic historians of the United States,' in Stephen Haber (ed.), *How Latin America Fell Behind* (Stanford, CA: Stanford University Press), 260–306.

Engineer, Asghar Ali (ed.) (1984), *Communal Riots in Post-Independence India* (Hyderabad: Sangam Books).

Engineer, Asghar Ali (1995), *Lifting the Veil: Communal Violence and Communal Harmony in Contemporary India* (New Delhi: Sangam Books).

Engineer, Asghar Ali (2004), 'Communal riots, 2003', *Economic and Political Weekly*, 39(1): 21–4.

Enke, Stephen (1971), 'Economic consequences of rapid population growth', *The Economic Journal*, 81(324): 800–11.

Epstein, Scarlett (1973), *South India: Yesterday, Today and Tomorrow* (London: Macmillan).

Eswaran, Mukesh, Ashok Kotwal, Bharat Ramaswami and Wilima Wadhwa (2009), 'Sectoral labour flows and agricultural wages in India, 1983–2004: has growth trickled down?', *Economic and Political Weekly*, 44(2): 46–55.

Evans, Peter (1995), *Embedded Autonomy: States and Industrial Transformation* (Princeton, NJ: Princeton University Press).

Faust, David and Richa Nagar (2001) 'English-medium education, social fracturing and the politics of development in postcolonial India', *Economic and Political Weekly*, 36(30): 2878–83.

Fearon, James and David Laitin (2003), 'Ethnicity, insurgency and Civil War', *American Political Science Review*, 97(1): 75–90.

Ferguson, James (2006), *Global Shadows: Africa in the Neoliberal World Order* (Durham, NC: Duke University Press).

Fernandes, Leela (2004), 'The politics of forgetting: class politics, state power and the restructuring of urban space in India', *Urban Studies*, 41(12): 2415–30.

Fernandes, Leela (2006), *India's New Middle Class: Democratic Politics in an Era of Reform* (Minneapolis, MN: University of Minnesota Press).

Fernandes, Leela and Patrick Heller (2006), 'Hegemonic aspirations: new middle class politics and India's democracy in comparative perspective', *Critical Asian Studies*, 38(4): 495–521.

Fernandes, Walter (nd), 'Background note' to petition against operation green hunt. Retrieved from: <http://www.sanhati.org> (last accessed 11 June 2010).

Folbre, Nancy (1986), 'Hearts and spades: paradigms of household economics', *World Development*, 14(20): 245–55.

Forbes, Geraldine (1996), *Women in Modern India* (Cambridge: Cambridge University Press).

Foster, James, Joel Greer and Erik Thorbecke (1984), 'A class of decomposable poverty measures', *Econometrica*, 52(3): 761–5.

Fosu, Augustin Kwasi (2009), 'Inequality and the impact of growth on poverty: comparative evidence for sub-Saharan Africa', *Journal of Development Studies*, 45: 726–45.

Frankel, Francine (2005), *India's Political Economy, 1947–2004* (Delhi: Oxford University Press).

Frieden, Jeffry (2006), *Global Capitalism: Its Fall and Rise in the Twentieth Century* (New York: W. W. Norton).

Friedman, Thomas (2005), *The World is Flat: A Brief History of the Twenty-first Century* (New York: Farrar, Strauss and Giroux).

Froerer, Peggy (2007), *Religious Division and Social Conflict: The Emergence of Hindu Nationalism in Rural India* (Delhi: Social Science Press).

Frøystad, Kathinka (2005), *Blended Boundaries: Caste, Class and Shifting Faces of 'Hinduness' in a North Indian City* (New Delhi: Oxford University Press).

Fuller, Christopher J. (1996), 'Introduction: caste today', in Chris J. Fuller (ed.), *Caste Today* (New Delhi: Oxford University Press), 1–31.

Fuller, Christopher J. (2001), 'The "Vinayaka Chaturthi" Festival and Hindutva in Tamil Nadu', *Economic and Political Weekly*, 38(19): 1607–16.

Fuller, Christopher J. (2003), *The Renewal of the Priesthood: Modernity and Traditionalism in a South Indian Temple* (Princeton, NJ: Princeton University Press).

Fuller, Christopher J. (2004), *The Camphor Flame: Popular Hinduism and Society*, 2nd edn (Princeton, NJ: Princeton University Press).

Fuller, Christopher J. and John Harriss (2005), 'Globalizing Hinduism: a "traditional" guru and modern businessmen in Chennai', in J. Assayag and C. Fuller (eds), *Globalizing India: Perspectives from Below* (London: Anthem Press), 211–36.

Fuller, Christopher J. and Haripriya Narasimhan (2007), 'Information technology professionals and the new-rich middle class in Chennia (Madras)', *Modern Asian Studies*, 41(1): 121–50.

Fuller, Christopher J. and Haripriya Narasimhan (2008), 'Companionate marriage in India: the changing marriage system in a middle-class Brahman subcaste', *Journal of the Royal Anthropological Institute*, 14(4): 736–54.

Galanter, Marc (1984), *Competing Equalities: Law and the Backward Classes in India* (New Delhi: Oxford University Press).

Ganapathy (2007), 'Interview with Ganapathy, General Secretary, CPI (Maoist)'. Retrieved from: <http://www.satp.org>.

Ganguly, Sanjoy (2010), *Jana Sanskriti: Forum Theatre and Democracy in India* (New York: Routledge).

Ganguly-Scrase, Ruchira and Timothy J. Scrase (2009), *Globalization and the Middle Classes in India: The Social and Cultural Impact of Neoliberal Reforms*. London and New York: Routledge

Gayer, Laurent and Christophe Jaffrelot (2009), *Armed Militias of South Asia: Fundamentalists, Maoists and Separatists* (London: Hurst and Company).

Geddes, Barbara (2003), *Paradigms and Sand Castles: Theory Building and Research Design in Comparative Politics* (Ann Arbor, MI: University of Michigan Press).

Ghate, Chetan and Stephen Wright (2009), 'The V-factor: distribution, timing and correlates of the great Indian growth turnaround', *Jena Research Papers in Economics, 2009–10* (Jena: Max Planck Institute of Economics).

Ghate, Chetan, Stephen Wright and Tatiana Fic (2010), 'India's growth turna-round', in Kaushik Basu and Annemie Maertens (eds), *The Concise Oxford Companion to Economics in India* (New Delhi: Oxford University Press), 33–40.

Ghertner, Asher (2010) 'Calculating without numbers: aesthetic governmentality in Delhi's slums', *Economy and Society*, 39(2): 185–217.

Ghosh, Asha (2005), 'Public-private or a private public? Promised partnership of the Bangalore Agenda Task Force', *Economic and Political Weekly*, 40(47): 4914–22.

Ghosh, Jayati (1998), 'Liberalization debates', in Terence Byres (ed.), *The Indian Economy: Major Debates since Independence* (New Delhi: Oxford University Press), 295–334.

Ghosh, Jayati (2011a), 'The cash option', *Frontline*, 28(5); at: <http://www.frontlineonnet.com> (last accessed 29 April 2011).

Ghosh, Jayati (2011b), 'Is the MNREGS affecting rural wages?', *Macroscan* (4 February). Retrieved from: <http://www.macroscan.org> (last accessed 2 May 2011).

Ghosh, Kaushik (2006) 'Between global flows and local dams: indigenous-ness, locality, and the transnational sphere in Jharkhand, India', *Cultural Anthropology*, 21(4): 501–29.

Gill, Kaveri (2010), *Of Poverty and Plastic: Scavenging and Scrap Trading Entrepreneurs in India's Urban Informal Economy* (New Delhi: Oxford University Press).

Goldman Sachs (2010), 'Is this the BRICs Decade?', *BRICs Monthly*, 10(3). Retrieved from: <http://www2.goldmansachs.com> (last accessed 5 May 2011).

Goody, Jack (1971), *Technology, Tradition and the State in Africa* (Cambridge: Cambridge University Press).

Gooptu, Nandini (2001), *The Politics of the Urban Poor in Early Twentieth-century India*. (Cambridge: Cambridge University Press).

Gooptu, Nandini (2007), 'Economic liberalization, work and democracy: indus-trial decline and urban politics in Kolkata', *Economic and Political Weekly*, 42(25): 1922–33.

Gooptu, Nandini (2011), 'Economic liberalization, urban politics and the poor', in Sanjay Ruparelia, Sanjay Reddy, John Harriss and Stuart Corbridge (eds), *Understanding India's New Political Economy: A Great Transformation?* (London: Routledge), 35–48.

Gorringe, Hugo (2010), 'Shifting the grindstone of caste? Decreasing dependency amongst Dalit labourers in Tamilnadu', in Barbara Harriss-White and Judith Heyer (eds), *The Comparative Political Economy of Development: Africa and South Asia* (London: Routledge), 248–66.

Gould, Harold (1972), 'Educational structures and political processes in Faizabad district, Uttar Pradesh', in Susanne Hoeber Rudolph and Lloyd I. Rudolph (eds), *Education and Politics in India* (Cambridge, MA: Harvard University Press), 83–94.

Government of India (1988), *National Perspective Plan for Women* (New Delhi:

Department of Women and Child Development, Ministry of Human Resource Development).

Government of India (2006a), *Eleventh Five Year Plan* (New Delhi: Planning Commission).

Government of India (2006b), *Economic Survey, 2005–2006* (New Delhi: Ministry of Finance).

Government of India (2008), *Statistical Pocket Book for 2008* (New Delhi: Planning Commission).

Government of India (2009a), *Gender Human Development Indices: Recasting the Gender Development Index and Gender Empowerment Measure for India: Summary Report* (New Delhi: Ministry of Women and Child Development).

Government of India (2009b), *Report of the National Commission for Enterprises in the Unorganised Sector* (New Delhi: National Commission for Enterprises in the Unorganised Sector).

Gragnolati, Michele, Meera Shekar, Monica Das Gupta, Casryn Bredenkamp and Yi-Kyoung Lee (2005), 'India's undernourished children: a call for reform and action', *World Bank Health, Nutrition and Population Discussion Paper* (Washington, DC: World Bank).

Graham, Bruce (1990), *Hindu Nationalism and Indian Politics: The Origins and Development of the Bharatiya Jana Sangh* (Cambridge: Cambridge University Press).

Gramsci, Antonio (1971), *Selections from the Prison Notebooks*, ed. and trans. Q. Hoare and G. Nowell-Smith (London: Lawrence and Wishart).

Gramsci Antonio and David Forgacs (1998), *A Gramsci Reader* (London: Lawrence and Wishart).

Grewal, P. M. S. (2010), 'Indian maoists: flawed strategy and perverted praxis', in Prasenjit Bose (ed.), *Maoism: A Critique from the Left* (Delhi: LeftWord Books).

Grindle, Merilee (2000), *Audacious Reforms: Institutional Invention and Democracy in Latin America* (Baltimore, MD: Johns Hopkins University Press).

Guha, Ramachandra (1983), 'Forestry in British and post-British India: a historical analysis', *Economic and Political Weekly*, 18(44): 1882–96.

Guha, Ramachandra (1989), *The Unquiet Woods: Ecological Change and Peasant Resistance in the Himalaya* (New Delhi: Oxford University Press).

Guha, Ramachandra (2007a), 'Adivasis, Naxalites and Indian democracy', *Economic and Political Weekly*, 42(32): 3305–12.

Guha, Ramachandra (2007b), *India after Gandhi: The History of the World's Largest Democracy* (London: Macmillan).

Guhan, S. (1980), 'Rural poverty: policy and play acting', *Economic and Political Weekly*, 15(47): 1975–82.

Gupta, Dipankar (2000), *Interrogating Caste: Understanding Hierarchy and Difference in Indian Society* (New Delhi: Penguin).

Gupta, Dipankar (2005), 'Whither the Indian village: culture and agriculture in "rural" India', *Economic and Political Weekly*, 40(8): 751–8.

Gupta, Smita (2010), 'Searching for a third way in Dantewada', *Economic and Political Weekly*, 45(16): 12–14.

Gupta, Tilak D. (2006), 'Maoism in India: ideology, programme and armed struggle', *Economic and Political Weekly*, 61(2): 3172–6.

de Haan, Arjan (2008), 'Citizens, identity and public policy: affirmative action in India', in Anis Dani and Arjan de Haan (eds), *Inclusive States: Social Policy and Structural Inequalities* (Washington, DC: World Bank), 225–47.

Habermas, Jurgen (1965), *The Structural Transformation of the Public Sphere: An Inquiry into a Category of Bourgeois Society* (Cambridge: Cambridge University Press).

Haggard, Stephan and Steven Webb (eds) (1994), *Voting for Reform: Democracy, Political Liberalization and Economic Adjustment* (New York: Oxford University Press and World Bank).

Hansen, Thomas. B. (1996a) 'Recuperating masculinity: Hindu nationalism, violence, and the exorcism of the Muslim "other"', *Critique of Anthropology*, 16(22): 137–72.

Hansen, Thomas B. (1996b), 'The vernacularisation of Hindutva: the BJP and the Shiv Sena in rural Maharashtra', *Contributions to Indian Sociology*, 30(2): 177–214.

Hansen, Thomas B. (1996c), 'Globalisation and nationalist imaginations: Hindutva's promise of equality through difference', *Economic and Political Weekly*, 31(10): 603–16.

Hansen, Thomas B. (1999), *The Saffron Wave: Democracy and Hindu Nationalism in Modern India* (Princeton, NJ: Princeton University Press).

Hansen, Thomas B. (2002), *Wages of Violence: Naming and Identity in Postcolonial Mumbai* (Princeton, NJ: Princeton University Press).

Hansen, Thomas B. and Christophe Jaffrelot (eds) (1998), *The BJP and the Compulsions of Politics in India* (Delhi: Oxford University Press).

Haque, T. (2003), 'Reforms for agricultural growth and rural development', *Economic and Political Weekly*, 38(48): 5031–3.

Harberger, Arnold (1993), 'Secrets of success: a handful of heroes', *American Economic Review*, 83(2): 343–50.

Harris, Jose (ed.) (2003), *Civil Society in British History: Ideas, Institutions and Identities* (Oxford: Oxford University Press).

Harrison, Selig (1960), *India: The Most Dangerous Decades* (Princeton, NJ: Princeton University Press).

Harriss, Barbara (1981), *Transitional Trade and Rural Development* (New Delhi: Vikas).

Harriss, Barbara (1985), 'Agrarian change and the merchant state in Tamil Nadu', in Tim Bayliss-Smith and Sudhir Wanmali (eds), *Understanding Green Revolutions: Agrarian Change and Development Planning in South Asia* (Cambridge: Cambridge University Press), 53–83.

Harriss, Barbara and Elizabeth Watson (1987), 'The sex ratio in South Asia', in Janet Momsen and Janet Townsend (eds), *Geography of Gender in the Third World* (London: Edward Arnold).

Harriss, John (1982), *Capitalism and Peasant Farming: Agrarian Structure and Ideology in Northern Tamil Nadu* (New Delhi: Oxford University Press).

Harriss, John (1987), 'The state in retreat. Why has India experienced such half-hearted liberalisation in the 1980s?', *IDS Bulletin*, 18(4): 31–8.

Harriss, John (1992), 'Does the Depressor still work? Agrarian structure and development in India: a review of evidence and argument', *Journal of Peasant Studies*, 19(2): 189–227.

Harriss, John (1993), 'What is happening in rural West Bengal? Agrarian reform, growth and redistribution', *Economic and Political Weekly*, 28(24): 1237–47.

Harriss, John (2002), *Depoliticizing Development: The World Bank and Social Capital* (London: Anthem).

Harriss, John (2003a), 'The great tradition globalizes: reflections on two studies of "the industrial leaders" of Madras', *Modern Asian Studies*, 7(2): 327–62.

Harriss, John (2003b), 'Do political regimes matter? Poverty reduction and regime differences across India', in Peter Houtzager and Mick Moore (eds), *Changing Paths: International Development and the New Politics of Inclusion* (Ann Arbor, MI: University of Michigan Press), 204–32.

Harriss, John (2003c), '"Widening the radius of trust": ethnographic explorations of trust and Indian business', *Journal of the Royal Anthropological Institute*, 9(4): 755–73.

Harriss, John (2006) 'Middle-class activism and the politics of the informal working class', *Critical Asian Studies* 38(4): 445–65.

Harriss, John (2007), 'Antimonies of empowerment: observations on civil society, politics and urban governance in India', *Economic and Political Weekly*, 42(26): 2716–24.

Harriss, John (2010a), 'Globalization(s) and labour in China and India: introductory reflections', *Global Labour Journal*, 1(1): 3–11.

Harriss, John (2010b), 'Participation and contestation in urban governance in India', *Simons Working Paper No.2* (Vancouver, BC: School for International Studies, Simon Fraser University).

Harriss, John (2011), 'How far have India's economic reforms been "guided by compassion and justice"? Social policy in the neoliberal era', in Sanjay Ruparelia, Sanjay Reddy, John Harriss and Stuart Corbridge (eds), *Understanding India's New Political Economy: A Great Transformation?* (London: Routledge), 127-40

Harriss, John and Stuart Corbridge (2010), 'The continuing reinvention of India', in Chandan Sengupta and Stuart Corbridge (eds), *Democracy, Development and Decentralisation in India* (New Delhi: Routledge), 38–59.

Harriss, John, J. Jeyaranjan and K. Nagaraj (2010) 'Land, labour and caste politics in rural Tamil Nadu in the 20th century: Iruvelpattu (1916–2008)', *Economic and Political Weekly*, 45(31): 47–61.

Harriss, John, Kristian Stokke and Olle Tornquist (eds) (2004), 'Introduction: the new local politics of democratisation', *Politicising Democracy: The New Local Politics of Democratisation* (Basingstoke: Palgrave Macmillan).

Harriss, R. L. (2003), 'Popular resistance to globalization and neoliberalism in Latin America', *Journal of Development Studies*,19: 365–426.

Harriss-White, Barbara (2003*), India Working: Essays on Economy and Society* (Cambridge: Cambridge University Press).

Harriss-White, Barbara (2005), *India's Market Society: Three Essays in Political Economy* (Gurgaon: Three Essays Collective).

Harriss-White, Barbara and Judith Heyer (eds) (2010), *The Comparative Political Economy of Development* (London: Routledge).

Harriss-White, Barbara and S. Janakarajan (eds) (2004), *Rural India Faces the 21st Century* (London: Anthem Press).

Harriss-White, Barbara and Kaushal Vidyarthee (2010), 'Stigma and regions of accumulation: mapping Dalit and Adivasi capital in the 1990s', in Barbara Harriss-White and Judith Heyer (eds), *The Comparative Political Economy of Development: Africa and South Asia* (London: Routledge), 317–49.

Harvey, David (2003), *The New Imperialism* (New York: Oxford University Press).

Harvey, David (2005), *A Brief History of Neo-liberalism* (Oxford: Oxford University Press).

Hasan, Rana and Aashish Mehta (2006), 'Under-representation of disadvantaged classes in colleges: what do the data tell us?', *Economic and Political Weekly*, 41(35): 3791–6.

Hasan, Rana, Devashish Mitra and Beyza Ural (2007), 'Trade liberalization, labor market institutions and poverty reduction: evidence from Indian states', *India Policy Forum*, 3(1): 71–122.

Hausmann, Ricardo, Lant Pritchett and Dani Rodrik (2005), 'Growth accelerations', *Journal of Economic Growth*, 10(4): 303–29.

Hawthorn, Geoffrey (1991), *Plausible Worlds: Possibility and Understanding in History and the Social Sciences* (Cambridge: Cambridge University Press).

Hayton, Bill (2010), *Vietnam: Rising Dragon* (New Haven, CT: Yale University Press).

Hazell, Peter, C. Poulton, S. Wiggins and A. Dorward (2007), *The Future of Small Farms for Poverty Reduction and Growth* (Washington, DC: International Food Policy Research Institute).

Heller, Patrick (2000) 'Degrees of democracy: some comparative lessons from India', *World Politics* 52(4): 484–519.

Heller, Patrick (2001), 'Moving the state: the politics of decentralization in Kerala, South Africa and Porto Alegre,' *Politics and Society*, 29(1): 131–63.

Heller, Patrick (2009) 'Democratic deepening in India and South Africa', *Journal of Asian and African Studies* 44(1): 123–49.

Heller, Patrick (2011), 'Making citizens from below and above: the prospects and challenges of decentralization in India', in Sanjay Ruparelia, Sanjay Reddy, John Harriss and Stuart Corbridge (eds), *Understanding India's New Political Economy: A Great Transformation?* (London: Routledge), 157–71.

Heller, Patrick. G. Harilal and S. Chaudhuri, (2007), 'Building local democracy: evaluating the impact of decentralization in Kerala, India', *World Development*, 35(4): 626–48.

Herbst, Jeffrey (2000), *States and Power in Africa: Comparative Lessons in Authority and Control* (Princeton, NJ: Princeton University Press).

Herring, Ronald (ed.) (2007), 'Transgenics and the poor: biotechnology and development studies', Special Issue of *Journal of Development Studies*, 43(1): 63–78.

Heuzé, Gerard (1992), 'Shiv Sena and national Hinduism', *Economic and Political Weekly*, 27(41): 2253–61.

Heuzé, Gerard (1996), *Workers of Another World: Miners, the Countryside and Coalfields in Dhanbad* (New Delhi: Oxford University Press).

Heyer, Judith (2010), 'The marginalisation of dalits in a modernising economy', in Barbara Harriss-White and Judith Heyer (eds), *The Comparative Political Economy of Development* (London: Routledge), 225–47.

Himanshu (2007), 'Recent trends in poverty and inequality: some preliminary results', *Economic and Political Weekly*, 42(6): 497–508.

Himanshu (2008), 'What are these new poverty estimates and what do they imply?', *Economic and Political Weekly*, 43(43): 38–43.

Himanshu (2010), 'Towards new poverty lines for India', *Economic and Political Weekly*, 45(1): 38–48.

Himanshu (2011), 'Employment trends in India: a re-examination', *Economic and Political Weekly*, 46(37): 43–59.

Himanshu and Abhijit Sen (2011), 'Why not a universal food security legislation?', *Economic and Political Weekly*, 46(12): 38–47.

Hirschman, Albert (1967), *Development Projects Observed* (Washington, DC: Brookings).

Hirschman, Albert (1981), *Essays in Trespassing* (Cambridge: Cambridge University Press).

Hopkins, Anthony (1973), *An Economic History of West Africa* (Oxford: Oxford University Press).

Huber, Evelyne, Dietrich Rueschemeyer and John D. Stephens (1997), 'The paradoxes of contemporary democracy: formal, participatory and social dimensions', *Comparative Politics*, 23(3): 323–42.

Huebler, Friedrich (2008), *Beyond Gender: Measuring Disparity in South Asia Using an Education Parity Index* (Kathmandu: United Nation's Children's Fund). Retrieved from: <http://www.unicef.org/rosa/New_BeyondGender_09June_08.pdf> (last accessed 6 May 2011).

Human Rights Watch (2009), *Broken System: Dysfunction, Abuse and Impunity in the Indian Police* (New York: Human Rights Watch).

Humang, Yasheng and Tarun Khanna (2003), 'Can India overtake China?' *Foreign Policy*, 8(137): 74–81.

Husain, Zakir and A.Chatterjee (2009), 'Primary completion rates across socio-religious communities in India', *Economic and Political Weekly*, 44(15): 59–67.

Ilaiah, Kanchan (1991), 'Upper caste violence: study of Chunduru carnage', *Economic and Political Weekly*, 26(37): 2079–2804.

Inden, Ronald (1990), *Imagining India* (Oxford: Blackwell).

Isaac, Thomas with Richard W. Franke Franke (2000), *Local Democracy and*

Development: People's Campaign for Decentralized Planning in Kerala (Delhi: LeftWord).

Jackson, Cecile (1993), 'Doing what comes naturally? Women and environment in development', *World Development*, 21(12): 1947–63.

Jaffrelot, Christophe (1996), *The Hindu Nationalist Movement and Indian Politics: 1925 to the 1990s* (New Delhi: Viking).

Jaffrelot, Christophe (2003), *India's Silent Revolution: The Rise of the Lower Castes in North India* (London: Hurst).

Jaffrelot, Christophe (2007), 'The Vishva Hindu Parishad: a nationalist but mimetic attempt at federating the Hindu sects', in Vasudha Dalmia and Henrich von Stietencron (eds), *The Oxford Hinduism Reader* (Delhi: Oxford University Press), 320–46.

Jaffrelot, Christophe (2010), 'The Hindu Nationalists and power', in Niraja Gopal Jayal and Pratap Bhanu Mehta (eds), *The Oxford Companion to Politics in India* (Delhi: Oxford University Press), 205–18.

Jaffrelot, Christophe and Sanjay Kumar (2009), *Rise of the Plebeians? The Changing Face of Indian Legislative Assemblies* (New Delhi: Routledge).

Jalal, Ayesha (1995), *Democracy and Authoritarianism in South Asia* (Cambridge: Cambridge University Press).

James, K. S. (2008) 'Glorifying Malthus: current debate on "demographic dividend" in India', *Economic and Political Weekly*, 43(25): 63–9.

Jamous, Raymond (1996) 'The Meo as a Rajput caste and a Muslim community', in Chris Fuller (ed.), *Caste Today* (Delhi: Oxford), 180–201.

Jaoul, Nicolas (2009), 'Naxalism in Bihar: from bullet to ballot', in Laurent Gayer and Christophe Jaffrelot (ed.), *Armed Militias of South Asia: Fundamentalists, Maoists and Separatists* (London: Hurst and Company), 21–43.

Jaoul, Nicolas (2010), 'The BSP and the Land Issue: Politics of Class Struggles without Class', unpublished ms.

Jayadev, Arjun, Sripad Motiram and Vamsi Vakulabharanam (2011), 'Patterns of wealth disparities in India: 1991–2002', in Sanjay Ruparelia, Sanjay Reddy, John Harriss and Stuart Corbridge (eds), *Understanding India's New Political Economy: A Great Transformation?* (London: Routledge), 81–100.

Jayal, Niraja Gopal (2011), 'The people and the law makers', *Indian Express*, 24 August: available at: http://www.indianexpress.com/news/the-people-and-the-lawmakers/836157.

Jeffery, Roger and Patricia Jeffery (1997), *Population, Gender and Politics: Demographic Change in Rural North India* (Cambridge: Cambridge University Press).

Jeffery, Patricia and Roger Jeffery (2008), '"Money itself discriminates": Obstetric emergencies in the time of liberalization', *Contributions to Indian Sociology*, 42(1): 59–91.

Jeffery, Patricia and Roger Jeffery (2010), 'Polio in north India: what next?', *Economic and Political Weekly*, 45(15): 23–6.

Jeffery, Patricia and Roger Jeffery (2011), 'Obstetric emergencies in the time of liberalisation', in Akhil Gupta and K. Sivaramakrishnan (eds), *The State in*

India after Liberalization: Interdisciplinary Perspectives (London and New York: Routledge), 133–52.

Jeffery, Roger and Jens Lerche (eds) (2003), *Social and Political Change in Uttar Pradesh: European Perspectives* (New Delhi: Manohar).

Jeffery, Roger, Patricia Jeffery and Craig Jeffrey (2005), 'Social inequality and the privatisation of secondary schooling in north India', in Radhika Chopra and Patricia Jeffery (eds), *Educational Regimes in India* (New Delhi: Sage), 41–61.

Jeffery, Roger, Patricia Jeffery and Craig Jeffrey (2006), '*Parhāī ka māhaul?* An educational environment in Bijnor, UP', in Geert de Neve and Henrike Donner (eds), *The Meaning of the Local: Politics of Place in Urban India* (London: Routledge), 116–40.

Jeffrey, Alex (2008), 'Zilho's journeys: displacement and return in Bosnia-Herzegovina', in Craig Jeffrey and Jane Dyson (eds), *Telling Young Lives: Portraits in Global Youth* (Philadelphia, PA: Temple University Press), 113–22.

Jeffrey, Craig (1999), 'Reproducing difference: the accumulation strategies of richer Jat farmers in Western Uttar Pradesh, India', PhD dissertation (Cambridge: University of Cambridge).

Jeffrey, Craig (2000), 'Democratisation without representation? The power and political strategies of a rural elite in North India', *Political Geography*, 19(8): 1013–36.

Jeffrey, Craig (2001), 'A fist is stronger than five fingers: caste and dominance in rural North India', *Transactions of the Institute of British Geographers*, 25(2): 1–30.

Jeffrey, Craig (2002), 'Caste, class and clientelism: a political economy of everyday corruption in rural North India', *Economic Geography*, 78(1): 21–42.

Jeffrey, Craig (2008), 'Kicking away the ladder: student politics and the making of an Indian middle class', *Environment and Planning D: Society and Space*, 26(3): 105–23.

Jeffrey, Craig (2009), 'Fixing futures: educated unemployment through a north Indian lens', *Comparative Studies in Society and History*, 51(1): 182–211.

Jeffrey, Craig (2010), *Timepass: Youth, Class and the Politics of Waiting* (Stanford, CA: Stanford University Press).

Jeffrey, Craig, Patrica Jeffery and Roger Jeffery (2004), '"A useless thing!" or "nectar of the gods"? The cultural production of education and young men's struggles for respect in liberalizing north India', *Annals of the Association of American Geographers*, 94(4): 961–81.

Jeffrey, Craig, Patricia Jeffery and Roger Jeffery (2008), *Degrees without Freedom? Education, Masculinities and Unemployment in North India* (Stanford, CA: Stanford University Press).

Jeffrey, Craig and Stephen Young (in press), 'Waiting for change: youth, caste and politics in India', *Economy and Society*

Jeffrey, Robin, Ronojoy Sen and Pratima Singh (2012), *More Than Maoism: Politics, Policies and Insurgencies in South Asia* (Delhi: Manohar).

Jehan, Kate (2009), 'Heroes or Hondas?: analysing men's dowry narratives in a time of rapid social change', in Tomalin E. Bradley and M. Subramaniam (eds), *Dowry: Bridging the Gap between Theory and Practice* (New Delhi: Women Unlimited), ch.4.

Jejeebhoy, Shireen (2001), 'Women's autonomy in rural India: its dimensions, determinants and the influence of context', in Harriet Presser and Gita Sen (eds), *Women's Empowerment and Demographic Processes: Moving Beyond Cairo* (Oxford: Oxford University Press), 205–38.

Jenkins, Robert (1998), 'The developmental implications of federal political institutions in India', in Mark Robinson and Gordon White (eds), *The Democratic Developmental State* (Oxford: Oxford University Press): 187–214.

Jenkins, Robert (1999), *Democratic Politics and Economic Reform in India* (Cambridge: Cambridge University Press).

Jenkins, Robert (2011), 'The politics of India's special economic zones', in Sanjay Ruparelia, Sanjay Reddy, John Harriss and Stuart Corbridge (eds), *Understanding India's New Political Economy: A Great Transformation?* (London: Routledge), 49–65.

Jenkins, Robert and Anne-Marie Goetz (1999), 'Accounts and accountability: theoretical implications of the right to information movement in India', *Third World Quarterly*, 20(3): 589–608.

Jewitt, Sarah (2000), 'Mothering earth? Gender and environmental protection in Jharkhand, India', *Journal of Peasant Studies*, 27(2): 94–131.

Jha, Praveen (2007), 'Some aspects of the well-being of India's agricultural labour in the context of the contemporary agrarian crisis'. Retrieved from: <http://www.macroscan.org/anl/feb07/anl220207Agrarian_Crisis.htm> (last accessed 21 June 2010).

Jha, Saumitra, Vijayendra Rao and Michael Woolcock (2005), 'Governance in the Gullies: democratic responsiveness and leadership in Delhi slums', *World Development*, 35(2): 230–46.

Jha, Vikas (2010), 'Evidence-based research mobilising action for policy-influencing in two provinces: policy changes under the Right to Information Act in India', *Overseas Development Network* (London: Overseas Development Institute); available from the Society of Participatory Research in India at: <http://www.pria.orgdocs/RTI/20%case%20Study(2).pdf>.

Jodhka, Surinder S. (2008), 'Caste and the corporate sector', *The Indian Journal of Industrial Relations*, 44(2): 185–93.

John, Mary (2007), 'Women in power? Gender, caste and the politics of local urban governance', *Economic and Political Weekly*, 42(39): 3986–93.

Jones, Gareth and Stuart Corbridge (2010), 'The continuing debate about urban bias: the thesis, its critics, its influence, and its implications for poverty reduction strategies', *Progress in Development Studies*, 10(1): 1–18.

Jones, Kenneth W. (1966), *The Arya Samaj in the Punjab: A Study of Social Reform and Religious Revivalism 1877–1902* (Berkeley, CA: University of California Press).

Jones, Reece (2009), 'Geopolitical boundary narratives, the global war on terror and border fencing in India', *Transactions of the Institute of British Geographers*, 34(3): 290–304.

Jose, Sunny and K. Navaneetham (2008), 'A factsheet on women's malnutrition in India', *Economic and Political Weekly*, 43(33): 61–7.

Jose, Sunny and K. Navaneetham (2010), 'Social infrastructure and women's under-nutrition', *Economic and Political Weekly* 45(14): 83–9.

Joshi, Sanjay (2001), *Fractured Modernity: Making of a Middle Class in Colonial North India* (New Delhi: Oxford University Press).

Joshi, Vijay (2009), 'Economic resurgence, lop-sided performance, jobless growth', in Anthony Heath and Roger Jeffery (eds), *Diversity and Change in Modern India, Economic, Social, Political Approaches* (Oxford: Oxford University Press), 73–106.

Joshi, Vijay and Ian Little (1994), *India – Macroeconomics and Political Economy 1964–1991* (Oxford: Oxford University Press and World Bank).

Kabeer, Naila (1994), *Reversed Realities: Gender Hierarchies in Development Thought* (London: Verso).

Kalecki, Michal (1972), *Selected Essays on the Economic Growth of the Socialist and Mixed Economy* (Cambridge: Cambridge University Press).

Kamat, Sangeeta (2002) *Development Hegemony: NGOs and the State in India* (New Delhi: Oxford Universiy Press).

Kamath, Lalitha and M. Vijayabaskar (2009), 'Limits and possibilities of middle class associations as urban collective actors', *Economic and Political Weekly*, 44(26–7): 368–76.

Kannan, K. P. and G. Raveendran (2009), 'Growth sans employment: a quarter century of jobless growth in Indian manufacturing', *Economic and Political Weekly*, 44(10): 80–91.

Kapadia, Karen (2010), 'Liberalisation and transformations in India's informal economy: female breadwinners in working-class households in Chennai', in Barbara Harriss-White and Judith Heyer (eds), *The Comparative Political Economy of Development* (London: Routledge), 267–90.

Kaplinsky, Raphael (2005), *Globalization, Poverty and Inequality: Between a Rock and a Hard Place* (Cambridge: Polity).

Kapur, Devesh (2005), 'Explaining democratic durability and economic performance: the role of India's institutions', in Devesh Kapur and Pratap Bhanu Mehta (eds), *Public Institutions in India: Performance and Design* (New Delhi: Oxford University Press), 28–76.

Kapur, Devesh (2007), 'The causes and consequences of India's IT boom', in Baldev Raj Naya (ed.), *Globalization and Politics in India* (New Delhi: Oxford University Press), 387–407.

Kapur, Devesh (2010), 'The Political Economy of the State', in N. Gopal Jayal and P. Bhanu Mehta (eds), *The Oxford Companion to Politics in India* (Delhi: Oxford University Press), 443–58.

Kapur, Devesh and Pratap Bhanu Mehta (eds) (2005), *Public Institutions in India: Performance and Design* (Delhi: Oxford University Press).

Kapur, Devesh and Pratap Bhanu Mehta (2007), 'Mortgaging the future? Indian higher education', *Brookings-NCAER India Policy Forum* paper. Retrieved from: <http://www.polisci.upenn.edu/faculty/CVs/cvkapur.pdf> (last accessed 26 July 2010).

Kapur, Devesh, Partha Mukhopadhyay and Arvind Subramanian (2008), 'More on direct cash transfers', *Economic and Political Weekly*, 43(47): 85–7.

Kaur, Ravinder (2010), 'Khap panchayats, sex ratio and female agency', *Economic and Political Weekly*, 45(23): 14–16.

Kaviraj, Sudipta (1984), 'On the crisis of political institutions in India', *Contributions to Indian Sociology*, 18(2): 223–43.

Kaviraj, Sudipta (1988), 'A critique of the passive revolution', *Economic and Political Weekly*, 23: 45–7, 2429–44.

Kaviraj, Sudipta (1991), 'On state, society and discourse in India', in James Manor (ed.), *Rethinking Third World Politics* (Harlow: Longman), 72–99.

Kaviraj, Sudipta (2001), 'In search of civil society', in Sudipta Kaviraj and Sunil Khilnani (eds), *Civil Society: History and Possibilities* (Cambridge: Cambridge University Press), 287–323.

Keefer, Philip and Stuti Khemani (2004), 'Why do the poor receive poor services?', *Economic and Political Weekly*, 39(9): 935–43.

Kenworthy, Lae and Melissa Malami (1999), 'Gender inequality in political representation: a worldwide comparative analysis', *Social Forces*, 78(1): 235–68.

Keynes, John Maynard (1973 [1936]), *The General Theory of Employment, Interest and Money* (London: Macmillan).

Khatkhate, Deena (2006), 'Indian economic reform: a philosopher's stone [review of Acharya]', *Economic and Political Weekly*, 41(22): 2203–5.

Khera, Reetika and Nandini Nayak (2009), 'Women workers and perceptions of the NREGA', *Economic and Political Weekly*, 44(43): 49–57.

Khilnani, Sunil (1997), *The Idea of India* (London: Hamish Hamilton).

Kiernan, Ben (1996), *The Pol Pot Regime: Race, Power and Genocide under the Khmer Rouge, 1975–79* (New Haven, CT, and London: Yale University Press).

Kiernan, Victor (1967), *The Lords of Humankind: European Attitudes towards the Outside World in the Imperial Age* (New York: Columbia University Press).

Kingdon, Geeta (1997) 'Private schooling in India: size, nature, and equity effects', *Economic and Political Weekly*, 31(51): 3306–14.

Kingdon, Geeta (2007) 'The progress of school education in India', *Oxford Review of Economic Policy*, 23(2): 168–95.

Kingdon, Geeta and Mohammad Muzammil (2003), *The Political Economy of Education in India: Teacher Politics in Uttar Pradesh* (Oxford: Oxford University Press).

Kinnvall, Catarina (2006), *Globalization and Religious Nationalism in India: The Search for Ontological Security* (London and New York: Routledge).

Kishor, Sunita (1993), '"May God give sons to all": gender and child mortality in India', *American Sociological Review*, 58(2): 247–65.

Klingensmith, Daniel (2003), 'Building India's modern temples: Indians and Americans in the Damodar Valley Corporation, 1945–60', in Kalyanakrishnan Sivaramakrishnan and Arun Agrawal (eds), *Regional Modernities: The Cultural Politics of Development in India* (Stanford, CA: Stanford University Press), 122–42.

Kochanek, Stanley (1995–96), 'The transformation of interest politics in India', *Pacific Affairs*, 68(4): 529–50.

Kochanek, Stanley (1996), 'Liberalization and business lobbying in India', *Journal of Commonwealth and Comparative Politics*, 34(3): 155–73.

Kochhar, Kalpana, Utsav Kumar, Rajan Raghuram, Arvind Subramanian and Ioannis Tokatlidis (2006), 'India's pattern of development: what happened, what follows?', *IMF Working Paper* (Washington, DC: International Monetary Fund).

Kohli, Atul (1987), *The State and Poverty in India: The Political Economy of Reform* (Cambridge: Cambridge University Press).

Kohli, Atul (1990), *Democracy and Discontent: India's Growing Crisis of Governability* (Cambridge: Cambridge University Press).

Kohli, Atul (1994), 'Centralization and powerlessness: India's democracy in a comparative perspective', in Joel Migdal, Atul Kohli and Vivienne Shue (eds), *State Power and Social Forces: Domination and Transformation in the Third World* (Cambridge: Cambridge University Press), 89–107.

Kohli, Atul (1998), 'Another enduring election: India defies the odds', *Journal of Democracy*, 9(3): 7–20.

Kohli, Atul (2001) 'Introduction', in Atul Kohli (ed), *The Success of India's Democracy*, (Cambridge and New York: Cambridge University Press), 1-20

Kohli, Atul (2006a), 'Politics of economic growth in India, 1980–2005: part I, the 1980s', *Economic and Political Weekly*, 41(13): 1251–65.

Kohli, Atul (2006b), 'Politics of economic growth in India, 1980–2005: part II, the 1990s and beyond', *Economic and Political Weekly*, 41(14): 1361–70.

Kohli, Harinder S. and Anil Sood (eds) (2010), *India 2039: An Affluent Society in One Generation* (New Delhi: Sage Publications).

Kothari, Ashish (2007), 'For lasting rights', *Frontline*, 23(26): 14–18.

Kothari, Rajni (1964), 'The Congress "system" in India', *Asian Survey*, 4(12): 1161–73.

Kothari, Rajni (ed.) (1970), *Caste in Indian Politics* (London: Sangam).

Krishna, Anirudh (2002), *Active Social Capital: Tracing the Roots of Development and Democracy* (New York: Columbia University Press).

Krishna, Anirudh (2010), *One Illness Away: Why People Become Poor and How They Escape Poverty* (Oxford: Oxford University Press).

Krishna, Anirudh and Devendra Bajpai (2011), 'Lineal spread and radial dissipation: experiencing growth in rural India, 1993–2005', *Economic and Political Weekly*, 46(38): 44–51.

Krishnan, K. P. and T. V. Somanathan, (2005), 'Civil service: an institutional perspective', in Devesh Kapur and Pratap Bhanu Mehta (eds), *Public Institutions in India: Performance and Design* (New Delhi: Oxford University Press), 258–319.

Krueger, Anne and Sajjid Chinoy (eds) (2002), *Reforming India's External, Financial and Fiscal Policies* (Stanford, CA: Stanford University Press).

Kumar, Krishna (1988), 'Origins of India's "textbook culture"', *Comparative Education Review*, 32(4): 452–64.

Kumar, Krishna (1993), 'Hindu revivalism and education in north central India', in M. Marty and R. Appleby (eds), *Fundamentalisms and Society* (Chicago, Il: University of Chicago Press).

Kumar, Krishna (1994), *Democracy and Education in India* (London: Sangam Books).

Kumar, Nilotpal (2010), 'Famer suicides in Andhra Pradesh, India', unpublished PhD dissertation (Department of International Development, London School of Economics and Political Science).

Kumar, Nita (2000), *Lessons from Schools: The History of Education in Banaras* (New Delhi: Sage).

Kunnath, George (2006), 'Becoming a Naxalite in rural Bihar: class struggle and its contradictions', in *Journal of Peasant Studies*, 33(1): 89–123.

Kunnath, George (2009), 'Smouldering Dalit fires in Bihar, India', *Dialectical Anthropology*, 33(4): 309–25.

Laitin, David (2007), *Nations, States and Violence* (Oxford: Oxford University Press).

Lake, Marilyn and Henry Reynolds (2008), *Drawing the Global Colour Line: White Men's Countries and the International Challenge of Racial Equality* (Cambridge: Cambridge University Press).

Lal, Deepak (1983), *The Poverty of 'Development Economics'* (London: Institute of Economic Affairs).

Lal, Deepak (1999), *Unfinished Business: The Indian Economy in the 1990s* (New Delhi: Oxford University Press).

Lal, Deepak, Rakesh Mohan and I. Natarajan (2001), 'Economic reforms and poverty alleviation: a tale of two surveys', *Economic and Political Weekly*, 36(12): 1017–28.

Lanjouw, Peter and Rinku Murgai (2009), 'Poverty decline, agricultural wages and non-farm employment in rural India: 1983–2004', *Policy Research Working Paper* 4850 (Washington, DC: World Bank).

Lanjouw, Peter and Nicholas Stern (eds) (1998), *Economic Development in Palanpur over Five Decades* (Oxford: Oxford University Press).

Laski, Harold J. (1921), *The Foundations of Sovereignty and Other Essays* (London: Harcourt, Brace and Company).

Legg, Stephen (2006), 'Governmentality, congestion and calculation in colonial Delhi', *Social and Cultural Geography*, 7(5): 709–29.

Lemanski, Charlotte and Stephanie Lama-Rewal (2010), 'The "Missing Middle": Participatory Urban Governance in Delhi's Unauthorized Colonies', unpublished ms.

Lerche, Jens (1995), 'Is bonded labour a bound category? Reconceptualising agrarian conflict in India', *Journal of Peasant Studies*, 22(3): 484–515.

Lerche, Jens (1999), 'Politics of the poor: agricultural labourers and political transformations in Uttar Pradesh', in Terence J. Byres, Karin Kapadia and Jens Lerche (eds), *Rural Labour Relations in India* (London: Frank Cass), 182–243.

Lerche, Jens (2008), 'Transnational advocacy networks and affirmative action for Dalits in India', *Development and Change* 39(2): 239–61.

Lerche, Jens (2010), 'From 'rural labour' to "classes of labour": class fragmentation, caste and class struggle at the bottom of the Indian labour hierarchy', in Barbara Harriss-White and Judith Heyer (eds), *The Comparative Political Economy of Development* (London: Routledge), 64–85.

Lewis, William Arthur (1955), *The Theory of Economic Growth* (London: George Allen and Unwin).

Li, Tania (2010), 'To make live or let die? Rural dispossession and the protection of surplus populations', *Antipode*, 41(1): 66–93.

Lieten, G. Kristoffel (1996), 'Panchayats in Western Uttar Pradesh: "namesake" members', *Economic and Political Weekly*, 31(39): 2700–5.

Lieten, G. Kristoffel and Ravi Srivastava (1999), *Unequal Partners: Power Relations, Devolution and Development in Uttar Pradesh* (New Delhi: Sage).

Linz, Juan and Alfred Stepan (1996) 'Toward consolidated democracies', *Journal of Democracy*, 7(2): 14–33.

Lipset, Seymour M. (1959), 'Some social requisites of democracy: economic development and political legitimacy', *American Political Science Review*, 53(1): 69–105.

Lipset, Seymour M. (1994) 'The social requisites of democracy revisited', *American Sociological Review*, 59(1): 1–22.

Lipton, Michael (1977), *Why Poor People Stay Poor: A Study of Urban Bias in World Development* (London: Temple Smith).

Lipton, Michael (2009), *Land Reform in Developing Countries: Property Rights and Property Wrongs* (London: Routledge).

Little, Daniel (2003), *The Paradox of Wealth and Poverty: Mapping the Ethical Dilemmas of Global Development* (Boulder, CO, and Oxford: Westview Press).

Lukose, Ritty (2010), *Liberalization's Children: Gender, Youth and Consumer Citizenship in Globalizing India* (Durham, NC: Duke University Press).

McCartney, Matthew (2009a), *India: The Political Economy of Growth, Stagnation and the State, 1951–2007* (London: Routledge).

McCartney, Matthew (2009b), *Political Economy, Liberalisation and Growth in India, 1991–2008* (London: Routledge).

McFarlane, Colin (2008) 'Sanitation in Mumbai's informal settlements: state, slum and infrastructure', Environment and Planning A, 40(1): 88–107

McFarlane, Colin (2009) 'Translocal assemblages: space, power and social movements', *Geoforum*, 40(4): 561–7.

McKean, Lise (1996), *Divine Enterprise: Gurus and the Hindu Nationalist Movement* (Chicago: University of Chicago Press).

McNay, Kirsty, Periasnayagam Arokiasamy and Robert Cassen (2003), 'Why are uneducated women in India using contraception: a multilevel analysis?', *Population Studies*, 5(1): 21–40.

Maddison, Angus (1998), *Chinese Economic Performance in the Long Run* (Paris: OECD).

Madhok, Sumi (2007), 'Autonomy, gendered subordination and transcultural dialogue', *Journal of Global Ethics*, 3(3): 335–57.

Madsen, Jakob, Shishir Saxena and James Ang (2010), 'The Indian growth miracle and endogenous growth', *Journal of Development Economics,* 93: 37–48.

Madsen, Stig T. (1998), *The Decline of the BKU,* mimeo, European Conference of Modern Asian Studies (Prague: Charles University).

Madsen, Stig T. and Staffan Lindberg (2003), 'Modelling institutional fate: the case of a farmers' movement in Uttar Pradesh', in Roger Jeffery and Jens Lerche (eds), *Social and Political Change in Uttar Pradesh: European Perspectives* (New Delhi: Manohar), 199–223.

Mains, Daniel (2007), 'Neoliberal times: progress, boredom, and shame among young men in urban Ethiopia', *American Ethnologist,* 34(4): 659–73.

Maiti, Dibyendu and Kunal Sen (2010), 'The informal sector in India: a means of exploitation or accumulation?', *Journal of South Asian Development* 5(1): 1–13.

Majumdar, Manabi and Jos Mooij (2011), *Education and Inequality in India: A Classroom View* (Routledge: London).

Mamdani, Mahmood (1973), *The Myth of Population Control: Family, Caste and Class in an Indian Village* (New York: Monthly Review Press).

Mamdani, Mahmood (1996), *Citizen and Subject: Contemporary Africa and the Legacy of Late Colonialism* (Princeton, NJ: Princeton University Press).

Mandelbaum, David G. (1970), *Society in India,* 2 vols (Berkeley, CA: University of California Press).

Mander, Harsh (2008), 'Living with hunger: deprivation among the aged, single women and people with disability', *Economic and Political Weekly,* 43(17): 87–98.

Mannheim, Karl (1972), 'The problem of generations', in Philip Altbach and R. Laufer (eds), *The New Pilgrims: Youth Protest in Transition* (New York: David McKay and Company), 101–38.

Manor, James (1987), 'Tried then abandoned: economic liberalization in India', *IDS Bulletin,* 18(4): 39–44.

Manor, James (1988), 'Parties and the party system', in Atul Kohli (ed.), *India's Democracy: An Analysis of Changing State-Society Relations* (Princeton, NJ: Princeton University Press), 62–98.

Manor, James (1995), 'The political sustainability of economic liberalization in India', in Robert Cassen and Vijay Joshi (eds), *India: The Future of Economic Reform* (New Delhi: Oxford University Press), 339–63.

Manor, James (2010a), 'Local Governance', in N. Gopal Jayal and P. Bhanu Mehta (eds), *The Oxford Companion to Politics in India* (Delhi: Oxford University Press), 61–79.

Manor, James, (2010b), 'Beyond clientelism: Digvijay Singh's participatory, pro-poor strategy in Madhya Pradesh', in Pamela Price and Arild Ruud (eds), *Power and Influence in India: Bosses, Lords and Captains* (London: Routledge), 193–213.

Manor, James (2011a), 'Epilogue: caste and politics in recent times', in Rajni Kothari (ed.), *Caste in Indian Politics* (Delhi: Oxford University Press).

Manor, James (2011b), 'The Congress Party and the "Great Transformation"', in Sanjay Ruparelia, Sanjay Reddy, John Harriss and Stuart Corbridge (eds), *Understanding India's New Political Economy: A Great Transformation?* (London: Routledge), 204–20.

Manuel, Peter (1993), *Cassette Culture: Popular Music and Technology in North India* (Chicago, IL: University of Chicago Press).

Marx, Karl (2008), *The Eighteenth Brumaire of Louis Bonaparte* (Washington, DC: Wildside Press).

Mathur, Archana, Surajit Das and Subhalakshmi Sircar (2006), 'Status of agriculture in India', *Economic and Political Weekly*, 41(52): 5327–36.

Mathur, Kanchan (2008), 'Gender hierarchies and inequalities: taking stock of women's sexual and reproductive health', *Economic and Political Weekly*, 43(59): 54–61.

Mayer, Adrian (1996), 'Caste in an Indian village: change and continuity 1954–1992', in Chris Fuller (ed.), *Caste Today* (Delhi: Oxford), 32–64.

Mazumdar, Ranjini (2007), *Bombay Cinema: An Archive of the City* (Minnesota, MN: Minnesota University Press).

Mehta, Pratap Bhanu (2006), 'Being middle class is okay', *The Indian Express* (7 June).

Mehta, Pratab Bhanu (2007), 'The rise of juridicial sovereignty', *Journal of Democracy*, 18(2): 70–83.

Mehta, Pratap Bhanu (2011), 'The politics of social justice', *Business Standard India 2011* (Delhi: BS Books).

Mendelsohn, Oliver (1993), 'The transformation of authority in rural India', *Modern Asian Studies*, 27(4): 805–42.

Mendelsohn, Oliver and Marieke Vicziany (1998), *The Untouchables: Subordination, Poverty and the State in Modern India* (Cambridge: Cambridge University Press).

Metcalf, Barbara D. and Thomas R. Metcalf (2006), *A Concise History of Modern India* (Cambridge: Cambridge University Press).

Michelutti, Lucia (2007) 'The vernacularization of democracy: political participation and popular politics in north India', *Journal of the Royal Anthropological Institute*, 13(3): 639–56.

Michelutti, Lucia (2008), *The Vernacularisation of Democracy: Politics, Caste and Religion in India* (New Delhi: Routledge).

Micklethwait, John and Adrian Wooldridge (2009), *God is Back: How the Global Revival of Faith is Changing the World* (New York: Penguin Press).

Miklian, Jason (2009), 'The purification hunt: the Salwa Judum counter-insurgency in Chhattisgarh, India', *Dialectical Anthropology*, 33(3–4): 441–59.

Miles, Rebecca (2002), 'Employment and unemployment in Jordan: the importance of the gender system', *World Development*, 30(3): 413–27.

Miliband, Ralph (1969), *The State in Capitalist Society: The Analysis of the Western System of Power* (London: Weidenfeld and Nicholson).

Miller, Barbara (1981), *The Endangered Sex: Neglect of Female Children in Rural North India* (Ithaca, NY: Cornell University Press).

Mills, C. Wright (1956), *The Power Elite* (New York: Oxford University Press).

Mines, Mattison (2006), 'Temples and charity: the neighbourhood styles of Komari and Beeri Chettiar merchants of Madras City', in Geert de Neve and Henrike Donner (eds), *The Meaning of the Local: Politics of Place in Urban India* (London: Routledge), 89–115.

Minhas, B. S. (1988), 'Validation of large-scale sample survey data: the case of NSS household consumption expenditure', *Sankhya*, 2(5): 1–63.

Mishra, Pankaj (2004), *The Romantics* (New York: Random House).

Mishra, Pankaj (2006), *Butter Chicken in Ludhiana: Travels in Small Town India* (London: Picador).

Mishra, Yamini and Bhumika Jhamb (2009), 'An assessment of UPA-1 through a gender budgeting lens', *Economic and Political Weekly*, 44(35): 61–8.

Misra, Banikanta (2010), 'Agriculture, industry and mining in Orissa in the post liberalisation era: an inter-district and inter-state panel analysis, *Economic and Political Weekly*, 45(20): 49–68.

Mistry, Rohinton (1995), *A Fine Balance* (Toronto: McLelland and Stewart).

Mitchell, Katharyne (2003), 'Liberating the city: between New York and New Orleans – a response', *Urban Geography*, 27(8): 722–8.

Mitra, Sonia (2006), 'Patterns of female employment in urban India: analysis of NSS data (1983 to 1999–2000)', *Economic and Political Weekly*, 41 (38): 500–8.

Mitra, Sidhartha and R. Nagarajan (2005), 'Making use of the window of demographic opportunity', *Economic and Political Weekly*, 40(5): 5327–32.

Mitra, Subrata and Malte Pehl (2010), 'Federalism', in Niraja Gopal Jayal and Pratap Bhanu Mehta (eds), *The Oxford Companion to Politics in India* (Delhi: Oxford University Press), 43–60.

Miyamura, Satoshi (2010), 'Labour market institutions in Indian industry: a comparison of Mumbai and Kolkata', unpublished PhD thesis (London: Department of Economics, School of Oriental and African Studies, University of London).

Mlodinow, Leonard (2008), *The Drunkard's Walk: How Randomness Rules Our Lives* (New York: Vintage).

Mohan, Rakesh (2008), 'Growth record of the Indian economy, 1950–2008: a story of sustained savings and investment', *Economic and Political Weekly*, 43(13): 61–71.

Moodie, Megan (2008), 'Enter microcredit: a new culture of women's empowerment in Rajasthan?', *American Ethnologist*, 35(3): 454–63.

Mooij, Jos (1999), *Food Policy and the Indian State: The Public Distribution System in South India* (New Delhi: Oxford University Press).

Mooij, Jos (2008), 'Primary education, teachers' professionalism and social class about motivation and demotivation of government school teachers in India', *International Journal of Educational Development*, 28(5): 508–23.

Mooij, Jos (2011), 'Redressing poverty and enhancing social development: trends in India's welfare regime', paper presented at Conference on Poverty in South Asia (Oxford: University of Oxford), 28–9 March.

Moore, Barrington (1966), *The Social Origins of Dictatorship and Democracy: Lord and Peasant in the Making of the Modern World* (Boston, MA: Beacon Press).

Moore, Donald (2005), *Suffering for Territory: Race, Place and Power in Zimbabwe* (Durham, NC: Duke University Press).

Mosse, David (2010), 'A relational approach to durable poverty, inequality and power', *Journal of Development Studies*, 46(7): 1–23.

Mukherji, Nirmalangshu (2010), 'Arms over the people: what have the Maoists achieved in Dandakaranya?', *Economic and Political Weekly*, 45(25): 16–20.

Mukherji, Rahul (2000), 'India's aborted liberalization, 1966', *Pacific Affairs*, 73(3): 375–92.

Mukherji, Rahul (2010), 'The political economy of reforms', in Niraja Gopal Jayal and Pratap Bhanu Mehta (eds), *The Oxford Companion to Politics in India* (New Delhi: Oxford University Press), 483–98.

Mukhopadhyay, Partha (2006), 'Whither urban renewal?', *Economic and Political Weekly*, 41(10): 879–84.

Mukhopadhyay, Swapna (ed.) (2007), *The Enigma of the Kerala Woman: A Failed Promise of Literacy* (New Delhi: Social Science Press).

Muller, Anders Riel and Raj Patel (2004), 'Shining India? Economic liberalization and rural poverty in the 1990s', *Policy Brief* No. 10 (Oakland, CA: Institute for Food and Development Policy).

Munshi, Kaivan and Mark Rosenzweig (2005), 'Why is mobility in India so low? Social insurance, inequality and growth', *Working Paper* 14850 (Cambridge, MA: National Bureau of Economic Research).

Muralidharan, Kartik and Michael Kremer (2006), *Private and Public Schools in Rural India*, mimeo (Cambridge, MA: Harvard University).

Muralidharan, Sukumar (2003), 'A new phase of adventurism', *Frontline*, 20(15). Retrieved from: <http://www.flonetcom.com> (last accessed 27 August 2010).

Murthi, Mamta, Anne-Catherin Guio and Jean Drèze (1995), 'Mortality, fertility, and gender bias in India: a district-level analysis', *Population and Development Review*, 21(4): 745–82.

Myint, Hla (1964), *The Economics of the Developing Countries* (London: Hutchinson).

Myrdal, Gunnar (1968), *Asian Drama: An Inquiry into the Poverty of Nations* (New York: Twentieth Century Fund).

Myrdal, Jan (1996), *India Waits* (New York: Lake View Press).

Myrdal, Jan and Gautam Navlakha (2010), 'In conversation with Ganapathy, general secretary of CPI (Maoist)'. Retrieved from: <http://sanhati.com/articles/2138/> (last accessed 28 November 2010).

Nagaraj, Karkada (2008), 'Farmers' suicides in India: magnitudes, trends and spatial patterns'. Retrieved from: <http://www.macroscan.org/anl/mar08/anl030308Farmers_Suicides.htm> (last accessed 21 June 2010).

Nagaraj, R. (2004), 'Fall in manufacturing employment', *Economic and Political Weekly*, 39(30): 3387–90.

Naipaul, Vidiadhar Surajprasad (1990), *India: A Million Mutinies Now* (Harmondsworth: Penguin).

Nair, Janaki (2005), *The Promise of the Metropolis: Bangalore's Twentieth Century* (Delhi: Oxford University Press).

Nambisan, Vijay (2000), *Bihar is in the Eye of the Beholder* (New Delhi: Penguin).

Nambissan, Geeta B. (1996), 'Equity in education? schooling of Dalit children in India', *Economic and Political Weekly*, 31(16–17): 1011–19.

Nambissan, Geeta B. and M. Sedwal (2002), 'Education for all: the situation of Dalit children in India', in R. Govinda (ed.), *India Education Report* (New Delhi: Oxford University Press), 72–86.

Nanda, Meera (2009), *The God Market: How Globalization is Making India More Hindu* (Delhi: Random House).

Naoroji, Dadabhai (1901), *Poverty and UnBritish Rule in India* (London: Sonnenschein).

NAPM (National Alliance of People's Movements) (2010), 'Preliminary observations by the national panel on SEZs'. Retrieved from: <http://napm-india.org> (last accessed 11 June 2010).

Narayan, Badri (2008), 'Demarginalisation and history: Dalit re-invention of the past', *South Asia Research*, 28(2): 169–84.

Narayan, Deepa, Lant Pritchett and Soumya Kapoor (2009), *Moving Out of Poverty: Success from the Bottom Up* (Washington, DC: Palgrave-Macmillan and World Bank).

Navlakha, Gautam (2010), 'Days and nights in the Maoist heartland', *Economic and Political Weekly*, 45(16): 38–47.

Navlakha, Gautam and Asish Gupta (2009), 'The real divide in Bastar', *Economic and Political Weekly*, 44(33): 20–3.

Nayab, Durre (2007), 'Demographic dividend or demographic threat in Pakistan', Pakistan Institute of Development Economics Working Paper Series. Available at SSRN: <http://ssrn.com/abstract=963426>.

Nayak, Pulin (2010), 'Privatization: Indian experience since 1991', in Kaushik Basu and Annemie Maertens (eds), *The Concise Oxford Companion to Economics in India* (New Delhi: Oxford University Press), 369–71.

Nayyar, Deepak (2006), 'Economic growth in independent India: lumbering elephant or running tiger?', *Economic and Political Weekly*, 41(15): 1451–8.

Nelson, Joan (ed.) (1990), *Economic Crisis and Policy Choice: The Politics of Adjustment in the Third World* (Princeton, NJ: Princeton University Press).

Nevill, H. R. (1922), *Meerut – a Gazetteer* (Lucknow: Government Branch Press).

Nigam, Aditya (2010), 'The rumour of Maoism', in *Seminar*, 607 (March 2010). Retrieved from: <http://www.india-seminar.com> (last accessed 6 December 2010).

Nilekani, Nandan (2008), *Imagining India: The Idea of a Renewed Nation* (London: Penguin).

Nilsen, Alf Gunvald (2010), *Dispossession and Resistance in India: The River and the Rage* (London and New York: Routledge).

Nisbett, Nicholas (2007) 'Friendship, consumption, morality: practising identity negotiating hierarchy in middle class Bangalore', *Journal of the Royal Anthropological Institute*, 13(4): 935–50.

Noorani, Abdul (2002), *Savarkar and Hindutva: The Godse Connection* (Delhi: LeftWord).

Noorani, Abdul (2009), 'BJP's Democracy Deficit', *Frontline*, 26(20): 80–5.

Norris, Pippa and Ronald Inglehart (2004), *Sacred and Secular: Religion and Politics Worldwide* (New York: Cambridge University Press).

North, Douglass (1990), *Institutions, Institutional Change and Economic Performance* (New York: Cambridge University Press).

Nunn, Nathan (2008), 'The long-term effects of Africa's slave trades,' *Quarterly Journal of Economics*, 123 (1): 139–76.

Nunn, Nathan (2009), 'The importance of history for economic development,' *Annual Review of Economics,* 1(1): 65–92.

Nussbaum, Martha (2002), 'Sex, laws and inequality: what India can teach the United States', *Daedalus*, 131(1): 95–106.

Oldenburg, Philip (2010), *India, Pakistan, and Democracy: Solving the Puzzle of Divergent Paths* (London: Routledge).

Olson, Mancur (1965), *The Logic of Collective Action: Public Goods and the Theory of Groups* (Cambridge, MA: Harvard University Press).

Omvedt, Gail (2003), *Buddhism in India: Challenging Brahminism and Caste* (New Delhi: Sage).

O'Neill, Jim (2001), 'Building better global economic BRICs', *Global Economics Paper No.66*, Goldman Sachs. Retrieved from: <http://www2.goldmansachs. com> (last accessed 5 May 2011).

O'Neill, Jim and Anna Stupnytska (2009), 'Long term outlook for the BRICs and N-11 post-crisis', *Global Economics Paper No.192*, Goldman Sachs. Retrieved from: <http://www2.goldmansachs.com> (last accessed 5 May 2011).

Osella, Filippo and Caroline Osella (2000), *Social Mobility in Kerala: Modernity and Identity in Conflict* (London: Pluto Press).

Pai, Sudha (2000), 'New social and political movements of Dalits: a study of Meerut district', *Contributions to Indian Sociology*, 34(2): 189–220.

Pai, Sudha (2002). *Dalit Assertion and the Unfinished Democratic Revolution: The Bahujan Samaj Party in Uttar Pradesh* (New Delhi: Sage).

Pai, Sudha (2010), *Developmental State and the Dalit Question in Madhya Pradesh: Congress Response.* (New Dehli: Routledge).

Panagariya, Arvind (2008), *India: The Emerging Giant* (Oxford: Oxford University Press).

Panda, Pradeep and Bina Agarwal (2005), 'Marital violence, human development and women's property status in India', *World Development*, 33(5): 823–50.

Pande, Rohini (2003), 'Can mandated political representation provide disadvantaged minorities influence? Theory and evidence from India', *American Economic Review*, 93(4): 1132–51.

Panikkar, K. N. (2001), 'Outsider as enemy: the politics of rewriting history in India', *Frontline*, 18(1). Retrieved from: <http://www.flonetcom.com> (last accessed 27 August 2010).

Parry, Jonathan P. (1999), 'Two cheers for reservation: The satnamis and the steel plant', in Ramachandran Guha and Jonathan P. Parry (eds), *Institutions and Inequalities* (New Delhi: Oxford University Press), 128–69.

Parry, Jonathan P. (2001), 'Ankalu's errant wife – sex, marriage and industry in contemporary Chhattisgarh', *Modern Asian Studies*, 35(4): 783–820.

Patel, Indraprasad Gordhanbhai (2002), *Glimpses of Indian Economic Policy: An Insider's View* (New Delhi: Oxford University Press).

Patel, Rita (nd), *The Practice of Sex Selective Abortion in India: May You Be the Mother of a Hundred Sons*, mimeo. Retrieved from: <http://cgi.unc.edu/research/pdf/abortion/pdf> (last accessed 14 June 2010).

Patnaik, Usha (2010, January 5), 'The Tendulkar committee report on poverty estimation'. Retrieved from: <http://idathupaksham.wordpress.com> (last accessed 11 May 2011).

Patnaik, Utsa (2007), *The Republic of Hunger and Other Essays* (Gurgaon: Three Essays Collective).

Pattenden, Jonathan (2005), 'Trickle-down solidarity, globalisation and dynamics of social transformation in a south Indian village', *Economic and Political Weekly,* 40(19): 1975–85.

Peabody, Norbert (2001) 'Cents, sense, census: human inventories in late precolonial and early colonial India', *Comparative Studies in Society and History*, 43(4): 819–50.

Pedersen, Jorgen (2000), 'Explaining economic liberalization in India: state and society perspectives', *World Development*, 28(2): 265–82.

Pinto, Sarah (2008), *Where There is No Midwife: Birth and Loss in Rural India* (New York: Berghahn).

Planning Commission (Government of India) (2008), *Eleventh Five Year Plan 2007–2012. Volume 1: Inclusive Growth* (Delhi: Oxford University Press).

Polanyi, Karl (1944/1957/2001), *The Great Transformation: The Political and Economic Origins of Our Time*, 2nd edn (Boston, MA: Beacon Press).

Pomeranz, Kenneth (2000), *The Great Divergence: China, Europe, and the Making of the Modern World Economy* (Princeton, NJ: Princeton Univeristy Press).

Popkin, Barry M., Susan Horton, Soowon Kim, Ajay Mahal and Jin Shuigao (2001), 'Trends in diet, nutritional status, and diet-related non-communicable diseases in China and India: the economic costs of the nutrition transition', *Nutrition Reviews*, 59(12); 379–90.

Poteete, Amy (2009), 'Is development path-dependent or political? A reinterpretation of mineral-dependent development in Botswana', *Journal of Development Studies*, 45: 544–71.

Potter, David (1986), *India's Political Administrators: From ICS to IAS* (Delhi: Oxford University Press).

Poulantzas, Nicos (1973), *Political Power and Social Classes* (London: New Left Books).

Pradhan, Mahesh Chandra (1966), *The Political System of the Jats of Northern India* (Bombay: Oxford University Press).

Pramanik, Rashmi (2008) 'Overburdened school-going children: reflections from a small city in India' in Deepak Behera (ed.), *Childhoods in South Asia* (Delhi: Pearson), 274–90.

Prasad, Archana (2007), 'Survival at stake', *Frontline*, 23(26): 4–10.

Prause, JoAnn and Dooley, David (1997), 'Effects of underemployment on school-leavers' self-esteem', *Journal of Adolescence*, 20(1): 243–60.

Prebisch, Raúl (1950), *The Economic Development of Latin America and its Principal Problems* (New York: United Nations).

Price, Pamela and Arild Ruud (2010), *Power and Influence in India: Bosses, Lords and Captains* (London: Routledge).

Pritchett, Lant (2008), 'Is India a flailing state? Detours on the four lane highway to modernization', *Working Paper RWP09-013* (Cambridge, MA: Harvard University, Kennedy School).

Pritchett, Lant (2009), 'A review of Edward Luce's "In spite of the Gods": the strange rise of modern India', *Journal of Economic Literature*, 47(3): 771–80.

Pritchett, Lant and Michael Woolcock (2004), 'Solutions when the solution is the problem: arraying the disarray in development', *World Development*, 32(2): 191–212.

Pritchett, Lant and Rukmi Murgai (2007) 'Teacher compensation: can decentralization to local bodies take India from perfect storm through troubled waters to clear sailing?', in S. Berry, B. Bosworth and A. Panagariya (eds), *India Policy Forum 2006–07* (Delhi: Sage), 123–78.

The Probe Team (1999), *Public Report on Basic Education in India* (New Delhi: Oxford University Press).

Przeworski, Adam (1991), *Democracy and the Market* (Cambridge: Cambridge University Press).

Przeworski, Adam (2004), 'Institutions matter?', *Government and Opposition*, 39(4): 527–40.

Przeworski, Adam, Michael Alvarez, Jose A.Cheibub and Fernando Limongi (1996), 'What makes democracies endure?', *Journal of Democracy*, 7(1): 39–55.

Putnam, Robert (2000), *Bowling Alone: The Collapse and Revival of American Community* (New York: Simon and Schuster).

Putnam, Robert, Robert Leonardi and Raffaella Y. Nanetti (1993), *Making Democracy Work: Civic Traditions in Modern Italy* (Princeton, NJ: Princeton University Press).

Quah, Danny (2011), 'The global economy's shifting centre of gravity', *Global Policy*, 2(1): 3–9.

Quigley, Declan (1993), *The Interpretation of Caste* (Oxford: Clarendon Press).

Radkar, Anjali and Sulabha Parsuraman (2007), 'Maternal deaths in India: an exploration', *Economic and Political Weekly*, 42(31): 3259–63.

Raheja, Gloria G. (1988), *The Poison in the Gift: Ritual Prestation and the Dominant Caste in a North Indian Village* (Chicago, IL: University of Chicago Press).

Rahman, Lupin and Vijayendra Rao (2008), 'The determinants of gender equity in India: examining Dyson and Moore's thesis with new data', *Population and Development Review*, 30(2): 239–68.

Raj, K. N. (1973), 'The politics and economics of "intermediate regimes"', *Economic and Political Weekly* 9: 1189–98.

Rajagopal, Arvind (2001), *Politics after Television: Hindu Nationalism and the Reshaping of the Public in India* (Cambridge: Cambridge University Press).

Rajalakshmi, T. K. (2002) 'Loaded against labour', *Frontline*, 19(16) : 99–101

Rajalakshmi, T. K. (2005), 'A scathing indictment', *Frontline*, 22(3). Accessed at: <http://www.hindu.com>, 31 August 2010.

Rajamani, Lavanya and Arghya Sengupta (2010), 'The Supreme Court', in N. Gopal Jayal and P. Bhanu Mehta (eds), *The Oxford Companion to Politics in India* (Delhi: Oxford University Press), 80–97.

Rajan, Raghuram (2010), *Fault Lines: How Hidden Fractures Still Threaten the World Economy* (Princeton, NJ: Princeton University Press).

Raju, Saraswati, Peter Atkins, Naresh Kumar and Janet Townsend (1999), *Atlas of Women and Men in India* (New Delhi: Kali for Women).

Ramachandran, Prema (2009), 'The double burden of malnutrition in India', *FAO Corporate Document Repository*. Retrieved from: <http://www.fao.org/docrep/009/a0442e0d.htm> (last accessed 26 May 2010).

Ramachandran, V.K. and Vikas Rawal (2010), 'The impact of liberalisation and globalisation on India's agrarian economy', *Global Labour Journal*, 1(1): 56–91.

Ramachandran,Vimala (ed.) (2004) *Gender and Social Equity in Primary Education: Hierarchies of Access* (New Delhi: Sage).

Ramakrishnan, Venkitesh (2000), 'An agenda of Indianisation', *Frontline*, 17(222). Retrieved from: <http://www.flonet.com>, last accessed 27 August 2010).

Ramakrishnan, Venkitesh (2005), 'A message from Chitrakoot', *Frontline*, 23(23): 33–4.

Ramakrishnan, Venkitesh (2006), 'Conflict zones', *Frontline*, 23(20): 4–8.

Ramakrishnan, Venkitesh (2009), 'Taking on the Maoists', *Frontline*, 26(22): 4–8.

Ramakrishnan, Venkitesh (2010a), 'Militant route to Hindu Rashtra', *Frontline*, 27(16): 4–7.

Ramakrishnan, Venkitesh (2010b), 'Flawed operation', *Frontline*, 27(9): 4–9.

Ramana, P. V. (2008), *The Naxal Challenge* (New Delhi: Pearson-Longman).

Rangan, Haripriya (2000), *Of Myths and Movements: Rewriting Chipko into Himalayan History* (London: Verso).

Rao, Marapalli Govinda and Nirvikar Singh (2005), *Political Economy of Federalism in India* (New Delhi: Oxford University Press).

Rao, Vijayendra and Paromita Sanyal (2009), 'Dignity through discourse: poverty and the culture of deliberation in Indian village democracies', *Policy Research Working Paper 4924* (Washington, DC: World Bank).

Rauch, James E. and Peter B. Evans (2000), 'Bureaucratic structure and bureaucratic performance in less developed countries', *Journal of Public Economics*, 75(1): 49–71.

Ravallion, Martin (2001), 'Growth, inequality and poverty: looking beyond averages', *World Development*, 29(11): 1803–15.

Ravallion, Martin (2003), 'Fanciful numbers and fictitious intrigues', *Economic and Political Weekly*, 34(44): 4653–4.

Ravallion, Martin (2009a), 'Why don't we see poverty convergence?' *Policy Research Working Paper 4974* (Washington, DC: World Bank).

Ravallion, Martin (2009b), 'A comparative perspective on poverty reduction in Brazil, China and India', *Policy Research Working Paper 5080* (Washington, DC: World Bank).

Ravallion, Martin and Shaohua Chen (2007), 'China's (uneven) progress against poverty', *Journal of Development Economics*, 82(91): 1–42.

Ravallion, Martin and Gaurav Datt (1999), 'When is growth pro-poor? Evidence from the diverse experiences of India's states', *Policy Research Working Paper 2263* (Washington, DC: World Bank).

Ravallion, Martin, Gaurav Datt and Dominique van de Walle (1991), 'Quantifying absolute poverty in the developing world', *Review of Income and Wealth*, 37: 345–61.

Rawal, Vikas (2008), 'Ownership holdings of land in rural India: putting the record straight', *Economic and Political Weekly*, 43(10): 43–7.

Rawat, Ram (2011), *Reconsidering Untouchability: Chamars and Dalit History in North India* (Bloomington, IN: Indiana University Press).

Ray, Rabindra (1988), *The Naxalites and Their Ideology* (Delhi: Oxford University Press).

Reddy, G. Ram and G.Haragopal (1985), 'The pyraveekar: the "fixer" in rural India', *Asian Survey*, 25(11): 1148–62.

Reddy, Sanjay and Thomas Pogge (2002), *How Not to Count the Poor*, mimeo (New York: Barnard College).

Registrar General of India (2006), *Delhi: Census Commissioner Tabulations*.

Right to Food Campaign (2011), 'Right to Food', *Economic and Political Weekly*, 46(33): 21–3.

Robinson, Joan (1962), *Economic Philosophy* (Harmondsworth: Penguin).

Robinson, Marguerite (1988), *Local Politics: The Law of the Fishes – Development through Political Change in Medak District, Andhra Pradesh (South India)* (New Delhi: Oxford University Press).

Rodden, Jonathan and Steven Wilkinson (2004), *The Shifting Political Economy of Redistribution in the Indian Federation*, mimeo. Retrieved from: <http://dspace.mit.edu/bitstream/handle/1721.1/18135/rodden.wilkinson.isnie2004.pdf?sequence=1> (last accessed 18 July 2010).

Rodrik, Dani (2003) 'Introduction: what do we learn from country narratives?', in Dani Rodrik (ed.), *In Search of Prosperity: Analytical Narratives on Economic Growth* (Princeton: Princeton University Press), 1–19.

Rodrik, Dani (2009), 'The new development economics: we shall experiment, but how shall we learn?', in Jessica Cohen and William Easterly (eds), *What Works in Development? Thinking Big and Thinking Small* (Washington, DC: Brookings Institution Press), 24–47.

Rodrik, Dani and Arvind Subramanian (2004a), 'Institutions rule: the primacy of institutions over geography and integration in economic development', *Journal of Economic Growth*, 9(2): 131–65.

Rodrik, Dani and Arvind Subramanian (2004b), 'Why India can grow at 7% a year or more: projections and reflections', *IMF Working Paper*, 4(118): 1–16.

Rodrik, Dani and Arvind Subramanian (2005), 'From "Hindu growth" to productivity surge: the mystery of the Indian growth transition', *IMF Staff Papers*, 52(2): 1–42.

Rogaly, Ben, Daniel Coppard, Abdur Safique, Kumar Rana, Amrita Sengupta and Jhuma Biswas (2002), 'Seasonal migration and welfare/ill-fare in eastern India: a social analysis', *Journal of Development Studies*, 38(5): 89–114.

Rogers, Martyn (2008). 'Modernity, "authenticity", and ambivalence: subaltern masculinities on a south Indian campus', *Journal of the Royal Anthropological Institute*, 14(1): 79–95.

Roitman, Janet (2004), *Fiscal Disobedience: An Anthropology of Economic Regulation in Central Africa* (Princeton, NJ: Princeton University Press).

Ross, Michael (1999), 'The political economy of the resource curse', *World Politics*, 51(2): 297–322.

Roulet, Marguerite (1996), 'Dowry and prestige in north India', *Contributions to Indian Sociology*, 30(1): 89–107.

Roy, Ananya (2009), 'Why India cannot plan its cities: informality, insurgence and the idiom of urbanization', *Planning Theory*, 8(1): 76–87.

Roy, Arundhati (2001), 'The greater common good', in Arundhati Roy (ed.), *The Algebra of Infinite Justice* (Delhi: Viking Books), 43–141.

Roy, Arundhati (2009), *Listening to Grasshoppers: Field Notes on Democracy* (New Delhi: Hamish Hamilton).

Roy, Arundhati (2010), 'Walking with the comrades', *Outlook* (29 March).

Roy, I., (2006), 'Representation and development in urban peripheries', *Economic and Political Weekly*, 40 (36): 4363–8.

RoyChowdhury, Supriya (2003), 'Old classes and new spaces: urban poverty, unorganised labour and new unions', *Economic and Political Weekly*, 38(50): 5277–84.

Rudolph, Lloyd and Suzanne Hoeber Rudolph (1967), *The Modernity of Tradition* (Chicago, IL: University of Chicago Press).

Rudolph, Lloyd I. and Susanne Hoeber Rudolph (1987), *In Pursuit of Lakshmi: The Political Economy of the Indian State* (Chicago, IL: University of Chicago Press).

Rudolph, Lloyd I. and Susanne Hoeber Rudolph (2001), 'Iconisation of Chandrababu: sharing sovereignty in India's federal market economy', *Economic and Political Weekly*, 26(18): 541–52.

Rudra, Ashok (1997), *Prasanta Chandra Mahalanobis: A Biography* (New Delhi: Oxford University Press).

Ruparelia, Sanjay, Sanjay Reddy, John Harriss and Stuart Corbridge (eds) (2011), *Understanding India's New Political Economy: A Great Transformation?* (London: Routledge).

Rushdie, Salman (1981), *Midnight's Children* (London: Jonathan Cape).

Rustagi, Preet (2004), 'Significance of gender-related development indicators: an analysis of Indian states', *Indian Journal of Gender Studies*, 11(3): 291–343.

Sachs, Jeffrey, Andrew Mellinger and John Gallup (2001), 'The geography of poverty and wealth', *Scientific American*, 284(3): 70–6.

Saez, Lawrence (2000), 'Economic liberalization and federalism: the case of India', in Stuart Nagel (ed.), *Global Economic Policy* (New York: Marcel Dekker Publishers), 195–217.

Saez, Lawrence (2002), *Federalism without a Centre: The Impact of Political and Economic Reform on India's Federal System* (New Delhi: Sage Publications).

SAHMAT (2001), *The Saffron Agenda in Education: An Expose* (New Delhi: Safdar Hashmi Memorial Trust).

SAHMAT (2002a), *Against Communalisation of Education* (New Delhi: Safdar Hashmi Memorial Trust).

SAHMAT (2002b), *Communalisation of Education: The Assault on History* (New Delhi: Safdar Hashmi Memorial Trust).

SAHMAT (2002c), *Saffronised and Substandard: A Critique of the New NCERT Yextbooks* (New Delhi: Safdar Hashmi Memorial Trust).

SAHMAT (2003), *Plagiarised and Communalised: More on the NCERT Textbooks* (New Delhi: Safdar Hashmi Memorial Trust).

Sala-i-Martin, Xavier (2006), 'The world distribution of income: falling poverty and . . . convergence, period', *Quarterly Journal of Economics*, 121(2): 351–97.

Samata Sanghatana (1991), 'Upper caste violence: study of the Chunduru carnage', *Economic and Political Weekly*, 26(36): 2079–84.

Sanyal, K. and R. Bhattacharyya (2009), 'Beyond the factory: globalisation, informalisation of production and the new locations of labour', *Economic and Political Weekly*, 44(22): 35–44.

Sarkar, Sumit, (1983), *Modern India, 1885–1947* (Delhi: Macmillan).

Sarkar, Sumit (1996) 'Indian nationalism and the politics of Hindutva', in David Ludden (ed.), *Contesting the Nation: Religion, Community, and the Politics of Democracy in India* (Philadelphia, PA: University of Pennsylvania Press), 270–93.

Sarkar, Sumit (2001), 'Indian democracy: the historical inheritance', in Atul Kohli (ed.), *The Success of India's Democracy* (Cambridge: Cambridge University Press), 23–46.

Sarkar, S. and B. S. Mehta (2010), 'Income inequality in India: pre- and post-reform periods', *Economic and Political Weekly*, 44(37): 45–9.

Savarkar, V. D. (1923/2003), *Hindutva: Who is a Hindu?* (Delhi: Hindi Sahitya Sadan).

Seminar (2003), No. 522 *The Teaching of History*. At: <http://www.india-seminar.com>.

Sen, Abhijit (2000), 'Estimates of consumer expenditure and its distribution: statistical priorities after NSS 55th round', *Economic and Political Weekly*, 35(51): 4499–4518.

Sen, Abhijit and Himanshu (2004a), 'Poverty and inequality in India – I', *Economic and Political Weekly*, 39(38): 4247–63.

Sen, Abhijit and Himanshu (2004b), 'Poverty and inequality in India – II. Widening disparities during the 1990s', *Economic and Political Weekly*, 39(38): 4361–75.

Sen, Amartya (1990), 'More than 100 million women are missing', *New York Review of Books,* 37(20): 17–22.

Sen, Amartya (1999), *Development as Freedom* (New York: Knopf).

Senthilkumar Solidarity Committee (2008), 'Caste, higher education and Senthil's "suicide"', *Economic and Political Weekly*, 43(33): 10–12.

Shah, Alpa (2006a), 'Markets of protection: the "terrorist" Maoist movement and the state in Jharkhand, India', *Critique of Anthropology*, 26(3): 297–314.

Shah, Alpa (2006b), 'The labour of love: seasonal migration from Jharkhand to the brick-kilns in other states of India', *Contributions to Indian Sociology*, 40(1): 91–116.

Shah, Alpa (2009), 'In search of certainty in revolutionary India', *Dialectical Anthropology*, 33(3–4): 271–86.

Shah, Alpa (2010a), 'Annihilation is the last choice', *Economic and Political Weekly*, 45(19): 24–9.

Shah, Alpa (2010b), *In the Shadows of the State: Indigenous Politics, Environmentalism and Insurgency in Jharkhand, India* (Durham, NC, and London: Duke University Press).

Shah, Alpa and Judith Pettigrew (eds) (2009), 'Windows into a revolution: ethnographies of Maoism in south Asia', *Dialectical Anthropology*, 33(3–4): 225–51.

Shah, Gyansham, Amita Baviskar, Satish Deshpande, Harsh Mander and Sukhdeo Thorat (2006), *Untouchability in Rural India* (New Delhi: Sage).

Shankar, Shylashri (2010), 'India's judiciary: imperium in imperio?', in Paul Brass (ed.), *Routledge Handbook of South Asian Politics* (London and New York: Routledge), 165–76.

Sharma, A.N. (2006), 'Flexibility, employment and labour market reforms in India', *Economic and Political Weekly* 41(21): 2078–85.

Sharma, Shalendra (2009), *China and India in the Age of Globalization* (Cambridge: Cambridge University Press).

Shastri, Vivek (1997), 'The politics of economic liberalization in India', *Contemporary South Asia*, 6(1): 27–56.

Sheth, D. L. (1999), 'Secularization of caste and the making of a new middle class', *Economic and Political Weekly*, 34(34): 2502–10.

Shils, Edward (1961), *The Intellectual Between Tradition and Modernity: The Indian Situation* (The Hague: Mouton).

Shiva, Vandana (1988), *Staying Alive: Women, Ecology and Survival in India* (New Delhi: Kali for Women).

Shukla, Shrilal (1992), *Raag Darbari: A Novel (translated by Gillian Wright)* (New Delhi: Penguin).

Silberschmidt, M. (2001), 'Disempowerment of men in rural and urban East Africa: Implications for male identity and sexual behaviour', *World Development*, 29(24): 657–71.

Simeon, Dilip (2010, March), 'Permanent spring', *Seminar* #607. Retrieved from: <http://www.india-seminar.com> (last accessed 6 December 2010).

Simon, Julian L. (1977), *The Economics of Population Growth* (Princeton, NJ: Princeton University Press).

Singer, Hans (1950), 'The distribution of gains between investing and borrowing countries', *American Economic Review*, 40(2): 478–96.

Singer, Milton (1972), *When a Great Tradition Modernizes: An Anthropological Approach to Indian Civilization* (New York: Praeger).

Singer, Milton and Bernard Cohn (eds) (1968), *Structure and Change in Indian Society* (Chicago, IL: Aldine Publishing Company).

Singh, Jagpal (1992), *Capitalism and Dependence: Agrarian Politics in Western Uttar Pradesh 1951–1991* (Delhi: Manohar).

Singh, Jagpal (ed.) (2005), *Women and Panchayati Raj* (Delhi: Sunrise).

Singh, Manmohan (1964), *India's Export Trends*, (London: Oxford University Press).

Singh, S. (2010), 'Implementation of FDI in food supermarkets', *Economic and Political Weekly*, 45(34): 17–20.

Singh, Shashi Bhushan (2005), 'Limits to power: Naxalism and caste relations in a south Bihar village', *Economic and Political Weekly*, 40(29): 3167–75.

Sinha, Aseema (2004), 'The changing political economy of federalism in India: a historical institutionalist approach', *India Review*, 3(1): 25–63.

Sinha, Aseema (2005a), *The Regional Roots of Development Politics in India: A Divided Leviathan* (Bloomington, IN: Indiana University Press).

Sinha, Aseema (2005b), 'Understanding the rise and transformation of business collective action in India', *Business and Politics*, 7(2): 1–34.

Smith, Neil (1996), *The New Urban Frontier: Gentrification and the Revanchist City* (New York: Routledge).

Sokoloff, Kenneth and Stanley Engerman (2000), 'History lessons: institutions, factor endowments, and paths of development in the New World', *Journal of Economic Perspectives* 14(3): 217–32.

Spodek, Howard (2010), 'In the Hindutva Laboratory: Pogroms and Politics in Gujarat, 2002', *Modern Asian Studies*, 44(2): 349–99.

Sridaran, E. (1999), 'Toward state funding of elections in India: a comparative perspective on possible options', *The Journal of Policy Reform*, 3(3): 229–54.

Srinivas, M. N. (1955), 'The social system of a Mysore village', in McKim Marriott (ed.), *Village India* (Chicago, IL: Chicago University Press), 1–35.

Srinivas, M. N. (1989), *The Cohesive Role of Sanskritization and Other Essays*, (Oxford: Oxford University Press).

Srinivas, M. N. (1996), 'Introduction', in M. N. Srinivas (ed.), *Caste: Its Twentieth Century Avatar* (New Delhi: Penguin), 9–38.

Srinivasan, Janaki (2009), 'Paradox of human development of women in Kerala', *Economic and Political Weekly*, 44(10): 23–5.

Srinivasan, Rukmini (2010), 'India has no middle class?', *The Times of India* (6 May).

Srinivasan, Thirukodikaval Nilakanta (2004), Comments on Rodrik and Subramanian, *From "Hindu Growth" to Productivity Surge: The Mystery of the Indian Growth Transition'*, mimeo. Retrieved from: <http://www.imf.org/external/pubs/ft/staffp/2004/00-00/sriniv.pdf> (last accessed April 2010).

Srinivasan, Thirukodikaval Nilakanta (2005), *Indian Economic Reforms: A Stocktaking*, mimeo. Retrieved from: <http://www.econ.yale.edu/~srinivas/Indian%20Economic'0%Reforms%20A%Stocktaking.pdf> (last accessed April 2010).

Srivastava, Manoj (forthcoming), 'Governing the poor in Bihar and Madhya Pradesh', unpublished PhD dissertation, London School of Economics.

Srivastava, Sanjay (1998), *Constructing Post-colonial India: National Character and the Doon School*. (London: Routledge).

Srivastava, Sanjay (2007), *Passionate Modernity: Sexuality, Consumption, and Class in India* (New Delhi: Routledge).

Stallings, Barbara (1992), 'International influence on economic policy: debt, stabilization and structural reform', in Stephan Haggard and Robert Kaufman (eds), *The Politics of Economic Adjustment* (Princeton, NJ: Princeton University Press), 41–88.

Stern, Nicholas, J-J. Dethier, and F. H.Rogers (2005), *Growth and Empowerment* (Cambridge, MA: MIT Press).

Stiglitz, Joseph (2002), *Globalization and Its Discontents* (New York: W.W.Norton and Co.).

Stokes, Eric (1980), *The Peasant and the Raj: Studies in Agrarian Society and Peasant Rebellion in Colonial India* (Cambridge: Cambridge University Press).

Subramanian, Arvind (2007), 'The evolution of institutions in India and its relationship with economic growth', *Oxford Review of Economic Policy*, 23(2): 196–220.

Subrahmaniam, Vidya (2009a), 'Violence and threats bring a government to its knees', *The Hindu* (16 December).

Subrahmaniam, Vidya (2009b), 'The system strikes back', *The Hindu* (17 December).

Subrahmaniam, Vidya (2010), 'Three pogroms held together by a common thread', *The Hindu* (4 September).

Subrahmaniam, Vidya (2011), 'An aam admi sarkar fights the poor', *The Hindu* (3 February).

Sudarshan, Ratna and Shrayana Bhattacharya (2009), 'Through the magnifying glass: women's work and labour force participation in urban Delhi', *Economic and Political Weekly*, 44(48): 59–66.

Sudha, S. and S. I. Rajan (1999), 'Female demographic disadvantage in India, 1981–1991: sex-selective abortion and female infanticide', *Development and Change*, 30(3): 585–618.

Sundar, Nandini (2002), 'Indigenise, nationalise and spiritualise' – an agenda for education?', *International Social Science Journal*, 54 (173): 373–83.

Sundar, Nandini (2004), 'Teaching to hate: RSS' pedagogical programme', *Economic and Political Weekly* 39(16): 1605–12.

Sundar, Nandini (2006), 'Bastar, Maoism and Salwa Judum', *Economic and Political Weekly*, 41(29): 3187–92.

Sundaram, K. (2007), 'Employment and poverty in India, 2000–2005', *Economic and Political Weekly*, 42: 3121–31.

Sundaram, K. and S. Tendulkar (2003), 'Poverty *has* declined in the 1990s: a resolution of the comparability problems in NSS consumer expenditure data', *Economic and Political Weekly* 38: 327–37.

Swaminathan, Madhura (2000a), *Weakening Welfare: The Public Distribution of Food in India* (Delhi: LeftWord).

Swaminathan, Madhura (2000b), 'The budget and food security', *The Hindu* (9 March).

Swaminathan, Madhura (2008), 'The case for state intervention', *UN Chronicle*, 45(2 & 3); available at: http://www.un.org/wcm/content/site/chronicle/home/archive/issues2008/pid/21607.

Swamy, Anand, Stephen Knack, Lee Young and Omar Azfar (2000), *Gender and Corruption*, mimeo. Retrieved from: <http://www.williams.edu/Economics/wp/Swamy_gender.pdf> (last accessed 7 June 2010).

Tambiah, Yasmin (ed.) (2002), *Women and Governance in South Asia: Reimagining the State* (Colombo: International Centre for Ethnic Studies).

Tatsumi, Kayoko (2009), 'Coalition politics, ethnic violence and citizenship: Muslim agency in Meerut, India, *c*.1950–2004', unpublished PhD dissertation (London: London School of Economics and Political Science).

Taylor, Charles (1990), 'Modes of civil society', *Public Culture*, 3(1): 95–118.

Teitelbaum, Emmanual (2006), 'Was the Indian labor movement ever co-opted? Evaluating standard accounts', *Critical Asian Studies*, 38(4): 389–417.

Tendler, Judith (1997), *Good Government in the Tropics* (Baltimore, MD, and London: Johns Hopkins University Press).

Tendulkar, Suresh and T. A. Bhavani (2007), *Understanding Reforms: Post 1991 India* (New Delhi: Oxford University Press).

Thorat, Sukhadeo and Katherine Newman (2007), 'Caste and economic discrimination: causes, consequences and remedies', *Economic and Political Weekly*, 42(41): 4121–24.

Thorat, Sukhadeo and Katherine S. Newman (eds) (2010), *Blocked by Caste: Economic Discrimination in Modern India* (New Delhi: Oxford University Press).

Thorner, Daniel (1956/1976), *The Agrarian Prospect in India*, 2nd edn (Bombay: Allied Publishers).

Tiwari, Nupur (2009), 'Rethinking the rotation term of reservation in panchayats', *Economic and Political Weekly*, 44(5): 23–5.

Tomlinson, Brian R. (1990), 'Economics: the periphery', in Andrew Porter (ed.), *The Oxford History of the British Empire: The Nineteenth Century* (Oxford: Oxford University Press), 53–74.

Tonnies, F. (1955), *Community and Association* (London: Routledge and Kegan Paul).

Topolova, Petia (2004), *Factor Immobility and Regional Effects of Trade Liberalization: Evidence from India*, mimeo (Cambridge, MA: MIT, Economics Department).

Topolova, Petia (2005), 'Trade liberalization, poverty and inequality: evidence from Indian districts', NBER *Working Paper* 11614. Retrieved from: <http://www.nber.org/papers/w11614>.

Topolova, Petia (2008), 'India: is the rising tide lifting all boats?', *IMF Working Paper* 08/54.

Topolova, Petia and Dan Nyberg (2010), 'What level of public debt could India target?', *IMF Working Paper* 10/7.

Toye, John (1988), 'Political economy and the analysis of Indian development', *Modern Asian Studies*, 22(1): 97–122.

Truelove, Yaffa and Emma Mawdsley (2010), 'Discourses of citizenship and criminality in clean, green Delhi', in Isabelle Clark-Decès (ed.), *A Companion to the Anthropology of India* (Oxford: Blackwell)., 407–25.

Turner, Simon (2009) '"These young men show no respect for local customs" – globalisation and islamic revival in Zanzibar', *Journal of Religion in Africa*, 39(3): 237–61.

Unni, Jeemol (2009), 'Gender differentials in education: exploring the capabilities approach', *Economic and Political Weekly*, 44(9): 111–17.

Unni, Jeemol and G. Raveendran (2007), 'Growth of employment (1993–4 to 2004–5): illusion of inclusiveness', *Economic and Political Weekly*, 42(3): 196–9.

Upadhya, Carol (2007) 'Employment, exclusion and "merit" in the Indian IT industry', *Economic and Political Weekly*, 42(20): 1863–8.

Upadhyay, Sugeeta (2007), 'Wastage in Indian higher education', *Economic and Political Weekly*, 42(2): 161–8.

Vaidyanathan, A. (2006), 'Farmers' suicides and the agrarian crisis', *Economic and Political Weekly*, 41(38): 4009–13.

Vaidyanathan, A. (2010), *Agricultural Growth in India: Role of Technology, Incentives and Institutions* (New Delhi: Oxford University Press).

Vakulabharanam, Vamsi (2005), 'Growth and distress in a south Indian peasant economy during the era of economic liberalisation', *Journal of Development Studies*, 41(6): 971–97.

Vakulabharanam, Vamsi and Sripad Motiram (2011), 'Political economy of agrarian distress in India since the 1990s', in Sanjay Ruparelia, Sanjay Reddy, John Harriss and Stuart Corbridge (eds), *Understanding India's New Political Economy: A Great Transformation?* (London: Routledge), 101–26.

Varadarajan, Siddharth (2010), 'Supreme Court should not go into the realm of policy formulation', *The Hindu* (7 September).

Varshney, Ashutosh (1995), *Democracy, Development and the Countryside: Urban–Rural Struggles in India* (Cambridge: Cambridge University Press).

Varshney, Ashutosh (1998), 'Mass politics or elite politics? India's economic reforms in comparative perspective', *Policy Reform*, 2(4): 301–35.

Varshney, Ashutosh (2000), 'Is India becoming more democratic?', *Journal of Asian Studies*, 59(1): 3–25.

Varshney, Ashutosh (2001), 'Ethnic conflict and civil society: India and beyond', *World Politics*, 53(3): 298–362.

Varshney, Ashutosh (2002), *Ethnic Conflict and Civic Life: Hindus and Muslims in India* (Delhi: Oxford University Press).

Vatuk, Sylvia (1972), *Kinship and Urbanization: White Collar Workers in North India* (Berkeley, CA: University of California Press).

Venkatesan, V. (2003a), 'The judicial response', *Frontline*, 20(18): 20–2.

Venkatesan, V., (2003b), 'A sevular veneer', *Frontline*, 20(2). Retrieved from: <http://www.flonet.com> (last accessed 27 August 2010).

Venkatesan, J. (2010), 'Courts apathetic to sacking under cover of globalization, says Supreme Court', *The Hindu* (30 January).

Virmani, Arvind (2006), *Propelling India from Socialist Stagnation to Global Power: Volume 1 – Growth Processes* (Delhi: Academic Foundation).

Visaria, Leela (2008), 'Violence against women in India: is empowerment a protective factor?', *Economic and Political Weekly*, 43(48): 60–6.

Wade, Robert (1982), 'The system of administrative and political corruption: canal irrigation in south India', *Journal of Development Studies*, 18(3): 287–328.

Wade, Robert (1985) 'The market for public office: why the Indian state is not better at development', *World Development*, 13(4): 467–97.

Wade, Robert (1988) 'Politics and graft: recruitment, appointment and promotions to public office in India' in Peter Ward (ed.), *Corruption, Development and Inequality: Soft Touch or Hard Graft?* (London: Routledge), 73–110.

Wade, Robert (1990), *Governing the Market: Economic Theory and the Role of Government in East Asian Industrialization* (Princeton, NJ: Princeton University Press).

Wade, Robert (2004), 'Is globalization reducing poverty and inequality?', *World Development*, 32(4): 567–89.

Wadley, Susan S. (1994), *Struggling with Destiny in Karimpur, 1925–1984* (New Delhi: Vistaar Publications).

Waghorne, Joanne Punzo (2004), *Diaspora of the Gods: Modern Hindu Temples in an Urban Middle Class World* (Oxford: Oxford University Press).

Wallack, Jessica (2003), 'Structural breaks in Indian macroeconomic data', *Economic and Political Weekly*, 38(41): 4312–15.

Walton, Michael (2010), 'Inequities and India's long-term growth: tackling structural inequities', in Harinder S. Kohli and Anil Sood (eds), *India 2039: An Affluent Society in One Generation* (New Delhi: Sage Publications), 67–99.

Wang, Shaoguang (2008), 'Double movement in China', *Economic and Political Weekly*, 43(52): 51–9.

Warrier, Maya (2003), 'Processes of secularization in contemporary India: guru faith in the Mata Amritanandamayi mission', *Modern Asian Studies*, 37(1): 213–53.

Warrier, Maya (2005), *Hindu Selves in the Modern World: Guru Faith in the Mata Amritanandamayi Mission* (London and New York: Routledge Curzon).

Washbrook, David (1988), 'Progress and problems: south Asian economic and social history c.1720–1860', *Modern Asian Studies*, 22(1), 57–96.

Washbrook, David (2004), 'South India 1770–1840: the colonial transition', *Modern Asian Studies*, 38(3): 479–516.

Watt, Carey (2005), *Serving the Nation: Cultures of Service, Association and Citizenship* (Oxford: Oxford University Press).

Watts, Michael (2003), 'Alternative modern: development as cultural geography', in Kay Anderson, Mona Domosh, Stephen Pile and Nigel Thrift (eds), *Handbook of Cultural Geography* (London: Sage), 433–53.

Webb, Martin (2010) 'Boundary paradoxes: the social life of transparency and accountability activism in Delhi', unpublished PhD dissertation (University of Sussex).

Weiner, Myron (1962), *The Politics of Scarcity* (Chicago, IL: University of Chicago Press).

Weiner, Myron (1967), *Party Building in a New Nation: The Indian National Congress* (Chicago, IL: University of Chicago Press).

Weiner, Myron (1991), *The Child and the State in India* (Princeton, NJ: Princeton University Press).

Weiner, Myron (1999), 'The regionalization of Indian politics and its implications for economic reform', in Jeffrey Sachs, Ashutosh Varshney and Nirupam Bajpai (eds), *India in the Era of Economic Reforms* (New Delhi: Oxford University Press), 261–94.

Weinstein, Liza (2009), 'Democracy in the globalizing Indian city: engagements of political society and the state in globalizing Mumbai', *Politics and Society*, 37(3): 397–427.

Whitehead, Judy (2003), 'Place, space and primitive accumulation in Narmada Valley and Beyond', *Economic and Political Weekly*, 38(4): 4224–6.

Whitehead, Laurence (2001), 'High anxiety in the Andes: Bolivia and the viability of democracy', *Journal of Democracy*, 12(2): 6–16.

Wilkinson, Steven (2004), *Votes and Violence: Electoral Competition and Ethnic Riots in India* (Cambridge: Cambridge University Press).

Wilkinson, Steven (ed.) (2005), *Religious Politics and Communal Violence* (Delhi: Oxford University Press).

Wilkinson, Steven (2007), 'Reading the election results', in Sumit Ganguly, Larry Jay Diamond and Marc F Plattner (eds), *The State of India's Democracy* (Oxford: Oxford University Press), 26–44.

Williams, Philippa (2007), 'Hindu–Muslim brotherhood: exploring the dynamics of communal relations in Varanasi, north India', *Journal of South Asian Development*, 2(2): 153–76.

Williamson, John and Roberto Zagha (2002), 'From the Hindu rate of growth to the Hindu rate of reform', *Working Paper 144* (Stanford, CA: Stanford University, Center for Research on Economic Development and Policy Reform).

Winters, Alan and Shahid Yusuf (2007), *Dancing with Giants: China, India and the World Economy* (Washington, DC: World Bank).

Wiser, William H. (1936), *The Hindu Jajmani System: A Socio-economic System Interrelating Members of a Hindu Village Community in Services* (Lucknow: Lucknow Publishing House).

Wittfogel, Karl (1957), *Oriental Despotism: A Comparative Study of Total Power* (New Haven, CT: Yale University Press).

World Bank (1989), *India: An Industrializing Economy in Transition* (Washington, DC: World Bank).

World Bank (2001), *World Development Report, 2000–2001: Attacking Poverty* (Wahington, DC: World Bank).

World Bank (2005), 'India and the knowledge Economy: leveraging strengths and opportunities'. Retrieved from: <http://ddp-ext.worldbank.org/EdStats/INDstu05.pdf> (last accessed 6 May 2011).

World Bank (2006), *India: Inclusive Growth and Service Delivery – Building on India's Success* (Washington, DC: World Bank).

World Bank (2008), *World Development Report 2008: Agriculture for Development* (Washington, DC: World Bank).

World Bank (2011), *Conflict, Security and Development: World Development Report* (Washington, DC: World Bank)

Wyatt, Andrew K. J. (2009), *Party System Change in India: Political Entrepreneurs, Patterns and Processes* (London: Routledge).

Yadav, Bhupendra (2009), 'Khap panchayats: stealing freedom?', *Economic and Political Weekly*, 44(52): 16–19.

Yadav, Yogendra (1996), 'Reconfiguration in Indian politics: state assembly elections 1993–1995', *Economic and Political Weekly*, 31(2–3): 95–104.

Yadav, Yogendra (1999), 'Electoral politics in the time of change: India's third electoral system: 1998–99', *Economic and Political Weekly*, 34(34–5): 2393–9.

Yadav, Yogendra (2004), 'The elusive mandate of 2004', *Economic and Political Weekly*, 39(51): 5383–98.

Yadav, Yogendra and Suhas Palshikar (2009) 'Between fortuna and virtu: explaining the Congress' ambiguous victory in 2009', *Economic and Political Weekly*, 44(39): 33–46.

Yadav, Yogendra and V. B. Singh (1996), 'Maturing of a democracy', *India Today* (15 August).

Yagnik, A. and Suchitra Sheth (2005), *The Shaping of Modern Gujarat: Plurality, Hindutva and Beyond* (Delhi: Penguin Books).

Yang Lian (2005), 'Dark side of the Chinese moon', *New Left Review*, 32(2): 132–40.

Young, Stephen (2010), 'The "moral hazards" of microfinance: restructuring rural credit in India', *Antipode*, 42(1): 201–23.

Zaidi, Annie (2005), 'Food, for education', *Frontline* 22(5): 49–52.

Zavos, John (2000), *The Emergence of Hindu Nationalism in India* (Delhi: Oxford University Press).

Zerah, Marie-Helene (2007), 'Middle class neighbourhood associations as political players in Bombay, *Economic and Political Weekly*, 42(47): 61–8.

Index

Above Poverty Line (APL), 48, 107,
    109
Abraham, Janaki, 226
'accumulation by dispossession',
    206
Acemoglu, Daron, 4–5
adivasis, 8, 77, 90, 246
    anti-Muslim violence, 185
    displacement of, 206, 207–9
    dowries, 284
    Hindu nationalism, 181, 186
    local government, 170, 171
    Maoism, 202, 212, 213, 215, 217
    structural violence against, 216
    underweight girls, 267
    see also Scheduled Tribes
Advani, Lal Krishna, 17, 183
affirmative action, 7, 8, 101, 140–1,
    305
    Constitutional provisions, 166
    public opinion, 129
    women, 260, 279–80, 282
Africa
    civil society, 222–3
    colonial legacy, 5
    cross-class mobilization, 234
    debt crisis, 122
    land/labour ratios, 6
    poverty, 59, 60
    sex ratios, 262

Agarwal, Bina, 261, 270–2, 273,
    274–5
Agarwala, Rina, 116
agriculture, 14–15, 26, 80, 82
    agrarian class relations, 203–5
    Dalits, 81
    distribution of GDP and
        employment, 83
    economic growth, 31, 39
    employment trends, 96
    female workers, 274
    Green Revolution, 15, 30, 66, 205,
        265, 284
    problems with, 85–91
    reforms, 38, 124
    shift to manufacturing, 286
    societal transition, 81–2
    solutions to the crisis in, 91–3
    state bureaucracy, 162
    subsidies, 90, 91, 163
Ahirs, Jats, Gujars and Rajputs
    (AJGAR) coalition, 250
Ahluwalia, Montek Singh, 86, 128
Ahmedabad, 97, 298
Alam, Javeed, 167
Aligarh, 193, 195
Alkire, Sabina, 51, 75
Ambedkar, Bhim Rao, 7, 152
Amritanandamayi, Mata, 191
Anagnost, Ann, 293

Communist Party of India (Marxist)
(CPI(M)/CPM), 9–10, 132–3,
146, 172, 199–200, 204–5,
209–10, 231
Communist Party of India (Marxist-
Leninist) (CPI(ML)), 200
Congress Party, 11, 111, 126, 127,
142
 agrarian problems, 204
 communal violence, 193
 corruption, 165
 decline of, 150, 165
 deinstitutionalization of, 12, 15
 dominant castes, 243
 economic reform, 132
 elections, 177–8, 186
 elites, 149
 failures of the, 181–2, 196
 funding to supportive states, 133
 hegemony, 146
 Madhya Pradesh, 155, 156
 patronage system, 150–1
Constituent Assembly, 6, 7
Constitution of India, 7, 8, 41, 143,
150
 affirmative action, 140–1, 166
 caste reservations, 245, 248
 decentralization, 168
 democracy, 140
 Directive Principles, 104, 105, 113,
140, 168
 education, 288–9
 Fundamental Rights, 11, 104, 140
 grants-in-aid, 133
 social justice, 114
 women, 259, 273
consumption, 52, 53–4, 64–6, 67
contract farming, 92
Corbridge, Stuart, 17, 231, 232, 244,
246, 303
corruption, 42, 157, 166, 216, 296,
301
 corporate capital, 138
 Hazare's campaign against, 228–9,
303–4
 'intermediate regime', 125

legislator, 165
Madhya Pradesh, 156
middle classes, 228
MKSS, 231
NREGS, 113
patronage system, 149, 150–1
public activism, 233
Public Distribution System, 107
Right to Information Act, 155–6
'side incomes', 151
toleration of, 159
women politicians, 283
women's experience of, 276
Corsi, Jessica, 104, 106, 111
crises, 122
Crook, Richard C., 170–1
Cross, Jamie, 297
cultural organizations, 232
currency devaluation, 37, 126, 132

Da Costa, Dia, 148, 232, 233, 234,
248, 256
Dalit Panther Iyakkam (DPI), 153–4
Dalits, 81, 90, 239, 242–3, 248, 257
 agricultural employment, 89
 civil society, 234, 235–6
 displacement of, 206
 education, 247, 251
 graduate employment, 298
 literacy rates, 208
 local government, 170, 171
 Maoism, 199, 200, 210–11, 214,
216, 217
 politics, 147, 250–1
 reservations, 246
 social oppression, 205
 structural violence against, 216
 substantive democratization, 152–6
 temple management, 191
 untouchability, 256
 work, 244–5, 252
 see also Scheduled Castes
dams, 11, 206–7, 214
Das, Gurcharan, 25, 40
Das, Jishnu, 73
Das, Tarun, 138

rape, 272
Rashtriya Janata Dal (RJD), 250
Rashtriya Swayamsevak Sangh (RSS),
    2, 178, 180, 183–4, 186–7, 292
Ravallion, Martin, 51, 54, 56–7
Raveendran, G., 95
Rawal, Vikas, 83, 90, 93
redistributive land reform, 92, 93
reforms, 25, 33–9, 41, 46, 136–9
    'audacious', 121–4, 137, 139
    balance of payments crisis, 126–7
    catalysts for, 127–8
    costs and benefits of, 122–3
    elite politics, 128–32, 137–8, 139
    Hindu nationalism, 183–4
    land redistribution, 92, 93
    middle classes, 43
    'Provincial Darwinism', 132–5, 136
    reform champions, 122, 128, 132
    see also policy
regulation see legislation
Reliance Industries, 134, 135, 138
religion, 97, 178, 179, 180
    civil society, 227, 238
    education, 292
    'political society', 225
    religious conversions, 183, 192
    resurgence of, 187–8, 190
    see also Hinduism
rent-seeking, 131, 162
reservations
    caste, 7, 8, 11, 17, 140–1, 147, 240,
        245–6, 248, 250
    women, 279
    see also affirmative action
Resident Welfare Associations
    (RWAs), 174–5, 226, 227, 230
resources, 134, 199
    exploitation of, 208–9, 217
    privatization of common, 206, 214
    resource curse effects, 3
Right to Information Act (RTI, 2005),
    155–6, 167, 233
rights, 102, 103–17, 144, 157
    citizenship, 150
    Constitution of India, 140

to education, 102, 105, 289
to food, 106–11, 117
'political society', 225
'rights-based development', 103–4
to work, 111–13
of workers, 114–15, 116
Rithambara, Sadhvi, 278
Robinson, James, 4–5, 26
Robinson, Joan, 3
Robinson, Marguerite, 144–5, 243,
    248
Rodrik, Dani, 25, 34, 35–6, 39, 41,
    45
Roy, Ananya, 236
Roy, Aruna, 112, 278–9
Roy, Arundhati, 213
RoyChowdhury, Supriya, 116
Rudolph, Lloyd and Susanne, 15, 125,
    150
rule of law, 25, 41, 43, 45
rural areas
    agricultural labourers, 116
    anti-Muslim violence, 185
    caste, 242–3, 245
    consumption growth, 66, 67
    economic reforms, 129
    education, 291
    election turnout, 145
    employment trends, 94, 96
    health care, 73, 293
    Hindu nationalism, 181
    inequalities, 61–2, 65
    land ownership, 83–4, 92–3,
        203–4
    Maoism, 203–5, 210–16
    poverty, 49, 53, 55, 56–7, 60, 61–2,
        64, 66–8
    untouchability, 256
    wage growth, 68
    women, 260, 274, 285
Russia, 270, 271, 278, 302

Sachs, Jeffrey, 7
Saez, Lawrence, 133
Salwa Judum, 214, 217
Samajwadi Party (SP), 152, 165, 250